The Psychology of Second Language Acquisition

The Psychology of Second Language Acquisition

ZOLTÁN DÖRNYEI

OXFORD
UNIVERSITY PRESS

OXFORD

UNIVERSITY PRESS

Great Clarendon Street, Oxford ox2 6DP

Oxford University Press is a department of the University of Oxford.
It furthers the University's objective of excellence in research, scholarship,
and education by publishing worldwide in

Oxford New York

Auckland Cape Town Dar es Salaam Hong Kong Karachi
Kuala Lumpur Madrid Melbourne Mexico City Nairobi
New Delhi Shanghai Taipei Toronto

With offices in

Argentina Austria Brazil Chile Czech Republic France Greece
Guatemala Hungary Italy Japan Poland Portugal Singapore
South Korea Switzerland Thailand Turkey Ukraine Vietnam

Oxford and Oxford English are registered trade mark of
Oxford University Press in the UK and in certain other countries

© Oxford University Press 2009

ISBN 978-0-19-442197-3
Printed and bound in Great Britain

Contents

List of Figures

Preface

> *The history of acceptance of new theories frequently shows the following steps: at first the new idea is treated as pure nonsense, not worth looking at. Then comes a time when a multitude of contradictory objections are raised, such as: the new theory is too fancy, or merely a new terminology; it is not fruitful, or simply wrong. Finally a state is reached when everyone seems to claim that he had always followed this theory. This usually marks the last state before general acceptance.*
> (Lewin 1943: 292)

I normally enjoy the process of writing a book, but this volume on the psychology of second language acquisition (SLA) has been an emotional roller-coaster at times. In fact, after I received the contract from Oxford University Press, I put off working on the manuscript for several years—I did have some good excuses, but the bottom line was that I was apprehensive about the enormity of the task: applied linguistics and second language research had clearly been shaken by a paradigmatic earthquake. This has been caused by (1) the rapidly growing influence of relevant brain research in psycholinguistics, neurolinguistics, neuropsychology, neurobiology, and more generally, in cognitive (neuro)science; and (2) the emergence of new cognitive approaches to the study of language acquisition, such as connectionism, emergentism, dynamic systems theory, complexity theory, and usage/exemplar-based theories. The resulting changes in our field have been so fast and profound that the word 'blitzkrieg' seems oddly fitting to describe what we are currently experiencing.

Soldiering on in the 'psycho-blitzkrieg'

I have spent most of my professional life at the interface of linguistics and psychology, yet even I was unprepared for the sudden emergence of the multitude of new metaphors, technical terms, measurement procedures, and theoretical orientations that cognitive and neuropsychological research has brought about. My first reaction was to ignore these new developments, saying that they do not apply to my specialization area, individual difference research. However, I had to realize that applied linguists simply do not have the option of ignoring the new psychological approaches because the advances in these areas are leading to a fundamental restructuring of our knowledge base of language acquisition and language processing. Disregarding these developments would lead to the marginalization of the field of applied linguistics/second language research—a process that has already begun to some extent with many of the recent cutting-edge findings produced under the relatively new (and somewhat vague) banner of the fast expanding field of bilingualism. Thus, while many of the contemporary SLA courses and texts worldwide are still confined to talking about issues such as the limitations of Krashen's comprehensible input hypothesis, the most exciting discussions 'out there' concern topics such as the potentials and limitations of distributed connectionist models or the interfaces and neurobiological substrates of explicit and implicit language knowledge.

Even if we recognize the importance of investing in the psychological aspects of applied linguistics, it still remains the case that the task of coming to grips with the wide variety of relevant research areas and directions may seem overwhelming. If you have read any recent writings of the foremost contemporary psycholinguists or neurolinguists, you may have felt you were undergoing a psychedelic experience, often with catastrophically disempowering effects. Second-language (L2) neuroresearch, for example, is vigorously trying its wings by developing an unprecedentedly rich new metaphor-repertoire while re-examining everything we have known (or thought we had known) about language attainment through the lenses of neuroimaging. And, as with so many new initiatives, it is not easy for readers to distil what is truly worthwhile and what are merely intellectual dead-ends; there is a lot of confusion, a lot of contradiction, and many gaping holes in the findings, which makes following this literature hard going even for the specialists.

With all the above in mind, I would like to invite the readers to an orientation tour in the new stream of 'psycho-SLA'. (This is bound to be the most awful term in this book, although you might be surprised.) This book does not offer an 'all-you-ever-wanted-to-know-about-the-psychology-of-SLA' summary but rather a 'what-you-definitely-need-to-know-about-the-psychology-of-SLA' crash course. In the following chapters, I will introduce the new language of 'Neuropsychologese', I will describe the main research methods in investigating the operation of the brain (Ch. 2), I will outline the most important psychological processes underlying second language attainment, and I will introduce several new emerging theoretical paradigms (Chs. 3–4). Building on these foundations, I will then summarize what we know about the language learner's role and impact in the SLA process (Ch. 5) and examine the effects of age (i.e. is younger really better?) (Ch. 6). Finally, I will discuss the psychological basis of 'instructed SLA', that is, language learning and teaching in educational contexts (Ch. 7).

All in all, this book is not unlike the diary of an explorer. I have done my best to visit what I thought were the most exciting and exotic places within this part of the (intellectual) world, and during my exploration I made extensive field notes to record and organize my experiences. *The Psychology of Second Language Acquisition* is in many ways the edited collection of these notes. As with other diaries, some of the insights are more discerning than others, and some might turn out merely to outline intriguing states of affairs without getting anywhere near to the bottom of those. For many readers, the region explored is likely to be a strange land, full of odd and perhaps menacing elements. Yet, the inescapable truth is that SLA researchers need to become skilled rangers in these territories—the psychological aspects will not go away but will take up an increasingly central position within the study of the acquisition of a foreign or second language. I do hope that this book will be useful in gathering the right equipment and gaining confidence before embarking on the next expedition.

What this book does and does not offer

Even fools are thought wise if they keep silent, and discerning if they hold their tongues.
(Proverbs 17: 28)

The Psychology of Second Language Acquisition is a book about language acquisition. Although this may sound self-evident, we will see in the first chapter that most of the SLA literature is not only, and often not even predominantly, concerned with how languages are learnt. This is because second language acquisition research is usually equated with second language research in general, and this latter domain involves two other key areas besides acquisition: second language representation (i.e. how L2 knowledge is structured in a formal system and stored in the brain) and second language processing (i.e. how an L2 is produced and comprehended). My interest, however, lies in the developmental aspect of L2 knowledge and this book, therefore, provides neither a detailed account of L2 representation nor one of processing.

Even after restricting the theme to the acquisition of an L2, the scope of the relevant topics is wide, ranging from Universal Grammar through the cognitive neuroscience of SLA to the psychological basis of language teaching methodologies. In covering the various areas, I will try to offer evaluative syntheses of the complex issues while also including numerous literal citations by leading scholars to represent multiple voices. The inherent difficulty of surveying the field was knowing that, given the speed of development in the area, a great deal of the current literature will be considered outdated or inaccurate in ten years' time. Thus, the challenge was to try and identify those aspects of our current knowledge that are likely to stand the test of time so that the summary is sufficiently forward-pointing.

Due to time and space limitations, and perhaps more importantly, due to my uneven knowledge, some potentially important areas have been omitted or covered only in insufficient detail. Examples include sociocultural theory, language transfer and fossilization, L2 attrition, and the psycholinguistics of literacy. In addition, I tended to spend the bulk of the time available for researching a particular topic reviewing the most recent literature, which left the historical background to some of the areas rather thin or sketchy. Even with these restrictions, I found that the further I progressed, the more obvious it became that I was unlikely ever to get there, a fact graphically illustrated by the growing piles of unread papers and books on my desk. I therefore sincerely apologize to scholars whose work will not be discussed in appropriate detail in the following chapters.

Acknowledgements

Over the years of preparing for, and then actually getting down to, writing this book, I have been encouraged and helped by many people. First and foremost, I would like to express my thanks to Cristina Whitecross from Oxford University Press, who has been much more than merely a good editor. She embraced the vision of this book right from the beginning and provided ongoing support throughout the whole process of completing the manuscript. Special thanks are due to Simon Murison-Bowie, who not only polished the text and sorted out all the commas and colons but who also made many valuable suggestions on how to improve the content. I am grateful to Natasha Forrest for making sure that the production of the book went so smoothly.

I have been fortunate to have several friends and colleagues willing to read the whole or various parts of the manuscript and give me detailed suggestions on how to improve the text. My warm thanks are due to David Birdsong, Robert DeKeyser, Nick Ellis, Jan Hulstijn, Diane Larsen-Freeman, Patsy Lightbown, Peter MacIntyre, Lourdes Ortega, John Schumann, Tom Scovel, Norman Segalowitz, Nina Spada, and Henry Widdowson for their valuable feedback. I have done my best to take as many of their comments on board as possible and I do believe that the manuscript has improved considerably as a result of their contribution. Needless to say, the remaining faults are entirely mine.

1

Introduction: mapping the terrain

The literature in various linguistic, psycholinguistic and neurolinguistic domains does not converge on an integrated, coherent view on L2 learning (and L1 learning).
(Hulstijn 2002a: 200)

Second language acquisition (SLA) research has traditionally been part of the broader field of applied linguistics, and even today, the main international organization sponsoring SLA research is the American Association of Applied Linguistics (AAAL). Hundreds of pages have been written about the fact that the label 'applied linguistics' does not do full justice to the field because of what it emphasizes and, more importantly, what it does not. Without going into detail, the curious fact is that many of today's best-known applied linguists do not seem to be doing research that is particularly 'applied' and they would not necessarily call themselves 'linguists' either. As already highlighted in the Preface, the study of the acquisition, processing, and mental representation of a second/foreign language (L2) is in a process of transition towards acquiring a new disciplinary identity that is increasingly linked to aspects of relevant psychological research.

A good starting point for understanding the emerging new identity of our field is to map the main theoretical currents and academic areas that are contributing to the ongoing restructuring process. Broadly speaking, psychological influences have affected SLA theory through two main channels: (1) learning lessons from the growing knowledge about the brain in cognitive psychology, psycholinguistics, neuropsychology, and cognitive neuroscience; and (2) drawing on the extensive research on first language (L1) acquisition, which has traditionally been studied by developmental psycholinguists. In this chapter, I will first inspect the various academic disciplines that address aspects of the linguistics–psychology interface, and then I will look at the various forms of language acquisition, from mother-tongue learning to instructed SLA.

Language, linguistics, and psychology: academic interfaces

The relationship between psychology and linguistics has been a curious one.
(Segalowitz 2001: 3)

In our changing academic climate it will not come as a surprise to hear that language—the central topic of its 'officially' designated discipline, linguistics—is also a key area in the field of psychology. This is because language is more than a mere communication code or a cognitive linguistic system; it stands at the centre of human affairs, from the most prosaic to the most profound, and it is a basic ingredient of virtually every social situation. Accordingly, as Lightbown and Spada (2006: 1) summarize, the acquisition of language is 'one of the most impressive and fascinating aspects of human development'. It is hardly surprising therefore that psychologists, whose mandate has been to try and understand the complexities of human behaviour and thinking, have spent a great deal of effort in the past analysing language-related phenomena—as of course have linguists. Yet, given this common interest, it is a curious fact of life that until very recently, scholars from the two fields had tended to work independently of each other, having no ongoing dialogue and without building on each others' findings. In a paper devoted to the analysis of the evolving connections between psychology and linguistics, Segalowitz (2001) explains that although in the 1960s—following Chomsky's work—the two fields had the potential of developing a close working association with each other, this potential never really materialized and 'psychological research on language today is far less driven by recent advances in theoretical linguistics than it was then; similarly, a great deal of work in theoretical linguistics makes little reference to current developments in psychology' (p. 3). Consequently, his overall conclusion was grim:

> The sad truth is that many psychologists interested in language have not kept up with recent developments in linguistics . . . and it would also seem that many linguists are not aware of what is happening in psychology, especially in cognitive psychology and cognitive neuropsychology. (p. 4)

One fundamental reason for the divide between linguists and psychologists specializing in language has been that they have traditionally looked at the same phenomenon—language—from two different perspectives: broadly speaking, linguists have studied the language *output* of the speech/language production process (i.e. people's oral and written discourse) without looking at how this output was generated. Accordingly, the main objective of linguistics has been to provide descriptive rules and patterns of the language system (e.g. 'grammar') without any concern for psycholinguistic validity, that is, whether the proposed system had any plausibility in terms of its neurological operation and development. Psychologists, on the other hand, have focused on the mental processes and structures whereby people understand, produce, remember, store, and acquire language, with little concern for the subtle linguistic patterns of the language code.

The breach between psychological and linguistic approaches has also been apparent within the field of applied linguistics. A decade ago Skehan (1998: 1), for example, stated that 'Psycholinguistics, the study of the psychological processes underlying language learning and use, has been insufficiently influential on our profession as a foundation discipline, losing out in importance to linguistics and sociolinguistics'. While I believe that ten years later this claim still carries some truth because applied linguistics is still characterized by a dominant linguistic orientation, during the past decade we have witnessed a gradual but profound transformation in the relationship of the two disciplines. According to Segalowitz (2001), this change was the result of parallel developments in psychology and linguistics. In the former, advances in brain sciences and in modelling associative learning systems shed new light on the mental representations of linguistic processes, while in linguistics new approaches emerged that explicitly tried to link models of language to cognitive psychological processes. Applied linguists have been sensitive to this new spirit of cross-fertilization. An increasing number of studies drawing on psychological theories have been presented at applied linguistics conferences or in mainstream L2 journals: starting with the 2001 issue of the journal *Annual Review of Applied Linguistics,* a series of special issues have appeared in leading international journals, specifically focusing on the intersection of language and psychology (e.g. *Applied Linguistics* 2006: 27/4; *Lingua* 2008: 118/4; *Bilingualism: Language and Cognition* 2007: 10/1; *Modern Language Journal* 2008: 92/2; *Studies in Second Language Acquisition* 2003: 24/2, 2005: 27/2). Furthermore, this tendency has shown signs of acceleration recently—when I was collecting material for this book I was struck by the unexpected richness of the psychologically oriented SLA research of the past few years.

Interestingly, the gradual convergence of linguistics and psychology has been part of a broader paradigm shift in the traditional division of academic fields, with cognitive (neuro)science emerging as a new academic 'top gun'. Baars (1997a: p. vii) describes this shift:

> Ever since the nova scientia of Galileo and Copernicus began the
> revolutionary rise of modern physics, new sciences have been proclaimed
> with some regularity. Most of these announcements turn out to be
> false alarms. But today we actually find ourselves at one of those rare
> nodal points in the evolution of human understanding: For the first
> time . . . serious brain and psychological scientists are exploring conscious
> experience—often under obscure labels, but now with far better evidence
> and theory than ever before.

Let us have a look at the most important language-related fields with the 'obscure labels' that Baars was referring to above—'cognitive linguistics', 'psycholinguistics', 'neurolinguistics', 'cognitive science', and 'cognitive neuroscience'—to see how they can inform applied linguists in the study of SLA.

Cognitive linguistics

Cognitive linguistics can be seen as a broad theoretical movement, subsuming different theories that share certain common features, the most important and most general of which being the commitment to work with constructs that have some psychological reality. (For SLA-specific overviews, see Achard and Niemeier 2004; Robinson and N. Ellis 2008*b*.) It is a relatively new area of linguistics, dating back to 1990, when the flagship journal of the approach, *Cognitive Linguistics,* was launched (N. Ellis and Robinson 2008).

Croft and Cruse (2004) list three major hypotheses that have guided the cognitive linguistic approach to language: (1) language is not an autonomous cognitive faculty; (2) grammar is conceptualization; and (3) knowledge of language emerges from language use. These principles are closely related to the usage-based theories of language acquisition discussed in Ch. 3 and, indeed, as Tomasello (2003) states, the new wave of usage/item/exemplar-based linguistic theories usually appear under the general banner of functional and/or cognitive linguistics.

The 'cognitive' label also reflects the general drive to make cognitive linguistic theories compatible with the main principles of cognition and, more specifically, with models in cognitive psychology, such as models of memory, perception, attention, and categorization. In the introduction to their recent comprehensive overview of the field, N. Ellis and Robinson (2008: 4) summarize this cognitive commitment:

> The additional cognitive commitment of CL [cognitive linguistics] is to specify the interface of linguistic representation (grammatical factors), which can be used to communicative effect in producing utterances, with other aspects of conceptual structure (e.g. semantic factors, such as our concepts of time, and spatial location), as well as with the constraints imposed by the architecture of cognitive processes, and the structure of cognitive abilities (e.g. psychological factors, such as those involved in the allocation and inhibition of attention).

Most of the past research in cognitive linguistics has focused on semantics (Croft and Cruse 2004), but syntax and morphology have also been addressed, and as we will see in Ch. 3, cognitive linguists have recently made substantial progress in exploring issues related to (mainly first) language acquisition. The semantic emphasis has been a consequence of the central belief in cognitive linguistics that words reflect broader underlying conceptual systems, not unlike the tip of an iceberg; in Fauconnier's (2003: 540) words: 'Hidden behind simple words and everyday language are vast conceptual networks manipulated unconsciously through the activation of powerful neural circuits.' This perspective explains the special significance attached to the study of *metaphors* in their role as powerful conceptual mappings that are central to both everyday language use and scientific terminologies. Metaphor theory, started by Lakoff and Johnson in the 1980s, proposes that by linking source domains of human experience to abstract concepts, metaphors contribute considerably to the development of thought. That is, except for talking about purely physical reality, our conceptual system is fundamentally metaphorical in nature, and therefore unpacking the conceptual meaning behind metaphors offers unique inroads into the understanding of cognition. (For summaries of metaphors, see Cameron 2003; Kövecses 2005.)

Psycholinguistics

According to Gernsbacher and Kaschak (2003), the term 'psycholinguistics' was coined in 1953 at a conference at Cornell University, but the field really took off only after the 1957 publication of Noam Chomsky's book *Syntactic Structures*. (It is interesting to note here that, as Altmann (2006) recounts, *Syntactic Structures* was based on Chomsky's lecture notes for undergraduate students, notes that he only wrote up in a book upon the encouragement of a friend who happened to visit MIT.) In many ways psycholinguists have been pursuing similar goals to those of cognitive linguists—namely, to expound the psychological reality and the cognitive mechanisms underlying language structure and use—yet the particular foci and research methods of the two disciplines are dissimilar due to their different disciplinary affiliation. Most cognitive linguists would consider themselves linguists first with an interest in cognition, while most psycholinguists would regard themselves primarily as psychologists with an interest in language. Accordingly, while cognitive linguistics has adopted the standard research methodology of linguistics, namely introspection in conjunction with theoretical analysis (Talmy 2007), psycholinguistics has been drawing on the research techniques of experimental psychology (described in detail in Ch. 2).

The first decade of psycholinguistic research was largely taken up by developing theories of language processing based on Chomsky's generative grammar, and this scope was broadened at the end of the 1960s by the influence of information processing theory. As Altmann (2006) explains, it was this period when the 'mind-as-computer' metaphor started to have a pervasive influence on both psycholinguistics and the study of cognition in general—which is a good illustration of the profound significance of metaphors discussed in the previous section. As a result of these developments, the 1970s saw enormous growth in psycholinguistics across a wide range of topics, including word recognition, sentence comprehension, and the mental representation of texts. This momentum further increased in the 1980s and 1990s with the spread of neuroimaging techniques (described in detail in Ch. 2); as MacWhinney (2001c) summarizes, the current emphasis is on trying to link experimental methodology to methods of imaging the human brain during language processing. Thus, we can observe an increasing integration of traditional psycholinguistic approaches and cognitive neuroscience (to be discussed below). Altmann (2006: 8) sums this up clearly:

> What we can be sure of is that the boundaries between the study of language and the study of other aspects of cognition are wearing thinner. No doubt there are already developments in 'neighbouring' fields of study (e.g. the computational sciences and non-cognitive neurosciences) that will also have an impact, but have yet to emerge as quantifiable influences on psycholinguistics.

A special subdomain of psycholinguistics that is particularly relevant to the topic of this book is *developmental psycholinguistics*. This field has tradition-ally focused on the study of child language acquisition and will be discussed in more detail later in this chapter. Here we need only note the peculiar aca-demic phenomenon that L1 acquisition has traditionally been seen as an area of psychology, whereas L2 acquisition has almost entirely been studied by (applied) linguists. Although this divide is still as a whole in existence, the recent converging trend of linguistics and language psychology has not been without effect and communication amongst scholars across the L1/L2 bound-ary has become more featured. (For a good illustration, see for example the discussion of L1 influences on SLA concerning age effects, such as 'language entrenchment', at the end of Ch. 6.)

Neurolinguistics

The previous section briefly mentioned the powerful contemporary drive of incorporating the methods and findings of neuroscience into more traditional approaches such as psycholinguistics and, in this sense, neurolinguistics can be seen as a linguistic companion to psycholinguistics. Neurolinguistics shares similar objectives with cognitive linguistics but draws on neuropsychology rather than cognitive psychology as the main source of psychological knowl-edge. In his comprehensive summary of the neurolinguistics of bilingualism, Paradis (2004) explains that the term 'neurolinguistics' was first used by French neurologist Henry Hécaen in the late 1960s, to denote a discipline that was to bridge a gap between the neurosciences (neurology, neuroanat-omy, neurophysiology, and neurochemistry) and human communication (linguistics and psycholinguistics). Originally, the main emphasis of the field was on studying verbal deficits resulting from cortical lesions (i.e. aphasia) and therefore neurolinguistics was initially closely associated with language pathology. For this reason, some scholars (e.g. Ahlsén 2006) put the genesis of neurolinguistics as being 1861, when Paul Broca presented his seminal findings on what was to be called 'Broca aphasia'. (See Ch. 2 for more details.) Recently, neurolinguistics has extended its scope well beyond aphasia studies and embraced the whole new spectrum of neuroimaging techniques, thereby blending gradually into the cognitive neuroscience of language—see below.

Cognitive science

The academic discipline *cognitive science* is the most prominent outcome of the 'great academic paradigm shift' described earlier. Its remit includes the 'scientific study of minds and brains, be they real, artificial, human or animal' (Nadel and Piattelli-Palmarini 2003: p. xiii). It is thus a rich and diverse area of the study of the mind that has been fuelled by the academic world's (and also laypeople's) unrelenting interest in the operation of the brain and the growing excitement about the fact that for the first time in human history there are realistic ways of peeping into what had been treated for centuries as a 'black box'. (For a discussion of a range of brain-related issues, see Ch. 2.) This momentum is palpable in the growing number of university programmes, faculty positions, international conferences, and publications such as academic journals, handbooks, and encyclopaedias that are explicitly related to cognitive science, and which are usually seen as the indices of the vitality of a field. The significance of the field is also measurable in the prestige of its main scholars and the amount of research funding and media coverage that is associated with it. All in all, it is good to be a cognitive scientist nowadays!

In an interview about the genesis of cognitive science, George Miller, one of the fathers of the field, stated that the birthday of the discipline was 11 September 1956, the date of a meeting at MIT where 'leading cognitivists from computer science, linguistics, and psychology all came together for the first time and began to realize they shared their interest in the human mind' (Gazzaniga, Ivry, and Mangun 2002: 18). Three talks in particular—Miller's 'The magical number seven' (Miller 1956), Chomsky's 'Three models of language', and Newell and Simon's 'Logic theory machine'—were influential in laying the foundations of a movement whose success story has exceeded even the most fervent enthusiasts' expectations. The four scholars also reflect the hugely interdisciplinary nature of the field—it draws on concepts and methods from linguistics, psychology, artificial intelligence, computer science, philosophy, neuroscience, and anthropology. One obvious attraction of the term 'cognitive science' for members of all these disciplines is that it helps to distinguish the field from both the humanities and the social sciences, making it appear more like the natural science of the brain.

The most dynamic current direction in cognitive research involves various forms of brain imaging. This area is often distinguished from cognitive science by the label 'cognitive neuroscience', although this is admittedly a rather permeable boundary. Interestingly, this permeability was not always in existence. For a good 25 years after its birth, classical cognitive science rejected the significance of the neurosciences because the dominant scientific pursuit concerned the generation of complex symbolic representations and computational models that required little or no contact with the brain. Neurons were relegated to the role of 'mere implementation' (Nadel and Piattelli-Palmarini 2003: p. xviii). Long and Doughty (2003) report on a survey that found that in the field's leading journal—*Cognitive Science*—and flagship conference—the annual conventions of the Cognitive Science Society—two subdisciplines, cognitive psychology and computer science, dominated the period between 1977 and 1995, accounting for over half the articles and papers. Even today, there are surprisingly few studies that are equally strong on cognitive theorizing and empirical neuroimaging. For this reason, I will discuss cognitive neuroscience separately below.

Cognitive science and SLA

In the concluding chapter of their comprehensive handbook of SLA, Long and Doughty (2003) argue that for many SLA researchers who are looking for a new identity or institutional home in the ongoing academic paradigm shift, the 'cognitive scientist' label is more attractive than that of 'social scientist'. Indeed, I assume that many, if not most, of the applied linguists cited in this book would agree with this claim. Research topics such as maturational constraints, explicit vs. implicit learning/memory, automatization, computer modelling of language processes, grammaticalization, aptitude complexes, and the like are obvious targets for cognitively minded scholars. As Long and Doughty argue, 'Underlying all their work is a shared conception of SLA as a cognitive process involving representations and computations on those representations' (p. 869). Consequently, their conclusion is straightforward:

> For SLA to achieve the stability, stimulation, and research funding to survive as a viable field of inquiry, it needs an intellectual and institutional home that is to some degree autonomous and separate from the disciplines and departments that currently offer shelter. Cognitive science is the logical choice. (ibid.)

The problem with this seemingly convincing contention is that due to the diverse role and nature of language in the world, it is equally possible to generate a similarly convincing list of key research issues that are targets for non-cognitively minded scholars. Topics such as identity, self, emotion, environment, social interaction, situational constraints, speech accommodation, caretaker talk, language policy, and the like highlight a completely different dimension of the complex dynamics of SLA; and we may even go one step further and compile a third, pedagogically grounded list comprising topics such as teaching methodology, learner groups, corrective feedback, curriculum, learning tasks, materials design, etc. Thus, it is hard to separate SLA from the social and instructional arena in which it takes place, an issue that has been argued passionately in a recent focus issue of *The Modern Language Journal* (Lafford 2007). Consequently, for many applied linguists the search for an identity may not end with cognitive science.

Cognitive neuroscience

> *Keeping up to date with cognitive neuroscience is much like surfing the Big Wave at Waikiki Beach. New findings keep rolling in and maintaining a stable balance is a big challenge. It is exciting, fun and, at times, a little bit scary.*
> (Baars and Gage 2007b: p. xiii)

The reason for talking about *cognitive neuroscience* separately from cognitive science is due to the unprecedented recent progress of neuroresearch as a result of major technological developments in neuroimaging techniques that have offered an entirely new window into the human mind, allowing the online study of the human brain while it is engaged in various cognitive tasks. As Nadel and Piattelli-Palmarini (2003: p. xxiv) summarize, the subsequent explosion of research on the brain mechanisms underlying human cognitive functions has been 'nothing short of phenomenal'. This intoxicating new potential (and the concerns with it) will be described in depth in the next chapter, so let me here merely outline the main parameters of the discipline. According to Gazzaniga, Ivry, and Mangun (2002), the term 'cognitive neuroscience' was coined in a New York City taxi in the late 1970s to give name to a 'new mission' (p. 19) to examine how the brain enables the mind. Interestingly, one of the passengers in this famous taxi was the very George Miller who played a key role at the 1956 MIT conference that is usually seen as the starting point of cognitive science.

The missionary spirit has not subsided over the past three decades. The following extract from the Preface of Baars and Gage's (2007*b*: p. xiii) recent summary of the field reflects the kind of excited confidence that accompanies successful expeditions:

> [W]e are seeing a marriage of the cognitive and brain sciences, building on historic advances over the last few decades. Cognitive and perceptual mechanisms that were inferred from behaviour can now be observed more directly in the brain, using a variety of novel brain imaging methods. For the first time, we can observe the living brain in real time, doing what it has evolved to do over hundreds of millions of years. The result is astonishingly rich, combining psychology and biology, medicine, biochemistry and physics.

In the Preface of another best-selling textbook on cognitive neuroscience, Gazzaniga, Ivry, and Mangun (2002: p. xv) address one of the key questions of the field head on: 'What constitutes the first principles that make cognitive neuroscience distinct from physiological psychology, neuroscience, cognitive psychology, or neuropsychology?' The authors' answer is that the characteristic feature of the new discipline is its well-balanced hybrid nature, integrating cognitive theory with neuropsychological and neuroscientific evidence, as well as computational techniques. This seems to be an idyllic 'marriage of the cognitive and brain sciences' (Baars and Gage 2007*b*: p. xiii).

Cognitive neuroscience and SLA

With language use being one of the most prominent human cognitive functions, a great deal of neuroscientific research has been directed at capturing 'in vivo' images of brain processes during a wide range of language tasks. Armed with powerful neuroimaging tools, several laboratories in the world have set out to map the language faculty in the human brain. (See Ch. 2 for more details.) Pulvemüller (2002: 9) justifies these neuropsychological efforts by pointing out that it is almost certain that language mechanisms in the brain are organized as nerve cells and their mutual connections, and a 'realistic model of language, therefore, must specify the putative organic basis of language use and language comprehension in terms of neurons, neuronal connections, and neuron circuits'. Arguing in a similar vein, Lamb (1999) asserts that a realistic theory of language needs to go beyond merely accounting for various processes and patterns in the output of the human linguistic system (which, as we have seen, has been the traditional practice of linguistic analysis) by also providing 'neurological plausibility'.

   While most scholars would agree in principle with Pulvemüller and Lamb's contention, Jacobs (2004) explains that a common objection to paying neuroscience more than mere lip service in language acquisition circles has been the claim that not enough is known about the brain to make significant contributions to our understanding of how language is acquired. In the light of the growing body of relevant research literature, however, this dismissive attitude is less and less tenable. (For a recent overview of the cognitive neuroscience of SLA, see Gullberg and Indefrey 2006.) While the picture emerging from cognitive neuroresearch on L1 and L2 issues has been admittedly rather 'noisy', we are getting an increasingly accurate sense of what kind of mental metaphors are simply *not* plausible in terms of their underlying neural foundation. This point is argued forcefully by Schumann (2004a) when he claims that in the twenty-first century we simply cannot afford not to impose certain neurobiological constraints on our conceptualization of language processes. The increasing amount of neuroscientific information available to SLA researchers about the bilingual brain (see e.g. Abutalebi, Cappa, and Perani 2005) offers sufficient munitions in this respect, and it is one of the main intentions of this book to provide the readers with enough background knowledge to be able to make use of this accumulating neuroscientific evidence.

Interim summary: the permeability of disciplinary boundaries

We have arrived at a new phase of studying the acquisition and processing of language, and one of the most obvious characteristics of modern times is the increasing fluidity of academic identities and the growing permeability of disciplinary boundaries. Nobody is surprised nowadays to see, for example, a former hardcore generative linguist becoming engaged in developmental psycholinguistic research (perhaps also doing some neuroimaging on the side), and it does not seem strange at all that a scholar might align him/herself simultaneously with applied, cognitive, and psycholinguistics. There is an increasing amount of common ground in the various subdisciplines, making it possible to straddle the borders between them or to completely cross the boundaries, dipping in and out. Thus, it seems to me that the main academic organizational force at present is not so much the inherent content of the various disciplines and strands as the individual scholars' subjective affiliation to professional organizations and conferences as their main reference points.

Interestingly, the academic community is behaving very much like a complex system would, with new directions and groupings emerging as a result of the field's self-organizing capacity. A classic example of this emergent feature is the appearance of 'bilingualism' as an academic rubric: strictly speaking it is not an academic discipline (and, accordingly, I will discuss it in more detail later under the various types of language attainment) and yet it has now its own journals and well-attended international conventions—in fact, an increasing number of scholars who used to call themselves applied linguists, psycholinguists, or SLA researchers now fly the bilingualism banner. It would be an intriguing study to apply dynamic systems theory (see Ch. 3) to the analysis of the evolution and sociology of SLA research. In any case, the main lesson for our current purpose is that we need not worry too much about the exact labelling of research directions. My personal feeling is that we are all inevitably becoming, at least partially, cognitive neuroscientists specializing in second language issues.

Main avenues to language attainment

The term 'language acquisition' often occurs in the language-related psychological literature without any specification as to whether the authors are talking about the acquisition of an L1 or an L2, let alone specifying the exact type of these broad categories. Looking more closely at these texts we will usually find that 'language acquisition' refers to mother-tongue attainment only, with relatively few language psychologists addressing the unique issues of L2 acquisition and processing. Although in their influential text on psycholinguistics, Berko Gleason and Bernstein Ratner (1998: p. v) state that a 'psycholinguistic discussion of language processing would not be complete without consideration of bilingualism and second language learning', this is not (as yet) the standard position in psychology.

It has been pointed out by many that the majority of the people living in the world speak more than one language and therefore the norm is not monolingualism but bilingualism. So why is there such an obvious reluctance in psychologists to consider second language issues? And how much can we generalize findings from L1 acquisition studies to SLA? What are the similarities and differences between the two processes? Are there situations (e.g. early learning) when SLA can be seen as virtually identical to L1 acquisition? Can we distinguish two types of SLA depending on whether the L2 is primarily acquired in the host environment or in a formal school setting? And more generally, what are the main types of bilingualism and how do they differ in psychological terms? These are some of the central questions that will be addressed in our exploration of the psychological basis of SLA in the following chapters. Let us have a preliminary overview of the main issues here.

First language acquisition

Infants learn language with remarkable speed, but how they do it remains a mystery.
(Kuhl 2004: 831)

Although in theory the study of L1 acquisition falls outside the SLA focus of this book, the following chapters will contain a surprisingly large amount of material that is derived from the study of mother-tongue learning. This is because the comparison between L1 and L2 acquisition is enlightening both when we find similarities and when the two processes display deviating features. Accordingly, the process of how infants master their first language will be a recurring theme throughout this book and therefore I would like to address four general issues here concerning L1 acquisition and its research: (1) *mysterious uniformity*; (2) *nature versus nurture*; (3) *the evolution of language acquisition research*; and (4) *early milestones in L1 development*.

Mysterious uniformity of L1 acquisition

One of the most common statements about L1 acquisition in the literature concerns the remarkable uniformity of the process. Indeed, there seems to be a general agreement amongst scholars that children acquire an impressive amount of language in a comparatively short time without much direct tuition and with remarkable commonality (Shatz 2007). This uniformity is quite mysterious in at least two ways: first, after decades of intensive research, we still do not know enough about the details of the acquisition process or why there is such little variability in its ultimate outcome. Berko Gleason (2005: 5), for example, concludes that 'explaining what it is that children acquire during the course of language development is easier than explaining how they do it', and N. Ellis (2005b: 3) adds that 'never has there been so much debate as there currently is concerning the mechanisms of first language acquisition'.

The second source of puzzlement concerns the fact that although there is a general emphasis in the literature on the uniformity of the L1 acquisition process, a closer look reveals a great deal of individual-level variation in how native speakers acquire and use their L1. We tend to talk about 'native-like proficiency' in a language, but the content of this term is rather difficult to define scientifically beyond Doughty's (2003: 258) specification that children learning their L1 are 'eventually indistinguishable from other native speakers of their speech community'. Yet, within the L1 speech community there appears to be a considerable diversity across L1 speakers' command of their mother tongue, from their pronunciation to their syntactic or pragmatic skills. A detailed analysis of the variability in L1 acquisition goes beyond the scope of this book, although some aspects of it will be addressed in Chs. 5 and 6; let me conclude here with a thought-provoking comment by Bohannon and Bonvillian (2005: 273):

> Admittedly, no developmental psycholinguist seriously believes that magic is at the root of language acquisition, despite our frustrated

attempts to identify the actual processes involved. One of the reasons that we have failed to discover simple and easily observable processes in language learning may be that they do not exist, owing to the importance of the phenomenon to the developing child. In other words, there is simply so much pressure placed on children to communicate successfully that there are probably many routes to the goal, and within each route, a great deal of variability may be tolerated.

Nature versus nurture

L1 acquisition researchers are divided in how they explain the remarkable language learning capability of infants. The question revolves around how much, if any, innate language knowledge children bring to the learning process, and whether the learning mechanisms they apply are *domain-specific* (i.e. dedicated to language processing) or *domain-independent* (i.e. non-language-specific general learning capacities). The former view is usually labelled as 'nativist' and the proposed innate language endowment is typically, but not always, associated with a 'Universal Grammar' within a generative linguistic framework. In contrast, the latter, non-nativist stance claims that L1 competence is fully emergent during development as infants apply general cognitive mechanisms to processing language input. Chapter 3 provides an overview of this debate, also outlining an interim, 'soft' position between the two extremes. As a preliminary, the current momentum in developmental psycholinguistics increasingly supports the position that our mother tongue can be learnt without being fitted with any special linguistic endowment as part of the human genome, but we should note—as will be made clear in Ch. 3—that almost all the main experts in the field acknowledge that the jury is still out regarding this question.

The evolution of language acquisition research

There has been a continuous stream of research into mother-tongue acquisition over the past century, displaying an evolution of research approaches. As Shatz (2007) describes, the first half of the twentieth century was characterized by largely descriptive work, and this period was followed by a phase when the researchers' main concern was to test the claims of theoretical linguistics about predispositions specific to language. Although the debate about the existence of any innate language-specific endowment is still ongoing, the past decade has seen a fascinating new line of inquiry in developmental psycholinguistics that examines the mechanisms that infants use to parse and make sense of the speech stream that constitutes the auditory world around them. Chapter 3 will describe the infants' extraordinary implicit statistical learning skills that they utilize to process the probabilistic distributional properties of the language input. Saffran, Aslin, and Newport (1996), for example, found that after listening to as little as two minutes of computer-synthesized nonsense speech that contained no breaks, pauses, stress differences, or intonation, 8-month-old infants were able to detect and learn certain syllable combinations that were statistically more probable than others in the string they had just heard.

Early milestones in L1 development

This book does not offer a review of the developmental stages of L1 acquisition but I would like to point out one key characteristic of this process. Regardless of any individual-level variation mentioned earlier, certain milestones of language development occur with an impressive regularity in the majority of children, particularly in the first year of life. For example, as Berko Gleason (2005) summarizes, around the same time that they take their first steps, many infants produce their first words much the same way all over the world. This happens approximately when they are 12 months old, and the speech production and perception timeline up to this point—including the process of 'locking in' the sounds of our L1 (MacWhinney 2004)—appears to be fairly universal. Tomasello (2003) adds that the last few months of our first year of life is also the time for developing certain language-specific social-cognitive skills related to intention reading and categorizing. Thus, by the end of the first year of an infant's life, the scene is set for getting down to acquiring the L1 in earnest, and indeed, over the subsequent 3–4 years, the acquisition of the basic linguistic system is largely completed for most children. Although children display increasing variation in both the pattern and the rate of language acquisition during this subsequent period, Singleton and Ryan (2004) conclude that at least with regard to the development of syntax, we can observe a stable sequence of milestones associated with reasonably well-defined age norms.

Bilingualism

> *[M]ultilingualism is humankind's norm. With perhaps 6,000 languages of the world, far more than the 200 or so countries, an equally rough-and-ready calculation suggests that human beings are more likely than not to be able to speak more than one language.*
> (N. Ellis 2005b: 3)

L1 acquisition research almost always looks at the attainment of our mother tongue in a monolingual framework, and SLA research typically takes an established L1 system as a starting point to which a distinct L2 dimension is added. Ortega (2007b: 246) is right in pointing out that in this respect SLA research actually carries a certain amount of 'monolingual bias':

> Ironically, the field of SLA takes as prototypical the idealized case of the individual who already possesses a mature monolingual grammar and who subsequently begins learning an L2 with the goal to add on a monolingual-like command of the additional language.

While there are many examples of a clear-cut separation of L1 and L2 acquisition, a significant proportion of people in the world display some sort of 'bilingualism' (a term that is often used to stand for multilingualism as well) as a result of a language learning history whereby the acquisition of at least two languages happen simultaneously or overlap considerably in childhood. The term 'bilingualism' does not refer to a uniform phenomenon but rather to a range of different patterns and combinations of acquiring and knowing multiple languages, depending on factors such as the number of languages involved, their acquisition timelines, the amount of opportunity for their use, and their relative dominance in different situations. In addition and to make things even more complicated, the term is often extended to postpubertal L2 learners—the main targets of SLA research—who master their second language in a formal educational environment as a school subject.

Thus, owing to the great variability amongst bilinguals, the literature contains a whole variety of definitions of the term 'bilingualism', some of which deviate from each other considerably. The two extremes are (1) *balanced bilingualism,* featuring native-like competence in two languages, typically resulting from double L1 acquisition in infancy (or 'bilingual first language acquisition'; see Genesee and Nicoladis 2007); and (2) a very broad interpretation of bilingualism that defines the term as 'the ability to produce complete meaningful utterances in two languages' (Herschensohn 2007: 4). Between these maximalist and minimalist criteria lies a whole range of possible definitions, based on language-specific differences in a span of dimensions such as the degree of proficiency (often broken down to components such as fluency, accuracy, comprehension, etc.); the time-frame of acquisition; the context of acquisition (age and manner); the context of use (e.g. relative frequency, purpose, modalities, sociolinguistic status); and the structural distance between the languages. An unfortunate consequence of the huge number of possible permutations of these dimensions is that it makes it difficult to compare studies that examine various types of bilingualism; accordingly, it is not quite clear what exactly 'bilingualism' means in one of the most cutting-edge contemporary research areas, the study of the 'neurobiological correlates of bilingualism'. Indeed, Grosjean *et al.*'s (2003) enlightening article entitled 'Imaging Bilinguals: When the Neurosciences Meet the Language Sciences' contains an intriguing exchange between neuroscientists and bilingualism experts in which the definition of bilingualism is one of the main topics of dispute.

I mentioned earlier in this chapter that 'bilingualism' appears to be emerging as an academic discipline independent of applied linguistics or SLA research. Bialystok (2007), for example, confirms that the growing number of publications on the topic demonstrate that bilingualism has enjoyed a particular surge in interest in the past decade, and Walters (2005: 4) also concludes that studies in bilingualism have 'proliferated so widely and rapidly in recent years that most scholars will now find it difficult even to keep up with the reading'. What explains this seemingly unwarranted boom? Or, to look at the question from the other direction, why would a scholar nowadays choose to be labelled a bilingualism expert? We can get a good sense of the field's academic

identity by looking at the stated objectives of the four leading academic journals specifically devoted to the study of bilingualism:

- *Bilingualism: Language and Cognition*: the official description on the journal's website characterizes the journal as one that focuses on 'bilingualism
  from a cognitive science perspective' and its aims are to promote research
  on 'bilingual language competence, perception and production, bilingual
  language acquisition in children and adults, neurolinguistics of bilingualism in normal and brain-damaged subjects, and non-linguistic cognitive
  processes in bilinguals'. While there is clearly some overlap with SLA
  research, this blurb positions the journal in the forefront of the cognitive
  paradigm shift described earlier. We should also note that although acquisition is listed as an area of interest, the emphasis of the journal is not on
  the developmental aspects of an L2 but rather on the representational and
  processing sides.
- *International Journal of Bilingualism*: this journal aims to promote research
  on the 'linguistic, psychological, neurological, and social issues which
  emerge from language contact', with a focus on the 'language behaviour
  of the bi- and multilingual individual'. These aims are similar to those of
  Bilingualism: Language and Cognition in that they emphasize neurocognitive approaches and the study of language use rather than development.
- *International Journal of Bilingual Education and Bilingualism*: as the title
  indicates, this journal represents an angle that is different from the profiles
  of the above two journals, namely bilingual education. This is a central
  issue is many countries, including the United States, in which large ethnolinguistic groups coexist.
- *The Bilingual Research Journal*: the official organ of the American
  'National Association for Bilingual Education' and covers a wide range of
  topics relating to 'bilingual education, bilingualism in society, and language
  policy in education'. As such, its profile is similar to that of the *International Journal of Bilingual Education and Bilingualism*.

In sum, the profiles of the main bilingualism journals indicate that the
'bilingualism' label is primarily used by two types of scholar: (1) those who
specialize in the (neuro)cognitive analysis of the bilingual mind/brain, with
an emphasis on language representation, processing, and performance
associated with bilingual competence; and (2) those whose interest lies in educational issues such as language contact and planning within multicultural
societies. These two rather disparate directions share the common theme of
investigating how two active languages interact and compete with each other
either at the cognitive or at the societal level. In recognition of this basic
duality, Hamers and Blanc (2000) distinguished the two levels by referring to
them as 'bilinguality' and 'bilingualism', respectively, but this distinction in
terminology has not become widespread, and in most cases 'bilingualism' is
used for both meanings.

Cost–benefit appraisal of being bilingual

This book does not discuss bilingual first language acquisition or the characteristics of balanced bilinguals in detail. However, there is one topic I would like to address briefly because of its more general relevance: the potential costs and benefits of growing up with two active languages. In a recent overview, Genesee and Nicoladis (2007) explain that bilingual children tend not to differ from their monolingual peers in the time-frame of reaching some important milestones of language development such as the appearance of the first words. Furthermore, their overall rate of vocabulary growth is typically also similar. On the other hand, some differences between bilingual and monolingual children have been observed, for example in their vocabulary size in each language (which is likely to be due to the differences in exposure) and delays in the discrimination of certain phonetic contrasts. According to Bialystok (2005), bilingual children generally score lower than respective monolinguals in each of their languages within the area of receptive vocabulary.

While parents nowadays tend not to be worried about whether a child who is growing up in a bilingual environment will develop native-like L1 skills, questions are often raised about the potential cognitive costs of bilingual schooling, with some influential voices cautioning parents that bilingual children are disadvantaged both educationally and cognitively. A series of studies by Bialystok and her colleagues (e.g. Bialystok 2005; Bialystok *et al.* 2004, 2006, 2007), however, has produced a substantial body of evidence showing that not only is the intellectual growth of bilingual children not retarded but these children can actually outperform their monolingual peers in certain cognitive tasks. This advantage is related to the fact that bilingual children are required from an early age to deal with two languages by switching and inhibiting the competition between them. This functions like intensive cognitive training, as a result of which bilinguals are better at solving problems in which 'conflicting information, especially perceptual information, interferes with the correct solution and requires attention and effort to evaluate and ultimately ignore one of the options' (Bialystok 2005: 425). In addition to being able to resolve conflicting information better, bilinguals have also been found to have superior creative thinking and flexibility of thought, which is assumed to emerge from being able to see things from two perspectives as a function of being in possession of two linguistic systems.

The Bialystok experiments did not stop at proving that bilingualism has beneficial effects in children; they also revealed that bilingualism slows down the decline of cognitive control processes that comes with age. What is more, the bilingual advantage found in adulthood increases with age as bilinguals maintain higher levels of cognitive control beyond 60 years of age. Thus, bilingualism offers widespread benefits across a range of complex cognitive tasks. In a recent headline-grabbing study, Bialystok, Craik, and Freedman (2007) also demonstrated that lifelong bilingualism is associated with a delay in the onset of symptoms of dementia by four years compared to those who speak only one language. The significance of this result is underscored by the fact that currently there are no pharmacological interventions that have shown a comparable impact.

Second language acquisition

According to Larsen-Freeman (2002), the genesis of SLA research as an autonomous discipline goes back to the turn of the 1960s/1970s: two land-mark articles are usually mentioned in this respect, Pit Corder's (1967) 'The Significance of Learners' Errors' and Larry Selinker's (1972) 'Interlanguage'. These and other works of the period emphasized the systematic nature of L2 development, featuring L2-specific regularities such as 'interlanguage developmental sequences'. Although the sequences concerned were largely restricted to a few morphemes in the English language (e.g. progressive -ing, plural -s, possessive -s, third person singular present -s) and the research meth-odology used in the so-called 'morpheme order studies' might be questioned (for a summary, see N. Ellis and Larsen-Freeman 2006), their significance lay in underscoring the existence of a unique L2 developmental order, thereby confirming that an L2 cannot simply be seen through research lenses and paradigms developed for L1 studies. Since these initial developments in the 1970s, the field of SLA has grown considerably, with an increasing number of universities all around the world starting postgraduate pro-grammes focusing on second language acquisition or English as a second language.

With second language acquisition being the main theme of this book, all the following chapters address various aspects of this process. Let me set the scene here for these subsequent discussions by defining the broad domain and boundaries of SLA. To start with, here is a recent definition of the field by some eminent Dutch scholars: 'The field of Second Language Acquisition research focuses on how languages are learnt' (de Bot, Lowie, and Verspoor 2005: 3). While this may sound like a self-evident, even trivial truism, the puzzling fact is that most texts aimed at describing SLA are not only, and often not even predominantly, concerned with how languages are learnt. (Indeed, this even applies to de Bot *et al.*'s book from which the above quote has been taken.) What typically happens is that second language acquisition research is equated with second language research in general, which involves two other key areas besides acquisition: second language *representation* (i.e. how L2 knowledge is structured in a formal system and stored in the brain) and second language *processing* (i.e. how an L2 is used).

As will be discussed in Ch. 3, formal linguistic theories have traditionally adopted a symbolic approach; they have focused on the analysis of language output conceptualized as a static state without a prominent developmen-tal or transitional component. In this tradition, language acquisition has been seen as a 'movement through successive grammars (interlanguages)' (Hulstijn 2007*b*: 785). Thus, with some exaggeration, linguists have tradi-tionally had little to say about how languages are learnt; to find a substantial body of research that is relevant to the acquisition and development of L2 competence, we need to cross over to the domain of psychology, where developmental psychologists have made successful inroads into understanding L1 acquisition over the past century. This curious situation—namely that linguistics offered little information on acquisition—has often posed a real problem when it came to writing SLA texts, because the majority of the first generation of applied linguists—who have been, by definition, the authors of the most influential SLA texts—had linguistics rather than psychology as their background training. So, in the absence of an elaborate acquisitional dimension, these scholars emphasized the representational and processing/use aspects of the L2, or more specifically, as Hulstijn (2007a) summarizes, (1) the representation and (2) the processing of linguistic information, (3) the communicative interaction among L2 learners or between L2 learners and native speakers of the L2, (4) learner attributes, and (5) social context.

The main argument for extending the domain of SLA beyond acquisition has been the assumption that 'We learn language while using language' (N. Ellis 2005a: 305) and accordingly, 'Scientific studies of language representation and competence and of language acquisition and use are complementary' (N. Ellis and Larsen-Freeman 2006: 558). While nobody would question the validity of these claims, in order to be able to reflect this complementary nature properly we would need a theoretical paradigm that offers dynamic interfaces for the complementary aspects, otherwise any talk about the interrelatedness of L2 acquisition and use remains superficial. In Ch. 3, I will argue that traditional symbolic linguistic theories have failed to offer such a dynamic framework and therefore their discussion of the formal architectures of language (i.e. grammar) was not overtly relevant to the understanding of the acquisition of an L2. However, recent non-symbolic theories that are often subsumed under the 'connectionist' banner have introduced an entirely new approach to studying language, one that aims to account for representation and acquisition in one and the same form (Hulstijn 2002a). This movement will be the topic of Ch. 3 along with various related approaches inspired by developments in cognitive science (e.g. emergentism and dynamic systems theory) that offer new avenues to exploring language development and change. Then, in Ch. 4, I will examine the contribution of cognitive psychological theories of explicit/implicit learning, declarative/procedural knowledge, as well as skill learning and automatization to SLA research.

Instructed versus naturalistic SLA

'Naturalistic SLA'—the primarily untutored learning of an L2, for example by picking it up during an extended stay in the host environment—and L1 acquisition share an important feature: the pacing and sequencing of the acquisition process is not consciously manipulated by human agents. In authentic and input-rich environments the gradual and incremental development of the learner's L2 proficiency emerges of its own accord. In contrast, 'instructed

SLA'—that is, the learning processes whereby an L2 is predominantly mastered within an educational context with no or only little contact with native speakers of the L2—follows a very different principle; here the course of L2 development is largely determined by formal curricula and syllabi, and even small details of classroom events are often controlled by man-made lesson plans. Thus, in such formal school contexts the role of human agency—that is, the impact of policymakers, curriculum designers, materials writers, language teachers, and testers—is paramount.

Owing to the dissimilar role of human agency, instructed and non-instructed SLA differ fundamentally from each other in a number of key issues. One prominent example that will be elaborated on in Ch. 6 (when we examine age effects) is that in naturalistic SLA environments the younger the learner the better, whereas in school contexts the younger is not only not better but is often worse. A second source of difference concerns the basic disposition of the learners. Most school learners have no real need to acquire the L2 at all, let alone to a native-like level, whereas in naturalistic SLA most people would feel a natural urge to master the language of the host environment.

At the research level, one of the most basic differences between naturalistic and instructed SLA concerns the strikingly different social settings for the language learning enterprise. Naturalistic SLA is embedded in authentic, real-life situations, whose language-specific characteristics have been described in the past by theories of acculturation and intergroup contact. For example, Giles and Byrne's (1982) famous *intergroup model* described the conditions under which the members of minority ethnic groups in multicultural settings can successfully acquire and use the dominant language in terms of 'group boundaries', 'multiple group membership', and the minority group's 'ethno-linguistic vitality'. Schumann's (1978, 1986) *acculturation theory* focused on the social and psychological distance between the L1 and L2 communities, as well as on the ways by which this distance could be bridged by some sort of an integration process.

In contrast, the educational setting of instructed SLA has been described by means of a completely different set of factors such as teacher and student roles, classroom management, inter-student relations and interaction patterns, group norms, classroom goal structures, and group cohesiveness, that is, variables describing a microcosm that is complex and self-contained but reflects the broader social reality only indirectly, through a unique lens. (See e.g. Dörnyei 2007a; Dörnyei and Murphey 2003; Gass and Mackey 2007; Harklau 2005; Lightbown 2000; Mackey and Polio in press; Toohey 2008; Zuengler and Mori 2002.) There has also been a growing body of knowledge of language teaching methodology accumulated by the large number of language teaching professionals employed at different levels of the L2 teaching industry; yet, all too often there has been a gap between this latter know-how of best practices and the data-based findings of SLA research. I will come back to this question in Ch. 7, which analyses instructed SLA.

Similarities and differences between first and second language acquisition

It is an undeniable fact that both L1 and L2 attainment involve the same target languages and the same learners (obviously in an aggregated sense) and therefore commonalities are to be expected. Yet, it is also an undeniable fact that the outcome of the two enterprises is vastly different, which suggests some substantial disparity between the two processes. Over the past decades the pendulum in SLA research has been swinging between emphasizing the similarities and emphasizing the differences, and by now it is clear that the truth lies somewhere in between the two poles: L1 and L2 acquisition share certain underlying psychological processes—for example, the method we use for learning new word forms (MacWhinney 2004)—and the transfer from L1 to L2 knowledge also plays a substantial role in SLA. For these reasons, MacWhinney (2004: 83) argues:

> Thus, rather than attempting to build two separate models of L1 and L2 learning, it makes more sense to consider the shape of a unified model in which the mechanisms of L1 learning are seen as a subset of the mechanisms of L2 learning. Although these L1 learning mechanisms are less powerful in the L2 learner, they are still partially accessible.

The last sentence of the above quote touches upon one of the central issues in the search for an understanding of the L1–L2 relationship: are the mechanisms that make L1 acquisition possible still operational, even if partially, when it comes to SLA? That is, do L1 and L2 acquisition differ from each other only quantitatively or are there more substantial qualitative differences related to the operation of different learning mechanisms? Our current answer is, admittedly, somewhat speculative due to the rather limited information available; the next decade is likely to bring about a much clearer understanding of the processes underlying L1 acquisition, which will then allow us to test the extent to which these contribute to the mastery of an L2. Drawing on our existing knowledge, it seems that L1 and L2 acquisition differ from each other both quantitatively and qualitatively. We shall see in Chs. 3 and 4 that some of the key learning processes underlying infant language attainment (e.g. statistical learning) can be observed in SLA as well, but their function is restricted; therefore, to achieve success, L2 learners need to complement these with L2-specific learning processes (most notably, explicit learning mechanisms). In fact, one influential argument supporting the 'Critical Period Hypothesis' in SLA (see Ch. 6) is specifically related to this qualitative shift from implicit to explicit learning. Let us have a look now at the most salient differences between L1 and L2 acquisition:

- *Differential success*: the most obvious difference between the attainment of an L1 and an L2 is that the former is invariably considered successful by the learners themselves (i.e. we do not hear people complaining about not speaking their mother tongue well enough), whereas most L2 learners never reach as high a level in the target language as they have originally hoped for. The issue of differential success is therefore central to any SLA theory construction, giving rise to the theory of Universal Grammar (see Ch. 3) and the Critical Period Hypothesis (see Ch. 6).

- *Automatic versus optional:* not only is L1 acquisition invariably successful, it also appears to be automatic in the sense that the learners' motivation does not play a role in whether or not they learn the language, or how far they proceed. In contrast, motivation is a basic issue in SLA, underpinning the operation of every other factor—a good illustration of the saying 'You can lead a horse to water, but you can't make it drink'.

- *Homogeneity versus heterogeneity of the learning process:* we have seen earlier that L1 acquisition is characterized by certain milestones of development that occur with an impressive regularity in the majority of children, particularly in the first year of life. I personally believe that we tend to overstate the uniformity of mother tongue learning as there is a fair amount of variability in both the processes and the final outcomes. Nevertheless, this is all relative because, compared to the great amount of individual-level variation we find in every aspect and at every level of SLA, L1 acquisition appears to be definitely homogeneous. SLA also involves many factors and processes that are not evident in the acquisition of a mother tongue (Juffs and DeKeyser 2003).

- *Knowledge of the language and knowledge of the world:* an important feature of L1 acquisition is that it goes hand in hand with the infant's learning about the world around him/her (N. Ellis 2002*a*). In contrast, SLA displays a marked imbalance between the developmental level of the L2 code and learners' pre-existing conceptual knowledge as well as their thinking and problem-solving skills. This background knowledge and the cognitive maturity associated with it inevitably affects the way by which L2 learners go about the language-learning task.

- *Expressing individuality:* L1 learners develop their basic identity through expressing their individuality and substantiating their membership in groups through the newly learnt L1 (Tomlinson 2007), thus forging a strong and intimate link with the language. While appropriating a new identity might be associated with the knowledge of an L2 in immigration contexts, this is an additional, often optional, identity that complements the learner's existing L1 identity, which makes the necessity of L2 learning far less compelling.

- *Pre-existing L1 knowledge:* an obvious L1/L2-learning difference with potentially far-reaching consequences is the fact that our first language is literally the first we learn, with no pre-existing language knowledge, whereas SLA builds on pre-existing L1 knowledge. The importance of the absence or presence of an underlying language substrate is well manifested in the significant role that L1 transfer plays in L2 learning and use. We still do not understand fully how the brain's commitment to an L1 affects its capacity to accommodate additional languages, but Ch. 6 will describe two interesting theories in this respect—MacWhinney's 'entrenchment' theory and Kuhl's 'native language neural commitment' (NLNC) theory—which both suggest that the pre-existing L1 knowledge can act as a serious constraint.

- *Language input and the amount of exposure:* although there is a fair amount of variation in the quality and quantity of language input learners are exposed to in both L1 and L2 acquisition, the two learning processes tend to differ greatly in these respects: both the quality and quantity of L1 input significantly exceed the L2 input that language learners are typically exposed to. In fact, L1 acquisition theories, and the interactive view of L1 acquisition in particular, emphasize the significance of the instances when parents/caregivers provide language exemplars that are particularly salient to the child. Social interactionists argue that the special nature of the speech directed at children—often called 'motherese' or 'child-directed-speech'—is a necessary condition for normal L1 development (see e.g. Bohannon and Bonvillian 2005; Jay 2003). In contrast, SLA either does not involve any systematically delivered 'learner-directed speech', or when it does, this tends to comprise artificial classroom discourse. In other words, unlike in L1 acquisition, the scaffolding of interlocutors is not guaranteed in SLA and even if the learner has succeeded in seeking out some support, the input received may not be accommodated to match the interactional needs of L2 learning process (Robinson and N. Ellis 2008a).

- *Implicit learning versus explicit learning:* perhaps the most researched theoretical distinction between L1 and L2 acquisition concerns the varying involvement of implicit and explicit learning mechanisms in the two processes. The ballpark view is that L1 acquisition relies on efficient implicit learning, which, for some reason, shifts at some point in our lives to less-than-efficient explicit learning that is characteristic of SLA. (See e.g. Paradis 2004; Ullman 2005.) As we will see in Chs. 3 and 4, the actual picture is more complex than this because L1 acquisition also involves explicit learning mechanisms (e.g. in vocabulary learning) and, similarly, L2 acquisition also includes a certain amount of implicit learning (e.g. as part of automatization), yet it is an incontestable fact that we find very little of the effortless and automatic nature of L1 acquisition in the L2 process. Possible reasons for this shift will be offered in Ch. 6 when we discuss age effects in language acquisition.

Third language acquisition and multilingualism

We have seen above that the traditional approach to first language acquisition has typically adopted a monolingual framework (i.e. it has usually been implicitly assumed that the child learns only one L1 without any interference from other languages), and SLA research has been similarly concerned with how one additional language can be added to the already attained single mother tongue. One reason for the emergence of the field of 'bilingualism' has been the recognition that this '1 + 1' situation is often simplistic because many people's language learning history is characterized by an ongoing competition of several languages the person is exposed to at various stages of his/her development. While a very broad understanding of bilingualism involves competence in two languages in general, regardless of their level of development, the more common interpretation of the term refers to cases when two or more languages happen simultaneously in early childhood, at the L1 acquisition phase. The relatively new term of 'third language acquisition' has been introduced to distinguish multiple L2 learning from multiple L1 learning that is subsumed by the bilingualism label. In other words, 'third language acquisition' can be seen as SLA + 1 (or SLA + 2, 3, etc.). Alternative names include 'trilingualism' and 'multilingualism', but these again tend to mix up the attainment of multiple languages in early childhood and at later stages of life.

Jessner and Cenoz (2007) emphasize that L3 acquisition is more complex than SLA because both the process and the product of acquiring an L2 can potentially influence the acquisition of additional languages. This makes sense: learners of an L3 have prior language learning knowledge and, as the authors point out, these learners possess metalinguistic skills and meta-cognitive strategies that a monolingual learner lacks. In this sense, the third language learner can be equated with the seasoned language learner. While most scholars would accept in principle Jessner and Cenoz's (2007) claim about the difference of L2/L3 acquisition, in actual reality the distinction is more often than not played down or ignored. De Angelis (2007: 4–5) summarizes this issue thus:

> At present the onus of highlighting meaningful differences between the
> acquisition of a second language and the acquisition of third or additional
> languages rests upon those who actively work on multilingualism
> and language acquisition, who generally support the view that some
> differences between types of acquisition exist and should be accounted
> for. In contrast, SLA scholars appear more willing to embrace a 'no
> difference' assumption in their work, and it is not uncommon to read
> statements to this effect.

The problem with the theoretical definition of L3 acquisition is that it is centred on the learner's 'prior experience of learning an L2' and this is a rather slippery concept. How long is 'prior': six months or five years? In their 'Dynamic Model of Multilingualism', Herdina and Jessner (2002) examine this issue in detail under the term 'threshold phenomena'. (For a recent summary, see Jessner 2008.) Drawing on the work of Cummins, the scholars show that the effects of the relationship between multiple languages can be explained by two proposed thresholds in the levels of the bilingual's competence: a low level of competence in a new language is likely to have negative effects, but beyond a certain threshold the negative consequences disappear. Then, beyond an upper threshold, the learner is likely to experience positive cognitive effects of multilingualism. Unfortunately, the authors note that the exact identification of these thresholds is problematic because the 'metalinguistic abilities still lack the necessary operationalization to be immediately empirically verifiable' (p. 116).

A further difficulty arises with regard to the exact meaning of 'experience': do we mean by this the length of exposure to a second language or the more individualistic and subjective acquisition of transferrable metalinguistic skills/awareness? If the former, can we assume that the length of prior exposure has, roughly speaking, the same effect for most multilingual speakers? If the latter, do these skills have to come from studying an additional foreign language in an L3 acquisition situation or do they also develop in SLA? That is, can we equate the prior metalinguistic experience of Learner A, who is about to start learning, say, Finnish with two years of past Hungarian-learning experience, and Learner B, who is about to start his third year of learning Hungarian, with two years of past Hungarian-learning experience? Here again, we run into the problem of the underspecified nature of what 'metalinguistic experience' involves; although Jessner (2008) provides an analysis of metalinguistic awareness, she leaves the issue of the source of this awareness open when she states that metalinguistic awareness develops 'in individuals living with two or three languages' (p. 277). Thus, questions abound and as Leung (2007: 99–100) concludes in a recent review article, 'We are still a long way from a definitive statement about how prior linguistic knowledge plays out in L3 acquisition, and there is still much for L3 researchers to explore.'

Summary

I began this chapter by looking at how the recent trend of the gradual convergence of linguistics and psychology in exploring language phenomena has produced a number of new, 'hybrid' disciplines, and how these fields have started to play an increasingly active role in informing the study of SLA. As a result of this ongoing paradigm shift, disciplinary boundaries have become increasingly blurred and permeable, and scholars who would traditionally have identified themselves as being aligned to applied linguistics—the original home of SLA research—started to adopt multiple academic identities. It was concluded that we are in the middle of a major academic restructuring process in which different research directions cross-fertilize each other in an unprecedented manner. MacWhinney (2006) pointed out that this cross-fertilization process has promoted innovation and dynamism, but at the same time, 'researchers and practitioners have often found themselves awash in a sea of conflicting claims and recommendations from these various theoretical sources' (p. 729).

Having mapped the terrain of the academic disciplines that have something to offer to the study of the psychology of SLA, we looked at the main avenues to language attainment. Between the two poles of monolingual L1 acquisition and multilingualism we can find several categories that describe various combinations of multiple language attainment processes. In the absence of any clear-cut terminological distinctions, I offered the broad organizing principle that the term 'bilingualism' tends to be associated with multiple and simultaneous L1 acquisition, whereas 'third language acquisition' with multiple and usually overlapping L2 acquisition. This, however, represents an admittedly crude distinction because we can find many exceptions and overlapping cases between conceptualizations of bilingualism and L3 acquisition in the literature.

2

Language and the brain

*It is a good idea to think about language in terms of brain
mechanisms—to spell out language in the language of neurons, so to
speak.*
(Pulvemüller 2002: 1)

For most applied linguists the normal reaction when coming across a sentence like the following one is panic: 'The NCC involve a coalition of forebrain neurons implicated in working memory and planning, interconnected via widespread cortico–cortico and cortico–thalamic feedback loops with sets of neurons in sensory and motor regions that code for particular features' (N. Ellis 2005a: 311). Yet, this sentence does not come from a *Manual for Emergency Neurosurgery on the Battlefield* but from the renowned applied linguistics journal *Studies in Second Language Acquisition*. Referring to a similar passage in a different article, N. Ellis (2002b: 299) commented:

> This might seem overly psychological for some readers, using concepts
> perhaps remote from conventional SLA discourse. If this proves so
> and you feel like you are losing the plot, then skip this section and move
> on to more traditional issues. Please return here later, though: We are now
> at a stage at which there are important connections between SLA theory
> and the neuroscience of learning and memory.

The word 'perhaps' in the first sentence above is quite an understatement: neurobiological concepts are totally remote from anything that is typically taught in an 'Introduction to Applied Linguistics' or 'TESOL' course. Yet, Ellis is right in pointing out that we have reached a stage when applied linguistics and neuroscience inevitably link up, and therefore this kind of language simply won't disappear. So, the only solution for us is to learn it. A good starting point may be the following brief introduction to what we can call 'Neuropsychologese'.

As a preliminary, Jacobs (2004: p. ix) warns us that a psychologically oriented approach 'is not for the neurobiologically timid, as it requires one to learn the language of the brain for effective academic discourse'. Schumann *et al.* (2004*b*: p. xii) explain that the prerequisite investment involves 'a course in neuroanatomy and one in the cell biology of learning and memory', which he forecasts optimistically 'will become more generally available to applied linguistics programs'. Whether or not this is true, Neuropsychologese is certainly based on an extensive vocabulary describing the neuroanatomy of the brain. Works adopting a neurolinguistic perspective place a real emphasis—and we may sometimes feel, *over*-emphasis—on such vocabulary, but this is not (only) motivated by the desire to show off the authors' 'neuro-savvy'. Rather, the introduction of the new terminology has to do with a more fundamental question, the use of metaphors in scientific discourse.

When scholars describe mental processes they inevitably use metaphors to grasp and pin down complicated and abstract issues. Scientific metaphors in general are an invaluable scaffolding, and as Baars (1997*a*: 53) points out, they have a 'long and honorable history in science as tools for making the perilous leap from the known to the unknown'. In applied linguistics, for example, metaphors such as 'comprehensible input', 'language acquisition device', or 'affective filter' have been highly useful in identifying central concerns and research directions in spite of the fact that the meaning of these terms has always carried a certain amount of vagueness. According to the well-known cognitive psychologist, Larry Squire (2007), history shows us that the problems associated with complex and fuzzy metaphors become less salient when these concepts are linked to biological information about structure and mechanism. For example, he argues, the term 'heredity' may be a little vague, but DNA is not. 'Whereas one might debate exactly what heredity means, there is no similar argument about DNA. In the case of DNA, one could call it something else' (p. 342). As he concludes, 'Biology provides leverage on the issue of classification and definition' (p. 342). It is in this light that we need to appreciate the significance of Neuropsychologese: scholars are attracted to it because it offers biological validation of many of our existing concepts and metaphors. We can argue as to whether this validation is overdone, but the basic justification of the use of some Neuropsychologese appears to be sound.

So, after this lengthy introduction, let us plunge into the world of neurons. I start below by describing the functional neuroanatomy of the brain, followed by a discussion of the nature of the human mind in the light of this neuroanatomical foundation. Then, in the second half of the chapter, we take a (critical) look at the intricate world of neuroimaging and brain scanning (alongside other research methods) to obtain an overview of the emerging new research methodology targeting the brain. This chapter will not provide a systematic review of research on SLA that has been conducted with the technology reviewed. Relevant results of such studies will be described in the following chapters, and readers are also referred to R. Ellis (2008: ch. 14) and Gullberg and Indefrey (2006).

The brain

> [T]he twenty-first century is going to be the century of the brain.
> (Hulstijn 2002*a*: 214)

Let me start by putting things into proper perspective: With tens of billions of neurons, connected by trillions of transmission points, the brain is one of the most complex structures in the known universe (Baars 2007*b*). This complex system has as much as 10 terabytes of information storage capacity (Murre 2005), which is a gigantic memory potential; Anderson (2000*a*), for example, compares the processing power of the brain to that of 100 billion intercon-nected and interacting personal computers!

In order to describe this vastly complex system, I will address three main issues. First, we will take an initial overview of brain anatomy. The brain is made up of some salient subcomponents (e.g. the two hemispheres) and this structural division seems to be universal amongst humans, cutting across gender and ethnic boundaries. Second, we will look at the neurobiological basis of brain functioning, that is, the operation of the neurons and other com-ponents, resulting in mental processes such as thinking, feeling, and sensing. Third, we will investigate one of the fundamental dilemmas in current brain research concerning the extent to which it is worth developing some sort of a functional anatomy of the brain (e.g. by trying to localize certain cognitive functions such as various language aspects). Some parts of the brain have tradi-tionally been associated with certain language functions, but how meaningful is this endeavour given that the neuron system is so heavily interconnected?

The anatomy of the brain

Discussions of human information processing do not start with the brain but with the broader *nervous system* that also includes the sensory/peripheral systems that gather information from parts of the body and the motor system that controls movement. At the heart of the nervous system is the *central nervous system*; this is composed of the *spinal cord*, which is the transmitting channel from the various sensory/peripheral organs, and the *brain*, which is the central processing unit. (There are many good descriptions of the brain; I have found the following works accessible and useful: Ahlsén 2006; Pulvemüller 2002; Ullman 2006; Uttal 2001.)

The brain itself is composed of the *cerebrum*—which we usually refer to when we speak about the 'brain' in everyday parlance—and below it the *cer-ebellum,* the 'little brain'; the spinal cord is connected to the brain through the *brain stem*—see Figure 2.1. Both the cerebrum and the cerebellum are made up of two *hemispheres*, but when we talk about the left and the right hemi-spheres of the brain, we usually only mean the hemispheres of the cerebrum, which are connected to each other by three cerebral commissures (i.e. links), of which the most important is the *corpus callosum.*

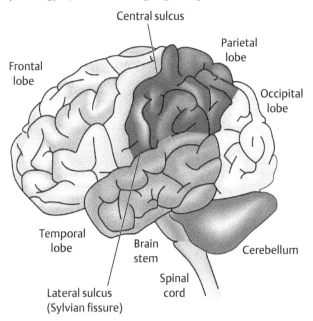

Figure 2.1 The macroanatomical landscape of the brain

The two hemispheres of the cerebrum appear to be mirror images of each other but they are actually not identical. They are covered all the way around with the *cortex,* whose name comes, very appropriately, from the Latin word for 'bark'. This cortex, just like the bark of a tree, is far from being smooth, but rather features various ridges and grooves, making it similar to the topography of a real landscape. The fissures or infoldings are called *sulci* (singular: sulcus) and the protruding parts or convolutions *gyri* (singular: girus). Although no two brains are identical, some of the salient landmarks of the brain topography are consistent enough to be given generic names—these often contain geographically directional terms such as superior (meaning up), inferior (meaning down), anterior (meaning in front of), and posterior (meaning behind) (Ullman 2006). One of the most prominent of the land-marks of the cortex is a groove on the cerebrum when viewed from the top, running from left to right, called the *central sulcus*. The area of the cortex that is anterior to the central sulcus is the *frontal lobe*, and the cortex on each hemisphere has traditionally been divided into three further lobes, the *temporal lobe* on the side and the *parietal* and *occipital lobes* on the back. A second prominent, 'universal' groove is the *lateral sulcus* (or Sylvian fissure), which separates the temporal lobe from the frontal and parietal lobes.

It is important to note that the various parts of the brain are not only divided by salient demarcation lines such as sulci but are also characterized by differences in their cellular anatomy or make-up (e.g. the anatomy and arrangement of their neurons), resulting in sharp and distinct boundaries (Uttal 2001). The most often used neuroanatomical division was originally proposed by German neurologist Korbinian Brodmann at the beginning of the twentieth century. He divided up the cerebral cortex into 52 numbered regions (some of which have been further subdivided since then); thus, we can talk about Brodmann area 10 or 23a (or simply BA10 or BA23a).

Although the cortex plays a prominent role in the cognitive functioning of the brain and is certainly the most relevant cerebral area for language, we must not ignore what is below the surface, that is, the various subcortical structures—see Figure 2.2. These include the *brain stem,* which regulates, for example, consciousness, and at the top of the brain stem the *thalamus,* which acts as a 'switchboard' (Ahlsén 2006) or 'traffic hub' (Baars 1997a), controlling all messages going in an out of the cortex in its communication with the different sensory/peripheral systems of the nervous system. Schumann's (1997; Schumann and Wood 2004) research on emotions and L2 motivation has highlighted another important subcortical structure, the *amygdala* (or rather amigdalae, because there is one in each hemisphere), involved, for example, in emotional memory and stimulus appraisal. Two other subcortical structures that are often mentioned in language-related neuropsychological studies are the *basal ganglia* and the *hippocampus* (or rather hippocampi), which are involved in a variety of important functions from motor control to memory.

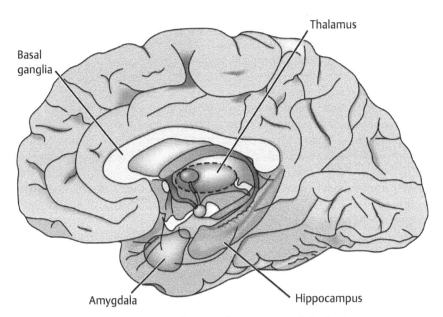

Figure 2.2 Some important subcortical structures of the brain

The neurobiological basis of brain activity

How does the brain work? The answer is simple: through the interactions of nerve cells called *neurons*. Simplicity, of course, stops at this point because the roughly 100 billion neurons in the brain are of several different types, organized in highly varied and complex patterns. For example, each nerve cell has about ten thousand inputs from other neurons, and the neurons in general are so interconnected that one can get from one cell to any other cell in the brain in seven steps or fewer. Add to this that neurons send out electrical pulses 40–1,000 times per second and that most of them are simultaneously active (Baars 1997*a*, *b*), and the picture could not be further away from being simple.

Neurons communicate with each other through *axons* and *dendrites*—see Figure 2.3. Each neuron has one or maximum a few axons, which are the transmitting (i.e. output) channels extending towards the dendrites of other neurons, which are the receiving ends (and of which, as said above, each neuron has about 10,000). The end of the axon, called the *axon terminal*, almost reaches the receiving neuron's dendrite, leaving a minuscule gap, which is called the *synapse*. Communication between neurons involves bridging the synapse by releasing various chemicals, called *neurotransmitters*, that cause a tiny electric nerve impulse; the most often mentioned neurotransmitter in language-related research has been *dopamine*. It is important to note that the axon branch of a neuron can be quite long, sometimes 10 cm or more, which means that it can be linked to neurons in relatively distant cortical or subcortical nuclei and not just in its immediate vicinity. The outer surface of the brain is gray because it consists of a thin (2–5 mm) layer of gray neuron cell bodies, whereas the subcortical matter is white because of the white insulating layers of the bundles of billions of axons this matter consists of.

Pulvemüller (2002) explains that the synaptic connections between cortical neurons are usually weak and therefore several simultaneous or near-simultaneous inputs are necessary to elicit an action potential in a neuron. That is, for most higher-order cognitive activities neurons must work in concert. This explains partly why we find specialized 'cell assemblies' or 'functional webs of neuronal links' associated with many language functions, supporting a modular view of the brain. (See the next section.) Another important characteristic of neuron activation is that, as proposed by Donald Hebb almost 60 years ago, repeated activity between two neurons strengthens the synaptic link between them, thereby in effect priming the connection.

The functional anatomy of the brain

Most of the human organs are linked to specific bodily functions; if we have, say, breathing problems, doctors will naturally first examine our lungs, which are the primary organs in charge of breathing. In other words,

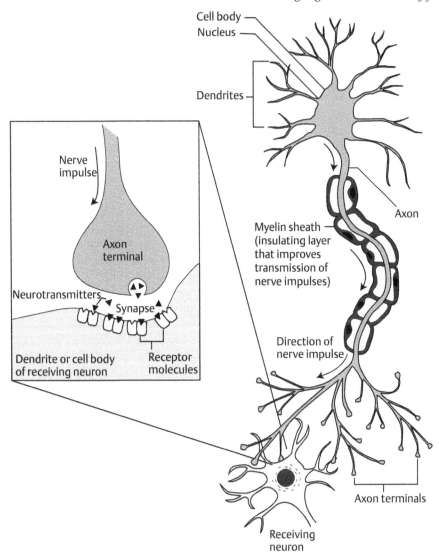

Figure 2.3 The constituents of a neuron (source: Ullman 2006: 239)

the human body displays a salient *functional anatomy*. We saw in the previous sections that our brain is made up of distinct parts and, following the general analogy of our overall anatomy, it would be logical to find that the various cerebral regions are responsible for different mental activities. If we manage indeed to identify different areas of the brain to have distinct functional properties, that would have far-reaching consequences because we could then argue for a functional localization of cognitive—and, thus, language—functions. This would mean that if we propose, for example, that 'grammar' is a distinct and salient aspect of language, we would be justified in starting to look for the cerebral region of the brain that is in charge of grammatical functions. And, consequently, if we cannot locate the area where grammar resides, this could be seen as an argument invalidating the concept of grammar as we know it.

So, does the brain feature a clear-cut functional anatomy? The standard view amongst neuroanatomists is that the architectural differences in brain structure are indeed linked to functional differences, and given the huge arsenal of brain imaging and scanning devices at scholars' disposal, as well as the vast amount of research done during the past 15 years in the area, we would be justified to trust this view. Unfortunately, the complete picture is not as straightforward as this: although with regard to certain mental functions we do find distinct regional specialization in the brain, the massively intercon-nected nature of millions of neurons working in a parallel and simultaneous manner, with the links between them often reaching as much as 10 cm, has raised doubts in some about the rationale for any attempts to localize higher-order cognitive functions such as language. In the following discussion, therefore, I will first summarize the arguments in favour of assuming a promi-nent functional anatomy—this can be considered the mainstream view—and following this I will present some of the most compelling counterarguments. Finally, to conclude the discussion of the functional anatomy of the brain, I will specifically address one particular localization issue that has received a great deal of attention in language psychology, the issue of 'language later-alization', that is, the extent to which the two hemispheres of the brain play distinct language roles.

As a preliminary, we should realize the issues at stake. The spectacular rise of cognitive neuroscience over the past decade has partly been driven by technological advances in brain scanning and neuroimaging instruments and techniques. Most of these techniques, however, assume some degree of localization of cognitive functions—after all, the typical outcome of such procedures is that a part of the brain image on the computer screen 'lights up' when the subjects of the experiments are engaged in a particular mental activity. Any theoretical ambiguities about the existence of a functional neu-roanatomy would therefore fundamentally undermine the validity of these approaches.

Arguments supporting the existence of a functional anatomy of the brain

In his overview of the neuroscience of language, Pulvemüller (2002) goes back to the absolute basics when he starts his arguments by stating that (1) there is no doubt that it is the human brain that provides the mechanisms for real-izing language; and (2) nobody would question either that brain mechanisms are organized by means of nerve cells and their mutual connections. There-fore, the author reasons, any realistic model of language needs to specify the putative organic basis of language functions in terms of neurons, neu-ronal connections, and neuron circuits. We saw in the previous section that higher-order cognitive functions are carried out by assemblies of neurons, and therefore the key question is how we can characterize the various neuron circuits involved in the various language functions.

Neurobiological examinations confirm that most of the neurons in the brain are organized in specialized patterns. Baars (1997*a*: 6) summarizes this very clearly:

> Most of the brain consists of small assemblies of brain cells, arrays, columns, maps, clusters, networks, functional routines, and great swaths of cable connections, all with highly specific functions. Some nerve cells pick up point sources of red light in a single location in the visual field. Others specialize in short lines oriented forty-five degrees above the horizontal. Still others recognize faces or coordinate sights with sounds. Specialization is the name of the game for most neurons.

We also saw above that the brain is not an undifferentiated mass but its anatomy can be divided into distinct regions and parts. Paradis (2004) emphasizes that this differentiation takes place not only at the gross anatomical level but also at the microanatomical level, that is, in the cellular and biochemical make-up of the various parts, which is due to the fact that different areas begin postnatal maturation at different times and develop at different rates. Therefore, many argue, it is almost inconceivable that the anatomical division is not associated with certain distinct functional properties. This assumption receives strong support if we consider certain primary mental processes, particularly those related to sensory and motor functions, about which we have detailed understanding: Even a cursory analysis reveals that the cerebral regions subserving the primary sensory modalities and the motor output portions of the brain are highly structured and localized. (Visual perception is, for example, centred in the occipital lobes.)

It seems therefore that certain key mental functions are associated with localized neurofunctional modules, and there have also been indications that language functions are no exceptions. For example, neuropsychological studies of patients with aphasia (i.e. language impairment caused by brain injuries as a result of a stroke or an accident—see later in detail) show that language loss can occur independently of other cognitive, sensory, or motor deficits (Paradis 2004). Ullman's (2006: 247) explanation is clear and convincing:

> If a person suffers from brain damage, and then loses the ability to do certain things, one might reasonably infer that the lost functions depended on the damaged structures. For example, if damage, or lesions, to particular temporal lobe structures consistently lead to impairments of lexical processing, one may infer that these structures underlie lexical processing. The identification of such structure–function correspondences underlies the basic logic of the lesion method. By analogy, if you damage your lungs, you will have trouble breathing, whereas if you damage your

stomach, you will probably have trouble with your digestion. This shows that one cannot perform these functions without these particular organs and so these organs are necessary for these functions.

Thus, a strong case can be made in support of the existence of localized neurofunctional modules that are domain-specific and that have a characteristic pattern of development. Based on decades of research on aphasia, Paradis (2004) argues that language (or more specifically, implicit linguistic competence) is represented in the brain as a neurofunctional system that can be divided into a number of neurofunctional modules, which respectively subserve phonology, morphosyntax, and semantics. Indeed, such a neurofunctional position is becoming the mainstream view both in language-specific and non-language-specific areas of neuropsychology, as reflected, for example, in this summary by N. Ellis (2005*a*: 314):

> Language representation in the brain involves specialized localized modules, largely implicit in their operation, collaborating via long-range associations in dynamic coalitions of cell assemblies representing— among others—the phonological forms of words and constructions and their sensory and motor groundings.

The most famous localized neurofunctional modules in the brain are the Broca and the Wernicke areas (Figure 2.4), which were identified at the genesis

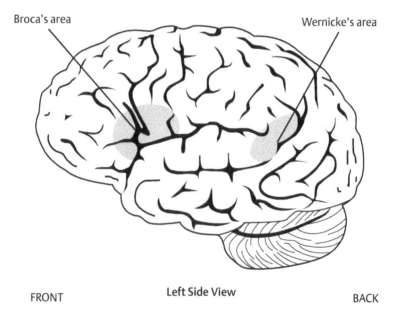

Figure 2.4 *The Broca and the Wernicke areas in the left hemisphere of the brain*

of aphasia research in the second half of the nineteenth century (and which are named after the scholars who discovered them). It was found that people suffering from damage to the Broca area cannot create grammatically complex sentences but can convey meaning in 'telegraphic' sentences made up primarily of content words, whereas people suffering from Wernicke aphasia can produce speech that has a natural-sounding rhythm and a relatively normal syntax without any real meaning. (Wernicke aphasics also have a pronounced impairment in comprehension.) The impact of the discovery of these two brain regions—once claimed to be the only language centres in the brain—was significant in stimulating neurolinguistic research even though we now know that both the anatomical identification of the areas involved and their language correlates were rather crude if not inaccurate—see Poeppel and Hickok (2004).

Using cutting-edge neuroimaging techniques, scholars have established that besides the classical language zones of the Broca and Wernicke areas there are several other regions of the brain that contribute to language processing. For example, the right cerebellum seems to underlie the search for lexical knowledge, whereas retrieving or selecting this knowledge involves the basal ganglia along with the broader region of the Broca area (Ullman 2006). However, at present we do not have a universally accepted, detailed language-specific topography of the brain, which may be due to the fact that the cognitive neuroscience of language is still in a relatively early phase of development. On the other hand, there is a possible alternative explanation, namely that our past failure to identify a distinct set of brain areas that are responsible for concrete language functions is due to the fact that some language functions are carried out by distributed networks of neurons that have no straightforward correlates to specific cerebral regions. We are now going to turn to this argument.

Arguments against the existence of a functional anatomy of the brain

> [T]he cognitive psychologist wishes to know how the mind works, not where the brain works. Of course, nobody would deny that there is a link between the two, but my point is that it is not a necessary one.
> (Page 2006: 429)

Although, as shown above, the mainstream view appears to accept the existence of a functional anatomy of the brain, this does not necessarily mean that this is a straightforward issue, let alone that localization efforts are conducive to the long-term development of the field. New technological advances (which will be discussed below in detail) have certainly set into motion a gigantic neuro-bandwagon, but several serious theoretical concerns have been raised about whether this wagon is moving in the right direction. Let us look at some of the main points here, and then revisit this question when evaluating the appropriateness of the various neuroimaging techniques at the end of this chapter.

To start with, even one of the strongest critics of the localization of mental processes, William Uttal (2001), accepts that in certain well-established domains (e.g. the sensory input channels and their respective receiving areas, or the motor regions and output pathways of the brain) there is ample and indisputable evidence to support the existence of homogeneous specialized regions of the central nervous system. What has been questioned is that this modular set-up can be generalized to higher-order cognitive constructs, including language functions. Indeed, if we look at some current overviews of first and second language representations of the brain, we find a great deal of vagueness, confusion, and contradiction disguised under the power-language of neuroscience. Abutalebi and Green's (2007: 242) starting sentence of their overview of the neurocognition of bilingual language representation can be seen as honest and realistic: 'Despite an impressive psycholinguistic effort to explore the way in which two or more languages are represented and control-led, controversy surrounds both issues.'

The claim that language is represented in distinct and easily identifiable locations in the brain has been questioned by a major meta-analysis of the neuroimaging literature by Vigneau *et al.* (2006). Drawing on 129 studies, the authors identified over 700 regions of peak activity in the left hemisphere associated with phonology, semantics, and text/sentence processing. The various activity centres are scattered in large areas that cover more than a third of the left hemisphere, and the various types of language functions consider-ably overlap. Accordingly, the authors have concluded that the results 'argue for large-scale architecture networks rather than modular organization of language in the left hemisphere' (p. 1414). In a recent authoritative overview of the field, Baars (2007*a*) characterized the overlap and wide scatter of peaks in Vigneau *et al.*'s meta-analysis as 'striking' and pointed out that this is not the kind of pattern we encounter in studying sensory regions such as vision. His conclusion therefore provides strong support for the anti-localization argument:

> These facts have a strong theoretical interpretation. They suggest that much of the brain works by way of distributed networks of language functions, like the worldwide web. An Internet chat group may work even if the participants come from many different parts of the world. The idea of distributed brain functioning seems to support the connectionist view of the brain. (p. 322)

Baars's (2007*a*) argument is very similar to Uttal's (2001) conclusion that certain parts of the neuron system are so heavily interconnected and the con-stituents interact with each other so strongly that we cannot isolate individual functional modules. Thus, even if we assume the existence of separable neu-rofunctional modules each of which 'is distinct from other neurofunctional modular systems, reacts only to certain specific types of stimuli, and works in accordance with its own set of computational procedures, which differ from, and are not permeable to, the computational procedures of other modules' (Paradis 2004: 125), these may often be non-contiguous, that is, not con-centrated in a specific cortical or subcortical location but are, instead, made up of a set of interlinked dedicated neurons distributed in a neural network. Thompson and Varela's (2001: 418) conclusion fully supports this view: 'Cognitive neuroscience now leaves little doubt that specific cognitive acts require the transient integration of numerous, widely distributed, constantly interacting areas of the brain.'

It seems therefore that the theoretical concerns about the current obsession of specifying a functional neuroanatomy with regard to certain higher-order cognitive functions such as language are strong and substantiated. Why, then, are thousands and thousands of scholars—indeed, the majority of neuroscientists—ignoring these points in their research practice? There are several possible answers. First, research is always methodology-driven—scholars will examine everything they can—and, as we will see below, we currently have an unprecedentedly sophisticated, rapidly developing, and immensely sexy technological repertoire of research instruments. The acquisition and running of these complex machineries require major financial, intellectual, and human resource investment on the part of universities, and once a lab has been set up, its main concern is usually to 'earn its wages' by producing study after study rather than contemplating the necessity of its own existence.

A second, more theoretical explanation is related to the fact that for many years the brain was considered a 'black box' (especially in language studies): we knew what went in (i.e. the input), and we could also measure the output (e.g. with language tests), but we had only very vague and indirect clues of what was happening inside. Even experimental and cognitive psychology was to a large extent confined to theoretical speculations and modelling work based on limited and indirect evidence. Given this long state of frustrating ignorance, we can imagine what a revolution it was to finally have the means to look directly into the brain, in a real-time manner. Neuroimaging offered the field a new avenue of discovery that had no obvious alternative; the new technology provided (and still offers) a great deal of hope and any emerging problems could easily be put down to the teething pains of a baby that is to grow into a beautiful adult in due time. The concluding sentences of the language chapter in Gazzaniga, Ivry, and Mangun's (2002: 399) well-known summary of cognitive neuroscience reflects this mood:

> Newer formulations based on detailed analysis of the effects of neurological lesions (supported by improvements in structural imaging), functional neuroimaging, human electrophysiology, and computational modelling now provide some surprising modifications of older models. But the human language system is complex, and much remains to be learnt about how the biology of the brain enables the rich speech and language comprehension that characterize our daily lives. The future of language research is promising as psycholinguistic models combine with neuroscience to elucidate the neural code for this uniquely human mental faculty.

The third point to explain the disregard of any theoretical concerns with language localization is related to the rapid improvement of the available instrumentation. As we will see, existing neuroimaging techniques can already provide data that go beyond pure localization, and technical developments in this area are so fast that scholars who have invested heavily in the field can always trust that within five to ten years a new generation of instruments will satisfy even the most critical expectations.

In sum, whatever the reason, the fact is that there is a nearly unstoppable momentum for mapping, scanning, and imaging the brain from every possible angle and viewpoint. The 2006 convention of the Society for Neuroscience in Atlanta, for example, attracted over 30,000 attendants, and almost all the presentations were based on neuroimaging studies. However, even this phenomenal interest does not hide the fundamental question: can the monumental efforts to map the terrain of cerebral topography lead to an understanding of how the brain works? I suspect that nobody knows the answer. The success of this process is taken as an axiom in mainstream research, but because of the non-linear nature and heavy interconnectedness of the various neural circuits, Uttal (2001: 205) considers this assumption 'to be the central weakness in this enterprise'. As mentioned above, I will revisit the various critical issues concerning neuroimaging at the end of this chapter.

Language lateralization

Arguably the earliest awareness of the function of the brain in L2 research concerned the differing functions of the two hemispheres. (For a recent review, see Hull and Vaid 2005.) This was the time—in the 1970s and 1980s—when we used to talk about 'left-brain-dominated' and 'right-brain-dominated' learners and it was almost universally accepted that for most humans language functions are handled by the left hemisphere (where the Broca and Wernicke areas are located). This claim, which goes back to early lesion studies that showed that only damage to the left hemisphere causes aphasias in most individuals (Pulvemüller 2002), is clearly one of the most basic and, at the same time, most researched of all neurofunctional localization issues and therefore warrants a more detailed discussion.

To start with, we must realize that the human brain displays many lateralized functions, that is, there is an asymmetry of several mental functions between the two hemispheres, with the language function being one of the prime candidates. The standard claim about language lateralization has been as follows: 'Most individuals, about 85 percent of the population, are right-handed, and almost all right-handers have their language functions represented in their left hemisphere' (Berko Gleason 2005: 16). Furthermore, even of the left-handed population, about half also have their language areas in the left hemisphere. Although it was acknowledged that the right hemisphere also contributed to language processing, this contribution was thought to concern only certain specialized functions such as verbal creativity or the recognition of the emotional tone of speech.

One of the main findings of language-specific neuroimaging research has been the realization that the right hemisphere plays a much larger role in language production than previously assumed, so that 'a modification of the virulent left-hemisphere imperialism characteristic of the field is in order' (Poeppel and Hickok 2004: 10). For example, the right hemisphere has been found to be active during speech perception, and Paradis (2004) argues that this hemisphere is also responsible for the pragmatic aspects of language. Furthermore, Pulvemüller (2002) reports on studies of patients whose brain hemispheres were disconnected by cutting the corpus callosum or in whom the dominant hemisphere was removed to cure an otherwise intractable epilepsy, and these subjects showed word-processing abilities in their isolated right hemisphere. Pulvemüller therefore concludes that although language lateralization is a well-established phenomenon, the non-dominant hemisphere not only contributes to, but in extreme cases can also be sufficient for, the optimal processing of language. This is in accordance with the general view in neuropsychology that both hemispheres are likely to be involved in the performance of any complex task, but with each contributing in its specialized manner (Gazzaniga, Ivry, and Mangun 2002). (For more details about laterality research and its educational misapplication, see the section on laterality research later in this chapter.)

The conscious and the unconscious mind

We have seen that the neural system of the brain is an amazingly complex, vast, and interconnected network of simultaneously active neurons. However, of all the neural processes happening at any given moment, the vast majority are unconscious. This massive imbalance of unconscious and conscious processes is one of the fundamental contrasts in neuropsychology and has important implications for language processing. Let us explore more closely what exactly 'consciousness' means in the light of a creative and instructive metaphorical model proposed by Bernard Baars (1997a, 1997b), the 'Global Workspace Theory'. (Further discussion of consciousness and its relationship with attention is provided in Ch. 4, when discussing explicit and implicit learning.)

Let us start the examination of consciousness with a puzzle. Given the incredible processing power of the brain—recall that Anderson (2000a) compared it to that of 100 billion interconnected and interacting personal computers—why is our conscious capacity so limited? For example, we find severe bottlenecks in our immediate memory and attentional focus: we can only keep about seven separate things in our working memory; we can only listen to one dense flow of information at a time; or we cannot do two demanding voluntary actions at the same time. Baars (1997b: 293) rightly concludes that if we look only at these limited mechanisms, 'the brain seems to be a rather slow, one-thing-at-a-time, error-prone organ'. Having said that, he also points out that one aspect of consciousness offers a compensating advantage, namely that it is a highly flexible gateway through which we can have access to virtually any part of the nervous system, from the mental lexicon to memory stores, and it also allows us to bring under voluntary control automatic action routines.

How can we envisage this starkly contrasting set-up—a vast and power-ful neural system that works without our consciousness in the background and a narrow, sharply focused, and flexible conscious 'window' into this system? Baars's (1997a, b) Global Workplace Theory compares this scenario to a working theatre, where 'consciousness acts as a "bright spot"' on the stage, directed there by the selective 'spotlight' of attention' (Baars 1997b: 292). This is indeed an appropriate metaphor in the sense that although in a theatre very specific and rather limited events take place on stage (e.g. one or two people talking), the organization would not be able to operate without the vast surrounding audience and a complex background apparatus. Baars highlights the almost unlimited capacity of our visual memory as a powerful illustration of how consciousness can act as the gateway to these unconscious sources of knowledge. We tend to be rather good at recognizing scenes from films we have seen only once in the past. This indicates that we must be storing unconscious records of millions and millions of images in our visual memory and the recognition of a specific scene is based on the ultra-quick scanning of this unconscious store to create a sudden sense of familiarity and to bring the single relevant image in the spotlight of consciousness. In a famous study, Standing (1973) for example estimated that one second of scanning time allows us to search for 51,180 pictures in memory!

Thus, Global Workspace Theory considers one of the main functions of consciousness to create global access in a brain of 100 billion neurons. For this reason, Baars (1997a, b) refers to consciousness as the 'publicity organ' of the brain, and we can perhaps see now that such a publicity organ is badly needed exactly because of the vast capacity of our neural system. The prerequisite to such a 'global access device' is speed for selection—which it has—and from this perspective the narrow focus is not a limitation but a necessary character-istic of the mechanism by which the spotlight is directed on the selected part of our unconscious mind.

Research methods for investigating language and the brain

When it comes to investigating the brain and the language-specific mental operations that take place within it, the traditional research methodologi-cal repertoire that applied linguists have been employing (see e.g. Dörnyei 2007b) needs to be complemented with a set of specialized techniques and observation methods. In the following, I describe the most important such methods used by psycholinguists and neuroscientists. For the sake of clarity of organization, I have divided these methods into four broad groups: (1) psycholinguistic investigations; (2) pre-neuroimaging methods of brain research; (3) neuroimaging; and (4) molecular genetic investigations. This is, however, only a rough classification, particularly because an emerging trend in contemporary research is to use several methods of different types in combination. For space limitations, my description of most of these methods will be rather brief, but I will devote more space to introducing the latest neuroimaging procedures, partly because they are less known in our field and partly because of their increasing impact on the development of language-specific research in psychology.

Psycholinguistic methods

Because psycholinguists used not to have any direct means of observing mental representations and processes, they have traditionally employed a range of creative indirect measures of mental operations within laboratory experiments; and they have also relied on computational modelling in trying to recreate language processes and their outcomes artificially. The three most established, classic research techniques in this area are *reaction-time studies*, *priming and masking,* and *self-paced reading,* and after a brief description of each I will conclude this part by discussing the basis of *computational modelling*, which will be revisited in Ch. 3 when we look at connectionism (for more detailed summaries, see Frenck-Mestre 2005; Juffs 2001; Marinis 2003; Papadopoulou 2005).

Reaction-time studies

Measuring *reaction times* has traditionally been the most common method of psycholinguistic experimentation, because it can be used in a wide variety of behavioural experiments and it has minimal hardware requirements—only a personal computer with some special software such as E-prime. 'Put flippantly, accuracy and reaction times have been the "meat and two veg" of experimental psychology' (Henson 2005: 195). The procedure is straightforward: participants are presented with some sort of linguistic stimuli (usually on a computer screen) and are asked to perform a task (e.g. make judgements or choose between two alternatives) by giving their responses by pressing a button (or one of two buttons). The reaction time is measured by the computer in milliseconds—the average human reaction time is between 200–270 milliseconds—and the results can be processed using standard statistical techniques. On the basis of these, researchers can make inferences about the nature of the processing that was involved in doing the task.

In a review of psycholinguistic studies in second language research, Juffs (2001) considers it 'slightly embarrassing' for the SLA research community that reaction-time measures have been considerably underutilized relative to their long history in mainstream psycholinguistics. In order to facilitate the use of the technique, Juffs not only describes the main procedures but also presents a variety of examples of studies where the technique can be applied to good effect, ranging from traditional grammaticality judgement tasks to sentence matching. In all these tasks the time element can be seen as an index of the extent to which some competence or skill has been established or automatized.

Priming

In many ways, *priming* embodies the prototype of the psycholinguistic experiment because it focuses on the mental mechanisms underlying cognitive functioning indirectly, without the participants of an experiment being aware of what is being examined. We know that if we are confronted with a stimulus that we attend to, it will always leave some residue in our brain, which can later be verified objectively (e.g. we remember it and attest to it)—priming refers to experiments when researchers set up an initial stimulus in such a way that the participants do not have an explicit memory or awareness of the residue it has left in them, yet their subsequent behaviour or responses show that the residue is there in their memory. Thus, the initial stimulus creates an 'unconscious' readiness in their mind by activating, for example, a semantic area (e.g. after hearing the word 'black', people are quicker to perceive the word 'white' than without hearing 'black' first) or by sensitizing the subject to a later presentation of the same or a similar stimulus. For example, if the first task is to read a long list of words that includes 'window', and the second task requires the participants to complete a word stem that starts with 'win...', the probability of producing the word 'window' rather than something like 'winter' or 'winner' is significantly higher than without having had the initial reading task, even if the participants cannot consciously recall that the first list contained 'window'. Such priming effects are common and can be illustrated easily. To prove this, Bohannon and Bonvillian (2005: 260) recommend this simple demonstration:

> Have a friend say the word silk out loud five times, then quickly answer this question: 'What do cows drink?' Most people readily respond with 'milk,' although upon reflection they realize that cows rarely drink what they produce. The word milk was doubly primed, first with the similar sounds in silk and then with semantic association to drink and cows.

In *cross-modal priming*, two sensory modes are activated at the same time (e.g. someone watching something and listening to something else through earphones), and even though the subject's attention is intentionally kept on one of the tasks (e.g. they have to concentrate because they need to answer comprehension questions), the stimulus they receive through the other sensory channel will still affect their responses. Priming has also been used in bilingual word recognition tasks examining the bilingual mental lexicon and lexical processing in general. (For a review, see Dijkstra and van Heuven 2002.) When, for example, bilingual speakers are presented with texts in the target language that contains some words that also exist in their other, non-target language (e.g. the word 'list' for bilingual English–Dutch speakers, since 'list' means 'trick' in Dutch), it has been consistently found—usually using various reaction-time experiments—that the prime words activate the participants' non-target language system without them being aware of this.

The importance of examining priming effects lies in the fact that, because the subjects are not aware of the researchers' manipulation and intentions, they cannot influence the results, and thus their underlying mental operations can be observed without any conscious human interference. Creatively designed priming experiments can be used to examine a wide range of psycholinguistic phenomena, particularly if they are combined with *masking*, which is a technique to hide some stimulus that would in normal conditions be consciously perceivable. For example, N. Ellis (2005*a*) points out that a visual word that is flashed for only a few tens of milliseconds remains readable, but if we present the same word in close spatial and temporal proximity with other visual stimuli, it becomes invisible and unnoticed. Yet, despite the unconscious nature of the masked stimulus, it can be proved empirically that the flashed word does activate part of the cerebral networks for word processing.

Self-paced reading

Reading tasks lend themselves to psycholinguistic experimentation because the input/stimulus (i.e. the text to be read) is easily controllable. *Self-paced reading* has been employed widely in the past to examine language processing as it occurs. Using a personal computer, subjects are asked to read a sentence in a word-by-word or phrase-by-phrase fashion by pressing a button to request the next word/phrase to appear on the screen. Each sentence is usually followed by a yes/no or true/false comprehension question in order to ensure meaningful rather than merely mechanical engagement. Variations of the technique include whether or not to indicate the length of the sentence initially with dashes (which are then transformed into words one by one), and whether the already seen words should remain on the screen in a cumulative fashion or disappear so that only one word can be seen at a time. (For a detailed overview, see Marinis 2003.)

During the task, the computer software records the reading time of each word/phrase, thus producing an online measure of reaction/processing speed as the sentence unfolds. Slower parts are indications of processing difficulties that, taken together with the content of the sentence in those points (e.g. grammatical or lexical complexity), allow the researcher to make a variety of inferences. A potential problem with the technique is the usually slower than normal reading pace and, in the case of the non-cumulative version, the need for the reader to remember the previous parts without the option of going back to reread words, which may result in short-term memory interference. Eye tracking (discussed below) does not suffer from these constraints, but in contrast to self-paced reading it requires expensive technology.

Eye tracking

Vision lends itself to psycholinguistic experimentation because eye movement can be measured very accurately, allowing researchers to identify precisely the point of gaze relative to what a person is looking at. To do so, we need a special instrument, the *eye tracker* (see Figure 2.5), which can be head-mounted or

Figure 2.5   Eye tracker in operation

may require the wearer's head to be kept in a fixed position with a chin rest. (There are several versions and the technology is continually improving.) This research method expanded rapidly in the 1970s, partly to study the process of reading but partly to examine more general mental operations through examining our visual attention. The advent of neuroimaging has curbed somewhat the popularity of the technique in psychology but eye tracking is still used to good effect for certain research purposes. After all, this technique allows us to monitor the precise functioning of one of our primary sensory organs with a high degree of accuracy.

Eye tracking results can include various statistical data concerning the quantity of visual observation targeting a particular area or point—we can distinguish, for example, between first-pass reading time, second-pass reading time, and total reading time—and the basic temporal data can also be used to compute more complex measures describing eye-movement patterns—for example, the percentage of forward to regressive saccades, or the likelihood either to regress to a previous word or to skip an upcoming word, and the precision of a regression (Frenck-Mestre 2005). In addition, eye-tracking findings can be displayed graphically, indicating gaze movement over the target (e.g.

reading a passage). These data can inform researchers about the sequence of text processing and, more generally, about the overt shifts of a person's attention in various tasks with a visual focus. As Frenck-Mestre (2005: 175) emphasizes, the 'complex trace of saccades, fixations and regressions that the eyes make while taking in a line of text is unquestionably one of the richest accounts available as concerns the process of reading'. As the author further argues, current instruments can provide to-the-letter, millisecond-precise reports of the readers' immediate syntactic processing and also allow researchers to asses the influence of various modifying factors, which would warrant a more extensive use of the technique in L2 research than the handful of studies conducted to date.

Computational modelling

Computational modelling is the culmination of the indirect psycholinguistic approach to investigate mental representations and functions. It involves explicitly summarizing everything we know of a certain cognitive operation and then setting up a model of this operation in the form of a computer program. The program is given similar input to that which the brain receives and then it simulates the psycholinguistic process in question to test if the rule-based operations that it performs can produce the same output as that of the brain. The procedure of designing and building an appropriately working computational model usually involves the process of successive approximation, that is, developing successively improved versions of the system by eliminating errors and inconsistencies until the program can approximate the output of real mental operations. When this happens, this can be seen as a powerful validity argument for the theoretical framework and the hypothesized mechanisms that the model was based on.

We must note, however, that computational modelling can mimic the operation of living nervous systems only in a rather limited way. As Gazzaniga, Ivry, and Mangun (2002) summarize, there are almost always radical simplifications in how neural mechanisms are modelled. The authors highlight three problematic points in particular: (1) while the units in a typical neural network model bear some similarity to neurons, the models are limited in scope, usually consisting of just a few hundred or so elements, and it is not always clear whether these elements correspond to single neurons or assemblies of neurons; (2) some technical aspects of the actual process of modelling are at odds with what we know occurs in biological organisms (e.g. 'back-propagation'; see the discussion of connectionism in Ch. 3 for more detail), and models are also prone to suffer 'catastrophic interference', that is, the loss of old information when new material is presented; and (3) most modelling efforts are restricted to relatively narrow problems; as such, they can provide useful tests of the viability of a particular hypothesis but are typically less useful in generating new predictions.

Thus, as with any research method, computational modelling has its own limitations, and some of these limitations are so serious that we cannot avoid asking the question: does this method yield any valid information? Indeed, de Bot (2008*a*) believes that it is a legitimate question to ask as to whether we need modelling and simulations at all. However, his answer is convincingly positive: currently there is simply no other way of testing out iterative processes that involve small incremental changes and multiple rerunning of specific procedures. A great deal of language development happens in such an iterative fashion, and yet it is simply not feasible to set up real-life experiments that can simulate such longitudinal growth functions. In Ch. 3 we will take a closer look at what computational modelling can achieve when discussing connectionist models of language representation and development.

Pre-neuroimaging methods of brain research

Besides the creative and often ingenious indirect methods used in the field of psycholinguistics, scholars from the early days started to examine the brain directly using a number of techniques. Initial information about the anatomy of the brain came from the *autopsy* of dead people, and until the introduction of recent non-invasive neuroimaging techniques (described later in detail), any method of directly observing live brain functioning required some form of brain surgery, which was, obviously, not feasible with human subjects for purely research purposes. Therefore, a great deal of information has been obtained from 'selective deactivation' studies carried out on experimental animals, in which certain parts of the brain are surgically removed, causing a well-defined lesion of the cerebrum or the brain stem. Human medical procedures include one special class of selective deactivation—the sectioning of the corpus callosum of split-brain patients with severe epilepsy—and neuropsychologists capitalized on this research opportunity in the 1960s by conducting *laterality studies* on these patients, which are the topic of the next section.

After discussing laterality studies, I will describe *neurophysiological research* that examines the impact of brain damage. In the nineteenth century, Paul Broca had to wait for his famous aphasic patient to die before his brain could be submitted to autopsy analysis and the exact region of the brain damage could be determined, but contemporary neurophysiological studies now utilize various imaging techniques for localizing the lesion. Finally, I present two interesting invasive techniques, *electrical cortical stimulation* of humans, which attracted significant media attention in the late 1970s, and *single-cell recording*, which is arguably the most refined way of neuroresearch, capable of recording the activity of a single neuron, but which is restricted to animals because of the need to insert a microelectrode into the skull.

Laterality research (left–right hemispheric differences)

It is an unfortunate fact that the aspect of brain research that has most succeeded in filtering through to the wider domain of public knowledge—the left brain–right brain discrepancy—and which has even crept into public education in terms of methodological considerations, is a highly problematic (and a somewhat outdated) area of cognitive neuroscience. This does not mean that there are no functional differences in the operation of the two cerebral hemispheres, but rather that the simplistic accounts of the differing cognitive styles associated with the dominance of each hemisphere belong more to the realm of 'pop psychology' than to scientific research proper. Indeed, even a quick search on the internet will produce websites such as the 'Hemispheric Dominance Inventory Test', which offers an analysis of the interested visitor's hemispheric set-up and then recommends using 'binaural beat technology for 3 weeks' to achieve considerable improvement. Or, in certain educational circles it is accepted as a given that students can be divided into left-brained and right-brained learners, the former being characterized as logical, rational, analytical, and objective while the latter are characterized as random, intuitive, holistic, synthesizing, and subjective. In fact, a whole industry has developed around catering for the hemispheric needs of our children, as attested to by the great number of books and training materials with such titles as *Teaching for the Two-Sided Mind: A Guide to Right Brain/Left Brain Education, Right-Brained Children in a Left-Brained World: Unlocking the Potential of Your ADD Child*, or *Teaching Creativity for Right Brain and Left Brain Thinkers*. For a highly critical review of these approaches, see Willingham's (2006) analysis, entitled 'Brain-Based Learning: More Fiction than Fact'.

As we will see below, laterality research was a burgeoning area within early neuroscience, but the left brain–right brain myth developing in popular culture has very little to do with facts: it is simplistic at best and utter hogwash at worst. I admit that the myth is built around an appealing dichotomy: the left hemisphere is the villain as it represents everything that is wrong with contemporary society: it is coldly logical and rational and it suppresses the tragic hero, the imaginative and creative right hemisphere. We are talking here about the unfair and tragic battle between the accountant and the artist! Indeed, there have been serious warnings against the moral and intellectual decay of left-brain modern society, and there was even a serious call for the reinsertion of 'whole brain' values into our over-mechanized culture—see Harrington and Oepen (1989). We also find newspaper adverts encouraging people to 'get in touch with your intuitive, creative right brain and find a whole other you'—see McCrone (1999).

Laterality research proper has grown out of the work of Nobel Prize winner Roger Sperry and his associates in the 1960s with 'split-brain' patients, that is, patients with intractable epilepsy whose corpus callosum (the link between the two hemispheres) had been cut as part of their surgical treatment. These operations are almost always successful as seizures generally subside immediately and there are no obvious side effects (Gazzaniga, Ivry, and Mangun 2002). However, psycholinguistic experiments revealed some intriguing consequences of the cortical disconnection. These experiments capitalized on the fact that our eyes and ears are cross-wired, that is, our left organs are linked to the right hemisphere and vice versa. This allowed researchers to restrict a visual or auditory stimulus to one hemisphere only by flashing, for example, an image in one visual field. It was found that the information did not transfer to the opposite hemisphere, and patients were unable to perform exactly the same functions with both hemispheres. A famous example is that subjects were able to name and describe objects seen through the right visual field (i.e. using their left hemisphere) but not when these objects were shown only to the left visual field (that is linked to the right hemisphere). This produced unambiguous evidence that some of the mental functions are lateralized to one hemisphere.

These initial findings were sufficiently exciting to trigger a whole wave of research in various areas of cognitive neuroscience, and as we have seen in an earlier section, language lateralization has traditionally been a key aspect of this. The search was on to find some fundamental dichotomy that characterizes cerebral lateralization. However, although it became clear that the two hemispheres of the brain do not represent and process information in an identical manner, the emerging picture turned out to be more complex and multicomponential than scholars had been hoping for. It was found that both hemispheres contribute to performance in any complex task, indicating that traditional laterality research is not elaborate enough to be able to explain the subtleties of joint hemispheric engagement.

Neurophysiological research of aphasics (lesion studies)

The target of *neurophysiological research* is 'aphasia', that is, language impairment that results from relatively circumscribed damage to the brain, usually caused by a stroke or a head injury. As we saw earlier, neuroanatomical research of the brain was initiated by aphasia research in the nineteenth century, and the study of clinical-pathological correlations with brain functions has been vibrant ever since. Furthermore, what is particularly important from this book's perspective, there has been a considerable body of research studying bilingual aphasia. (For reviews, see Green 2005; Paradis 2004.)

For a neurolinguist, interesting cases of aphasia are those when a relatively small lesion causes the loss of a specific language function without affecting the rest of the patient's linguistic abilities. The two classic types of aphasia described before—Broca and Wernicke aphasia—were particularly exciting because the former led to the deterioration of grammar while maintaining meaning in speech; the latter to the loss of meaning in grammatically correct sentences. However, we increasingly find that nothing is so simple regarding the neuroanatomy of the brain: more fine-tuned research revealed that although the classic language centres do play an important role, they are supplemented by many other parts of the brain (both cortical and subcortical) in both hemispheres. In the light of these recent findings, neurophysiological research appears to be rather crude. Having said that, some unique (and from the neurolinguist's point of view, lucky) cases of aphasia do offer unprecedented insights. Just to give one example, Fabbro, Skrap, and Aglioti (2000) reported on an aphasic patient (with a lesion to the left anterior cingulate cortex and to the frontal lobe) who demonstrated pathological switching between his two languages in the absence of any other linguistic impairment. He was aware that he had to speak in only one language, but he switched to the other even though he knew it was inappropriate and apologized for it immediately after doing so. Thus, regardless of any reservations about aphasia research (see below), this is interesting and potentially important information, and it could not have been produced by any other research method.

Let us now consider some possible shortcomings of neurophysiological research. (See Abutalebi, Cappa, and Perani 2005; Pulvemüller 2002; Ullman 2006.) To start with, researchers are dependent on the 'experiments of nature', without any control over what kind of symptoms the patients they have access to will display. This is somewhat counterbalanced by the fact that, as Green (2005) argues, as a result of migration patterns and intermarriage, the incidence of bilingual aphasia will increase, resulting in a fairly large patient pool. (There are, for example, in the United States alone, tens of thousands of new bilingual patients every year.) A second concern is that lesions are usually diffuse, overlapping multiple cerebral regions and brain structures, and even patients with similar damage cannot be automatically pooled under one category because the exact spread of the damage is never identical. A third issue concerns the timing of the assessment. Ullman (2006) explains that if one tests a patient too quickly after a stroke or head injury, the loss of function can be much greater than is attributable to the damaged regions—nearby regions can be temporarily affected (e.g. by tissue swelling or decreased blood flow). On the other hand, if one waits too long, other structures may take over some of the functions that the damaged structure used to perform. A further problem related to the latter point concerns the age of the patients: children's brains are still developing and are highly plastic, which means that in their case the confounding effect of the compensatory function of other brain regions is particularly acute.

The most problematic issue with aphasia research is concerned with the highly interconnected nature of the central nervous system. If we find that damage to a specific region of the brain is associated with a specific language impairment, it is questionable as to whether we can conclude that the impaired function is localized in that area. Let us suppose that the bulk of a neurofunctional module or a specialized assembly of neurons is located in Region A but a certain regulatory switch is in Region B. If we find that a certain aphasia involves the impairment of the language function in question, we simply cannot tell with our present state of knowledge whether the area affected by the aphasia was Region A or B. Put frivolously, the failure of a car to start because of a broken ignition key does not entail that the engine is in the keyhole. Thus, we are back to the central problem with the localization approach discussed before: in the case of broad distributed systems it is difficult to decide what the exact role of the constituent components is.

Electrical cortical stimulation

Similarly to laterality research with split-brain patients, *electrical corti-cal stimulation* also needs to accompany medical brain surgery on epileptic patients, though this time it is not the corpus callosum that is targeted but the epileptic tissue that is the source of the seizures. In operations like this the surgeon removes portions of the skull to make the brain accessible and then examines with electrodes the brain activity in the uncovered region to locate the tissue to be removed. Electrical cortical stimulation utilizes the period during which the cortex of the brain is accessible to probe various cogni-tive functions. The technique involves the temporary inactivation of specific cortical regions by stimulating the brain tissue with a small electric current while the patient is asked to perform some task. For example, Ojemann and Whitaker (1978, cited by Abutalebi, Cappa, and Perani 2005) asked bilingual patients to name pictures while the researchers stimulated the lateral cortex of the patients' dominant hemisphere and mapped the regions that were involved in the naming task (as indicated by the fact that when these regions were inactivated by the electric current, the patients could not name the pic-tures). Interestingly, in all bilingual patients studied, each language involved some common sites of naming and some specific areas in which naming was interrupted only for one language. Furthermore, the naming areas associated with the L2 were generally larger than those for the L1.

One obvious shortcoming of this method is that—similar to split-brain patients—the subjects of the procedure are not healthy individuals but severely epileptic patients. We simply do not know the extent to which their overall brain functioning differs from that of a healthy population. Further-more, a potentially more serious problem is curiously related to what used to be seen as the strength of the method: the accurate localization of the targeted cerebral region by placing the detector directly on it. Uttal (2001) explains that it is not at all clear to what extent the electric current might be leaking or short-circuiting to regions other than the one directly stimulated: the electric current applied requires two electrodes, an anode and a cathode, and the wet, heterogeneously packed tissue of the central nervous system may modify the path between them.

Single-cell recording

Although due to its invasive nature, *single-cell* recording can be applied only to laboratory animals, Gazzaniga, Ivry, and Mangun (2002) still consider the development of the method the most important technological advance in neu-rophysiology and perhaps even in the whole of neuroscience. The reason for this is the fact that single-cell recording has taken the assessment of neuron activity to the utmost level of accuracy as it allows the recording of single neurons with great precision. In this way the technique has the highest reso-lution of all brain imaging techniques and, as Gazzaniga, Ivry, and Mangun assert, 'With this method, the understanding of neural activity jumped a quantum leap' (p. 106). For the first time, neuroscientists have been enabled to go beyond describing functional regions of the brain by focusing on the characteristics of individual elements.

The procedure involves inserting a thin electrode into an animal's brain outside the targeted neuron, which allows for the measurement of changes in voltage or current while the animal receives some, for example, visual stimuli. Initially, focusing on a single cell also has the drawback that the cell was taken out of context, whereas cognitive functions tend to be achieved through the aggregate operation of assemblies of cells. However, new techniques now allow scientists to record simultaneously the activity of as many as 150 neurons. Gazzaniga, Ivry, and Mangun (2002: 111) believe that 'Multiple single-cell recording may bring about the next revolution in neurophysiology.'

Neuroimaging

Neuroimaging is definitely the hottest topic in cognitive science. If you produce a study that is accompanied by at least one high-resolution scan of some aspect of the brain, preferably also with some parts of it lit up (and all of it, of course, in vivid colours!), people will know that this is serious matter. Indeed, Ramsøy, Balsley, and Paulson (2007) report that in 2005 of all papers published in brain studies one in five included neuroimaging results, and this proportion is likely to grow in the future. And even if you are not one of the select few who have access to some expensive brain scanning or neuroimaging device, you can still redeem the situation somewhat by mentioning in your writings at least a good variety of acronyms such as fMRI, CAT, PET, or ERP (particularly if you also talk about N400!). Overdone as it may be, this enthusiasm for neuroimaging is understandable: scientists have been waiting for the opportunity to glimpse behind the curtains of human cognition and see how our brain works online for so long that now the first such opportunities have finally arisen they jumped at the chance. And the public response was equally positive: there is a widespread feeling both in academic circles and in the popular media that hi-tech neuroscience is the real thing, with unlimited potential for the future.

In the following discussion, I would like to achieve two somewhat contradictory goals. On the one hand, I would like to provide an informative summary of the various neuroimaging techniques and measurement procedures to justify why so many people are ready to put their trust, or at least their hope, in them. On the other hand, I would also like to step back a little from the enthusiastic frenzy that surrounds neuroimaging and take a more critical look at what its real potential is and what is merely hype or wishful thinking. In a recent review article, de Bot (2008a: 111) offers a sobering message when he concludes that 'while the number of neuro-imaging studies on multilingual processing has exploded over the last few years, the contribution of such studies to enhance our understanding of the process of multilingual processing has not been very substantial'. To be fair, we need to remember as we start our discussion that neuroimaging in language research is a very recent development. Although the brain's electric potential was first measured in animals as early as the 1910s and in humans in the 1920s, and although medical science has been using high-resolution scanning devices since the 1970s, the widespread application of neuroimaging in language-related research started only in the 1990s and L2 applications have really taken off only during the past decade. Thus, this is a field which is still very much in flux and major new technological advances are introduced regularly every few years.

As we will see below, there are several different neuroimaging techniques— I will describe nine of these—each with their unique capabilities and constraints. They can be used for two different purposes:

- *Structural imaging* produces high-resolution static pictures of the structure of the brain and is useful, for example, for the diagnosis of tumours and injuries. For obvious reasons, this type is common in medical practice but it is also used in neuropsychology when, for example, we want to determine the extent of brain damage for aphasics. (See the section on neurophysiological research above.)
- *Functional neuroimaging* involves measuring some aspect of brain function in order to understand the mental operations associated with it. That is, in this case the purpose of the imaging procedure is not merely to produce an accurate picture of the required section of the brain but also to gain insights into mental operations by producing images of the brain in action.

Accordingly, while the key aspect of structural imaging is *spatial resolution* (i.e. to obtain high-resolution images of the brain), functional imaging is also concerned with *temporal resolution* (i.e. to gain accurate real-time records of neural processes).

Based on the technology they apply, neuroimaging methods can be divided into three different groups: *CT scanning, electrophysiological methods,* and *haemodynamic methods.* The first is based on X-ray technology in taking high-quality structural images, the second type records the electrical activity of neurons in a functional manner, and haemodynamic methods can produce both structural and functional images by measuring changes in the blood flow in the brain.

CT or CAT scanning

Strictly speaking, *CT* (computed tomography) or *CAT* (computed axial tomography) *scanning* is not a neuroimaging technique because it produces no more than a detailed, three-dimensional structural image of parts of the brain without providing any specific information about neurons or neural activity. However, ever since the development of the technique in the 1970s it has been applied in conjunction with other methods by neuroscientists, for example in neurophysiological research to determine the exact location of brain damage that causes aphasia or in neuroimaging studies to complement functional PET images (see below) that have inferior spatial resolution with anatomical information. (There are now integrated CT-PET scanning devices.) The method is based on using conventional low-level X-rays, but by taking several pictures of the same region from slightly different angles and viewpoints that the resulting two-dimensional images can be processed by a computer to achieve a full three-dimensional reconstruction of the targeted body part. The procedure takes only a few minutes, which makes it a very useful tool for the medical profession to obtain anatomical information.

Electrophysiological methods

Electrophysiological methods are based on the recognition that the small changes in voltage around active synapses (i.e. the areas where neurons connect with each other) can be recorded by nearby electrodes (through electroencephalography (EEG)) or by measuring the small magnetic fields they create (through magnetoencephalography (MEG)). The strength of these methods lies in their temporal resolution: they can provide precise real-time measures in the range of milliseconds. However, due to technical constraints of measurement, their spatial resolution and versatility is less accurate and in this respect haemodynamic methods are superior.

EEG (electroencephalography)

Electroencephalography was developed in the first two decades of the twentieth century and since then the technology has continually improved. Being the first method to examine and measure the activity of the human brain directly, it is understandable that its impact on various branches of medicine and psychology has been enormous. EEG is a non-invasive technique, safe for experimentation or repeated application, and it has been successfully used to diagnose various brain disorders. The necessary equipment—a set of scalp detectors (see Figure 2.6)—is relatively cheap, which has also helped the widespread application of the method in neuroscience.

The weakness of EEG is its spatial resolution: because the skull acts as a strong electric insulator, detectors placed on the scalp can measure neural activity directly only for a relatively large population of neurons of (at least 1,000 to 10,000 for the smallest recordable signal) oriented in roughly the same direction and not too distant from the scalp. (For detailed descriptions, see Green 2001; Kutas, VanPatten, and Kluender 2006.) Thus, this method is selective in the kind of signals it can record and it is also insensitive to subcortical brain activity.

ERP (Event-related potential)

Although the acronym 'ERP' (standing for 'event-related potential') looks similar to all the other acronyms representing neuroimaging techniques, the term does not refer to a research method but rather to a certain type of electrophysiological result obtained by means of EEG (thus, it would probably be more appropriate to call an ERP an 'ERP measure'). EEG records the neural activity of thousands of ongoing mental processes and yields therefore

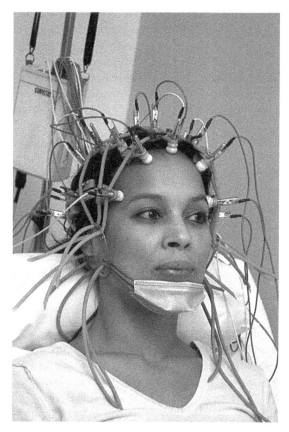

Figure 2.6 Scalp detectors for EEG (reproduced with permission:
A J Photo/Hop Americain/Science Photo Library)

only gross correlates of overall brain functioning. From a research point of view, it would clearly be more beneficial to be able to obtain accurate recordings of the neurological activity associated with specific cognitive tasks. ERPs provide exactly this kind of outcome—hence 'event-related'—and are therefore extensively utilized in language-related neuroresearch.

The main technological difficulty of recording electrical activity associated with a specific cognitive process lies in the fact that at the scalp level the signal produced by an individual activity is substantially smaller in amplitude than the large background oscillations of the EEG trace (about one-tenth; Kutas, VanPatten, and Kluender 2006). The ingenious way of extracting the isolated signal involves producing the same 'event' (e.g. giving the same stimulus or asking the subject to perform the same mental activity) many times and then applying computer averaging to identify the systematic signal amongst the spontaneous and random noise. The required number of trials

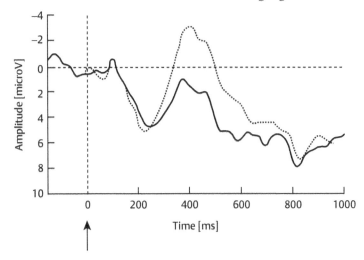

Figure 2.7 Sample output of an ERP waveform, with the vertical axis representing the amplitude of the voltage and the horizontal axis time (in milliseconds); the arrow points at the experimental stimulus and the two lines in this particular output represent separate results from two types of event.

varies according to the amplitude of the signal that the event produces, but usually ranges from several dozen to several hundred (30–50 on average). The outcome of the averaging procedure is a waveform of voltage (see Figure 2.7 for an example), in which the starting point is synchronized with the event that is measured, and the waveform of the electric activity shows (similar to a line diagram) the amplitude and direction (negative or positive voltage) of the systematic neural activity following the event. Thus, ERP output typically consists of the waveform of voltage plotted against post-stimulus time.

In the ERP output (waveform), the important aspect is the series of *negative* and *positive peaks* relative to the baseline (which is usually a short, 100–200 ms, record of signals immediately preceding each experimental stimulus). As Kutas, VanPatten, and Kluender (2006) explain, these peaks are typically labelled according to their polarity (negative = N, positive = P) and latency in milliseconds relative to stimulus onset (e.g. N400, P300); thus, N400 indicates a negative peak 400 ms after the stimulus. Occasionally, peaks are designated by some other characteristic such as their most reliable scalp location (e.g. LAN or left anterior negativity).

The assumption underlying the interpretation of an ERP is that the various peaks reflect different functional processes by different parts of the central nervous system. Thus, the ERP represents a series of stages of neural activity underlying the subject's response to the target stimulus or event; in many ways it can be seen as the temporal blueprint of the unfolding of neural processing. Interpretations have been helped by the fact that salient stimuli of the same type (e.g. visual stimuli) appear to elicit reliable ERPs from the subjects (i.e. similar ERPs are consistently reproduced across sessions), following the same time pattern. Therefore, when scientists find a recurring peak in the waveform (e.g. P300) that accompanies somewhat different stimuli, this would suggest that the particular peak represents some higher cognitive process triggered by the events. It is up to the scholars, then, to try to identify the nature of this process. The most famous such later peak is the N400, which will be discussed in more detail below.

ERP experiments typically involve subjects performing some cognitive task and it is important to note that these tasks are normally receptive: ERPs cannot be recorded during natural speech production because the neural activity involved in co-ordinating articulatory muscles would interfere with the results (Mueller 2005). In fact, even blinking or slightly moving one's head or eyes create substantial noise that needs to be screened out later by computer averaging.

N400 and other salient language-specific ERP components The most researched ERP component directly linked to language issues is the N400, first reported by Kutas and Hillyard (1980, cited by Kutas, VanPatten, and Kluender 2006). As the label suggests, it refers to a salient negative voltage peak around 400 milliseconds (300–500ms) after the stimulus, which in the 1980 study was the comparison of predictable and semantically incongruent/improbable sentence-final words. Kutas and Hillyard found that the incongruent words elicited a large negative wave, pointing to a semantic context effect. Since then many studies have successfully reproduced the N400 by eliciting unexpected linguistic stimuli. However, as Mueller (2005) summarizes, the relatively straightforward initial explanation that the N400 is a marker of the difficulty of semantic integration processes has been questioned because it was found that 'Outright semantic violations are neither necessary nor sufficient for the occurrence of an N400' (p. 156). Kutas, VanPatten, and Kluender (2006: 706) now agree that the explanation is more complex because recent studies 'have begun to blur the lines of this once pleasantly simple picture'. As they explain:

> The correct characterization of the N400 context effect is thus not that anomalous or unrelated words elicit unusual brain responses, but rather that a large negativity between 200 and 500ms or so (N400) is the default response, and that its amplitude is reduced to the degree trial context aids in the interpretation of a potentially meaningful stimulus. (p. 668)

Because of the low spatial resolution of ERPs, there is also some ambiguity around the localization of the cerebral region that produces the N400. It appears that the largest source of the N400 is the left temporal lobe with a substantial but lesser contribution from the right temporal lobe.

Other ERP components that have received attention in neurolinguistic research include negative peaks occurring after certain syntactic violations detected by left anterior electrodes (ELAN with a latency of 100–300 ms; and LAN with a latency of 300–500 ms) and the P600 component, which has been interpreted as reflecting processes of reanalysis and syntactic repair. (For an overview, see Mueller 2005.) We must note, however, that all these identifications are still rather speculative and often ambiguous (e.g. Kutas, VanPatten, and Kluender 2006 point out that certain manipulations of pragmatic plausibility at the lexical level have also been found to elicit P600s). The problematic nature of interpreting ERPs is well illustrated by the fact that although we have known the N400 for almost 30 years now, we are still not entirely certain about what causes it and where, which has been acknowledged by Kutas, VanPatten, and Kluender (2006: 707) with commendable frankness: 'Clearly, we still do not understand completely what the N400 indexes, let alone the exact nature of the more recently discovered language-related ERP components.' This deep-seated ambiguity warrants a closer look at the sources of the uncertainties regarding ERP measures in general.

Some concerns with ERPs As has been mentioned earlier, a general problem with electrophysiological methods is their poor spatial resolution, which means that even if we record some consistent and salient signal (e.g. N400) it is very hard to localize its source or generator. This shortcoming is further augmented by the selective nature of the EEG method: on the one hand, we can use it only with language perception tasks because of its sensitivity to interference from neural activity associated with muscle movement that is required for speech or writing; on the other hand, the electrodes placed on the scalp can pick up signals only coming from relatively large cell assemblies that are located in certain regions of the cerebral cortex.

As a result of these constraints, it is fair to admit that we are not completely sure about what ERPs reflect. All we know is that they can systematically indicate voltage peaks following certain cognitive tasks, which are then taken for measures of increased neural activity. We do not know, however, the nature or the exact place of this neural activity, and we do not know either what other neural processes are employed in the targeted task in areas of the brain that the method is insensitive to. Thus, we simply cannot tell, for example, whether ERPs represent the main neural activity evoked by the task, or whether the recorded voltage peaks are merely the tip of the iceberg. This is a rather curious situation: we have stable and highly interesting findings but no one really knows what these findings actually show, let alone the conditions they are linked with.

With so much uncertainty surrounding ERPs, how can they be included in meaningful (and often highly fruitful) research? We need to realize that psychologists tend not to be too fazed by uncertainties about what a research instrument measures; the guiding principle is that as long as the results appear to be consistent, there is a realistic hope that extensive empirical research will sooner or later uncover the phenomenon that has been tapped into. Research methodology in psychology has often not been driven by theory but by tri-al-and-error experimenting—for example, when intelligence tests were first introduced at the beginning of the twentieth century, nobody really knew what they were measuring except that they worked because they were effective in separating bright and slow children in schools, and it took several decades of gathering data with these tests before the first comprehensive models of cognitive abilities were proposed.

There is, however, also a specific feature of ERPs that has added to its research utility—the consistency with which certain voltage peaks accompany certain stimuli. This allowed researchers to fall back on the long-established strategy of dealing with ambiguous data, namely *comparative analysis*. The rationale for this procedure is that, if we find a salient electrophysiological response pattern with a certain type of input, we ought to check whether it also emerges with a slightly different type of event. If it does, we can start thinking of what is common between the event types and then draw up a theoretical hypothesis that can be tested by giving input that is conceptually contrasted with the original input. If the new input does not reproduce the previous ERP, we can start speculating that the neural activity reflected by the original ERP is indeed related to the hypothesized linguistic aspect. Alternatively, but following the same contrasting logic, we can compare native speakers' and non-native speakers' responses and draw conclusions about certain aspects of bilingualism. As Ullman (2006: 248) describes, this is exactly the approach ERP studies have followed:

> The general experimental approach is to take images of brain activity while subjects perform tasks that engage cognitive processes of interest. Typically one compares brain activation between two or more conditions that are designed to differ only with respect to the specific functions of interest.

Thus, as pointed out by Frisch, Hahne, and Friederici (2004), in L1 ERP research syntactic violations and semantic anomalies have been the target of the majority of studies following the recognition that such violations seem to produce especially clear changes in the electrical activity of the brain. However, the authors go on, such tasks represent rather artificial paradigms, which in turn question the generalizability of any findings, a view supported by other scholars including Kutas, VanPatten, and Kluender (2006: 707) when they concluded: 'As a research strategy, continuing to pursue the study of violation types may not necessarily answer as many questions as it raises.'

A final problem with pursuing voltage patterns and contrastive differences without really knowing the nature of the phenomena involved concerns the fact that detecting similar ERP patterns does not necessarily mean that the underlying neural processes are identical. In theory, several different combinations of sources can generate similar patterns (Mueller 2005; Ullman

2006), and therefore even the consistently recorded ERP components such as the N400 or the P600 may indicate fundamentally different neural activities in different studies.

MEG (magnetoencephalography) and MSI (magnetic source imaging)

EEG measures the voltage field produced by electric current flow, but the same flow also generates small magnetic fields that can be recorded by means of *magnetoencephalography* (MEG). Because it measures the same electric flow as EEG, the method has a similarly potent temporal resolution but much better spatial resolution (although still inferior to that of haemodynamic methods). One reason for this is that although the skull is a good electric insulator, bone is magnetically transparent and therefore causes no magnetic blurring. However, the strength of the magnetic fields created depends on the geometrical orientation of the electric current flow, and as a result, MEG does a much better job at detecting cortical activity in the sulci than in the gyri, the latter representing about one-third of the total cortical sheet (Kutas, VanPatten, and Kluender 2006). Unfortunately, the necessary equipment for MEG (ultrasensitive 'SQUID' detectors) is prohibitively expensive relative to the hardware needed for EEG. (Gazzaniga, Ivry, and Mangun 2002 point out that a system with 150 to 300 sensors that covers the entire head costs over a million dollars.) Additionally, the testing room needs to be heavily shielded against magnetic interference from computers, power lines, passing trains, etc. (Ullman 2006). As a result, relatively few neuropsychological studies—let alone studies focusing on language issues—have been conducted applying MEG.

An extension of MEG is *magnetic source imaging* (MSI), whereby MEG results are superimposed on an anatomic image of the brain (typically an MRI scan), to produce an integrated functional/structural record that arguably offers the best combination of spatial and temporal resolution and has therefore definite potential for the future. This is all the more so because the method also allows for the generation of *event-related fields* (ERFs) similar to the ERPs produced by EEG. (For a review and a summary of research, see Billingsley *et al.* 2003.)

Haemodynamic methods

We saw above that electrophysiological methods measure the electrical currents that are generated when neurons communicate with each other (i.e. by synaptic activity). *Haemodynamic methods* are based on an entirely different principle: they map the changes in the blood supply of the neurons. It has been observed that increased neural activity requires a local increase in the cerebral blood flow to provide the necessary energy for the increased neural firing rate. The intensity of regional blood flow can therefore be taken to be an index of a particular cerebral area's metabolic demand and, consequently, the level of its engagement in mental activities. This approach has turned out to be very accurate in terms of spatial resolution (i.e. it helps to localize increased neural activity precisely), resulting in extremely high quality structural images. Technological developments have also made it possible to combine this strength with functional imaging capacity (i.e. recording the process of mental activity), but the temporal resolution achieved is nowhere near as good as the millisecond-level precision of electrophysiological methods.

SPECT (single photon emission computed tomography)

Single photon emission computed tomography (SPECT)—along with PET (see below)—is a radioactive neuroimaging method. It uses a tracer isotope that is injected into the bloodstream so that the gamma ray that it produces can be measured by special detectors ('gamma cameras') to provide an image of the blood flow. Although the first SPECT imaging device was constructed in the early 1960s, it was a rather crude instrument that produced low-resolution (and often distorted) pictures. It took almost two decades before the technology improved sufficiently to produce good quality three-dimensional images of active brain regions. However, as Ullman (2006) concludes, functional neuroimaging with SPECT is now rare, which is due to the fact that PET offers better resolution (although it is more expensive) and the newer technique of MRI (to be discussed below) can measure the blood flow in a non-invasive way, that is, without exposing the subjects to radiation.

PET (positron emission tomography)

Introduced very soon after the development of CT scanning in the 1970s, *positron emission tomography* (PET) soon became the preferred method of functional neuroimaging. Although the appearance of fMRI (see below) at the beginning of the 1990s somewhat overshadowed PET scanning, it is still widely used worldwide. The technology is similar to SPECT in that a radioactive tracer isotope, which, in this case, emits positrons as it decays, is injected into the bloodstream; the emission data is recorded by PET scanners (see Figure 2.8) and is processed by a computer in order to reconstruct two- or three-dimensional images that indicate brain activity.

PET has been the most accurate of all metabolic imaging methods and it is widely used in medicine to diagnose brain tumours, strokes, and other brain diseases (such as Alzheimer's disease). In language-related research its use typically involves collecting images of blood flow before and during a targeted cognitive task so that by comparing these we can draw conclusions about task-specific brain engagement (Abutalebi, Cappa, and Perani 2005). This functional approach can be combined with high-resolution structural images (CT or MRI scans) to compensate for the method's relatively poor spatial resolution. A great advantage of PET over many other functional methods (e.g. ERP or fMRI) is that it is not selective in picking up signals only from certain brain regions. On the other hand, the number of observations on a subject is restricted because of the radiation involved, which puts a severe limitation on research design. Furthermore, PET cannot offer the kind of temporal resolution that electrophysiological methods can—it requires the

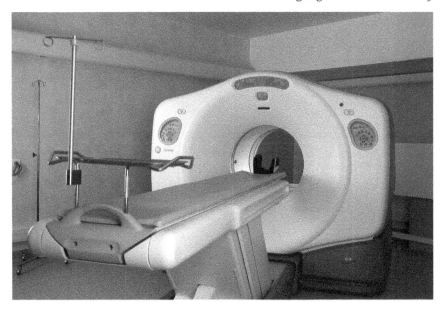

Figure 2.8 PET scanner (reproduced with permission: Science Photo Library)

subjects to be engaged continuously in a given experimental task for at least 40 seconds, and metabolic activity is averaged over this period—and even other haemodynamic methods such as fMRI are far superior in this respect (the temporal resolution of fMRI is about 3 seconds—see below).

MRI (magnetic resonance imaging) and fMRI imaging

Magnetic resonance imaging (MRI) is not a haemodynamic method but it is discussed here because it has been adapted for the purpose of *functional magnetic resonance imaging* (fMRI) so that it can produce accurate recordings of the blood flow. MRI is a method of constructing highly detailed structural images similar to CT scanning, but the outstanding spatial resolution and the non-invasive nature of the procedure (it uses magnetic fields and radio waves rather than X-rays) make it one of the most important medical inventions of the past three decades. The central part of the MRI scanner (see Figure 2.9) is a large cylindrical magnet that creates a magnetic field around the subject (who has to lie still in it during the scanning), which is then exposed to a beam of radio waves and the resultant signal is picked up by detectors. While the MRI scanner is not unlike CT scanners, it takes much longer—often as long as one hour or more—to produce the necessary MRI image than the few minutes needed for a CT scan and therefore MRI scans often require general anaesthesia for people with even mild claustrophobia.

Although MRI was developed at the end of the 1970s, it took over a decade for MRI technology to be successfully adapted to examine brain

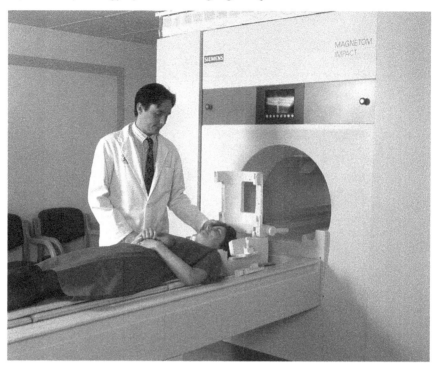

Figure 2.9 MRI scanner (reproduced with permission: Jean-Claude Revy, ISM/Science Photo Library)

activity. The fMRI procedure was introduced in 1991 and soon became the dominant research method used in neuroimaging studies. As with all other haemodynamic procedures, it measures neural activity through recording changes in blood flow in the brain, but it does not do so through the injection of radioactive isotopes into the bloodstreams as SPECT and PET do, but rather by focusing on the oxygen content of the haemoglobins of the brain. It was found that the haemoglobin has different magnetic properties depending on whether or not it is oxygenated, and during neuronal activity the haemoglobin becomes deoxygenated, thereby changing from a form that is not magnetically susceptible to one that is (Uttal 2001). In this way, fMRI can record brain activity with excellent spatial resolution (of about 1–3 mm), and this capacity to localize brain activity accurately is likely to get even better in the future as high-powered magnets become more available for use with human subjects (Gazzaniga, Ivry, and Mangun 2002). However, we must note that in neuronal terms even a 1 mm resolution is still rather crude.

In order to be able to investigate various mental processes, fMRI scanners have the facility to present subjects with visual and aural stimuli, and the participants can even respond by pressing a button or moving a joystick.

The non-invasive nature of the process allows for repeated administration of experiments to the same subjects, thus reducing a significant limitation on research design.

Over the past decade fMRI has transformed the landscape of neuroscience, with fMRI studies dominating the relevant journals and conferences. Gazzaniga, Ivry, and Mangun (2002) attribute this partly to the practicality of the method: MRI scanners are becoming much more common in hospitals than PET scanners, and because no radioactive isotope is involved, they require a smaller technical staff. As a result, an increasing number of research laboratories worldwide can either arrange access to MRI scanners or purchase their own device.

Some concerns with fMRI The greatest weakness of fMRI is its temporal resolution—about 2–3 seconds—because the haemodynamic changes that take place in response to neuronal activity are simply too slow to allow for the detection of real-time changes at the millisecond level. This severely restricts the applicability of the procedure in the study of language processing where high temporal resolution is a crucial factor (Ullman 2006). Furthermore, because of the long response time (relative to the speed of neuronal activities), the increased blood flow captured by an MRI image is unlikely to be associated with only one specific activity in the brain but rather with a mixture of several mental operations—that is, the haemodynamic signal in fact reflects the integration of several seconds of neural activity (Henson 2005). Dobbs (2005: 27) provides a vivid illustration of what this means in practice:

> This situation makes viewing an fMRI image something like listening to a string quartet by hearing (condensed into a single noise after the music has ended) only the total amount of sound each instrument produced during the piece, rather than hearing how the players accompany and respond to one another.

The temporal shortcoming of fMRI cannot be helped because it is inherent in the procedure. The only way to get around this problem is by combining the method with other techniques that offer good temporal resolution. While there are several technological difficulties to overcome, there have been promising initiatives that combine MRI with EEG and MEG technologies to get the best of both worlds (i.e. spatial and temporal).

Besides the poor temporal resolution, a further shortcoming of the method is that it is not equally sensitive to every part of the brain. Adjacent structures such as the middle ear can cause magnetic interference and therefore some regions (in particular, the orbitofrontal and inferior temporal regions and the temporal pole) cannot be visualized adequately (Abutalebi, Cappa, and Perani 2005). Thus, the method is selective in the signals that it can pick up. However, here again there are indications that technological advances may be able to bring about real improvement.

A third problem that needs to be pointed out concerns most neuroimaging techniques to some extent, namely that currently we can only detect signals produced by large groups of neurons. As Henson (2005) summarizes, haemodynamic techniques measure changes in metabolic demands that are associated with the activity of probably as many as millions of neurons at a time. However, we have no way of being certain that a small group of neurons cannot perform crucial cognitive functions, yet their activity will not be recorded in our neuroimaging data (Dobbs 2005). Furthermore, unwelcome variation might be caused by the fact that some types of neuron are more 'blood-economical' and therefore all these factors could mean that 'an fMRI image misrepresents actual neurodynamics' (ibid. 27).

Thus, just as with the other neuroimaging techniques, the overall picture about fMRI is a little bit like the glass that is half full: we can choose to focus on the absence of one half or the presence of the other. This is well illustrated by the conclusion of a review entitled 'What does fMRI tell us about neuronal activity?' (Heeger and Ress 2002: 149), in which the authors start by stating: 'This review has raised more questions than answers.' This is definitely not what we would expect of a review and yet this kind of approach is quite common in the general neuroscience literature. Yet, following the all too familiar trend, Heeger and Ress then decide to focus on the full half of the glass in their final sentences:

> With any new technique, it takes some time to sort out the methodological details.... fMRI provides a new and different picture of brain function, complementary to other techniques; although this presents a challenge, it will also prove to be of great benefit. (ibid.)

Optical imaging

The latest neuroimaging method (developed at the end of the 1990s) added to the neuroscientist's toolbox with great potential for future applications is *optical imaging*. It is based on beams of near infrared laser light, which diffuses through the tissues and allows us to 'see'—by means of sensors placed on the skull—blood volume and oxygenation changes. Because it utilizes light, the technique has excellent temporal resolution, and as Gazzaniga, Ivry, and Mangun (2002) conclude, its spatial resolution is comparable to that of modern MRI scanners. An optical imaging system is far less expensive than technologies that require scanners, and if the technology develops further so that the detectors can measure structures beyond the vicinity of the cortical surface, this method may become the neuroimaging star of the future.

Issues and concerns with neuroimaging

> *Despite the progress that has been made in linking the functional and the neuro-level, we do not know what it is that we measure with NI [neuroimaging] techniques. There is a signal, but what is the source?*
> (de Bot 2008a: 124)

Even this brief overview of the various neuroimaging techniques will have conveyed the existing momentum in the field, with a dazzling range of high-tech procedures already at our disposal and with further developments in the pipeline. These computerized tools have stimulated an enormous amount of interest and laboratory research, and have thus been to a large extent responsible for the establishment of cognitive neuroscience as one of the most vibrant contemporary academic disciplines. Curiously, Coltheart (2006) is right when he points out that within the huge volume of recent literature reporting the results of cognitive neuroimaging studies, there are surprisingly few papers that have attempted a critical appraisal of this methodology in terms of its theoretical yield. However, amongst the few works that have offered an evaluation, there are some that present rather negative conclusions, questioning the overall usefulness of neuroimaging. Although these concerns are not shared by the majority of scholars and the general atmosphere is still optimistic, they are sufficiently serious to warrant a more detailed discussion. After all, the issues raised by them touch upon some of the fundamental questions concerning the validity and the future of neuroscience in general. Let us look at the main points in some detail.

Unduly seductive nature

There is no question about the fact that neuroimaging is a highly appealing methodology. As Paradis (2004: 153) succinctly puts it, 'Neuroimaging is new, exciting, and colourful; it is also very expensive, and hence prestigious.' According to one of the most fierce critics of the approach, Uttal (2001: p. x), it displays 'an exuberance typical of a science suddenly provided a powerful new tool—or, perhaps, of a child given a new toy'. Bloom (2006) thinks that we are also affected by the fact that neuroimaging seems and feels like 'real' science: 'It has all the trappings of work with great lab-cred: big, expensive, and potentially dangerous machines, hospitals and medical centres, and a lot of people in white coats.'

This popularity in undeniable: newspapers, magazines, TV programmes nowadays often take a psychological angle to discuss 'theoretical' issues concerning politics, sports, advertising, and even sex, all supported by colourful neuroimagery (usually fMRI images). But as Bloom (2006) points out, even scientific journals such as *Science* or *Nature* give undue preference to papers that are accompanied by pretty colour pictures of the brain. As he concludes,

> The media, critical funding decisions, precious column inches, tenure posts, science credibility and the popular imagination have all been influenced by fMRI's seductive but deceptive grasp on our attentions. It's a pervasive influence, and it's not because the science is better.

Is this popularity justifiable? This is the point where opinions diverge. While the fans applaud, critics argue that neuroimaging runs the risk of being 'overrated and used for purposes beyond its true scope' (Paradis 2004: 153).

Uttal (2001) argues that the neuroimaging frenzy is going on at the expense of conventional psychological research and, indeed, some of the most prestigious American universities have already replaced their traditional cognitive/experimental psychology programmes with cognitive neuroscience programmes. This is a real problem, particularly if we consider the warning of Henson (2005: 228), who is himself a leading neuroscientist and a principled defender of neuroimaging:

> I think there is a real danger that pictures of blobs on brains seduce one into thinking that we can now directly observe psychological processes ('reifying' theoretical constructs). To the neuroscience undergraduate in particular, imaging data may seem to offer a more direct window on the mind than do behavioural data. Yet such high hopes are unlikely to be met. Indeed, from a pragmatic point of view, one could argue that, given the expense of acquiring imaging data and a finite amount of research funding, imaging experiments are of less value than behavioural experiments when the experimental hypothesis can be addressed by both.

Coloured pictures hide many sins

Critics argue that the colourful images of the brain are not just unduly attractive and awe-inspiring, but they are also deceptive in that they imply much more precision than there actually is. The imagery's power hides the fact that the actual pictures are the product of a great deal of 'doctoring' based on various subjective decisions. Raw imaging data is usually rather noisy and therefore different labs use different methods to filter out some of the noise and to enhance the signal-to-noise properties of the images. Techniques include, for example, averaging several different images pixel by pixel, setting somewhat arbitrary activation thresholds, or performing various data transformations and standardizations. A particularly powerful procedure is *subtraction*, whereby images obtained in two conditions (e.g. before and after a task) are subtracted from each other to create a difference image. There is nothing wrong in principle with such data management if it is not overdone—although, Ganis, Thompson, and Kosslyn (2005) produced worrisome evidence that the results of subtraction in a carefully designed and executed study were not the same as those obtained with another method—but several scholars believe that the only way to get the crisp images that are usually published is by dangerously and artificially reducing the variance in the data. (See e.g. Paradis 2004; Uttal 2001.)

The basic difficulty lies in the fact that no matter what neuroimaging method we use, it will produce plenty of results and in the absence of clear-cut theories and established procedural standards, it is to some extent up to the researchers to decide what of these results is meaningful. Accordingly, Paradis (2004) argues emphatically, if the final image suggests that there is no activation in a particular region, this does not mean at all that the particular area was not active. The activation may not have been detected because of the selective nature of the particular method (which I indicated in my descriptions of the individual procedures), the artificially set thresholds or baselines, or the masking effect of an inadequate task or research design—see below. Thus, we are dealing with significant method and researcher effects, yet the coloured pictures with bright spots suggest unambiguity and objectivity.

Shortcomings of the specific techniques

In the previous sections, where I reviewed the specific neuroimaging methods, I pointed out more than once that each procedure is constrained in some ways. Just to mention the most salient issues, they selectively pick up signals from a subset of brain regions and from certain types and groupings of neurons; none of them offers adequate spatial *and* temporal resolution; and the type of cognitive tasks that the participants can perform while undergoing neuroimaging is severely limited by the technologies. While we can veil these deficiencies with the convenient excuse of 'this is still a new area of science and therefore some teething troubles are natural', there is an equally justifiable alternative appraisal, namely that even if we find a salient activation pattern, we do not really know how it relates to the total activation of the relevant neural circuits at the time. In this respect, we can expect a breakthrough when future technological advances allow the fusion of the various imaging tools.

Ambiguity of the functional meaning of the detected signal

An important issue that is only rarely mentioned in the literature concerns the fact that, even if we successfully detect signals of neuronal activity, we cannot be certain whether the activity is excitatory or inhibitory (Crowell 2004). Paradis (2005) points out that because there are more inhibitory neurons than activating ones, there is a good chance that some of the observed activation reflect inhibition. Furthermore, Kutas, VanPatten, and Kluender (2006) explain that the current flow around the synapses can not only activate the target neuron's action potential or reduce its firing rate but it can also cause longer-term outcomes, making the neuron more or less responsive to future inputs. And, to make things worse, even if there is activation detected in an area, this does not necessarily mean that it plays a critical role in the task but may only be 'listening' (Gazzaniga, Ivry, and Mangun 2002). Thus, using neuroimaging techniques we currently cannot tell the exact functional contribution of a detected metabolic or electrophysiological signal.

Limited tasks

Functional neuroimaging studies are aimed at gathering information of the brain while the subjects are engaged in certain mental operations. These operations are evoked by specific experimental tasks, which have been limited in two major ways. First, as we saw earlier, the technological constraints of the various neuroimaging methods restrict the language tasks that could be utilized. For example, ERPs are disrupted by the neural activity of co-ordinating speech or movement, and therefore the targeted events can only involve tasks using listening and reading. Similarly, there is only so much one can do while lying in an MRI scanner.

The second source of task limitation is theoretical rather than technical. In the early, exploratory phase of neuroimaging that we are currently going through, there is little point targeting complex language tasks because we simply cannot even begin to match the cognitive processes subsumed by these tasks with the neuronal activation observed. Therefore, the typical research strategy in both L1- and L2-related neuroresearch has been focusing on simple, discrete tasks such as the recognition of single words, the detection of syllables, or the recognition of syntactic and semantic violations. While such limited tasks do provide a certain degree of control, they run the risk of tapping into something other than what is used in a natural linguistic task (Paradis 2004). We saw, for example when we discussed ERPs, that the standard paradigm of investigating various types of rule violations has recently come under criticism and Kutas, VanPatten, and Kluender (2006: 707) concluded that it 'may not necessarily answer as many questions as it raises'. Indeed, it is questionable how generalizable the information is that we gain from studying discrete language elements in isolation. Paradis, for example, argues convincingly that such tasks are unlikely to involve the implicit procedural computations that underlie the processing of a verbal message either in comprehension or production.

Simplistic research designs

In a reaction-time study where the only data we can obtain is some sort of response speed in milliseconds, only highly sophisticated research designs can offer meaningful result—after all, the milliseconds in themselves do not mean much. In neuroimaging studies, however, where the raw data is a colourful image of a segment of the brain, one is greatly tempted to be satisfied with this outcome; accordingly, the actual research design is often limited to a mere descriptive process of trying to draw up simple brain–cognition correlations. In what way is this illuminating? We have already discussed (and will come back to this below) that localization studies struggle with inherent theoretical problems. And even if our main goal is not simply to image evoked mental operations but rather to compare the reactions to different stimuli, it is questionable whether we can draw parallels between similar response patterns (Gazzaniga, Ivry, and Mangun 2002; Mueller 2005). For example, if we ask subjects to evaluate politicians and find that in looking at a particular person's picture the same brain region is activated as when the subject smells burning gunpowder, can we infer anything substantial from this? Although this is an imaginary example, the majority of neuroimaging studies regrettably do not exceed this level of design 'sophistication'.

Thus, I believe that many of the problems with neuroimaging studies stem from the inadequate research designs they employ. For example, in an enlightening exchange between bilingualism experts and neuroscientists discussing a paper published in the prestigious journal *Nature* on 'Brain Potential and

Functional MRI Evidence for How to Handle Two Languages with One Brain'
by Rodriguez-Fornells *et al.* (2002), Grosjean *et al.* (2003) present both sides
of the coin. It is interesting to see how the linguists (Grosjean and Li) home
in on what they see as salient problems with the research design (especially
sample selection) and the linguistic characteristic of the stimuli; they conclude
their commentary in general terms which are nevertheless clearly addressed
to the neuroscientists:

> The gap between the neurosciences and the language sciences of
> bilingualism will be narrowed if both sides define and choose their
> bilinguals with care, use carefully selected stimuli, control for language
> mode, employ tasks that tap into normal language processing, and build
> together coherent theories of bilingual language representation and
> processing. (p. 161)

In response, besides arguing a few technical points, the neuroscientists (Münte
and Rodriguez-Fornells) defend themselves thus:

> In any biological or psychological experiment, a particular limited
> phenomenon is studied under particular limited conditions. Our
> experiment suggests how certain bilingual subjects behave in a certain
> situation (reading of mixed word lists with one language relevant). Other
> mechanisms might help bilinguals to keep their languages separate in
> other situations. Thus, our experiment is limited like virtually every other
> brain imaging and psycholinguistic experiment. (p. 161)

This is clearly a clash of two cultures with different priorities. To put it
broadly, one side argues that from a linguistic point of view the results are
highly contestable, while the other side openly admits some shortcomings
but displays the confidence of researchers whose article contains both ERPs
and fMRI images and has been awarded the ultimate prize, a publication in
Nature. At the end of the debate Münte and Rodriguez-Fornells make this
position quite explicit:

> On a more practical note, first-time (psycholinguistic) users and
> consumers of neuroimaging or electro-physiological techniques may
> find that their experimental possibilities are limited by methodological
> constraints, e.g. the necessity to have many trials per category or the
> problem of artefacts produced by vocalizations. These drawbacks are
> offset, in our opinion, by the fact that these techniques can deliver
> multidimensional spatio-temporal data on the timing, localization
> and parcelling of cognitive processes underlying bilingual language
> processing. (p. 162)

In other words, the multidimensional neuroimages compensate for any possible design limitations, a view that seems to be covertly shared by many
neuroscientists (including the editors of *Nature*). To be fair, we must note that,
although ineffective use of neuroimaging is a general problem for the field, it

is not impossible to design creative and sophisticated neuroimaging investigations. (For a highly technical analysis of the efficient experimental design for fMRI, see for example, Henson 2007.) In a paper entitled 'If Neuroimaging is the Answer, What is the Question?', the renowned neuropsychologist Stephen Kosslyn (1999: 1293) for example argues:

> Neuroimaging is an enormously exciting field because of the possibilities of new discoveries about fundamental relations between mind and brain, and the chance to make concrete what have hitherto been very abstract ideas. However, if we are to do this correctly, we must know what questions we are asking and just how far we can go in answering them with these techniques. Simply finding that certain areas of the brain are active when someone performs a task is not enough.

In conclusion, I strongly believe that in functional neuroimaging studies—as in any other research method—the quality of the outcome depends on the quality of the subtle details of the research design. Such studies use, in effect, brain signals as dependent variables ('If I do this, the brain responds like this') and with such a sensitive system as the brain, it is clear that even minute changes in the research design, stimulus materials, and task characteristics can lead to very different patterns of brain activation. This underscores Page's (2006) more general point that, while it may be a good thing to add neuroimaging data to our potential list of dependent variables, sound research principles would suggest that we 'restrict ourselves to measuring dependent variables about which the theories under test have something necessary to say' (p. 429).

Thus, in order to ensure success, we need highly focused and theoretically driven research questions as well as tightly controlled experimental designs—something not yet characteristic of the neuroimaging field in general. As de Bot (2008a: 117) confirms with regard to L2-specific studies, 'Age of acquisition, level of proficiency and language contact appear to be the main variables that are included in the research reported on. These factors are operationalized in different and mostly inadequate ways'. Yet de Bot also adds that such design flaws are not a problem for neuroimaging studies only, because the 'majority of psycholinguistic studies on multilingual processing show the same weaknesses' (p. 117).

Having highlighted possible design shortcomings in neuroimaging studies, let me reiterate that, as with experimental studies, there is no reason why a solid research design focusing on a theoretically driven research question should not produce important and valid results. For example, in an important fMRI study, Naccache and Dehaene (2001) used a masked priming procedure in a series of carefully matched subsets of trials in which the relationship between prime and target was varied randomly in each trial. They found that the same brain circuits that were at work during conscious number processing were also involved when the information was presented subliminally (i.e. in a masked condition), producing thereby evidence for the existence of implicit cognition, which is a highly contested issue in cognitive science. (See Ch. 3 on implicit learning.) This study is a good example of how the methodological strength of a psycholinguistic method, masked priming, can be combined to good effect with cutting-edge neuroimaging.

Network versus localization

We saw in an earlier section (on the functional anatomy of the brain) that the neural system is a vast, complex, and massively interconnected network of simultaneously active neurons, which questions the rationale for any localization effort, since any but the lowest level (sensory or motor) cognitive functions will almost certainly involve more than a single area (Uttal 2001). However, this is at odds with one of the central objectives of neuroimaging in general, namely the achievement of accurate spatial resolution. Coltheart (2006) likens this situation to the relationship between computer hardware and software and argues that no amount of knowledge about the hardware will tell us anything serious about the nature of the software that the computer is running.

Indeed, as Schumann (2006) points out, past language-specific neuro-research has demonstrated that the areas of the brain activated in L2 processing are very similar to those involved in first language processing, and those areas include large parts of the temporal lobe and the frontal lobe. So, he asks (p. 316), given this extensive substrate for language acquisition, 'what parts of the brain can be shown to play NO role in language?' In a similar vein, as Ganis, Thompson, and Kosslyn (2005: 235) summarize, 'Neuroimaging has revealed that even apparently simple perceptual and cognitive tasks are carried out by numerous interconnected brain areas and that different tasks typically rely on partially overlapping sets of brain areas.' Of course, even if we accept this argument, we must not forget that neuroimaging goes beyond localization efforts—for example, ERPs do not involve any function–structure mapping.

Group- versus individual-level analysis

Quantitative research in the social sciences typically conducts group-level analyses, which aim to identify the common variance amongst participants, treating the idiosyncratic variation around the central tendency as mere 'noise' that is to be eliminated. This practice has been increasingly questioned in applied linguistics (e.g. de Bot, Lowie, and Verspoor 2007a; Larsen-Freeman 2006) and we will come back to this issue when we discuss individual differences in Ch. 5. However, the problem is perhaps even more acute in neuroimaging research, since cognitive neuroscience draws its validity to a large extent from its seemingly solid neurobiological foundation, which is supported by colourful images as evidence. In this context, we need to question the validity of data averaging (which, as we have seen above, is regularly done to produce clearer images). What exactly is 'anatomical averaging'? If we propose a functional anatomical regularity and a small per cent of the participants fails to display this, is it wise to simply ignore this fact? Are functional neuroanatomical differences merely noise? How shall we deal with inter-individual differences in neuroanatomy?

Paradis (2004) argues, I believe correctly, that we ought to be able to account for the considerable inter-individual variation observed in neurobiology, yet as Kosslyn *et al.* (2002) summarizes in a paper specifically discussing the question of individual- versus group-based analysis, most studies on the biological foundations of mental processes try to minimize and ideally eliminate any deviations from the central tendency. In short, 'Cognitive neuroscientists construct theories about the relation between the average brain and the average behaviour' (Thompson-Schill, Braver, and Jonides 2005: 115). This, according to Kosslyn *et al.* (2002), can be a mistake given that our biological systems are notoriously redundant and complex, affording many different ways towards the same goal. Conducting only group-level analyses may hide any alternative mechanisms or the reasons why certain individuals rely on them at times. Furthermore, Kosslyn *et al.* (2002) emphasize that in a situation where there are two groups of subjects who rely on different goal-specific strategies, pooling data from both groups may be uninformative at best and outright misleading at worst.

So, to reiterate the question, how shall we deal with inter-individual differences in neurobiology? There is no simple answer. Modell (2003) explains that the success of neurobiology at the levels of molecular and cellular biology demonstrates that individual differences at these levels can be safely ignored as 'noise'. When considering the higher level of cognitive functions, individual variation assumes greater significance, yet some neuroimaging techniques (e.g. PET or fMRI) mask this individual difference while others (e.g. MEG) reveal it—something that the uninitiated viewer of the published brain images will not be aware of. Those who argue for a group-level approach claim that although individual human brains do differ, there are some general organizing principles that transcend these differences. While there is reason to believe that certain tasks, especially simple ones, are performed by all individuals in roughly the same way, substantial individual-level variation has been documented in many cognitive domains. (For an interesting relevant study, see e.g. Parasuraman and Greenwood 2006.) Therefore, brain regions that are not activated consistently across individuals may still be key contributors to the performance of interest in spite of the fact they are unlikely to be detected in a standard group average analysis (Ganis, Thompson, and Kosslyn 2005). This interview extract by a leading neuroscientist, Marcus Raichle (cited in Gazzaniga, Ivry, and Mangun 2002: 141), is certainly intriguing in this respect:

> I find it amusing to reflect on the fact that our initial work was aided by the relative crude resolution of PET scanners. The blurring of the data brought responses common across individuals together and allowed us to 'see' them. Early on, even robust responses could be caused to 'disappear' when one attempted to go to too high a resolution.

Confusing and contradictory results

A common experience in reading reviews of neuroimaging research is to be faced with confusing or contradictory results, accompanied by the usual proviso that these are mere teething troubles that will disappear with time. What if, however, they are not simply teething pains but rather the reflections of a fundamentally unfruitful research approach? The fact that, as discussed earlier, even after almost 30 years we still do not know what the most researched electrophysiological signal, the N400, truly indexes is certainly worrying and substantiates Paradis's (2004: 153) conclusion:

> At best, neuroimaging provides us with circumstantial evidence, and like all circumstantial evidence, its credibility rests on the amount of converging data from other sources. There may come a point when there are so many coincidences that they affect our belief—even if each piece of evidence is circumstantial. However, the problem with neuroimaging studies of bilingual speakers is that they provide evidence that conflicts considerably and is sometimes incongruent with evidence from other sources.

The Other Side of the Coin

The famous biologist Richard Lewontin was so right when he pointed out (Lewontin 2000) that scientists in general tend to use whatever research tools are available to them. He further argued that once new experimental techniques exist they have great power in determining the questions that scientists ask. As an illustration, he mentioned the invention of automatic DNA-sequencing machines; these were originally a response to a growing demand for sequence, but their availability in making the sequencing of DNA relatively easy also meant that the problems targeted by geneticists have become those that can be answered from DNA sequences. Neuroimaging methodology has the same novelty appeal as DNA sequencing in biology and therefore it is quite understandable that the research community has embraced the technology with gusto. And it is unavoidable that the technology, in turn, has been shaping the direction of development. Whether this direction is right or wrong, nobody quite knows at present. And in any case, as Baars (1997*b*: 292) concludes, 'In science we never know the ultimate outcome of the journey. We can only take whatever steps our current knowledge affords.'

Furthermore, regardless of the various possible reservations with neuroimaging methodology, the truth is that neuroimaging is generating tons of data about the brain, about which we have known very little before. Although traditional experimental psychological methods such as reaction-time studies or eye tracking are valuable and should certainly not be discarded, the research community seems to have come to the collective belief that these methods did not offer a sufficiently viable avenue to the discovery of such a complex organism as the human brain. As Schumann (personal communication) has pointed out,

> determining process or mechanism from behavior (as is done in psychology) is unconstrained; it leaves too much to the imagination

in the characterization of cognitive processes. We have to remember that researchers have not simply turned to neurobiological research because it is sexy and has high status. They also did it because of growing dissatisfaction with the inferences that must be made when doing behavioral research.

Paradis (2005: 413) is probably right that the neuroimaging enterprise feels a little bit like a 'fishing expedition' along the lines of 'let's poke here and see what happens'; as a result, researchers are often left in a quandary when it comes to interpreting the often unexpected data. However, quite frankly, Raichle (cited by Dobbs 2005: 28) also has a point when he claims: 'Imaging lets us probe it to generate new hypotheses. Some of the probing will look silly in retrospect. But much of it is very productive.' In addition, we also need to realize that neuroimaging is a hugely exciting journey into exploring the relations between mind and brain. It also gives us the chance 'to make concrete what have hitherto been very abstract ideas' (Kosslyn 1999: 1293). In short, researching the brain this way can be a thoroughly engaging, worthwhile enterprise.

Interim summary

The promises of cognitive neuroimaging are enormous, albeit quite unrealistic.
(Paradis 2004: 185)

The purpose of this fairly detailed overview of various issues and concerns that have been raised with regard to the validity of neuroimaging methods was not the desire to undermine this research direction and encourage readers to disregard its findings. I have made it clear above that in the absence of powerful alternatives, neuroimaging is likely to remain the driving force in the development of cognitive neuroscience. Instead, my objective was to show that as with any other research method, neuroimaging techniques have both strengths and weaknesses and we should not take everything for granted even if it is accompanied by colourful images of the brain. It seems to me that the current tide of intellectually thin papers dressed up in neuro-techno-language is worrying and I have yet to be convinced that the neuroimaging studies conducted in the field of second language studies can deliver the much-awaited breakthrough in our understanding of psycholinguistic phenomena. It was therefore reassuring to read that in his overview cited earlier, de Bot (2008a: 111) shares a similar view: 'The conclusion is that as yet NI [neuroimaging] has not fulfilled the high expectations raised by the technical progress and the large number of studies that have been carried out.' However, there is no doubt that we can obtain valuable findings if neuroimaging methods are coupled with good ideas and elaborate research designs; it is also clear that there are certain results that only such methods can yield. Thus, Tomasello's (2003: 328) conclusion about new experimental methods in child language-acquisition research also applies to the area of neuroimaging: 'But these new methodological techniques will be of long-term benefit to the field only if we get our theoretical house in order.'

Molecular genetic investigations and imaging genetics

Although neuroimaging has made a triumphant entry into brain research, it could well be that the days of its unchallenged dominance are numbered; a new star is already waiting in the wings to take the stage by storm. The candidate is *molecular genetic research* of cognition, and it comes with strong credentials: those of the 'Human Genome Project', which has successfully mapped the genetic make-up of the human species by determining the DNA sequence of the human genome. To be fair, such a takeover is unlikely, because molecular genetics is seen as complementary to imaging, which is reflected in the newly introduced term 'imaging genetics'. This aims at integrating imaging data with the rich genetic information resulting from the human genome project in order to enhance our understanding of brain functions. It is easy to predict that the coming decade is likely to witness an explosion in this research area.

Although genetics is an established scientific discipline, its application to the understanding of cognition is a very recent enterprise, with a history of less than a decade. The appeal of molecular genetic investigations is the recognition that genes act as the main building blocks of neurons and therefore individual differences in our genetic makeup are expected to influence the functioning of the brain (Ramsøy, Balsley, and Paulson 2007). It is our genes that determine how the human brain develops into the amazingly complex system it is, and therefore a genetic analysis can be potentially highly fruitful as a means of understanding the characteristics of this system.

As Parasuraman and Greenwood (2006) summarize, much of what we know about the genetics of cognition has come from behavioural genetic studies of twins, and the long history of twin studies has provided evidence, for example, about the extent of heritability of various traits. Molecular genetics differs from this approach as it aims to identify genes that are associated with a certain trait. Although the human genome contains 30,000–35,000 genes, 99 per cent of these do not differ between individuals and can therefore be excluded from being determinants of individual differences in cognition. The focus of this research approach, therefore, is the small percentage of DNA base pairs that show variation. There have already been interesting findings, for example with regard to a gene associated with attention and the working memory. Also, Plomin, Kovas, and Haworth (2007) argue that genetics contributes importantly to learning abilities and disabilities, which makes the field particularly relevant to future SLA research.

Summary

This book has been written in the belief that future studies of second language acquisition need to embrace psychologically oriented research. However, for most L2 professionals, the domain of psychology is a strange land where they speak a foreign language. This chapter has offered a travel guide and a crash course in the local tongue to enable the readers to travel around in this exotic land freely, without constraints. The emphasis has been on becoming familiar with the brain and the main methods of researching it. I do hope that the overview of the various psycholinguistic and neuroimaging techniques has made the big picture less confusing and that offering a critical analysis of the strengths and weaknesses of the methods has helped to demystify them. As Ullman (2006: 246) concludes, 'today a wide range of methods are available. However, none is perfect, and each method has a different set of strengths and weaknesses. Researchers try to choose the most appropriate techniques for answering a given question'.

Unfortunately, most of the methods described require special and often hugely expensive equipment as well as thorough training. Perhaps this explains the inclusion of the verb 'try' in the final sentence in Ullman's quote: Although we may try to choose the method that we think would suit our research design best, we are usually limited by what is available and accessible to us. Researching the brain is a highly specialized area that can realistically be done only if we are attached to a lab with the necessary hardware and know-how. The good news, however, is that some traditional psycholinguistic research methods such as reaction-time studies or self-paced reading are exceptions to this restriction as they can be set up with relatively little investment. And, as we have seen earlier, they can produce valuable results that are often more relevant and theoretically more sound than the dazzling images of the high-tech instruments.

It is hard to predict where the field is going. The technology is developing fast, with improved instruments introduced each year. Thus, we can expect current technologies to become increasingly sophisticated, existing methods to be combined with each other in meaningful ways, and brand new approaches to emerge. So, Ramsøy, Balsley, and Paulson (2007: 511) are probably right: 'Continuous innovations, both within hardware and software, make any prediction of the future of neuroimaging hazardous.'

3

Psychological processes in language acquisition I: symbolic versus connectionist accounts

> *There is little doubt, from the historical perspective, that although the emergence of connectionism has offered a powerful theoretical tool, its emergence has also polarized sections of the psycholinguistic community, between 'connectionists' on the one hand, and 'symbolists' on the other.*
> (Altmann 2006: 6)

Let us start our exploration of the maze of overlapping contemporary theories of language learning by looking at one of the most basic distinctions in the psychology of language that concerns both the representation and the acquisition of language competence, the *symbolic* versus *connectionist* contrast. In a comprehensive account of the L2 aspects of this topic, Hulstijn (2002*a*) explains that symbolic accounts represent knowledge as a collection of symbols accompanied by rules that specify the relationship between them. By 'symbol' we mean a unit that exists independently of the context; thus, traditional grammatical categories such as phonemes, syllables, and nouns are symbolic in nature. Although on the basis of this categorization it is tempting to believe that language as we know it must surely be entirely symbolic—since it is made up of discrete units—we can also think of a radically different type of architecture of knowledge—a connectionist account—whereby knowledge is not represented as sums of tiny information-packed units but rather as *activation patterns* in a neural network. According to this view, the main components of this network are not aligned to a fixed piece of information in a permanent manner but it is the various combined activation of the components that carries the meaning. Thus, if a network consists of three elements, A, B, and C, then a connectionist account would not assign any specific symbolic meaning to any of the three components—that is, they would be regarded as meaningless in isolation—but such an account would claim that it is in the combinations such as AB or BC that knowledge resides. We do not need to think hard to realize that the original inspiration for connectionist accounts has come from the brain, where the basic building blocks, the individual neurons, are believed to be content-independent (i.e. there is no neuron permanently assigned to mean, for example, the letter 'o', let alone the word 'orange'). This brain analogy is very clearly expressed by MacWhinney (2001*a*: 79–80):

> The human brain is basically a huge collection of neurons. These neurons are connected through axons. When a neuron fires, it passes activation or inhibition along these axons and across synapses to all the other neurons with which it is connected. This passing of information occurs in an all-or-none fashion. There is no method for passing symbols down axons and across synapses. Brain waves cannot be used to transmit abstract objects such as phrase structures. Rather, it appears that the brain relies on a type of computation that emphasizes patterns of connectivity and activation.

Unfortunately, things become more complicated in actual practice because we find that many primarily connectionist accounts do carry some 'hidden' symbolic units at lower, secondary levels of the network, and there are also some genuinely 'hybrid' accounts. However, let us not worry about these at this point but focus rather on the pure symbolic-connectionist distinction: in the former we assume the existence of independent knowledge; in the latter we assume that knowledge is stored in some sort of deconstructed way and is built up when the right buttons in the network are pressed. It is important to note that almost all linguistic theories so far have formulated their accounts in the form of symbolic architectures, whereas connectionist accounts have originally come from more abstract psycholinguistic theories of learning. With the growing convergence of linguistics and psychology, however, we must start to bring the two approaches together, which is not without teething pains (and given the enormity of the difficulties and the resistance on both sides, the term 'birth pain' would probably be more appropriate).

Hulstijn (2002*a*, 2007*a*) suggests that linguistic cognition can be described as a combination of symbolic and non-symbolic (or as is often called, 'subsymbolic') knowledge, because different aspects of language competence lend themselves more to either a symbolic or a connectionist account. As he explains, some cutting-edge recent research in psycholinguistics is trying to accommodate both types of representations, for example by assuming that some parts of a dynamic network can get so stabilized that these network parts attain the status equivalent to 'symbols' (with lexical units being prime examples of this). Pulvemüller (2002) points out that the network type most commonly used to model language is a kind of 'symbolic connectionist' model, which contains 1) low-level 'local representations'—usually single artificial *nodes* (as the constituent units of a network are usually referred to)—that represent elementary acoustic or visual features, phonemes, or graphemes, as well as (2) more complex entities such as word forms and word meanings. Thus, there is a variety of different approaches to trying to align connectionist and linguistic approaches. Elman (2001: 297) summarizes thus:

> The exact choice of how particular connectionist systems represent linguistic information varies dramatically. At one extreme, a word could

be represented by a single, dedicated input unit (thus acting very much like an atomic symbol). At the other extreme, the entire ensemble of input units might participate in the representation, with different words having different patterns of activation across a shared set of units.

Seen from the perspective of this book's main theme—the acquisition of a second language—one obvious problem with linguistic-symbolic accounts of language is that although they give a clear and elaborate description of the main components of language and their properties, they have little to say about the gradual process by which these symbols are developed and how symbolic knowledge changes. The process of L2 acquisition, for example, is seen by most linguistic theories as a movement through successive grammars (interlanguages), without specifying the transition (Hulstijn 2007b). This lack of an acquisitional aspect is very clearly expressed by White (2007: 46) with regard to the best-known nativist linguistic account, Universal Grammar (UG):

> It is important to understand that UG is a theory of constraints on representation... UG determines the nature of linguistic competence; principles of UG (constraints) guarantee that certain potential analyses are never in fact adopted. This says nothing about the time course of acquisition (L1 or L2) or about what drives changes to the grammar during language development. Similarly, the theory of parameter setting does not, in fact, provide a theory of language development even though it is often seen as such. The concept of parameter resetting in L2 presupposes that some kind of change takes place in the interlanguage grammar, from the L1 parameter value to some other parameter value... However, the precise mechanisms that lead to such grammar change are not part of the theory of UG.

In contrast, psycholinguistic-connectionist accounts lend themselves to be used for explaining language development because they aim to account for representation and acquisition in one and the same system. For this reason, after introducing briefly the most coherent linguistic approach to language acquisition—nativism and Universal Grammar—I will spend the rest of this and the whole of next chapter describing the various psychological theories of learning as applied to SLA.

Nativism and Universal Grammar

In the previous section, we looked at the symbolic versus connectionist contrast—let us now examine how this dichotomy is related to another frequently mentioned contrast in the field, that between *nativist* and *non-nativist* approaches, referring to whether the infant is assumed to bring a genetically coded linguistic endowment to the language acquisition process or not. The standard claim is to equate nativism with symbolism and non-nativism with connectionism. This general trend is by and large true: Chomsky's prominent symbolist theory of generative grammar is explicitly nativist, whereas for connectionists the idea of innate predeterminism with no process explanation seems to be at odds with current theories of the development and the functioning of the brain (N. Ellis 2001). Furthermore, non-nativists do not consider it necessary to postulate that children are endowed with language-specific knowledge at birth because, as we will see later, they regard the children's general learning capacities and mechanisms as entirely sufficient to develop L1 competence. However, we must note here that the different theories under the broad connectionist umbrella are not uniform in explaining how these underlying learning mechanisms are geared at language acquisition.

Because this book is about the psychology of SLA, the coverage of predominantly linguistic approaches such as nativist theories in general and Universal Grammar (UG) in particular will not be extensive but will focus only on the key organizing principles and the main strengths and weaknesses; for more detailed summaries of UG, please refer to Crain and Thornton (2006) or White (2003, 2007). As a preliminary, let me also add that although the psychological emphasis in this book might lead one to believe that the nativist/non-nativist debate has been won by the non-nativist camp, this is not so. Scholars in both camps would agree that the jury is still out on this question because each side can present powerful arguments to which at the moment there is no proper response from the other side. N. Ellis (2007a: 89) expresses this clearly:

> We do not have explanations of the emergence of all of the linguistic representations that play their part in UG accounts of language competence, any more than generativists have explained the inheritance and neural instantiation of these. The future will tell whether the logical problem will be solved better by inheritance or emergence.

Thus, at present, we simply do not know whether infants possess dedicated domain-specific learning mechanisms evolved for language acquisition (i.e. the innatist view) or whether they utilize existing learning mechanisms that are not domain-specific to discover the structure of human language (Saffran and Thiessen 2007).

Universal Grammar

As is well known, Noam Chomsky's theory of generative grammar (in its various evolving forms such as Government and Binding Theory or Minimalism) has been the dominant linguistic theory of the second half of the twentieth century, even though de Bot, Lowie, and Verspoor (2005) are right in pointing out that the majority of linguists in the world do not (or no longer) work exclusively within this paradigm. This theory contains a salient nativist component by proposing the existence of an innate human endowment, which can be seen as the blueprint for any human language (DeKeyser and

Juffs 2005). Accordingly, the capacity to learn language is a unique property of the human mind, and this innate endowment—or 'language acquisition device' in Chomsky's (1965) original proposal—has been conceptualized within the theory of 'Universal Grammar' (UG). UG is thus thought to be biologically fitted as part of the human genome (Crain and Thornton 2006) and it contains the core *principles* underlying any human language and the *parameters* for any allowable variation that these languages can manifest. These principles and parameters, thus, help to accommodate both the commonalities and the differences among languages in a systematic framework and, as Crain and Thornton (2006: 1073) summarize, they establish the 'boundary conditions on what counts as a possible human language'. Accordingly, the authors argue, children navigate within these boundaries in the course of language development.

As mentioned earlier, UG theory is not a theory of language acquisition because it does not spell out how the biologically driven process of developing the native-like system of grammar (conceived in terms of syntax, phonology, morphology, and semantics) takes place. As White (2007) explains, a key aspect of L1 acquisition is for the child to determine which of the possible parametric values pertain to the particular language to be learnt; however, since the differences are encoded in UG, the input data is supposed to trigger this parametric choice automatically. Thus, UG sets certain constraints, but beyond these constraints much of the relevant language knowledge does not actually have to be learnt in the traditional sense because it is derived from UG rapidly and effortlessly, without formal instruction and despite considerable differences in linguistic experience. This latter point leads us to the 'poverty of stimulus paradox', which is usually regarded as one of the most convincing arguments to support nativist accounts. Let us look at this paradox more closely.

The poverty of stimulus paradox

The *poverty of stimulus paradox* (also known as the 'logical problem of language acquisition' or 'Plato's problem'), concerns the fact that learners come to know more about language than they observe from experience. In other words, there is a considerable mismatch between the input that children are exposed to and their ultimate attainment: we simply seem to know more than we could have possibly learnt, which can be proved by our ability to decide that certain structures are ungrammatical without having any explicit knowledge of the reason for this and sometimes even without having come across the particular structure before. The universality of acquiring the L1 is indeed remarkable, particularly with children who come from environments which offer meagre input. What fills the input gaps? How can it be that the fundamental grammatical competence of some children is not patchier than others'? How can it be that there does not seem to exist a threshold of the minimal level of richness of the input for effective language acquisition to take place? Generative linguists believe that the answer to these questions is offered by the built-in knowledge of UG, and, indeed, UG derives its intuitive convincing power largely from this paradox. However, as we will see below when discussing the weaknesses of UG theory, non-nativist scholars have proposed several possible alternative answers to explain this puzzling phenomenon.

Other support for UG

Although the poverty of stimulus paradox is usually seen as the strongest evidence for UG, it is not the only one. Another frequently mentioned point is the 'no negative evidence in input' argument. It is well known that children make mistakes during the course of acquiring their mother tongue, yet they are neither corrected (or not often and certainly not everybody), nor do they pay much attention to these corrections. If this is the case, how do they recover from their mistakes? which they do, as proved by the adults' ability to use error-free language (Shatz 2007).

It also makes one wonder about the existence of a predetermined language faculty when considering how universal and uniform the L1 acquisition process is. As we saw in Ch. 1, infants produce their first words at around the same age as they take their first steps, and like walking, early language competence appears at around the same age and in much the same way all over the world. So, how can there be such regularity if the mechanisms of acquisition depend on individual learning processes and environmental input? Isn't this regularity a powerful evidence for the fact that infants are primed to acquire their L1?

Crain and Thornton (2006) list several more subtle points in support of UG, which are nevertheless similarly powerful. Most of these are highly technical and follow the pattern that a specific linguistic structure or rule is so complex that it could not possibly have emerged spontaneously as a product of experience, without some innate regulation. Those examples are particularly convincing where the correct structure is such that general-purpose learning algorithms would actually be expected to tempt children to violate them (e.g. by overgeneralizing). As Crain and Thornton conclude, experience-based accounts of such complex phenomena (e.g. the displacement of wh-phrases or the consequences of wh-movement for contraction) seem highly implausible to nativists, because

> the relevant distinctions that children would need to keep track of are
> so subtle and so numerous. The kinds of record keeping that is needed
> to mimic linguistic constraints would seem to be beyond the capacity of
> certain statistical learning mechanisms, such as connectionist or parallel
> distributed processing networks. (p. 1086)

Of course, the inherent weakness of this type of argument is that, just because we do not know the nature of the process that causes people to observe a particular rule, it does not mean that the process does not exist or that we have to assume therefore an innate, predetermined familiarity with the rule. This is, in fact, an example of what is sometimes called the 'poverty of imagination' fallacy, whereby a lack of knowledge of a phenomenon is taken as evidence for refuting the phenomenon. Bohannon and Bonvillian (2005: 249) rightly point out that 'concluding that grammar is not learnt through any known principles is not equivalent to concluding that it is innate'.

Problems with UG

Let us now look at five particularly salient criticisms of UG theory. Some of the points are rather compelling, but we must bear in mind throughout that the alternative, non-UG-based explanations also have gaping holes and weaknesses (to be discussed later).

1 *Lack of neurobiological validity:* from a psychological perspective the fundamental concern with UG is summarized by Schumann (2004*b*: 1) in a short statement when he concluded that research on the brain has found it very difficult to identify 'any areas or circuits that might constitute UG'. Paradis (2004: 36) summed up this point as follows:

> The actual computational procedures that generate sentences, though not undiscoverable in principle, are unlikely to correspond to any of the linguists' theoretical constructs, known as 'underlying structures,' or to the various pedagogical grammars available for L2 instruction, if only because the descriptions of underlying structure are varied and ever-changing—a testimony to the tenacious opacity of the actual form of implicit linguistic competence.

2 *The innatism issue:* a second aspect of UG that has raised—fairly predictably—considerable controversy is the tendency for UG theoreticians to resort to innateness as a default position whenever there is no obvious alternative explanation. This point has already been mentioned above when describing the 'poverty of imagination' fallacy. Bohannon and Bonvillian (2005: 274), for example, argue that this practice is, in effect, an easy and unconstructive way to ignore the problem:

> When an observer is at a loss to explain the origin of a form in children's speech, it would behove them to realize that simply labelling it as innate neither helps us determine its relation to other forms, nor to predict when it should appear in the developmental progression.

> In agreement with this position, N. Ellis (2001) regards predeterminism as a bit of unnecessary 'magic' brought into the scientific discourse when simpler explanations might suffice. As we will see below, a real development in this somewhat stalemate debate occurred when some connectionist-type procedures were found to successfully reproduce nativist-like results.

3 *Speed of language acquisition:* it has been taken as an axiom in support of UG that language development is unusually rapid. However, a closer look offers a different picture, and we can even find strong arguments to contend

that L1 acquisition is rather slow. Even if we focus only on grammar, the acquisition of complex rules and the subtleties of syntax continue well into the child's school years. And given the gradual, often life-long progress in other key linguistic areas such as vocabulary and pragmatics, this development rate is anything but fast. Of course, there are well-rehearsed and convincing responses to this issue, but the point to be made here is that this whole question is not so unambiguous that it can be cited in an unqualified manner as basic support for UG.

4 *The selective nature of UG:* a general concern of several linguists (applied linguists and psycholinguists alike) is that the UG theory tends to concentrate on grammar and relegate large areas of language structure to the 'periphery' (MacWhinney 2006).

5 *Grammaticalization and other experience-based processes:* Tomasello (2003) provides a detailed account of how certain grammatical rules that have traditionally been thought of as being part of the innate human linguistic heritage can actually emerge as a result of humans stringing together language components into consolidated and often conventionalized patterns. This process of producing grammatical constructions through usage has been referred to as 'grammaticalization' and it takes a central place in the newly developed usage-based theory of language acquisition—see separate section later. Similarly, N. Ellis (2007*b*) also discusses certain defining features of language (e.g. structure-dependence and hierarchical organization) as being naturally emergent properties because they are the products of sequential routines, scripts, and motor behaviours. These recent theoretical developments challenge the key tenets of UG, and so do all the efforts, described by Shatz (2007: 5), that aim at identifying general capacities in children for extracting from the language input over time 'a deeper set of relations than are revealed superficially in the input'. If successful, such findings could be used to refute the poverty of stimulus argument. We will come back to these issues at the end of the chapter when we look at usage-based theories.

UG and SLA

UG admittedly does not aim to account for language acquisition processes and this is increasingly so with regard to the learning of a second language. SLA lacks the relative ease and invariable success of L1 acquisition, which are powerful arguments in favour of UG. Instead of commonalities, SLA is characterized by variation at multiple levels, which White (2007) explains by the existence of factors that come into play in L2 acquisition and that do not arise in L1 acquisition, including prior knowledge of another language and possible deficiencies in the input. We could add to these the impact of social factors concerning the environment and psychological factors concerning the learners that UG is oblivious to. Whatever the exact reason, the fact is that UG has very limited explanatory power concerning the main questions that L2 theoreticians and practitioners face. This is augmented by the fact that many of the sentence-bound grammatical issues that UG focuses on are often seen as somewhat peripheral from the perspective of L2 communicative success. Thus, as Lightbown and Spada (2006) summarize, several proponents of UG openly admit that the theory is not a good explanation for the acquisition of a second language, especially by learners who have passed the critical period or who receive formal L2 instruction.

This limited relevance has been clearly illustrated in White's (2007) contribution on UG to a recent anthology on *Theories in Second Language Acquisition*. The editors of this volume, Bill VanPatten and Jessica Williams (2007), asked experts on specific SLA theories to address ten salient observations about L2 learning in the light of each particular theory. White discussed only five of the observations and justified this limited response as follows: 'In seeking to characterize the unconscious underlying linguistic competence of L2 learners, the generative perspective on L2 acquisition cannot and does not aim to account for all of the observable phenomena discussed in this volume' (p. 50).

A weak form of nativism

Even if one rejects the strong form of nativism that presupposes some built-in language-specific processing module such as UG, there might be a case for a weaker form of nativism that would state that some initial human disposition for language learning is required. It is interesting that in the concluding paper of a special issue on dynamic systems theory, de Bot, Lowie, and Verspoor (2007*b*: 52) explicitly repositioned their originally negative view on this question:

> We would like to reposition ourselves by taking an agnostic view: for language development to take place, UG is not necessary, but it may well be possible that there are aspects of human cognition, social behaviour, and interaction with the environment that help bring about common or universal features in language. However, this does not automatically mean that language, and grammar or syntax specifically, is innate.

Such a weak form of nativism would assume that although language development utilizes various domain-general (i.e. non-linguistic) learning mechanisms, some of these are so closely associated with the acquisition of an L1 that we can think of them as exclusively language-specific (though not grammar-specific). In other words, this view would suggest that the human language processor has properties that are not linguistic in the traditional Chomskyan sense yet that are not found in any other module of mind. Examples of such mechanisms might include the infant's ability to break down acoustic stimuli into discrete parts, to find similarities in these stimuli, and to store and process such stimuli in unique ways. (See e.g. Hulstijn 2002*a*; for a recent discussion presenting arguments in favour of domain-generality, see Saffran *et al.* 2007.) However, regardless of the exact nature of the mechanisms that extract linguistic knowledge from experience, non-nativist approaches would always insist that they are 'resolutely non-linguistic' (Hawkins 2008*a*: 614). This is what unites the various non-nativist positions and distinguishes them from the work of linguistic nativists. We will come back to this question when we discuss non-nativist theories below.

Non-symbolic psychological theories

The term 'non-symbolic psychological theories' is used here for the lack of a better umbrella term to refer to theories representing an alternative perspective to traditional symbolic-nativist-linguistic approaches. This alternative view has been gathering momentum over the past two decades outside the mainstream of linguistics in the fields of cognitive science, psycholinguistics, and developmental psychology, and has been increasingly applied to language acquisition and recently also to SLA. Within this broad movement, I will describe five interrelated but distinct theoretical approaches: (1) *connectionism*; (2) *the competition model*; (3–4) *dynamic systems theory* and *emergentism*, which are two key strands within *complexity theory*; and (5) *usage-based theories*. Extending Thelen and Bates's (2003) conclusion about the link between connectionism and dynamic systems theory, we can say that all the five theories are 'working the same side of the street' (p. 390). They all represent non-linear dynamic approaches to the understanding of development in general and language development in particular, and they all stand in some sort of an opposition to the classic symbolic view of cognition and nativism.

As Smith and Samuelson (2003) explain, human cognition has traditionally been seen as residing in symbolic representations (a view that, as we saw earlier, also applies to traditional linguistics) and because 'no one has any idea how such symbolic representations might be initially formed, theories that take this classic representational stance end up as nativist theories of development' (p. 434). Rejecting this stance, the five theories to be discussed argue that cognition is an emergent phenomenon, grounded in lower, simpler, non-symbolic processes such as—according to Larsen-Freeman and Cameron (2008)—the general cognitive capacities that enable humans to establish joint attention, to understand the communicative intentions of others, to form categories, to detect patterns, to imitate, to notice novelty, and to have the social drive to interact with conspecific caregivers.

We should note at this point that the names of the above five theoretical approaches are often used loosely, with varying degrees of precision, covering overlapping content. Furthermore, although these theories display differences in their specific goals and research methodologies, their proponents refer to each others' work widely and, in fact, some of them simultaneously align themselves to more than one of these theories. Connectionism, dynamic systems theory, and emergentism (and more generally, complexity theory) were originally developed for non-language-specific domains, but they have also been applied to the attempt to understand language acquisition and processing, including SLA. The competition model (and its extension, the 'unified model of language acquisition') can be seen as an attempt to draw up a coherent connectionist account of language acquisition, and usage-based theories apply emergentist principles to the understanding of (primarily first) language acquisition.

As N. Ellis (2003) summarizes, working within the broad remit of cognitive science, these theories—which he refers to as 'constructivist' because they all assume that a child's linguistic knowledge is constructed rather than triggered (see also Fernald and Marchman 2006)—share the following general features:

- They hold that simple, domain-general learning mechanisms applied to language data are sufficient to drive the emergence of complex language representations in humans (i.e. there is no need to assume any innate language-specific knowledge or language-processing apparatus).
- They hold that the structural regularities of language (i.e. rules and regulations that are normally considered under the term 'grammar') emerge from the learners' analysis of the distributional characteristics of the language input (with an emphasis on frequency analysis) and are in the ongoing process of change as the learner is exposed to new input.
- Because of the belief that language structure emerges from language use, the emphasis in these theories is on the study of the language acquisition processes rather than on the final state of the language system.
- They work within the broad remit of cognitive science to seek functional and neurobiological descriptions of the language learning processes and the subsequently emerging linguistic representations.

In the next section, I discuss the five theories separately, with regular cross-references to each other.

Connectionism

Let us start our exploration of the non-symbolic theories of learning with *connectionism*, since this is the most widely known and used term in this area; it is also highly relevant to all the other theories discussed later in this chapter. Connectionism refers to a broad approach in cognitive science that utilizes computational modelling as its main research tool (see the discussion of this method in Ch. 2) and aims at explaining various mental processes within the framework of simple interconnected units (hence the term). These units (or *nodes* as they are often referred to) form *neural networks*, which are intended to simulate, in a highly simplified manner, the network of neurons in the brain. The approach has been used to apply to a whole range of mental areas from face recognition to number learning, with language-related processes being particularly prominent amongst the connectionist modelling efforts. Although, as we will see later, there are various hybrid models containing both non-symbolic and symbolic elements, connectionist architectures are considered primarily non-symbolic because a great deal of what the system 'knows' is captured by the nature and pattern of connectivity across the nodes (Elman 2001). The networks can receive input, produce output, and, during the course of processing, they can 'self-adjust', that is, change the activation level of the processing units and the connection weights between them, which is seen as analogous to 'learning'.

Connectionist principles in neurology and psychology can be traced back to the end of the nineteenth century, but the coming of age of connectionism was marked by the publication of Rumelhart and McClelland's seminal book, *Parallel Distributed Processing,* in 1986. (For a historical overview, see Altmann 2006.) We should note here that although 'parallel distributed processing' (PDP) is the dominant form of connectionism, there are other types of connectionist networks as well—see later.

Connectionist simulation of language processing

As N. Ellis (2006a: 106) succinctly summarizes, 'Connectionist simulations are data-rich and process-light.' The essence of connectionist modelling is to devise systems that are able to find patterns in rich linguistic stimuli fed into the model with only a few relatively uncomplicated algorithms. A successful connectionist model can exhibit rule-like behaviour even though no rules are explicitly represented and no symbols are passed around in the network. If a computational model can thus simulate learning and induce various aspects of the language system without any preprogrammed information, this can be seen as evidence that infants should be able to do the same thing using similarly simple learning mechanisms without any innate language knowledge. Connectionist models in SLA, then, try to extend this process to model the acquisition of an L2, but as Murre (2005) concludes, very few models for bilingual or L2 acquisition have been developed to date.

One of the most powerful determiners in a connectionist architecture simulating language acquisition is the *frequency* of the various elements in the language input. Items that are frequent in the input increase the connection weights between the nodes in the network, and the output of such models can show that seemingly rule-like behaviour can emerge simply from the processing of input, as a function of the consistency and frequency of various input properties (N. Ellis 2003). We should realize here that the observed impact of the language experience (i.e. language input) in computer simulations is not merely an abstract principle that is confined to computational algorithms but it is also a widely observed phenomenon in real-life situations by language theoreticians and practitioners alike: the volume of input and the statistical distribution of the various linguistic elements in it is a central issue in the usage-based (or cognitive-functional) theories that will be discussed at the end of this chapter, and the significance of frequency effects in general is well-known to anybody who has ever learnt a second language.

Thus, the main connectionist principle of language acquisition is that 'simple learning algorithms may be far more powerful than were previously recognized' (Elman 2001: 305): they can, in theory, offer an alternative to symbolic-nativist linguistic paradigms in that they can explain the emergence of rule-like regularities without a reference to an innate mental language system. Having said that, we must immediately add a caveat: along with others, Hulstijn (2002*a*) cautions that the learning achievement of existing connectionist networks has so far been largely limited to simulating simple linguistic phenomena such as the past tense forms of regular and irregular verbs, grammatical gender of nouns, and case endings in German and Russian noun phrases. At this stage it is not at all clear whether the inductive learning mechanisms used in these limited exercises can be extended to the successful mastery of more subtle and highly abstract aspects of linguistic knowledge. To a large extent, the secret in connectionist modelling lies in the details; this warrants a closer look at the nature of connectionist architectures.

Connectionist architectures or neural networks

A connectionist system, which is often called a *neural network*, consists of a large number of processing units (i.e. nodes) that are linked together in some way—see Figure 3.1. We can usually distinguish at least three types of nodes: *input nodes,* which receive information, *output nodes,* which represent the outcome of the model's processing work, and *hidden nodes*, which are within the network, between the input and output nodes, often in various layers. The operation of the neural network is not unlike a complex canal system regulated by locks and watergates, opening up or closing down routes, thereby controlling the amount of water that reaches each node (i.e. controlling the extent of activation of each node).

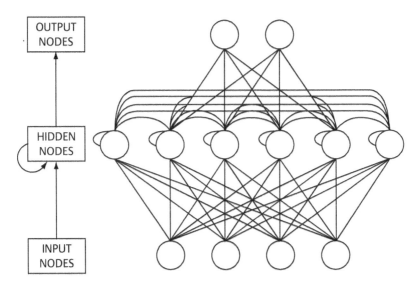

Figure 3.1 Sample connectionist network

Depending on the nature of the nodes, neural networks can vary greatly. In the purest form of *parallel distributed processing* (PDP), the nodes themselves do not represent any distinct piece of information because it is the pattern of activation that carries knowledge. In this network type, therefore, any piece of information is made up of the contribution of many processing units (hidden nodes) contributing to it. Hulstijn (2007*b*: 786–7) illustrates this with the following example: in a PDP network the word 'ball' is not represented with one symbolic node but rather in a distributed way over many nodes at levels lower than the word level; it can be seen, for example, as a constellation of four letters, each of which in turn consists of a number of letter features (straight–curved, long–short, horizontal–vertical, etc., lines).

The distributed, non-symbolic representation within connectionist networks is often thought of as the fundamental connectionist principle. However, this is not quite accurate because we can also have a connectionist network in which single, dedicated units represent distinct pieces of information (e.g. a node represents a word or a letter) without any hidden nodes in between. This would be an example of a *localist network* and such a system can be considered connectionist if it allows for the spreading of activation from one unit to the next in a parallel manner.

In a neural network we can adjust the connection weights between each pair of linked nodes. 'Learning', then, is conceived of as the gradual fine-tuning of these adjustments in the network, in small incremental steps, so that the system produces increasingly meaningful output. Elman (2001) explains that part of the main appeal of connectionism was the development of algorithms that allowed networks themselves to learn the weights of the connections between the nodes to optimize their operation. This meant, in essence, that the network was made capable of 'self-programming', which was particularly useful in the light of the fact that the learning process was inductive, that is, the network could extract regularities from the language input to which it was exposed. Once the network has been thus trained, it was in a position to generalize its performance to novel stimuli.

The incremental adjustment of the connection weights in a network to reach a certain level of output accuracy is called 'error correcting' or 'supervised learning'. The most common form of this learning type is *backpropagation* (which is an abbreviation of 'backwards propagation of errors') and the bulk of the work in the modelling of language processes has used this approach (MacWhinney 2001*c*). Backpropagation involves a stepwise process, whereby the output of the network is compared to the desired output, and the error—that is, the mismatch—for each output neuron is calculated. Then, moving backwards from the output nodes, the weights of the connections for the nodes on the previous levels are adjusted according to the amount of error the node is responsible for, and so on. Thus, backpropagation is an algorithm that recalibrates the connection weights in the light of the discrepancy between the actual and the desired output, and a back propagation network is a network that can learn with the benefit of hindsight to approach optimal output in small iterative steps.

Hybrid models

In the next chapter (Ch. 4), we shall look at a rather different theory of learn-ing, highlighting the explicit/implicit and declarative/procedural distinctions, which suggest that there are at least two main types of knowledge (including language knowledge). Hulstijn (2002*a*) suggests that one of these types, the explicit, declarative knowledge of form-meaning parings (e.g. vocabulary), can be better described by means of symbolic rather than PDP-type (i.e. sub-symbolic) representations. Without wanting to pre-empt the discussion of the two knowledge types, let me just mention here one of Hulstijn's arguments for the dual treatment, namely that explicit knowledge appears to be less susceptible to the influence of frequency than is implicit knowledge—which is evidenced by the fact that we can master a new lexical item upon a single encounter—and therefore such knowledge is not directly within the jurisdic-tion of frequency-driven connectionist architectures.

Given the different attributes of the two types of language knowledge, it might be justifiable to assume that a comprehensive neural network simulat-ing language processing might include *hybrid*—that is, both symbolic and subsymbolic—elements, resulting in a combination of a parallel distributed and a localist network. There are several ways of conceptualizing such hybrid connectionist models. One would be to view symbols as highly stabilized networks of subsymbolic components, acting as one unit with its own acti-vation level in a hierarchical network. This would mean, in effect, that the subsymbolic part of the model displays system functionality that is normally associated with symbolic systems. Paradis (2004) believes that language representation in the brain is characterized by such hybrid networks. As he argues, once a system has thus established a portion of the general network that is uniquely devoted to the performance of a specific task through dedi-cated pathways, it has in effect developed a module. This provides support to neurofunctional modularity, which was discussed in Ch. 2. Furthermore, if we assume that the established symbol-like subsystems contain nodes in proximity to each other, that could be used as an argument justifying locali-zationist attempts in brain research.

Problems with connectionism

Although connectionism has several attractive features, most notably its dynamic nature and ability to accommodate acquisition and change, critics have highlighted three areas where the approach is highly vulnerable: (1) the questionable neurobiological plausibility of connectionist models; (2) the unproved assumption that simple associative learning mechanisms can extract higher order regularities from the language input; and (3) the models' inability to incorporate non-linguistic cues and constraints concerning the social context of language use.

- *Questionable neurobiological plausibility:* one of the main arguments supporting connectionist architectures is that they follow the same principles—most notably the distributed co-operation of multiple inter-linked processing units—on which the neuronal system of the brain operates. However, we must recognize that this resemblance is only super-ficial. Paradis (2004) emphasizes that even if the computational model accurately simulates a specific language phenomenon, this cannot be taken as evidence that the processes used by the model and the brain to reach the same outcome are identical. One important difference, for example, concerns the fact that in contrast to the uniformity of the nodes in compu-tational models, the brain contains several different types of neurons and neurotransmitters, which differ in their functions. Another obvious target for criticism is the process of backpropagation, since it has no obvious analogue in human learning and it is highly unlikely that mental processes include such a reverse correctional algorithm (Eubank and Gregg 2002).

- *The limitations of simple associative learning mechanisms:* it was a real eye-opener for scholars to realize that simple learning mechanisms can simulate rule-like language behaviours, but it is not at all clear just how far-reaching this pattern-finding capacity is. (See e.g. Harrington and Dennis 2002.) For example, are these mechanisms also capable of extracting higher order syntactic knowledge or discourse structure? Or can they handle form-meaning pairing? If so, these need to be demonstrated because, as mentioned earlier, past connectionist studies have typically focused on the processing/acquisition of relatively straightforward and finite sets of forms. Indeed, Chater and Manning (2006) conclude that computational linguistics has typically taken a 'fairly cavalier approach' (p. 337) to exist-ing linguistic theory. They argue that, largely for computational purposes, computational linguists have tended to disregard the complex representa-tions and principles that traditional symbolic linguistics has generated in its attempt to account for linguistic patterns across languages, and focused instead on simple formalisms that allowed for handling real corpora (rather than small artificial languages). However, Chater and Manning believe that the introduction of probabilistic models to computational modelling has opened up new avenues in prioritizing the language aspects that are to be included in models of language processing. (For more details on probabil-istic issues, see the section on 'Frequency effects and probabilistic learning' in the discussion of usage-based theories below.)

- *Lack of contextual sensitivity:* connectionist models are primarily con-cerned with the acquisition of formal patterns and it is not clear how such networks can incorporate non-linguistic cues and constraints, as well as linguistic functional information that are so important with regard to real-life language acquisition. On the basis of these, Tomasello (2003: 325) raises serious doubts about the adequacy of connectionism:

Moreover, it is extremely difficult to see how...connectionism could ever deal adequately with the appropriate use of the many pragmatic grounding devices by means of which people take account of the knowledge, expectations, and perspective of their listeners. These are an integral part of everyday linguistic communication, and they are in fact the *raisons d'être* for many important morphological and syntactic constructions of the language. Are these to simply be left out of account?

The competition model and the unified model of language acquisition

The first versions of the *competition model* were proposed by Elizabeth Bates and Brian MacWhinney at the beginning of the 1980s (for a personal history, see Thelen and Bates 2003), but it has been associated mainly with the work of MacWhinney over the past two decades—see for example MacWhinney 2001b. Recently, MacWhinney has extended the model considerably and proposed a 'unified model of language acquisition' that would apply to both L1 and L2 acquisition (MacWhinney 2004, 2005, 2008). As the naming of the extended model suggests, the model has moved on from the early conceptualization—which was 'a minimalist model designed to predict exact numerical values in controlled studies' (MacWhinney and Bates 1994: 1)—to a general connectionist account of language acquisition and processing. Thelen and Bates (2003: 384) summarized this process thus:

> As MacWhinney has stated many times in the past, the Competition Model was a 'paleo-connectionist theory'. In fact, the model has now merged directly into the river of connectionism that came by after the authors' first fledgling efforts to work out a theory of this kind.

Thus, we can view the competition model as a concrete attempt by leading psycholinguists to apply connectionist theories to language, and this is certainly the most widely known connectionist SLA model.

The competition model

The core of the competition model is a distributed connectionist network that links the form of an input sentence to the function of that form, that is, its meaning in context. In deciphering the sentence function, the listener/reader is unconsciously looking for various *cues* in the input stream. There are multiple cues that compete with each other (hence the original name of the theory) and the winner takes all, that is, the winning clue determines the perceived meaning of the sentence.

What sort of cues are we talking about? Possible cues can be related to various levels of the language system, from word order (e.g. in English the positioning of the subject before the verb marking the agent) and grammatical markers, to semantic plausibility, particularly the animacy of the nouns in the sentence (e.g. the dog can chase the cat but the bone cannot). In their experiments MacWhinney and Bates (1994) specified the following four cue types (but we can conceive of other potential cues): (1) the linear surface position of the argument *vis-à-vis* its head; (2) the affixes attached to the argument;

(3) the affixes attached to the head; and (4) the inherent lexical semantic features of the argument. It is interesting to note that the model combines lexical and syntactic features and it proposes, ultimately, that language development is function-rather than rule-driven.

From this perspective, language development involves the process whereby children gradually match their interpretations and responses to the adult speech they hear, as a result of which the cues that correspond to adult patterns of speech get strengthened and the erroneous patterns disappear (Bohannon and Bonvillian 2005). This development is evidenced by the fact that as children get older, their reaction time in selecting cues gradually gets shorter in accord with the adult pattern (MacWhinney 2004). Interestingly, the basic process of recalibrating cue strengths in the light of ideal (adult) language samples is not unlike the backpropagation process in connectionist models.

A key characteristic of the competition model is the assumption that linguistic knowledge is 'probabilistic all the way down' (Thelen and Bates 2003: 383). Cue strength depends entirely on the cue's reliability and availability in the input. This would explain why the strength of cues shows cross-cultural variability, an issue that has been tested across several languages, including Hungarian (MacWhinney and Pléh 1988; MacWhinney, Pléh, and Bates 1985). Thus, the competition model offers, in effect, a theoretical explanation of how the distributional properties of the input control language learning and language processing (MacWhinney 2001*b*). As we will see later in this chapter, current usage-based linguistic theories follow the same basic principle, namely that language is learnt from the input in a statistical or probabilistic way.

With regard to the empirical testing of the theory, we should recall that the competition model grew out of a minimalist model designed to predict exact numerical values in controlled studies. As MacWhinney (2008) summarizes, this experimental work focused on the measurement of the relative strength of various cues to the selection of the agent. These experiments involved straightforward reaction-time studies using a simple sentence interpretation procedure: subjects listened to a sentence with two nouns and a verb (e.g. 'The dog chases the cat') and were asked to identify who the actor was. The sentences were constructed in a way that different potential cues were set in conflict with each other to check how much this cue conflict slowed down the comprehension process.

The unified model of language acquisition

With the *unified model of language acquisition*, MacWhinney (2005, 2008) made an attempt to broaden the scope of the competition model, which was not designed to give a full account of SLA and multilingualism, so that it can cover the acquisition and processing of both L1 and L2 in a unified model (hence the name). Although the new theory builds on the foundations of the earlier model and maintains its core elements, there are two major differences: (1) several new components were added to the paradigm; and (2) instead of a PDP network, MacWhinney used a different type of neural network, a *self-organizing map* or 'Kohonen map', as the underlying organizational framework.

Added components

Similar to its predecessor, the unified model assigns special significance to the concept of cues, cue strength, and the competition between cues. Yet, as part of a more elaborate treatment, the construct of *cue cost* is added, referring to limited cue evaluation when quick, online decisions are called for. This concept has grown out of one of the main findings of competition model experiments, namely that the cumulative validity of all the relevant cues is reflected in the subjects' decisions only when they are given plenty of time to consider the particular sentence. However, if these offline conditions are restricted (e.g. because of the speed of decisions required by the task), the ability of the subjects to sample all relevant cues is equally limited, resulting in cue cost factors (MacWhinney 2008).

A further new component in the model is the intriguing concept of *resonance*, which MacWhinney (2008) considers the most important area of theoretical development. It was inspired by the neurobiological understanding of effective vocabulary learning. Practitioners know that a simple repetition of the L1 and L2 versions of a lexical item is not too effective in itself unless the initial exposure is followed by practice. This, according to MacWhinney, is caused by resonant neural connections between cortical areas. As he explains,

> While two cortical areas are coactive, the hippocampus can store their relation long enough to create an initial memory consolidation. Repeated access of this trace can serve to further consolidate the memory. Once the initial consolidation has been achieved, maintenance only requires occasional reactivation of the relevant retrieval pathway. This type of resonance can be used to consolidate new forms on the phonological, lexical, and construction levels. (p. 360).

MacWhinney (2008) further argues that a fuller form of resonance occurs during covert inner speech. This involves resonance used not so much to acquire new forms as to activate conceptual interpretations and plan actions. Resonance is also thought to be involved in code-switching: if a language is repeatedly accessed, it will be in a highly resonant state, delaying or interfering with the activation of another language.

The final point that I would like to highlight creates a link to the self-organizing maps discussed below. MacWhinney (2008) argues that the process of 'learning' in the unified model is grounded on self-organization within these maps. The impact of various subprocesses such as chunking and resonance is also accommodated in the process of consolidating representations within the maps.

Self-organizing maps

The unified model views long-term linguistic knowledge as organized into a series of *self-organizing maps*, also called 'Kohonen maps' after their Finnish inventor (Kohonen 2001). These are neural networks that differ from PDP networks in that the nodes with the highest activation are moved in the direction of the input pattern, thus creating a spatial structure that reflects the activation pattern. Thus, these maps generate a representation of the input sample with additional topographical visualization. It can be seen as a kind of projection of complex data onto a usually two-dimensional grid (not unlike multidimensional scaling). The neurobiological validity of such an organizational structure is provided by the existence of such topological maps of neurons in the brain involved, for example, in the auditory and visual functions.

MacWhinney (2008) explains that the spatial concentration of nodes with a similar function leads to the specialization of neurons to become responsive to highly specific inputs, down to the level of the individual word or morpheme. Thus, what emerges is a localist network with symbolic nodes, which makes lexical items and parts of speech available for syntactic computation. The important feature of these networks is, however, that they are emergent, yet they also display increased entrenchment with the progression of the local organization. This aspect will be relevant when discussing age effects in SLA. Furthermore, because the training of the network does not include matching actual and ideal outcomes (i.e. the network performs unsupervised learning), the system works without the neurobiologically controversial backpropagation algorithms.

The unified model currently postulates the existence of self-organizing maps at three levels: the level of the syllable, the lexical item, and the construction. The introduction of these maps as well as the additional theoretical constructs discussed above certainly make the model a unifying framework with considerable future potential.

Problems with the competition and the unified models

Evaluating the unified model, MacWhinney (2008: 363–4) concludes: 'Many of the pieces of this model rely on separate theories that have been worked out in some detail.... Other areas provide targets for future work.' We could rephrase this conclusion in a less positive light by characterizing the unified model as a patchwork of theoretically uneven tenets, some of which are little more than intellectual speculation. In this sense, the model is not so much unified as fragmented, which makes it questionable as to whether it can be called a model at all. MacWhinney concludes his paper by saying that the 'unified model provides us with a high-level road map to guide our ongoing explorations of these topics' (p. 364), but while this may be true, the fact that even its author calls a supposedly unified, comprehensive psycholinguistic theory merely a 'roadmap' may be seen as indirect criticism.

Having such a broad remit, the ultimate appraisal of the model depends on the evaluator's personal orientation. Gibson (1992), for example, offered a scathing criticism of several aspects or the original competition model, but MacWhinney and Bates (1994: 1) put this down to the existing schism in linguistics between UG-based and non-nativist theories:

Gibson's review...exposes a set of deep fracture lines separating two competing approaches to psycholinguistics. One side of the fault zone, the competition model focuses on the construction of a minimalist model designed to predict exact numerical values in controlled studies. In this approach, an initial candidate model is not responsible for predicting all levels of all variables for all sentences in all languages. Instead, the model is developed inductively on the basis of a constrained set of sentence types and certain limited predictions. On the other side of the psycholinguistic fault zone, the UG model that Gibson espouses avoids minimalism and emphasizes the complexity of the theory of formal principles of language structure motivated by binary acceptability judgements generated by small numbers of professionally-trained theoreticians.

With regard to specific concerns, critics such as Eubank and Gregg (2002) followed Gibson's lead and zoomed in on what they considered the inadequate specification of the key concept 'cue'. Similarly to Gibson's argument that there are an 'infinite number of possible cues' (p. 829), Eubank and Gregg claim that the characterization of the class of possible cues is unprincipled and thus 'totally vacuous' (p. 239). This, however, means that an 'explanation of acquisition that appeals to cue frequency is doomed to arbitrariness and circularity' (p. 239). We should note that—unsurprisingly—MacWhinney and Bates (1994) forcefully rejected such claims, but it is undeniable that the experimental evidence and the theoretical groundedness of the model have gaps that scholars who do not believe in the connectionist approach can convincingly exploit.

Dynamic(al) systems theory

A DST (Dynamic Systems Theory) characterization of L2 acquisition as an emergent process marks the coming of age of SLA research.
(N. Ellis 2007b: 23)

Dynamic(al) systems theory (DST) is closely related to three other theories, 'complexity theory', 'chaos theory', and 'emergentism'. Of these four paradigms complexity theory is the broadest, denoting an overarching approach to studying complex, dynamic systems, with DST, chaos theory, and emergentism usually seen as three loosely related strands under it. (For a recent, book-length discussion of complexity theory, see Larsen-Freeman and Cameron 2008.) Chaos theory is a branch of mathematics that examines the frequently occurring unpredictable behaviour—termed 'chaos'—displayed by non-linear systems such as weather. Its relevance to SLA was first highlighted by Larsen-Freeman (1997), but recent discussions of the principles of chaos theory in SLA have usually been subsumed by analyses of DST and emergentism, and therefore I will concentrate on these two latter approaches below. We should also note here that while the four terms (complexity theory, DST, chaos theory, and emergentism) are linked to somewhat different research traditions and priorities, they have not been used consistently across disciplines and in most cases they converge in the same general non-linear systems approach.

In a recent position paper championing dynamic systems theory, de Bot, Lowie, and Verspoor (2007*a*) explain that DST has been developed as a branch of mathematics and successfully applied in many scientific disciplines both in the natural sciences (most notably in biology) and the social sciences, and most recently also in cognitive science. The mathematical origin is well reflected in the generous scattering of impenetrable equations in most 'serious' works describing the theory, and it is reassuring for us mortals to find that even leading DST researchers such as van Geert and Steenbeek (2005*a*: 408–9) complain about this:

> Being a developmental psychologist and applying dynamic systems theory is almost like begging for trouble. A quick look through handbooks on dynamic systems theory reveals an amassment of abstract terms and mathematical equations most of which are simply not accessible for the mathematically untrained reader, which the developmental psychologist is likely to be. . . . the mathematician will treat the developmentalist's dynamic models the same way as a kindergarten teacher evaluates a toddler's proudly made scribbles, knowing that the child in question deserves encouragement and that the way leading to a decent drawing of say, a horse, is still extremely long and arduous.

In spite of this seeming complexity, the initial idea behind the theory is relatively easy to grasp: Take a simple system in which there are at least two variables impacting the outcome, for example a paradigm in which a language learner's willingness to communicate (WTC) in an L2 is conceptualized as being dependent on his/her levels of L2 proficiency and linguistic self-confidence. A static model of the system would describe the outcome as the composite function of the two variables, which is relatively straightforward to compute. A dynamic systems representation, however, would take into account the fact that while the two variables exert their effect on WTC, they themselves also change (e.g. successful communication can improve the learner's L2 proficiency and enhance his/her confidence), which in turn impacts the outcome further, thus starting a chain reaction—it is easy to see how this dynamic take on the initially straightforward static model can become massively complicated by adding the time element (especially if the two variables pull the outcome in somewhat different directions). Thus, as Howe and Lewis (2005: 248) define it in the introduction to a special issue of *Developmental Review*, 'a system is dynamic if the value of x generated at time t depends on its history (or values at earlier times). That is, the term dynamic is synonymous with phrases such as "time evolution".'

A classic graphic illustration of the highly complex behaviour of a simple dynamic system is the movement of the double pendulum, which is a two-dimensional system with two variables—see Figure 3.2. Double pendulums

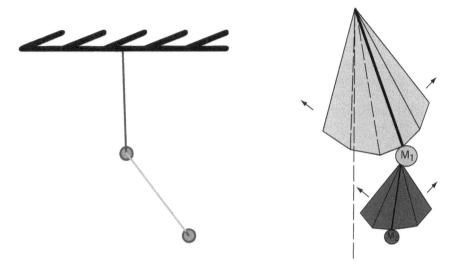

Figure 3.2 The double pendulum

are common in interactive science exhibitions for children, because of the spectacular consequence of simply starting the pendulum: as the upper arm starts moving, the lower arm seems to be going berserk, moving all over the place, which then upsets the initially regular movement of the upper arm, which of course causes further havoc in the whole system. We can well imagine how difficult it must be to precisely describe the dynamic trajectory of the whole arm in mathematical terms, and the task is even more daunting with systems comprising more than two dynamic variables.

De Bot, Lowie, and Verspoor (2007*a*) emphasize that we do not have to become mathematicians to understand the principles of DST—indeed, Esther Thelen, one of the leading DST theoreticians, freely admitted that she had never in her life 'programmed a computer, written an original equation, or run a computer simulation' (Thelen and Bates 2003: 378). While this might sound surprising, the main benefit that DST offers SLA researchers is definitely not the possibility of being able to compute the trajectory of the mental pendulum in the language learners' heads, but rather to introduce a new and more realistic perspective on the language acquisition process which can explain several phenomena that have traditionally been swept under the carpet. De Bot *et al.* summarize thus:

> What DST provides is a set of ideas and a wide range of tools to study complex systems. We can no longer work with simple cause-and-effect models in which the outcome can be predicted, but we must use case studies to discover relevant sub-systems and simulate the processes. (p. 19)

Dynamic systems theory and connectionism

Before we look at some of the details of DST, let me address a more general question: how is DST related to connectionism? That is, how does DST fit into the family of the various non-UG-based theories discussed in the second half of this chapter?

In a paper devoted specifically to discussing the similarities and differences of DST and connectionism, Thelen and Bates (2003) argue emphatically that dynamic systems do play a role in connectionism, because by their very nature, non-linear neural networks are non-linear dynamic systems; Smith and Samuelson (2003) add to this that DST and connectionism display a similarity in their mathematical background. Thus, it is fair to conclude that the two theories belong to the same general class, which Thelen and Bates describe as a 'new, synthetic theory of development that unites insights from developmental neurobiology, physics, mathematics, and computer science in the service of an increased understanding of human development' (2003: 390).

On the other hand, in spite of the obvious similarities, the relation between dynamic systems and connectionist models is not one of equivalence. To start with, some dynamic systems are not connectionist models and there are some connectionist models that are not dynamic systems, and, more generally, there is a marked difference between the two theoretical approaches in their emphases. DST focuses on explaining the nature of change in behaviour—in Thelen and Bates's (2003: 389) words, the 'entire coalitional contributions to behaviour'—examining the special mechanisms and time-related trajectories involved. In contrast, connectionism is primarily concerned with changes in mental representations, that is, how elementary neural building blocks can form a dynamic network. Smith and Samuelson (2003: 436) draw attention to a further deep-seated difference between the two theories concerning the way these view developmental change:

> Connectionist theories are about systems that learn statistical patterns. They take the regularities that exist in the world and internalize them in connection weights. This is a very specific claim about the nature of development. Dynamic systems theory, with its view of multiple causality and levels of interactions, encompasses a wider variety of kinds of causes—from strengthening of muscles, to exploration, to energy consumption, to memory.

Dynamic systems theory and SLA

> *Language development is a complex and dynamic process. Although this statement can be regarded as common knowledge for many researchers in the field of applied linguistics, most studies on language acquisition are nevertheless still placed within a theoretical framework working with static or linear presuppositions.*
> (Jessner 2008: 270)

Larsen-Freeman and Cameron (2008) suggest that complex, dynamic systems can be found throughout applied linguistics; examples they mention include the language used by a discourse community, the interactions of learners and their teacher in a classroom, or the language-specific functioning of the human mind. Indeed, the language learning enterprise in general can be conceived as a highly complex and dynamic system, impacted by a host of variables related to attributes of the target language, the language learner, and the learning situation. In applied linguistics we tend to use static linear models (e.g. based on correlations) to analyse the outcome of this system—that is, the L2 learning achievement of the learners—but I believe that the pendulum example above illustrates well that a simplified linear analysis of a dynamic system does not necessarily do justice to what really happens in real-life situations. So how can DST be applied to our understanding of SLA?

As mentioned earlier, the link between the seemingly random performance of a complex, dynamic system and the non-linear and sometimes chaotic nature of SLA has been first noted by Diane Larsen-Freeman (1997), who offered chaos/complexity theory as a perspective that had the potential to shed new light on a variety of issues related to the complexity of how people use, learn, and teach languages, and to offer new ways of investigating L2 behaviour and development. Recently, Cameron and Larsen-Freeman (2007: 227) argued in a similar vein:

> The descriptions of systems with many different elements in continuous flux and how they change over time seem to resonate with the problem spaces of applied linguistics. A language learning community can be thought of as a complex system, as can the brain/mind of an individual language user, and conventional ways of thinking of language as a system can be extended to seeing language as a complex system. Complex systems theory seems to make better sense of our experience as applied linguists and to offer fascinating new tools for thinking and for research.

The key concern of DST is examining any change over time and, with this being the case, this approach is highly relevant to the complex system of the sustained L2 learning process. We know that the variables affecting SLA are highly interrelated and therefore changes in one variable will have an impact on all other variables that are part of the system (de Bot, Lowie, and Verspoor 2007a). DST can provide a framework to accommodate the role of interaction of these multiple components at different levels of the system, which is why de Bot *et al.* conclude: 'Dynamic Systems Theory is proposed as a candidate for an overall theory of language development' (p. 7). In agreement with this view, in Ch. 5 I will reframe the concept of individual L2 learner differences in dynamic systems terms.

Main features of dynamic systems theory

The general picture of a dynamic system that DST suggests is one of complexity, with all the parts of the system being interconnected, and of ongoing change that results from the multiple interacting influences. If we apply this specifically to language, we obtain the image of language as a

> complex dynamic system where cognitive, social and environmental factors continuously interact, where creative communicative behaviours emerge from socially co-regulated interactions, where there is little by way of linguistic universals as a starting point in the mind of *ab initio* language learners or discernable end state, where flux and individual variation abound, where cause-effect relationships are nonlinear, multivariate and interactive, and where language is not a collection of rules and target forms to be acquired, but rather a by-product of communicative processes. (N. Ellis: 2007*b*: 23)

While this big picture makes good sense and will undoubtedly resonate with many language practitioners, the question is whether there are any more specific lessons that we can learn from DST. Interestingly, one relevant word that comes up in various accounts of what DST can provide is 'tools' (e.g. de Bot, Lowie, and Verspoor 2007*a*: 19; Cameron and Larsen-Freeman 2007: 227; Larsen-Freeman 2007*a*: 36; Larsen-Freeman and Cameron 2008: 41; Thelen and Bates 2003: 390). At the moment, it seems to me, the tools we can borrow from DST are more conceptual than research methodological in nature. (I will come back to the question of research methodology below.) Indeed, the theory offers a range of useful insights and metaphors that can enrich our perspective. Let us have a look at some of the key aspects of DST.

Sensitive dependence on initial conditions

One of the most distinctive characteristics of dynamic systems is their *sensitive dependence on the initial condition*. In chaos theory this feature is called the 'butterfly effect' and refers to the fact that relatively small differences in the initial conditions (such as a butterfly flapping its wings in a meteorological study) can in theory cause surprisingly large variations on the behaviour of the system. This would suggest, for example, that the common practice in SLA research of pooling subjects with mixed proficiency levels in a heterogeneous sample might lead to inaccurate generalizations, since the different initial starting values may result in diverse growth trajectories across individuals in the sample. (See Howe and Lewis 2005.) On the other hand, a dynamic system may also absorb major perturbations without much change. And, to make things even more complicated, we should recall that in a dynamic system the initial condition itself is also in an ongoing state of change, subject to an iterative process, which makes the system sensitive to specific input at one given point in time and some other input at another (de Bot, Lowie, and Verspoor 2007*a*).

Non-linear nature of development

From a dynamic systems perspective, language development is seen as a function of the moment-to-moment trajectory of the complex system, that is, a fluid, transient, and contextually sensitive process that displays a non-linear growth curve (Evans 2007). The key term here is 'non-linear', which means that a change in one element does not produce a proportional change in other elements. As mentioned above, sometimes a slight influence from an element may lead to considerable consequences, whereas at other times even a seemingly strong impact may have negligible effects (Vallacher and Nowak 1999). In other words, the resultant system behaviour is disproportionate to its causal factors (Larsen-Freeman and Cameron 2008). The seemingly random performance of language learners' L2 production mechanisms (i.e. the hugely fluctuating level of their effectiveness) is indeed a frequent experience as learners apply their L2 proficiency in real life and real time. Therefore, along with others, de Bot, Lowie, and Verspoor (2007a) claim that the dynamic flux of a complex system simply cannot be predicted exactly, an issue we will come back to when discussing possible problems with DST.

Self-organization

A key concept associated with dynamic systems is their *self-organizing* capacity. It refers to 'the spontaneous formation of patterns and pattern change in open, nonequilibrium systems' (Kelso 1995: p. xi). A good and often-mentioned illustration is the emerging ecological balance of a desert island on to which we have introduced a number of animal species: after some fluctuation, an equilibrium is likely to be reached, be it the total extinction of all the animals (i.e. a predator species eats all the others and then dies of hunger) or a habitat-friendly balance in terms of the number of specimens of each species. Thus, self-organization is used to explain how the fluid, transient, and non-linear developmental process of a dynamic system often results over time in the emergence of crystallized patterns, skills, and schemas. These, according to DST, are not hard-wired but are the outcomes of self-organization, associated with some attractor state—see below. Talking about physical movement but generalizable beyond, Thelen and Bates (2003: 381) describe this clearly:

> Such physical and biological structures literally 'self-organize' to form patterns: that is, the individual parts, none of which contain any program or blueprints, produce a more complex organization as a result of their interrelations. Thus, when the many, heterogeneous elements that produce movements—nerves, muscles, joints, metabolic processes— cooperate together in a task, they cohere together in a way that is more complex than the sum of the parts.

Thus, patterns emerge from the complexity of the system spontaneously, without any single component being in charge, having priority or privilege, or containing a pre-programmed 'instruction manual' for the behavioural performance of the whole system—self-organization is the driver of change. In Evans's (2007: 132) words, self-organization is 'the spontaneous emergence of complex forms of behaviour due to the cooperation of the multiple heterogeneous parts of the system that produce coherent complex patterned behaviour'.

While the essence of self-organization—namely that a system organizes itself without external direction or control—is straightforward, this conceptualization leaves a fundamental theoretical question open: does self-organization always lead to a new system with emergent (i.e. qualitatively new) properties? We will come back to this contentious issue in a separate section below as part of the discussion of emergentism, but let me propose as a preliminary that although self-organization and emergentism usually occur together, they do not denote exactly the same process. In a paper entirely devoted to this question, De Wolf and Holvoet (2005) argue that self-organization proper always leads to an increase in the order of the system behaviour to promote a specific function, but this function may or may not be emergent in nature.

Attractor and repeller states

We find that even in highly complex systems that display a great deal of variation and change over time, there are times of seeming stability, to the extent that the system can be seen as static or fossilized. How can we explain these non-dynamic, settled states? The answer lies in the concept of *attractors* and the subsequent *attractor states*. Attractor states are preferred—but not necessarily predictable—states to which the system is attracted (hence the name); their dispreferred counterparts are referred to as *repeller states*. As Nowak, Vallacher, and Zochowski (2005) explain, in a system governed by attractor dynamics, a relatively wide range of starting points will eventually converge on a much smaller set of states because the process unfolds in the direction of the attractor. De Bot, Lowie, and Verspoor (2005) offer a good illustration of how attractors work. Let us imagine a ball rolling over a surface with holes and bumps. The ball's trajectory is analogous to development, the holes can be seen as the attractor states and the bumps as the repeller states. If the ball is a light beach ball that is blown around by a fresh breeze on the beach, we can easily visualize that the movement of the ball will be shaped by the joint impact of the terrain and the environment, and the overall trajectory will include phases of stillness when the ball is settled into attractor states (i.e. holes). A linguistic example offered by Larsen-Freeman and Cameron (2008: 185) concerns the dynamic process of conversation; in these the attractors include 'conventionalized patterns of talk that shape the landscape and emergent features such as local routines, conceptual pacts, and shared metaphors'. Plaza-Pust (2008) regards L1 parametric options as attractors in L2 production, thereby reframing L1 transfer in dynamic systems terms.

When a complex system self-organizes, it can settle into a preferred pattern in which the elements are coherent and resist change. The ensuing stability of behaviour indicates that the system is in a strong attractor state. The steadiness of this stability is reflected by how resistant the system is to being pushed out of the attractor state by perturbations from outside—thus, attractor strength can be measured by the magnitude of the 'push' needed to send the system out of its equilibrium (Larsen-Freeman and Cameron 2008). When the multiple internal and external forces shaping the system form a combination that is powerful enough to disrupt the coherence of the elements, the metaphorical beach ball will be shoved out of the hole in which it has settled and, as a result, the system will reorganize into a new and possibly more stable state (Thelen and Bates 2003). This new state indicates a qualitative shift in the system's functioning, and, indeed, every dynamic system can be viewed as a series of shifts between periods of stabilization and periods of destabilization (Howe and Lewis 2005). Stable phases are guided by attractors, making the behaviour of the system more predictable, whereas unstable phases are characterized by weak or changing attractors. (I will provide a more elaborate description of the role of attractors—and also of 'attractor basins'—in Ch. 5, where I draw a parallel between individual difference variables and attractors.)

Co-adaptation

Dynamic systems are often characterized by the interaction of subsystems that gradually get aligned with each other. Larsen-Freeman and Cameron (2008) refer to this negotiation and adjusting process between systems as 'co-adaptation' and describe it as a 'kind of mutual causality, in which change in one system leads to change in another system connected to it, and this mutual influencing continues over time' (p. 233). They emphasize that many salient issues in applied linguistics feature co-adaptation; for example, the speech accommodation process of infants and caregivers or communication partners such as native and non-native speakers; students' and teachers' emerging classroom behaviour and discourse; or the phenomenon of 'washback' involving the co-adaptive move by teachers and schools in response to changes in the assessment system.

'Noise' is important

The highly individualistic nature of growth curves in DST would suggest that traditional quantitative statistical methods of data analysis are inadequate to be used with dynamic systems because these procedures are based on group averages and thus iron out idiosyncratic details. In contrast, the dynamic systems logic suggests that such details are crucial for the understanding of what really happens. Larsen-Freeman (2006), for example, found that when she disaggregated group data of five Chinese learners of English, several different developmental paths emerged that were lost in the composite results. In a similar vein, de Bot, Lowie, and Verspoor (2007a: 19) also concluded that 'It is very well possible that if we look closely enough, we find that the general developmental stages that individuals go through are much less similar than we have assumed thus far.' This means, in effect, that what has been considered as 'noise' in quantitative studies does matter and should not be eliminated through the quantitative focus on the central tendency at the group level.

In agreement with the need for replacing or complementing quantitative procedures with in-depth qualitative analyses, van Geert and Steenbeek (2005a) address the question that is at the heart of any quantitative concerns with qualitative analyses: how can one obtain valid information about development by studying a very unrepresentative sample of a few subjects? Their answer is that DST studies are interested in *how* one state is transformed into another and *by what mechanism* this occurs, and this can only be discovered by studying an actual developmental process in its entirety on an individual basis.

Researching dynamic systems

> *The behaviour of a complex system is not completely random, but neither is it wholly predictable.*
> (Larsen-Freeman and Cameron 2008: 75)

We saw in the previous section that DST has important research methodological implications. So, how can we operationalize the new dynamic systems approach in research terms? Do we need to make any significant changes in our research practices, and if so, what are the key issues to modify? Unfortunately, DST-based research in the social and cognitive sciences is a relatively uncharted territory and therefore currently we do not have a definitive answer to these questions, let alone any specific research methodological guidelines or templates on how to conduct language-specific DST studies. However, we can start formulating certain guiding principles to aid DST-based applied linguistic research along these lines:

- *The issue of cause–effect relationships:* the first principle we need to observe is that within a dynamic systems framework there are no simple cause–effect explanations between variables examined in isolation, which is the standard research focus in most quantitative applied linguistic research. As Larsen-Freeman and Cameron (2008) emphasize, dynamic systems are by definition not fully predictable and, therefore, rather than pursuing a reductionist agenda, any study in the dynamic systems vein should emphasize instead the processes of self-organization with regard to the whole of the interconnected system.
- *Focus on attractors (and repellers):* we have seen earlier that stable phases in a system's development are guided by attractors, making the behaviour of the system more predictable, whereas unstable phases are characterized by weak or changing attractors. This would suggest that one fruitful direction in researching dynamic systems is to focus on potential attractors (and also on repellers), assessing how powerful they are and which way they tend to move the system. However, even if we identify some salient attractors of considerable strength, we need to resist the temptation to propose direct linear links between them and the system outcome.
- *Focus on context and environment:* we have seen above that DST takes a socially grounded approach in which neither the internal development

of the organism nor the impact of the environment is given priority in explaining behaviour and its change—the context is part of the system (Larsen-Freeman and Cameron 2008). Accordingly, research paradigms need to extend beyond focusing merely on the L2 learner and his/her L2 learning achievement so that we can also gain adequate measures of the role of the context and the environment. I will come back to this question of ecological validity at the end of Ch. 5, when we look at the interaction of learner characteristics and the environment.

- *Focus on a qualitative rather than quantitative approach:* although DST has an extensive mathematical basis in applications in the natural sciences, a dynamic systems approach in SLA does not lend itself so easily to quantitative investigations because the number of confounding variables is extensive and some of them cannot be measured at the level of precision that is required for mathematical analyses—see, however, Byrne's (2002) inspiring attempt to synthesize quantitative data analysis and the main principles of complexity theory. On the other hand, several aspects of qualitative research make this approach suited to DST studies: (1) qualitative research is emergent in nature, that is, the research design is kept open and fluid so that it can respond in a flexible way to new details or openings that may emerge during the process of investigation; (2) qualitative studies aim to capture a sufficient level of detail (i.e. 'thick description') about the natural context and therefore such investigations are usually conducted through an intense, situated, and prolonged contact with the research environment; (3) qualitative research is particularly useful for the 'longitudinal examination of dynamic phenomena' (Dörnyei 2007b: 40); and (4) qualitative research takes an individual-level analysis, and therefore we can avoid the potential problem that 'the fact that an association holds over a population or sample does not necessarily imply that such an association holds for a time evolution or trajectory, that is, a dynamic system' (van Geert 2008: 188). For these reasons, Larsen-Freeman and Cameron (2008: 242) conclude that 'In many ways, qualitative research methods, such as ethnography, would appear to serve the understanding of language as a complex dynamic system.' The obvious challenge in such studies will be to go beyond merely providing a 'thick description' by also offering analysis and explanation.

- *Focus on mixed methods research:* I have argued elsewhere (Dörnyei 2007b) that *mixed methods research,* that is, the meaningful combination of qualitative and quantitative approaches, offers a radically different, new strand of research methodology that suits the multi-level analysis of complex issues, because it allows investigators to obtain data about both the individual and the broader societal context. (For an example of a mixed-methods study of dynamic L2 development, see Larsen-Freeman 2006.)

- *Focus on change rather than variables:* Larsen-Freeman and Cameron (2008) point out that social scientists tend to focus on well-defined and generalizable *variables* to describe the social world around them. A dynamic systems approach would shift the emphasis from this variable-centred, reductionist practice to studying *change*. Thus, the authors' recommendation is: 'Think in terms of dynamic processes and changing relationships among variables. Consider self-organization, feedback, and emergence as central....Consider variability as central. Investigate both stability and variability to understand the developing system' (pp. 241–2).

- *Focus on longitudinal research:* in his influential book on longitudinal research, Menard (2002) argues that longitudinal research should be seen as the default when we intend to examine any dynamic processes in the social sciences. Such dynamic processes are obviously involved in human learning/growth or social change, but they can also be associated with various interactions of different levels of an issue (e.g. micro or macro) or of different types of variables (e.g. learner traits and learning task characteristics). Indeed, it is difficult to imagine a DST study that does not have a prominent longitudinal aspect.
- *Focus on system modelling:* drawing up quantitative models of dynamic systems may not only be mathematically too demanding but arguably also unrealistic and inadequate for cognitive and social systems (van Gelder and Port 1995). Yet, modelling is an important aspect of DST because it considers, by definition, the co-ordinated operation of the whole system and allows for various cyclical processes, feedback loops, and iterations. Therefore, any attempts to devise at least qualitative models are steps in the right direction, in accordance with the dynamic systems logic. Larsen-Freeman and Cameron (2008) describe an interesting qualitative modelling approach that they call 'complexity thought modelling'. This comprises a series of steps: (1) identifying the different components of the system; (2) identifying the timescales and levels of social and human organization on which the system operates; (3) describing the relations between and among components; (4) describing how the system and context adapt to each other; and (5) describing the dynamics of the system, that is, how the components and the relations amongst the components change over time.

Problems with dynamic systems theory

I believe that the emphasis on viewing the SLA enterprise in terms of dynamically interacting complex systems and investigating each facet of learning in relation to each other is one that many SLA theoreticians and practitioners would endorse. However, at this stage we have few specifics as to how this broad sweep would allow a better understanding of the actual processes that we observe amongst language learners. N. Ellis (2007b: 24) is quite right when he points out that 'the challenge is to test the details of this faith, how do these patterns emerge from the interaction of these forces integrated over the processing of each and every utterance and exemplar of language?' Even some scholars from a UG background admit the potential contribution of the DST framework to the field of SLA, but they also have a point when they conclude that 'such contributions are at this point largely hypothetical' (Ionin 2007: 27).

A second general issue concerning DST is that it is far more successful in explaining the unpredictable nature of the system and individual variability than regularities and universals. Yet, there are general tendencies in SLA that are generalizable; as de Bot, Lowie, and Verspoor (2007*b*: 52) summarize, 'With so many variables playing a role in first and second language acquisition, language development could easily lead to totally random behaviour, but it doesn't.' How can we account for these commonalities in DST terms? Are they related to similarities in the beginning states or parallel environmental conditions? Or do we need to seek the answer in some common and perhaps universal attractors as suggested above?

A third concern, which is arguably the most acute current problem with DST in SLA research, and has already been addressed in the previous section, is the difficulty and uncertainty of how to conduct empirical studies in a dynamic systems vein. There are obvious difficulties with: (1) modelling non-linear, dynamic change (especially quantitatively); (2) observing the operation of the whole system and the interaction of the parts rather than focusing on specific units in it; and (3) replacing conventional quantitative research methodology and statistics with alternative methods and tools. Some scholars even stipulate (e.g. de Bot *et al.* 2007*a*; Howe and Lewis 2005) that it is theoretically impossible to measure the state of a dynamic system with precision. Larsen-Freeman (2007*a*) adds that currently we lack the dynamic terms in SLA to replace old static divides such as, for example, the performance–competence distinction. Therefore, as she predicts, the challenge for DST researchers will be to find the optimal 'interconnected units of analysis' (p. 37) that can do justice to the dialectical relation between parts and wholes.

On the other hand, Kelso (1995: p. xiii) points out that one of the greatest appeals of DST is that it can potentially offer a conceptual framework and vocabulary that is 'just as natural for the mind as it is for the processes going on in the brain or behaviour in general', creating natural connections among neural, mental, and behavioural events. In other words, this approach may allow us in the long run to adopt a radically new perspective on SLA that reflects the convergence of linguistics and psychology. However, while this may be welcomed by scholars who have found more traditional approaches unsatisfactory in terms of the results and explanations they yield (I for one will endorse DST in describing individual differences in Ch. 5), finding ways of talking fluently and meaningfully in a totally new conceptual system is not easy. In de Bot's (2008*b*: 171) words, 'new ideas take time to settle, and a fundamental shift in perspective such as this is difficult', and even Larsen-Freeman and Cameron (2008: p. x) admit that developing the new perspective has posed real language challenge as it is 'easy to fall back into old ways of thinking, and requires continual monitoring to ensure that ways of talking (or writing) reflect complex dynamic ways of thinking'.

To finish on an optimistic note, I genuinely believe that all the above obstacles are surmountable and that exploring DST is definitely worth the trouble. The stakes are high because, as van Geert (2007: 47) predicts, DST might turn out to be the dominant framework for future research:

> I consider the dynamic systems approach as the quintessential future approach to human action, cognition and behaviour, including language. All these phenomena are about change, about process in time. And this is exactly what dynamic systems approaches provide: an explicit model of change of some phenomenon of interest.

Emergentism

> *[U]se emergentism often, but with great care.*
> (MacWhinney 2006: 731)

Emergentism (or as it is also called, 'emergence') is currently a popular term in cognitive science, and its significance has also been highlighted in second language research. For example, the journal *Applied Linguistics* has recently published a special issue on 'Language emergence' (N. Ellis and Larsen Freeman 2006), and in this issue MacWhinney (2006: 731) stated explicitly that 'Emergentism is the most promising new trend in language studies'; another special issue on 'Current emergentist and nativist perspectives on second language acquisition' has just been published by the journal *Lingua* (Hawkins 2008*b*). We have seen several examples of the term 'emergent' in the previous sections on connectionism and dynamic systems theory—indeed, even the initial quote by N. Ellis (2007*b*: 23) on DST stated 'A DST characterization of L2 acquisition as an *emergent* process marks the coming of age of SLA research' (my emphasis). We also saw that the DST concept of self-organization is very close to the concept of emergence and the two terms are, indeed, sometimes used interchangeably. Thus, a crucial issue to be addressed here is whether emergentism is a theory in its own right or rather merely a broad property or approach that can characterize different theoretical models or stances. And if the former, what are its distinctive features and how is it related to other non-symbolic psychological theories?

What does 'emergent' mean?

It is clear that the term 'emerge/emergence' has been used in the literature in both a technical and a general sense, with the latter simply referring to the appearance of something. It is also clear that even when the term was used to indicate a more specific process of something qualitatively new coming into being, the usage has not been uniform across scholars and academic fields, and even the same scholar can apply the term in different places to have somewhat different meanings. For example, in the quote cited above, MacWhinney (2006: 731) describes emergentism as the 'most promising new *trend* in language studies' (my emphasis), but later in the same paper he also viewed emergentism 'as equivalent to basic scientific *methodology*' (p. 732;

my emphasis). And, to complicate things further, he adds in his conclusion, 'Emergentist thinking provides *general guidelines* for studying the mechanisms generating complex phenomena' (p. 739; my emphasis). So, where does the term come from and what exactly does it mean?

The basic idea of emergence can be found in Western thought going back to the time of the ancient Greeks (Goldstein 1999) and, as O'Grady (2008) explains, the actual roots of emergentism can be traced back to at least the mid-nineteenth century, to the work of the British philosopher John Stuart Mill. He proposed formally that a system can have properties that amount to more than the sum of its parts—which has been seen as the essence of emergentism ever since—and the actual term was coined to express this notion by another nineteenth-century British philosopher, George Henry Lewes, in 1875 (Corning 2002). Thus, the concept has a venerable history and is currently being applied to a surprisingly wide range of fields, from cognitive psychology and stock market research to evolutionary biology and cybernetics.

The attraction of emergentism to all these diverse fields is the concept's capacity to explain change and development that is not directly orchestrated by human agents. We live in a complex world in which a lot of unexpected things happen, and emergentism offers a framework that can explain some of the unusual occurrences around us. Having said that, we must realize that this framework is not rock solid; and the criteria by which emergent properties are to be distinguished from non-emergent properties are controversial (Stephan 1999). As a result, the online *Stanford Encyclopedia of Philosophy*, for example, characterizes the term as 'notorious' (O'Connor and Wong 2006), and Corning (2002: 18) as having 'an elusive, ambiguous standing'.

The most common, and often rather vague, description of 'emergence' concerns a process in which the interaction between the local parts of the system produces some global system behaviour (De Wolf and Holvoet 2005). To put it broadly, simple operations produce complex results in what is the ultimate bottom-up process. The emergent structure appears to have some underlying design even though it is the product of straightforward, iterative interactions of relatively uncomplicated mechanisms. In addition to the intricacy of the outcome, genuine emergence is usually associated with three further interconnected properties, all related to the important feature that the emergent global behaviour cannot be traced back to the individual parts of the system. (For good analyses, see De Wolf and Holvoet 2005; Stephan 1999.) These three properties are:

- *Novelty:* the emergent structure or pattern is novel with regard to the individual parts of the system.
- *Irreducibility:* the overall system's properties are not reducible to the arrangement and the properties of the system's parts.
- *Unpredictability:* the emergent properties could not have been predicted before their first appearance.

Emergentism and dynamic systems theory

As mentioned earlier, emergentism is closely related to dynamic systems theory and, indeed, the above specifications could also be cited to describe change in a dynamic system. So, given that they refer to similar, typically non-linear system developments, are DST and emergentism distinct theories? The best answer is a qualified yes. The two theories have different flavours in that DST is rooted in mathematics whereas emergentism originates in philosophy; and the two approaches also emphasize somewhat different aspects of a complex system's behaviour. Self-organization in DST underscores the functionality of the new state of the system (i.e. a new adaptive order of the constituent parts so as to promote a specific function), whereas emergence highlights the unpredictable novelty of the emergent structure. In principle, we can have a highly functional self-organized pattern that is non-emergent (i.e. a case when only DST applies) and a system exhibiting emergent chaos without promoting a specific function (i.e. a case when only emergentism applies), but we should note De Wolf and Holvoet's (2005) observation that in most systems that are considered in the literature, emergence and self-organization occur together. Thus, in actual practice when we talk about either theory we usually describe their combination. This is why definitions of DST-based self-organization and emergence often overlap.

Emergentism and connectionism

Emergent properties are often mentioned when talking about connectionist networks and the competition model. There is no question that neural networks have systemic properties in the sense that their constituent parts do not. However, we need to examine whether network functioning meets the criteria of real emergence. Stephan (1999) argues that with networks of the parallel distributed processing (PDP) type this may not be the case. The network develops global properties only after it has been trained, and the acquired soft structure of the network is a function of the organization of the network in question, the activation formulae, and the characteristics of the links between the processing units. As a consequence, if these quantities are known, the behaviour of the network can be predicted and the network properties are fully deducible from the network's structure. Thus, Stephan concludes, connectionist networks do not instantiate any strong type of emergence.

We saw earlier that the extension of MacWhinney's competition model, the unified model of language acquisition, utilizes a different type of connectionist network, 'self-organizing maps'. As their name suggests, these maps are truly self-organizing and therefore qualify as dynamic systems (in DST terms). Do they also have emergent properties? MacWhinney's (2001*b*) answer is affirmative:

> The formation of these local neural architectures is an emergent
> phenomenon, determined by processes such as inductance, the preference
> for short connections, cell differentiation, cell migration, competition

for input, and lateral inhibition. Self-organizing feature maps provide a particularly useful way of expressing our current knowledge of this local level of neural structure. (p. 453)

Emergentism and language acquisition

In recent years the term 'emergentism' has increasingly appeared in proposals about both L1 and L2. O'Grady (2008) explains that although there is currently no comprehensive emergentist theory of language or its acquisition, the various proposals converge in a well-defined emergentist programme for language analysis. The central tenet of this programme states that the core properties of language are best understood with reference to the interactive function of more basic non-linguistic factors, processes, and learning mechanisms. Admittedly, our knowledge of these emergent processes is still limited and it does not make the situation easier that—as with the broader practice discussed above—the term 'emergent' is understood and used in various ways in the field.

Non-linguistic means producing linguistic outcomes is a genuinely emergentist position and, as such, is non-nativist by definition. It is clearly motivated by the growing recognition that any theory of language acquisition has to specify how infants parse the auditory world to make the critical units of language available (Kuhl 2000). Emergentist linguists such as O'Grady (2008) see the solution in assuming the existence of a language processor that children employ in processing the input they encounter. So far the research focus has been predominantly on one property of this processor—its ability to identify and calculate distributional regularities in the input—and the linguistic theory associated with this line of research has been referred to as 'usage-based' or 'item-based' learning. Because of the special status of this probabilistic approach, I will discuss it in a separate section below. As a preliminary, we must note that most of the relevant studies focus on L1 acquisition, with work on an emergentist theory of SLA still being in its infancy. However, the momentum for paradigm shift is there and Larsen-Freeman (2006: 615) warns us that applied linguists may soon find themselves explaining SLA in the following way:

> Patterns in interlanguage emerge from the complexity and frequency in the L1 and L2 and their energetic status, shaped by individual learner orientations and contextual variables. As such, no particular subsystem of language has a priori priority, and no dimension of language proficiency has a priori privilege.

Larsen-Freeman (2002) believes that viewing language as an emergent, non-linear, dynamic system in which cognitive representations are highly affected by experience and input will soon yield practical benefits. She maintains it will help SLA researchers better to understand many phenomena, such as idiolects, individual linguistic creativity, and the instability of L2 performance, as well as the interdependence of language acquisition and language use. MacWhinney (2001*b*) adds a further interesting point, namely that the diachronic changes that languages undergo across centuries can also be viewed in emergentist terms. From this perspective, language evolution can be understood as a succession of emergent states that introduce new forms and contrasts, or iron out old distinction and contrasts.

Problems with emergentism

Because of the close links between emergentism and dynamic systems theory, emergentism has the same problems as DST, most notably (1) its limited capacity to explain regularities and universals rather than the unpredictable nature of the system and individual variability; (2) a lack of established research methods, templates, and even appropriate metaphors to describe the dynamic processes; and (3) as yet too few specific details about emergent processes—particularly with regard to SLA—to evaluate their explanatory power.

   This last point is further augmented by the fact that emergent processes are by definition unpredictable. This, according to MacWhinney (2006), carries the danger of scholars not even trying to specify where a complex linguistic behaviour comes from or how it comes about. As he warns us, it is easy to come up with emergentist accounts for complex phenomena that are appealing but wrong. For this reason, he recommends that we understand what emergentism can offer us 'while maintaining a certain scepticism regarding its immediate applicability' (p. 449). Goldstein (1999) takes this point even further when he reminds us of the standard criticism levelled at the idea of emergence—that an emergent explanation is merely a provisional cover-up for not knowing the nature of a process, and as soon as an adequate explanatory theory comes along, appeals to emergence are abandoned as they are no longer necessary. And, of course, the challenge of producing convincing emergentist accounts is particularly serious in areas where traditional forms of grammatical analysis have offered seemingly convincing hypotheses (O'Grady 2008). Thus, it is appropriate to reiterate MacWhinney's (2006: 731) caution in conclusion: 'use emergentism often, but with great care'.

Usage-based (or item-/exemplar-based) theories

Usage-based theories (also called *item-based* or *exemplar-based theories*) constitute a cluster of related linguistic approaches to the understanding of (primarily first) language acquisition and processing. They share the common belief that grammatical structures do not come directly from the human genome but are the outcome of an emergent process both at the macro level of language change/variation throughout the centuries and the micro level of a child mastering an L1. Although the various strands under the 'usage-based' rubric conceptualize the human language processor somewhat differently, they all attach special significance to the distributional frequency of the language input that a child is exposed to (i.e. the 'frequency effect'). Thus, these theories all subscribe to a *probabilistic model* of learning and processing language that draws on a store of concrete linguistic experiences rather than on innate abstract linguistic rules such as Universal Grammar.

Usage-based theories are becoming widespread in virtually all areas of linguistics—they have made contributions to research domains as diverse as phonetics, phonology, morphology, historical linguistics, semantics, syntax, computational linguistics, and language acquisition. In line with the general orientation of this book, the following overview focuses on the psycholinguistic processes underlying these models; for detailed reviews of the linguistic aspects, see for example Bod, Hay, and Jannedy (2003*a*), Bybee (2007), Bybee and Hopper (2001*a*), Chater, Tennebaum, and Yuille (2006), Gahl and Yu (2006), and Tomasello (2003); for summaries from an applied linguistic perspective, see N. Ellis (2008), Hawkins (2008*b*), and *Studies in Second Language Acquisition* 24/2 (2002) on frequency effects.

A good starting point for understanding the core principles of usage-based approaches is to look at child language acquisition, because recent research in this area has generated an increasing amount of evidence that the linguistic knowledge that children develop is different in significant ways from the kind of grammatical competence that had been suggested by generative linguistics.

Child language learning and usage-based theories

There is no doubt that children are successful in acquiring the syntactic structure of their mother tongue, and yet the way this is achieved is not at all straightforward because, as Tomasello (2000) argues, they do not hear adults speaking in abstract syntactic categories but only in concrete words and expressions. We saw at the beginning of this chapter that nativist theories propose that the core grammatical knowledge of language is inherited as part of the human genome. However, recent empirical investigations of child language learning have produced results that challenge this view. Tomasello summarizes these developments as follows:

> Most important is the discovery that virtually all of children's early linguistic competence is item-based. That is to say, children's early utterances are organized around concrete and particular words and phrases, not around any system-wide syntactic categories or schemas. Abstract and adult-like syntactic categories and schemas are observed to emerge only gradually and in piecemeal fashion during the preschool years. (p. 156)

Arguing in a similar vein, Bybee and Hopper (2001*b*) highlight the fact that there is a serious mismatch between the results of quantitative studies of child language acquisition and grammatical accounts that rely exclusively on imaginary data. In an era when large corpora allow researchers to gain an accurate overview of the child's evolving language competence, the existing data suggest that the child's language processor is not equipped biologically with the main principles and parameters of grammar that will be automatically activated through exposure to natural language input, but instead functions in a radically different way. The alternative proposal claims that the starting point of language development is the acquisition of concrete linguistic items (words and expressions) from the language that children hear around them as they engage in functional communication with the people in their environment (hence the 'usage-' or 'item-' or 'exemplar-based' label in the name of the new approach). Language competence in this sense is not so much based on a 'core grammar' as on a structured inventory of learnt *language constructions.*

How does the language processor work in usage-based theories? According to Tomasello (2003), all the constructions of a language—whether they are more rule-based or more idiosyncratic—are acquired through the same basic set of acquisitional mechanisms that fall under two main categories, *intention-reading* and *pattern-finding*. Tomasello highlights three specific processes that are central to language acquisition. First, all linguistic constructions are mastered through *imitative learning*, which is more than mere mimicking in that it involves the child's meaningful and functionally appropriate repetition of adult language. Second, using general cognitive skills, children go beyond the individually learnt item-based constructions by *finding patterns* in them, that is, categorizing and schematizing them. Third, children also *combine* various constructions creatively, using a number of different procedures. Thus, Tomasello's proposal integrates the role of relevant communicative intent with the analysis of the properties of the input, which amounts, more generally, to the synthesis of functional meaning and linguistic form. In this sense, usage-based theories are very different from both generativist and connectionist approaches, because the latter make no reference to communicative function.

Most research in this area has been directed at the pattern-finding process, exploring how children induce abstract regularities in the memories of all of the utterances encountered in communicative situations. There is a general agreement amongst usage-based linguists that the frequency distribution of the items in the language input has considerable impact on the emergence of grammar, and this focus on statistical distribution has led to interesting probabilistic accounts of learning. I will summarize these issues in more detail below, but let me first discuss a related concept—*grammaticalization*—which is a key notion in usage-based theories in explaining how the actual grammatical structures of modern languages have historically emerged from language use. In many ways, grammaticalization is the macro-level counterpart of the micro-level process of the child's acquiring the syntactic structure of language. From this perspective therefore, language acquisition can be seen as the process whereby children apply their general cognitive learning mechanisms to the historical products of grammaticalization (Tomasello 2000).

Grammaticalization

The term *grammaticalization* was first introduced at the beginning of the twentieth century to refer to a specific process whereby content words change into function words such as prepositions and auxiliaries, or even become grammatical markers such as affixes. However, the concept has also been used in a more general sense to denote the transformation whereby a lexical item gradually acquires grammatical status. Ramat (2001) points out that the implicit notion of grammaticalization goes back as far as the nineteenth century when it was used within a historical linguistic framework to indicate one of the most characteristic developments languages may undergo. It is this broader sense of the term that usage-based linguists have used to explain the emergence of grammar from functional language use. Tomasello (2003) argues that during the process of communication words are strung together into sequences, forming patterns of use that become consolidated into grammatical constructions. Non-nativist linguists offer this process as the alternative to the seeing the origins of grammatical structures in some sort of inherent human linguistic endowment:

> Grammaticalization processes are well-attested in the written records of numerous languages in their relatively recent pasts, and it is a reasonable assumption that the same processes were at work in the origin and early evolution of language, turning loosely organized sequences of single symbols into grammaticized linguistic constructions. (Tomasello 2000: 162)

N. Ellis and Larsen-Freeman (2006) argue that the grammaticalization process involves, in effect, the automatization of frequently occurring sequences of linguistic elements, which results in the emergence of syntactic constructions and then in subsequent shifts in their function due to frequency effects. Thus, frequency plays a crucial role in the diachronic development and change of languages. It is important to note that this diachronic evolution is a gradual process, which has been indicated in linguistic accounts by using metaphors such a 'graded scales' or 'grammaticalization chains'.

Frequency effects and probabilistic learning

We saw above that frequency plays an important role in the macro-level emergent process of grammaticalization, and with regard to the micro-level operation of the child's language processor, frequency effects constitute the single most studied factor. This is because there is a broadly shared assumption amongst usage-based linguists that the pattern-finding function of the child's language processor, that is, the abstraction of the regularities from the memorized constructions, is heavily frequency-biased; in other words, frequency underpins regularity effects in the acquisition of linguistic form. In a position paper that revisited frequency issues with the explicit aim of instigating further research in this area, N. Ellis (2002a: 143) summarized thus:

> Frequency is thus a key determinant of acquisition because 'rules' of language, at all levels of analysis (from phonology, through syntax, to discourse), are structural regularities that emerge from learners' lifetime

analysis of the distributional characteristics of the language input.
Learners have to *figure* language out. (emphasis in original)

In response to N. Ellis's (2002*a*) paper, Bybee (2002) confirms that a wide
range of contemporary linguistic approaches—corpus-based analysis, computational linguistics, discourse analysis, cognitive and functional linguistics,
and psycholinguistics—converge in the recognition that linguistic knowledge
is based firmly on language experience, and frequency of use is a foundational
determinant of the grammatical properties of language. Indeed, it seems now
unquestionable that frequency permeates language. In an overview of the
history of psycholinguistics in *The Encyclopedia of Language and Linguistics,* Altmann (2006: 262) summarizes this new phenomenon thus:

> Critics notwithstanding, statistical approaches to language (both with
> respect to its structure and its mental processing) are becoming more
> prevalent, with application to issues as diverse as the 'discovery' of
> words through the segmentation of the speech input, the emergence
> of grammatical categories, and even the emergence of meaning as a
> consequence of statistical dependencies between a word and its context.

Let us look at four particularly important frequency-related areas of the
usage-based approach: (1) children's parsing of the auditory strings of language they are exposed to; (2) the way frequency statistics are computed in
the mind; (3) the impact that frequency has on various language processes;
and (4) the more general issue of probabilistic learning.

Parsing the language input

An unavoidable question for any theory of language acquisition is how
infants parse the speech streams that make up the auditory world around
them. Kuhl (2004) points out that this is a formidable problem as indicated
by the difficulty computers have in segmenting speech. It is true that we now
have highly accurate voice recognition software, but this has to be calibrated
for each person before use and without this the various accent-, gender-, and
age-based variations dramatically reduce the effectiveness of the program's
performance. In contrast, infants at a very young age already display sensitivity to the sequential dependencies of language and perform complex parsing
operations to segment and recognize connected speech. As Kuhl sums up,
'Cracking the speech code is child's play for human infants but an unsolved
problem for adult theorists and our machines' (p. 831). Thus, children bring
to this task a highly sophisticated talent months before they are able to understand meaning in the words they hear (Fernald and Marchman 2006). This is
genuinely amazing and it is very likely that the 'language learning miracle' that
every human being displays has some of its key foundations in these hidden
processes. Indeed, there seems to be a growing consensus that the linguistic
knowledge acquired during the first year is largely the result of attending to
distributional information in speech.

A study by Saffran, Aslin, and Newport (1996), already mentioned briefly in Ch. 1, illustrates perfectly the extent of infants' remarkable capacity to process input. The researchers played to 8-month-old infants 2-minute strings of computer synthesized speech (e.g. 'tibudopabikugolatudaropi') that contained no breaks, pauses, stress differences, or intonation. These meaningless sequences were carefully designed to include certain syllable combinations more frequently than others. It was found that after as little as two minutes of exposure the infants were able to detect and learn these recurring sound patterns, attesting to their word-learning potential.

The parsing process is not unidimensional: N. Ellis (2002a) explains that categorization research in psychology has demonstrated that the internal tallying takes place on many multiple dimensions at once (e.g. tallying the token, the type, and the immediate context of an item). Thus, the only way for infants to perform the complex cognitive task of tracking, recording, and exploiting frequencies of various kinds is through an unconscious process. Furthermore, because parsing starts right after birth—if not in the womb—this is not a learnt but rather an innate skill. Indeed, as we saw in the discussion of nativism at the beginning of this chapter, some scholars believe that the parsing properties of the human language processor are so closely related to auditory language input that they are not found in any other module of mind, which would imply, in effect, a weak form of nativism ('weak' in the sense that the innate properties of the language processor are not linguistic in the traditional Chomskyan sense).

Computing frequency statistics in the mind

As we will se in the next section, frequency effects are widespread and salient, which raises the question of how the mind computes frequency statistics. The only way our brain can keep track of frequencies is by recording in our memory a trace of every occurrence of every item we hear, resulting in an accumulated count. Bod (2003) points out that this requires such a massive storage capacity of linguistic information that scholars in the past doubted whether this was a true explanation. However, the increasing amount of psycholinguistic evidence points consistently to this conclusion, and, as we saw in Ch. 2, the brain has an incredible information processing capacity, comparable, according to Anderson (2000a), to the processing power of 100 billion interconnected and interacting personal computers! We also saw that our visual memory capacity is almost limitless, and Standing (1973), for example, estimated that in one second we can search over 51,000 pictures in our memory. Therefore, unconscious storage requirements, even if they are enormous, simply do not constitute a bottleneck for our cognitive functioning.

How does an experience update the statistical representation of an item? N. Ellis (2002a) mentions several variants of possible tallying; as he explains, exemplar-based models have multiple instances in memory, one for each exemplar; prototype models count features and derive statistical abstractions of the central tendencies; connectionist accounts assume that each reoccurrence of an item increases the strength of the connections between the relevant processing units. Whichever way it happens, an important feature of the statistical recording process is that the resulting representational changes are gradual, which suggests that the tallying is instance-based (i.e. every instance leaves a memory trace and thus makes some difference).

Finally, which properties of the distribution of the items in the language input are tracked? The two most obvious properties are the frequency of the *tokens* and the *types* of the items. The former indicates the actual number of times an item occurs, the latter refers to the frequency of the broader pattern or category that specific items belong to; for example, the token frequency of the item 'harnessed' is likely to be low because this is a rare verb, but the type frequency that this token is an example of—the regular past tense (-ed) structure—is very high because the same construction can occur with thousands of different verbs (N. Ellis and Larsen-Freeman 2006).

Besides token and type frequencies, individuals are also assumed to keep track of further, more complex distributional properties of the input. These properties concern aspects of the context in which a particular item occurs and the frequency of other constructions with which it co-occurs (Harrington and Dennis 2002). Based on these counts, the human language processor computes various probabilistic expectancies (i.e. combinatorial sequential probabilities; N. Ellis 2002*a*) that affect every facet of language processing. (See below for a more detailed account of this.)

Frequency effects

How does the frequency of the distributional properties of an item or construction affect linguistic behaviour? Bybee and Hopper (2001*b*) listed the following six main effect types:

1 *Phonological reduction in high frequency words and phrases:* it has been widely observed in several languages that words of higher frequency tend to undergo sound change at a faster rate than words of lower frequency (for example the reduction to schwa in English). This process is the result of the automatization of neuro-motor sequences that comes about with repetition.

2 *Functional change due to high frequency:* the functional change in high frequency constructions underlies the process of grammaticalization discussed earlier.

3 *The formation of constructions:* the more often two elements occur in sequence, the tighter will be their constituent structure to the extent that they can fuse. This fusion (often accompanied by phonological reduction) leads to new emergent constructions that are stored as one unit based on their phonological and semantic coherence (e.g. 'don't know' → 'dunno'; 'want to' → 'wanna').

4 *Accessibility:* a robust effect that has been replicated across various languages is that high-frequency words are processed faster than low-frequency

words. In connectionist terms, the more often an item has been used, the lower its activation threshold.

5 *The retention of conservative characteristics:* high-frequency items resist analogical change, such as the regularization of irregulars (for example plurals or past tense verb forms), because their frequency makes them easy to access whole and there is no need to re-form them by regular rule. This means that high-frequency units become entrenched and thus resistant to re-formation on the basis of productive patterns.

6 *Experience-based stochastic grammar:* frequency effects are seen as the basis of the emergence of grammar in that grammatical generalizations are probabilistic in nature, and derived from the user's experience with language (hence the term 'stochastic', which means in this context 'subject to probabilistic behaviour'). Bybee and Hopper (2001b: 19) are explicit in their claim that people's intuitions about grammaticality are based on their past language experience:

> An utterance is judged as grammatical if it is highly similar to other frequently heard utterances; if an utterance has a part which bears no resemblance to any previously experienced constructions or fixed phrases, it will be judged to be ungrammatical.

Needless to say, these principles are not shared by all linguists and particularly the last point is contestable because it, in effect, undermines the main analytical methodology of Chomskyan generative grammar, in which identifying ungrammatical sentences was based entirely on the linguists' intuition. However, Manning (2003) illustrates it convincingly through corpus-based evidence that there is no well-defined distinction between sentences that are generally regarded as 'grammatical' in the literature and those regarded as ungrammatical. Instead, it is more useful to think of well-formedness as a cline in which we can differentiate between constructions that are highly preferred, constructions that are used less frequently, and constructions that are not used at all. Bod, Hay, and Jannedy (2003b) emphasize that nowhere in the cline is there a dramatic drop in frequency, which makes the grammatical/ungrammatical distinction relatively arbitrary; and while extreme cases (such as the ones that are used as examples in generative linguistic analyses) are clearly distinguishable, the middle territory has seldom been incorporated into formal models of syntax.

N. Ellis (2002a: 173) conceives frequency effects as the 'tuning of the language system through use'. These effects undoubtedly influence the operation of the system, but Larsen-Freeman (2002) stresses that simple frequency in itself is insufficient to explain everything about language acquisition (to which N. Ellis 2002b readily agrees—see below the discussion of the problems with usage-based theories). It is, however, very likely that fluent language performance is associated with some sort of probabilistic knowledge, a recognition that has given rise to a whole subdiscipline within linguistics: *probabilistic linguistics*. The psycholinguistic relevance of this research direction warrants a closer look at it.

Probabilistic learning

We saw above that frequency effects pervade language representation, processing, and language change. We also saw that categories and well-formedness are gradient. According to Bod, Hay, and Jannedy (2003*a*), these two features—frequency effects and gradience—are the hallmarks of a probabilistic system, and therefore the authors argue for the existence of a probabilistic language faculty: 'Knowledge of language should be understood not as a minimal set of categorical rules or constraints, but as a (possibly redundant) set of gradient rules, which may be characterized by a statistical distribution' (p. 10). In terms of grammar, this would mean that grammatical rules are associated with probabilities of use, thereby capturing what is linguistically likely (i.e. gradience) and not just what is linguistically possible (i.e. constraints). Probability linguistics exploits the assumed link between frequency and probability, using well-articulated mathematical methods of estimating the probability of complex events (such as sentences) by combining the probabilities of their subparts. Bod *et al.*'s claim is well summarized in the introduction of their seminal anthology that offers a collection of papers examining different linguistic areas from a probabilistic perspective (for another collection, see Chater, Tennebaum, and Yuille 2006):

> Clearly, there is a need to integrate probabilities into linguistics—but where? Taken together, the chapters in this book answer, 'Everywhere.' Probabilities are operative in acquisition, perception, and production. Moreover, they are not merely a tool for processing: linguistic representations are probabilistic, as are linguistic constraints and well-formedness rules. Probabilities permeate the linguistic system. (p. 7)

If probabilities are such a salient aspect of language, why have they not been more prominent in linguistic studies of the past decades? The answer lies in the fact that probabilistic ideas have been seen as incompatible with the Chomskyan representational system of grammar, and Chomsky himself has explicitly rejected probabilistic explanations. Interestingly, the behaviourist view of language that Chomsky (1959) virtually demolished in his critique of Skinner's (1957) *Verbal Behaviour* did emphasize concepts such as reinforcement though repetition—that is, frequency and entrenchment—but the cognitive view advocated by Chomsky, including complex linguistic representations such as feature matrices and tree diagrams, 'has crowded out probabilistic notions' (Chater and Manning 2006: 335). However, in the light of the various theories presented in this chapter, applied linguists might re-examine these early concepts. N. Ellis (2002*a*), for example, presents a detailed rediscovery of Lado's (1957, 1964) theory of second language learning that was built on the behaviourist principles of learning and which conceptualized grammatical structure as a system of habits. Thus, behaviourist views are similar to usage-based approaches in that language acquisition is seen to occur through experience. As N. Ellis points out in an admittedly surprised recognition, Lado's final view of language learning involved a lexico-semantic rather than a syntactic approach, highlighting the significance of the acquisition of lexical items and formulaic sequences, with the grammatical system seen to be emerging from these.

To add some further surprise element, some recent approaches to probabilistic learning actually claim to be compatible even with generative linguistics and nativism. According to Chater and Manning (2006), for example, probabilistic analysis can be utilized to asses the relative contributions of innate constraints in language acquisition. Bod, Hay, and Jannedy (2003*b*) also conclude that the two seemingly opposing views may go well together, as formal linguistic approaches focus on the endpoints of the distribution of linguistic phenomena, while probabilistic approaches focus on the gradient middle ground.

Problems with usage-based theories

Usage-based linguistic theories differ radically from traditional formal linguistic theories in their approach to understanding language acquisition and rule-like features of language behaviour. Most applied linguists would agree that the learners' language experience matters, which means that this experience is computed somehow in the brain. The question is how and where? Currently, the bulk of the research in this area focuses on one property of the usage-based language processor, its capacity to estimate the distributional characteristics of items in the language input. However, even usage-based theoreticians agree that simplistic frequency counts do not do full justice to the system. N. Ellis (2002*a*: 178), for example, acknowledges that 'frequency is not a sufficient explanation ... There are many other determinants of acquisition'. In his view, frequency effects work in interaction with other determinants of acquisition such as perceptual salience, semantic complexity, morphophonological regularity, and syntactic category.

The problem is that very little is known or said about these interactions, and therefore Hulstijn (2002*b*) is right when he points out that N. Ellis's claim that frequency is a necessary but insufficient explanation is a 'give-and-take statement' (p. 269) that is hard to argue with. Therefore, he calls for a more precise specification of the nature of the human language acquisition device, one which is embedded within a comprehensive theory of the representation, processing, and acquisition of linguistic knowledge of both first and second languages. Of course, at the moment there is no language theory that meets this requirement and therefore the most we can currently say in appraising usage-based approaches is that they help to explain certain important linguistic features without offering a comprehensive account.

Usage-based and probabilistic linguistics is still a minority view, which means that the majority of linguists take issue with many aspects of it. These concerns range from general questions—for example, how the emerging syntactic system can work without abstract linguistic categories such as 'word', 'verb', or 'direct object', or if such abstractions are needed, how they emerge from the analysis of the input (Shatz 2007)—to very specific issues such as the finding that statistical learning mechanisms cannot reliably segment sequences of monosyllabic words, though such sequences make up the majority of the input that is directed to children (Crain and Thornton 2006). A frequently questioned issue concerns the features of the special language input that children receive and the incompatibility of certain aspects of the children's non-adult linguistic behaviour with this input.

One of the most challenging lines of criticism questions the capacity of statistical learning mechanisms to account for the great complexity of language phenomena that formal linguistics has uncovered over the past 40 years. When discussing support for a nativist approach at the beginning of this chapter, we already saw Crain and Thornton's (2006) argument that certain linguistic structures or rules are so intricate that they could not possibly have emerged spontaneously, as a product of experience, without some innate regulation. As Hulstijn (2002b: 272) concludes, 'the jury is still out on the question of whether such architectures are capable of capturing the acquisition of many highly abstract forms of linguistic knowledge, for example, the binding principles, as defined by Chomsky'.

To add to the list of different types of worries, Harrington and Dennis (2002) question the very basis of usage-based learning, the reliability of the frequency counts. They review research findings which show that judgements of frequency can be affected by heuristics, or systematic biases in judgement. In a study they cite, for example, subjects consistently misjudged the most common occurrence of consonants in English words. We can argue that there is a difference between the subconscious process of computing mental distributional statistics and the explicit assessment of conscious frequency estimates, but the more general point such results raise is that we have insufficient knowledge about how the brain keeps track of the various item frequencies.

While Larsen-Freeman (2002) generally supports the frequency-based perspective, she raises the tricky question of how probabilistic is a probabilistic account? Probabilistic, by definition, is not absolute and therefore we are talking here about tendencies. So far very little has been said about the boundaries of the acceptable variation within such tendencies, and neither do we know the main sources of individualistic deviation. This point, then, takes us back to the absence of enough information about the interaction between the distributional frequency properties of the language experience and other determinants of acquisition.

Finally, let us consider the relevance of usage-based theories to SLA. These theories have been developed with reference to L1 acquisition and the mechanisms for computing item frequencies have typically been seen as part of an implicit process. N. Ellis (2002a: 173) is quite explicit about this: 'Because the conscious experiences of language learning do not revolve around counting, to the extent that language processing is based on frequency and probabilistic knowledge, language learning is implicit learning.' The problem with this purely implicit approach, however, is that while it makes good theoretical sense to argue for the existence of unconscious probabilistic learning mechanisms in mother tongue acquisition, it is less clear how relevant these mechanisms are for SLA, because even if they do contribute to the learning of an L2, they are only of limited effectiveness. (For a recent analysis, see N. Ellis 2008.) Past theories of L2 learning have invariably included explicit components (see e.g. the noticing hypothesis or the role of instruction), and there is a growing recognition in the field that implicit, usage-based accounts will need to be integrated with such explicit processes. Larsen-Freeman (2002), for example, points out that we are not simply imprinted by frequency as indicated by the fact that frequently occurring L2 items that are not noticed 'remain noise and likely do little to further the SLA process' (p. 280). Thus, this issue raises the broad question of the interface of implicit and explicit learning, a matter that will be discussed in the next chapter and which will then be revisited in Ch. 7 on instructed SLA.

Summary

This chapter started out by explaining that formal linguistic theories have traditionally adopted a symbolic approach, assuming the existence of context-independent units with specific properties (e.g. phonemes or syllables), organized into categories (e.g. nouns or verbs), and connected to each other by various rules (i.e. grammar). This approach is clearly useful for analysing language output, but it assumes a static state without a prominent developmental or transitional component. No wonder therefore that linguistic theories have been rather unhelpful in explaining language acquisition beyond considering it as a movement through successive grammars (interlanguages). Related to this absence of an elaborate acquisitional dimension, linguistic-symbolic theories have tended to be nativist, partly motivated by the fact that they were not geared to offer any explanation of the emergence of the subtle and highly complex language behaviour of humans; instead they tended to propose an innate language endowment—some sort of a language acquisition device—that has inbuilt linguistic knowledge and that also contains an automated processing system that allows the effortless mastery of any human language within certain constraints. The most elaborate theory of this endowment is Universal Grammar theory, associated with Chomsky's generative grammar.

While the virtually invariable success of the L1 acquisition enterprise for children coming from massively different language environments does suggest some sort of an innate language prerequisite, psycholinguists have been reluctant to subscribe to the idea of genetically motivated symbolic mental representations because this contradicted their dynamic view of the brain seen as a connectionist network of neurons where activation patterns rather than fixed units carry the information. Therefore, alternative theories have been proposed based on connectionist principles. The problem with such theories, however, is that if we apply a non-symbolic, connectionist approach consistently, it will in effect undermine most of the traditional linguistic categories. Few linguists would go so far because it does not seem right to relegate most of our linguistics understanding obtained over the last century as an intellectually fabricated, neurobiologically invalid dead-end. Therefore, the most promising attempts within the connectionist approach have been those that tried to create hybrid systems in which general connectionist organizing principles are accompanied by lower-level symbolic elements.

While linguistic-symbolic approaches are more suited to uncovering the subtleties of the linguistic system than connectionist architectures, the latter are more informative about the nature of language acquisition because the dynamic conceptualization of the networks can easily accommodate developmental processes. Therefore, the richest source of information for SLA currently comes from psychological-connectionist approaches, particularly in the light of the fact that the flagship symbolic theory in this respect, UG, has admittedly relatively little to say about L2 learning. Having said that, we should also note that the various cognitive psychological theories of learning (e.g. explicit versus implicit) and memory (e.g. declarative versus procedural) to be discussed in the next chapter contain strong symbolic components and, as will be stated below, one of the main challenges for future theorizing is likely to be to integrate these with connectionist accounts. What we can safely conclude at this stage is that currently neither the symbolic nor the connectionist approaches are in a position to account for the big picture in a comprehensive and coherent manner.

In the second part of this chapter we explored the broad contemporary non-symbolic movement by looking at five specific research directions: connectionism and the competition model; then two strands within complexity theory: dynamic systems theory and emergentism; and finally usage-based theories. These are all related to each other to some extent but are not equivalent. They can be seen as attempts to explain language change and development with different focuses and emphases, yet at the same time also sharing some common principles. They consider non-linguistic cognitive learning mechanisms as the main driving forces of language acquisition (although, as we saw, some limited attempts have been made to include nativist elements into the accounts) and they hold that grammatical knowledge emerges, at least partly, from the learners' unconscious analysis of the distributional characteristics of the language input.

The problem with the non-nativist theories in their current developmental stage is that they do not add up to a coherent and detailed account, and the linguistic insights they offer are no real match to the sophistication of the linguistic system that traditional linguistic approaches have generated. N. Ellis (2006a) talks about the amalgam of the new theories as the 'Associative-Cognitive CREED' (Construction-based, Rational, Exemplar-driven, Emergent, and Dialectic) and concludes that such 'broad frameworks suffer a number of difficulties. They are hard to pin down, to operationalize, and to test.' They are also diverse and wide-ranging, 'variously spanning psychological, linguistic, neurological, social, and educational phenomena, and these different areas adopt widely different research techniques and standards of research quality' (p. 113). In my view, the greatest benefit of the reform approaches has been their role in dramatically extending the scope of linguistics, opening up novel avenues, and offering a wide range of theoretical and methodological tools. It is true that they are rather patchy in what they can and what they cannot explain currently, but they set the scene for a total make-over of the linguistic landscape that is likely to take place over the next decades.

From the point of view of the main topic of this book—second language acquisition—the applicability of any approach discussed in this chapter, nativist and non-nativist alike, is rather limited. It seems that L1 acquisition presents so many challenges that scholars in the past have been, by and large, reluctant to tackle the even more complex and challenging SLA process. Fortunately, there are indications that this situation is changing with the number of studies applying the new theories to SLA having increased dramatically over the past few years, reaching (it is hoped) a point of no return. However, for any really meaningful results to emerge, the various non-symbolic psychological accounts will need to be integrated with another major theoretical strand in psychology, the issue of explicit versus implicit learning and the related dichotomy of procedural versus declarative knowledge. These topics are the subject of the next chapter.

4

Psychological processes in language acquisition II: explicit versus implicit learning

The primary focus of Ch. 3 was on exploring the process of development and change in cognitive systems such as language from a non-symbolic, connectionist perspective. Most of the material concerned first language acquisition and it was argued that the complex mechanisms that generate linguistic knowledge in the infant are largely implicit in nature. I pointed out more than once that in their present form the findings of the various research directions discussed in the chapter had only limited relevance to SLA, which is partly due to the fact that SLA also involves a prominent explicit component that needs to be taken into account when trying to understand the overall nature and course of learning an L2. Although we all wish that SLA were an implicit process that happens automatically and effortlessly, for most L2 learners this is regrettably not the case.

A second reason why connectionist accounts have been of only limited significance to SLA is that connectionist theories are typically concerned with the processing and acquisition of forms (i.e. grammar) as opposed to form–meaning pairings such as the learning of new vocabulary. Along with others, Hulstijn (2002a) argues that this latter type of knowledge is profoundly different from the knowledge of form-focused structural regularities, and this distinction has been typically analysed in the literature using the explicit–implicit or the declarative–procedural knowledge paradigms. This chapter, therefore, complements the previous one by focusing on the broad distinction between implicit versus explicit learning and the different types of knowledge that result from these processes.

The initial difficulty we face when starting to explore the explicit–implicit paradigm is the number of closely related but not identical terms. We read, for example, about implicit learning, implicit memory, implicit knowledge, and their explicit counterparts. Then we also come across references to incidental versus intentional learning. When we think that we have finally come to terms with these concepts, we realize that they are also related to a different paradigm, the contrast between declarative versus procedural knowledge, which has its own literature. And to make things really complicated, these explorations inevitably lead us to a number of related issues such as the question of consciousness and attention, the noticing hypothesis, the process of automatization, and skill learning theory. Therefore, the main objective of this chapter is to create some order in this terminology maze. However, we must realize that the concepts we will be looking at are some of the grand themes in cognitive science and have therefore been the subject of thousands of publications each; and, as is common with such hugely popular terms, their usage has not been consistent across subdisciplines and individual scholars.

Consciousness and attention

> *Consciousness remains one of the key puzzles confronting the scientific worldview.*
> (Koch 2004: 1)

Let us start our orienteering exercise by looking at two psychological concepts—*consciousness* and *attention*—that appear under various disguises in almost all our discourse on SLA. We already touched upon these two notions briefly in Ch. 2 when we looked at Baars's (1997a, 1997b) Global Workspace Theory, but there the purpose of the discussion was to describe the main facets of brain functioning within an extended metaphor; in this chapter we need to go further by providing definitions of the two terms and specifying their constituents.

Consciousness and attention are clearly interrelated, because what we are conscious of is usually what we attend to. However, Koch (2004) argues that it is important to separate these two notions because they refer to distinct processes that do not always coincide. Let us look at consciousness first.

Consciousness

Consciousness is a notoriously vague term with many usages in the fields of philosophy, psychology, neuroscience, and cognitive science. This is largely due to the fact that although tens of thousands of pages have been written on the subject over the past two thousand years, quite frankly nobody really knows what consciousness is exactly and why it exists. Therefore, Koch and Crick (2001) believe that the term will eventually be replaced by a vocabulary that more accurately reflects the contribution of different brain processes. The fundamental question, according to Koch (2004: 1–2), is this: 'What is the relation between the conscious mind and the electrochemical interactions in the body that give rise to it?' He argues that the mystery deepens when we realize that much of what goes on in the brain bypasses consciousness. For example, electrophysiological experiments have proved conclusively that we can have furious neuronal activity going on in our brains without it registering on our conscious radar. For example, with reflex actions we act first and think later, and psychologists have argued ever since Freud's ground-breaking work in this area that even high-level decision-making and creativity can occur without conscious thought.

What we do know about consciousness is that it is a property or character-istic of the mind, associated with qualities such as subjectivity, self-awareness, emotions, and reflectiveness. Baars (1997b: 293) refers to the content of con-sciousness as the 'immediate perceptual world' that includes inner speech and visual imagery; bodily feelings such as pleasure, pain, and excitement; surges of emotion; memories when they are remembered; intentions, expec-tations, and actions; as well as explicit beliefs about oneself and the world. Although there are only speculations about the main functions of this prop-erty, its purpose is often seen to help to focus the brain's vast unconscious resources and make them available for specific cognitive or motor use (e.g. Baars 1997a, b; Koch and Crick 2001). Following Baars, N. Ellis and Larsen-Freeman (2006) consider consciousness the 'publicity organ of the brain' (p. 570), whose job is to access, disseminate, and exchange information, and to exercise co-ordination and control.

As already mentioned in Ch. 3, one of the most peculiar features of con-sciousness is the narrowness of its limits compared to the vast and almost limitless unconscious processing capacity at out disposal. This bottleneck of capacity, however, makes sense if we look at consciousness as a gateway, a moving window that can create access to any part of our unconscious mind. We can be conscious of only one unified experience at a time, which means that, using Baars's (1997a, b) metaphor, on the stage of the theatre of our unconscious mind there is only one brightly lit area—consciousness. In this sense, this narrow focus is not a limitation but the main function of con-sciousness. Let us now look at how 'attention' can be fitted into this picture.

Attention

Ever since Aristotle described the phenomenon of selective attention, the notion of attention has been seen as the cognitive mechanism that controls access to consciousness (Schmidt 2001); using Baars's (1997b: 303) theatre metaphor, attention is the spotlight and 'only events in the bright spot on stage are strictly conscious'. Through our attention, we can selectively con-centrate on one issue while ignoring other things. In an environment of multiple stimuli, we can direct the spotlight of our attention at specific things (e.g. listening in on a conversation at the next table) and the spotlight can even slip out of our hands and we can catch ourselves 'mind-wandering'.

Although there is an intimate relationship between attention and conscious-ness, Koch and Tsuchiya (2007) caution us not to consider them inextricably interwoven. As they argue, the two processes need not necessarily occur together; in certain cases, for example, we can become conscious of a specific object despite the near absence of top-down attention—that is, conscious perception can occur outside the spotlight of attention. Usually, however, the two concepts go hand in hand.

What is the main function of attention? Earlier I argued that many scholars see the purpose of consciousness being to focus our vast unconscious resources on one particular issue. This selective function is typically highlighted with regard to attention: Koch and Tsuchiya (2007) argue that it is a top-down, task-dependent control mechanism the purpose of which is to help avoid information overload by focusing on a small fraction of the input in real time. Although Schmidt (2001) reminds us that bottom-up exogenous cues (e.g. a sudden loud noise) can hijack our attention—attesting to the existence of a passive, involuntary form of attention—we can use our internal voluntary attentional control to disregard these external distractions.

Attentional components and features

Schmidt (2001) explains that within the broad controlling function, attention refers to a variety of mechanisms or subsystems, including alertness, orientation, detection, facilitation, and inhibition. Robinson (2003: 633) also highlights the multicomponential nature of the concept when he identifies three current themes in attention research: (1) auditory and visual information intake and processing; (2) central control and decision-making functions, such as allocation of attention to competing task demands, and automatization; and (3) response execution and monitoring via sustained attention.

In order to describe the interrelationship of the various attentional functions and to link them to the much-researched concept of working memory (see Ch. 5), Knudsen (2007) has put forward a conceptual framework that proposes that attention reflects the combined contributions of four distinct processes: (1) working memory; (2) competitive selection; (3) top-down sensitivity control; and (4) automatic filtering for salient stimuli. It is assumed that a multitude of factors (resources, information, stimuli, etc.) compete continuously for gaining access to the working memory and thus for the spotlight of our consciousness. The *competitive selection* component, which is under the control of the working memory, carries out the main gatekeeping function, while *top-down sensitivity control* regulates the relative signal strengths of the different information channels that compete for access. The role of the *salience-filter* is to enhance automatically the strength of environmental signals that are likely to be important (e.g. they are of instinctive or learnt biological importance) and, according to Knudsen, the nervous system responds to such prioritized signals automatically (e.g. reflex reaction). Thus, the final strength of the competing signals reflects the combined effects of the quality of the encoded information, the top-down bias signals, and the bottom-up salience filters. The information with the greatest signal strength enters our working memory to be processed.

Of course, as with every cognitive model, Knudsen's (2007) proposal is only a rough approximation of the complex operation of attention, but it is helpful in highlighting its main functional components and operationalizing specific submechanisms that can, in turn, be tested. From our perspective, the key assumptions concerning the concept are, as summarized by Schmidt

(2001: 11–12), 'that it is limited, that it is selective, that it is partially subject to voluntary control, that attention controls access to consciousness, and that attention is essential for action control and for learning'.

The explicit–implicit dichotomy

The explicit–implicit dichotomy appears in many forms in research on language acquisition, and it has frequently been applied to SLA research as well. The gist of the contrast is clear: 'explicit' has something to do with consciousness, while 'implicit' is associated with unconscious, automatic, or indirect processes. However, when we look at the details, we find that within these broad rubrics the two terms have been used for a variety of purposes with differing meanings. Furthermore, in the SLA literature explicit and implicit language learning are sometimes also defined rather loosely as learning with or without the aid of grammar rules.

Reading the literature we soon realize that the explicit–implicit dichotomy is applied to three different concepts—learning, knowledge, and memory— and it is only very rarely explained how these are interconnected. Perrig (2001: 7244) describes this situation in the *International Encyclopedia of the Social and Behavioral Sciences* as follows:

> The fluent switch between notions like 'implicit knowledge,' 'implicit learning,' and 'implicit memory' either confronts us with the fact that psychology has—despite precision at the operational level—weaknesses at the terminological level, or it asks for synthesis in the explanation of implicit phenomena or implicit cognition.

So, let us start with a brief initial summary, followed by a more detailed discussion of each of these three facets of the learning process in separate sections. As a preliminary, let me point out that there are recent arguments that claim that with our increasing understanding of the cognitive operations in the brain, many existing distinctions previously described in purely functional, binary terms, such as the explicit–implicit or the declarative–procedural distinctions, can now be characterized anew in a more graded manner (Cleeremans 2003). Thus, it is likely that the explicit–implicit duality will be replaced by a more refined framework before long; at present, however, the distinction is useful for highlighting two very different aspects of cognition.

In the most general terms, 'learning' refers to the process of acquiring or encoding new information—that is, 'knowledge'—and 'memory' reflects the storage and retrieval of this knowledge. This would suggest two straightforward statements: explicit knowledge is acquired through explicit learning and is stored in explicit memory; and implicit knowledge is acquired through implicit learning and is stored in implicit memory. Unfortunately, the actual learning sequences that we can observe in real-life situations are not always as pure as these two relational chains would suggest. While the first statement is usually considered problem-free, the second statement about implicit knowledge/learning/memory raises several issues. Cleeremans, Destrebecqz, and Boyer (1998) point out that the field is significantly divided in what exactly constitutes 'implicit' or 'unconscious' knowledge and how it can be operationalized in measurement terms. In addition, as we will see below, assuming the existence of an independent and distinct 'implicit memory' also raises serious questions, with some scholars arguing that the concept has outlived its purpose and should be abandoned.

Definitions of explicit–implicit learning/knowledge/memory show a great deal of variance, and it is common practice to define some of the constructs in reference to each other, for example, 'Implicit knowledge can then be defined simply as knowledge that is not explicit' (Davies 2001: 8126), or defining learning with relation to its outcome as in the (correct) definition of explicit learning as 'the construction of explicit, verbalizable, metalinguistic knowledge in the form of symbols (concepts) and rules, specifying relationships between concepts' (Hulstijn 2002*a*: 206). However, because of the ambiguities surrounding each component of the above learning chains (i.e. learning–knowledge–memory), I will try to define each concept focusing on its own unique features rather than contrasting it with another concept. Let us start with the most straightforward notion: explicit learning.

Explicit learning

Explicit learning is usually treated as a conceptually unambiguous process characterized by the learner's conscious and deliberate attempt to master some material or solve a problem. From an information-processing perspective it involves the conscious intention to find regularities and to identify rules and concepts that are useful to capture these regularities (Hulstijn 2005). This is the learning type emphasized by most school instruction, either by presenting the learners with concepts and rules upfront or by encouraging them to derive and test hypotheses themselves. In a comprehensive review of the literature, N. Ellis (2005*a*) emphasizes that the effectiveness of explicit learning is correlated with the elaborateness and depth of the cognitive processing the material is subjected to (e.g. learning techniques, controlled practice, in-depth analysis), which is in line with standard educational guidelines of how to enhance good teaching. As Baars (1997*b*: 304) sees it, learning is a 'magical process' in the sense that it requires us only to 'point' our consciousness at some material we want to learn, and learning occurs magically, 'carried out by some skilled squad of unconscious helpers'. In this perspective, the key to explicit learning is to find the best ways of directing our biological spotlight of consciousness at the target material and keeping it focused on it.

Explicit learning thus takes effort and strategic expertise, but—as said above—the theory is straightforward. Or is it? In a paper reviewing what we know about learning complex bodies of knowledge (i.e. learning knowledge that goes beyond simple form–meaning associations, for example when preparing for an exam on a complex subject), Chi and Ohlsson (2005) point out that the process involves the combination of several components such as integrating information from multiple sources, generating inferences, connecting new information with existing knowledge, retrieving appropriate analogies, producing explanations, and co-ordinating different representations and perspectives, as well as abandoning or rejecting prior concepts that are no longer useful. As the authors argue, many of these component processes are still poorly understood and therefore further research is needed in this area. In addition, and somewhat related to this point, Reber (2003) emphasizes that real-life tasks cannot be regarded as 'pure' in terms of requiring either explicit or implicit mechanisms because they almost always involve a mixture of these. He concludes:

> This polarization tendency is almost certainly a mistake and has clouded issues in unhappy ways. Virtually everything cognitively interesting that people do is a complex blend of consciously controlled processing that is declarative in nature and implicit, automatic functioning that lies largely outside of awareness. Task purity is going to be hard to find. (p. 488)

Implicit learning

It was noticed (and researched) already at the beginning of the twentieth century that some of the skills and knowledge that make humans competent in dealing with each other and with their environment are not acquired through explicit learning processes but without conscious awareness. However, the modern interest in non-explicit learning was instigated by Reber's (1967) seminal paper that reported experiments in which people memorized meaningless letter strings that were generated by a simple pattern (i.e. 'rule') and then classified novel strings as following the same system of patterns (i.e. 'grammar') or not. What made this research exciting was that people were able to perform this classification task better than chance despite the fact that they were unable to describe the rules of the grammar in subsequent verbal reports. (For more details about such 'artificial grammar learning' tasks, see separate section below.) Thus, they learnt the rules at an unconscious rather than conscious level. Reber coined the term *implicit learning* to describe this process.

It was soon found that implicit mechanisms operated in a wide variety of domains, ranging from the somewhat simplistic concept of classical conditioning in behaviourism to compellingly complex areas such as language acquisition. As Baars (1997b) put it, we rarely become conscious of abstract patterns such as the regularities of grammar, the harmonic progressions of a symphony, or the delicate brushwork of the painter Vermeer: 'Most knowledge is tacit knowledge; most learning is implicit' (p. 305). This does sound intriguing and convincing, and the field of cognitive psychology was soon caught up with this excitement: implicit learning became a much researched issue—even a quick search of the term in the PsychInfo database produces over 400 results. So what exactly does the process involve?

Definitions of implicit learning

In a paper the title of which says it all—'One concept, multiple meanings: On how to define the concept of implicit learning'—Frensch (1998) argued that scholars in the past 30 years had been using the term in several meanings and, therefore, in order to move on it is necessary to tighten the definition of the concept. He also highlighted the issue that I already referred to earlier, namely that those meanings of implicit learning should be given preference that emphasize only the learning/encoding process rather than the retrieval process (which is linked to implicit knowledge and memory). So, let us have a look at the main properties of implicit learning:

- *Bottom-up mechanism:* Reber (2003) explains that implicit learning mechanisms are 'bottom-up' systems, that is, 'they function by picking up patterns of covariation in environmental displays' (p. 487). This growing sensitivity to certain regularities in environmental stimulus is exactly the kind of implicit learning process that has been hypothesized to underlie infants' probabilistic learning of their L1 (discussed in the previous chapter). The bottom-up process lends itself to representation in connectionist architectures, which can relatively easily capture the covariation in the input (Reber 2003), and following this logic, Hulstijn (2002a: 205) redefined implicit learning as 'the construction of knowledge in the form of neural networks'.
- *No conscious attempt to learn the target material:* implicit learning takes place naturally, with no conscious attempt on the part of the individual to learn the specific target material. This was one of the two key properties of implicit learning that Frensch (1998) has come up with in his review of the multiple definitions of the term.
- *Lack of awareness of learning:* during the course of implicit learning not only do people not make a conscious attempt to learn the target material, but they are not even aware that learning is taking place.
- *Automatic process:* it follows from the lack of any conscious learning operations that implicit learning is automatic. Frensch (1998) posited this property as the second defining criterion for implicit learning.
- *Lack of awareness of the result:* almost all definitions of implicit learning emphasize that the process leads to results that the individual is unaware of. This means, in effect, that implicit learning leads to 'implicit knowledge' (which is discussed below in detail).

Although this list might suggest that implicit learning is fully implicit (i.e. unconscious) at every possible level, this is not quite so. While it is still a contested issue, the weight of evidence today suggests that for effective implicit learning to take place, the learner needs to pay attention to the environmental stimulus that is to be processed implicitly. In other words, implicit learning is not *unattended* learning. In Baars's (1997b: 305) words, '*all learning requires conscious access to what is to be learnt*' (emphasis in the original).

Characteristics of implicit learning

The first characteristic of implicit learning to note is that it can result in highly effective performance but reaching this stage can take a long time. This point will be elaborated on in the second part of this chapter, where we discuss implicit L2 learning.

Reber (2003: 487) highlights a second characteristic of implicit learning mechanisms that has relevance to SLA: 'These acquisitional mechanisms are not particularly effective in settings that involve problem solving, hypothesis testing, or creative extrapolation. In short, they are mechanisms typically not associated with processes normally thought of as "smart".'

A third important characteristic of implicit learning is its robustness. As Litman and Reber (2005) summarize, implicit learning mechanisms show relatively little change over the life span (compared with explicit cognitive functions) and neither do they display considerable individual-to-individual variation. Furthermore, the implicit system demonstrates a rather remarkable robustness in the face of neurological and psychiatric disorders (e.g. amnesia) that severely restrict explicit mechanisms. Regrettably, this robustness seems to disappear when it comes to learning an L2; thus, when we discuss the process of SLA, we will need to account for the anomaly that L2 learning appears to be hugely affected by age and individual differences, suggesting some profound interference with the implicit aspects of language acquisition. Hulstijn (2002a: 206) formulates the fundamental question very clearly: 'If implicit learning is unstoppable, how can we account for the fact that L2 learning, despite massive exposure, training and motivation often does not lead to native-like performance, instead exhibiting persistent L1 interference or fossilization?'

Main types of implicit learning experiments

Implicit learning mechanisms are assumed to operate in a wide variety of domains. Yet, many of the claims made in the literature are based upon the results of a rather limited number and type of laboratory experiments. Let us briefly examine the nature of the main learning tasks that these experiments employed. According to Cleeremans (2003), implicit learning research has typically utilized three experimental paradigms: *artificial grammar learning*, *sequence learning*, and *dynamic system control*. These all involve first exposing the learner to some complex rule-governed environment under incidental learning conditions and then administering two follow-up measures: assessing the subjects' newly learnt knowledge/skill through some performance index and measuring the extent to which subjects are conscious of the knowledge they have acquired. The demonstration of improved performance without any conscious knowledge of the underlying system is seen as evidence that the participants have acquired knowledge about the structure of their environment seemingly without full awareness of what they have learnt.

- *Artificial grammar learning* was the classic experiment type that Reber (1967) used in his seminal study that introduced the term 'implicit learning', and his research has been replicated with similar results many times since then. In this paradigm, as already described briefly, participants are usually asked to memorize strings of consonants that conform to the patterns generated by a finite rule system (the 'artificial grammar'). Having memorized the strings, participants are then asked to discriminate novel strings that conform to the grammar involved in the memorized strings from strings that are not grammatical in this sense. The typical result is that subjects are able to do so better than chance would predict (although only with a maximum of 70 per cent accuracy; DeKeyser and Juffs 2005) without actually understanding the rules of the 'grammar' (as indicated by post-experimental interviews) upon which their judgements were based, attesting to unconscious, implicit learning.

- *Sequence learning* experiments typically use 'serial reaction-time' tasks, in which, for example, participants execute sequential finger movements (pressing specific keys on a keyboard) in response to visual cues that appear on the screen one after another. The sequence is made up of a combination of random and repeated stretches (of course without the participants knowing about this), and the typical finding in such experiments is that the participants exhibit improved response times during the execution of the recurring sequence compared to the random ones. Alternatively, the sequence is governed by a set of rules, which again results in faster reactions after a while. These improvements are attributed to implicit learning.

- *Dynamic system control* tasks are computer simulations of an interactive system—the best-known of these being an imaginary sugar factory—in which the participant is the 'boss' who controls the system's production by manipulating the input (in the sugar factory's case, the number of workers employed), which then determines the output of the system (the sugar output the factory produces). The relationship between input and output is non-linear and therefore participants cannot consciously discover the rule that governs the system. Yet, by simply participating in the computer simulation trials they tend to quickly achieve a good level of control of the system. A further indication of the implicit learning process is that when participants are asked to search for the rules underlying system behaviour, this can actually decrease their performance, suggesting that participants do not generally learn in an analytic way (Dienes and Fehey 1995).

Incidental versus intentional learning

In SLA research, and in L2 vocabulary acquisition studies in particular, we often come across the dichotomy of 'intentional' versus 'incidental' learning, which bears a strong resemblance to the explicit–implicit dichotomy. In *intentional learning conditions* participants are forewarned that they will be tested on the material to which they are exposed, that is, they are aware of the fact that they are participating in a formal learning task; by contrast, learning is considered *incidental* when participants are not expecting a memory test (Mäntylä 2001). In this sense, incidental learning denotes the usual 'test-free', natural learning processes of everyday life, outside the looming shadow of assessment typical of studying within educational institutions.

What motivates the use of these terms? At first glance they might not seem anything more than a domain-specific peculiarity typical of vocabulary studies, but a closer look reveals a more meaningful answer. We saw in the previous chapter that all too often when scholars talk about 'language acquisition' what they really mean is the development of grammar, that is, the rule-based system underlying language processing. Such structural regularities can be studied meaningfully using the explicit–implicit paradigm (e.g. when talking about explicit grammar teaching in language classes or the implicit process of probabilistic learning in infants). The case with vocabulary learning, however, is quite different due to the prominent symbolic and explicit character of the development of form–meaning pairings and the explicit nature of the resulting vocabulary knowledge. (For psychologically slanted overviews of vocabulary learning, see e.g. N. Ellis 1994*b*; Hulstijn 2003, 2005; Kirsner 1994.) This made scholars cautious in describing the formal versus natural dichotomy of vocabulary learning (e.g. learning vocabulary as part of language instruction in preparation for a proficiency test versus learning vocabulary through extensive L2 use such as extensive reading) using the explicit–implicit paradigm in spite of the obvious conceptual link. The main problem with using the explicit–implicit dichotomy would concern the description of the highly common form of learning lexis through being engaged with meaning-focused receptive language use such as reading books or magazines, listening to the radio, or watching TV, films, or videos. Compared to the explicit memorization of vocabulary in preparation for a test, processing input in such a meaning-focused manner is obviously less explicit, yet this learning process cannot be called implicit either because the outcome, lexis, is explicit knowledge.

In the light of the above, adopting the new terminology of incidental–intentional learning for this specific purpose makes sense, but the problem with the actual terms used (i.e. 'incidental' and 'intentional') is that they are too powerful and resonate too closely with explicitness–implicitness; therefore it was almost inevitable that the usage of these terms would be generalized beyond the specific methodological sense related to the presence or absence of warning about testing. Thus, as Hulstijn (2003: 349) summarizes, the terms have been given 'various interpretations, sometimes indistinguishable from two more widely used terms, namely implicit and explicit learning' (p. 349). As he further argues, although there is a vast literature of empirical studies in incidental and intentional vocabulary learning, these studies address a wide variety of theoretical and educational questions and they, therefore, 'do not constitute a coherent research domain'.

Can we conceive incidental learning as a specific subset of implicit learning? As we saw above, it is certainly the case that incidental learning is less explicit than intentional learning in that the latter by definition raises the learner's awareness of the learning process through the warning about testing; however, being less explicit does not necessarily make incidental learning completely unintentional and implicit. This is particularly true if we are talking about language learning within academic settings, which carries some inherent intentionality. Hulstijn (2003) specifically states that both incidental and intentional learning require some attention and noticing and, interestingly, he even recommends keeping a distinction between intentional and explicit learning as they, too, involve different emphases. Indeed, intentional learning highlights the goal-related nature of the process and in that sense it is more of a motivational than a cognitive psychological term. Mäntylä (2001) reports a study by Hyde and Jenkins that supports this observation. These researchers found that the main difference in the outcome of incidental and intentional learning lay in the processing strategies that the learners chose to employ; thus, the researchers concluded that the impact of the learning type was attributable to the difference in the participants' orientation toward the stimulus and the subsequent encoding strategies they applied. We will come back to the question of incidental learning towards the end of this chapter when discussing its implications for SLA.

Explicit versus implicit knowledge

Explicit–implicit knowledge refers to the outcome of the learning process. With most learning models it is possible to separate this end-product from the learning process itself, but we should note here Hulstijn's (2002a) warning that in a connectionist perspective implicit learning and knowledge cannot be separated. However, because the explicit–implicit paradigm is not usually explained in connectionist terms (although parallels are often drawn) and most scholars in this area do employ the learning/knowledge distinction, I will follow this practice.

A second point that needs to be made in advance is that explicit–implicit knowledge is often used interchangeably with declarative–procedural knowledge (to be discussed later). Although some schools or scholars make a distinction between the two sets, the usual reason for using one or the other paradigm is related to the specific research tradition that a study is associated with: investigations focusing on explicit–implicit learning tend to use the terms explicit–implicit knowledge, whereas studies that adopt a skill learning theory or Anderson's ACT-R (both to be discussed later in detail) tend to use the declarative–procedural dichotomy.

Finally, this section will be confined only to describing and defining the concepts of explicit and implicit knowledge; the crucial questions as to how the two knowledge types interact with each other and whether there is access from one to the other will be discussed in a separate section on the explicit–implicit interface below.

Definition and content of explicit and implicit knowledge

The most common and elegant definition of *explicit knowledge* is that it is knowledge that the individual can express in a verbal statement. Thus, this is conscious knowledge that can be consciously searched and recalled into memory on demand. It is stored in the form of symbols (concepts, categories) and rules that specify inter-symbol relationships (Hulstijn 2007*b*); in L2 proficiency the most prominent types of explicit knowledge involve form–meaning pairs, such as lexical units, and the knowledge of grammar rules.

With regard to *implicit* (or *'tacit'*) *knowledge,* we have already seen that Davies (2001) defines it simply as knowledge that is not explicit, and although this is clearly less than informative, it might turn out to be the most accurate characterization at present because the concept is riddled with problems. Nobody questions the existence of some sort of a non-explicit, non-expressible knowledge—the standard illustration concerns cycling because even though so many of us know how to ride a bicycle, nobody except for a few physicists can explain what this knowledge actually involves. Indeed, we all have knowledge of a variety of skills without being able to give a verbal account of how the performance is achieved. Moreover, implicit knowledge is not limited to motor skills but also extends to higher-level cognition. Cleeremans (2003) argues that expertise in domains such as medical diagnosis or aesthetic judgements all involve intuitive knowledge to which one seems to have little introspective access.

The first question to ask is whether these implicit skills and expertise constitute real 'knowledge' in the true sense of the word. According to Davies (2001), the answer is probably no. 'Knowing' means being aware of something and therefore the term 'knowledge' does not seem to be applicable in cases where the person is unaware of the presence or influence of the information, as is the case with implicit knowledge. Reber (2003) admits that what has been termed implicit knowledge is akin to the everyday notion of intuition. But, he argues, when people make intuitive judgements they are actually using considerable knowledge about the particular situation within which the judgements are made.

Even if we accept that some sort of implicit knowledge exists, what does it consist of? How is it represented in the mind? The field is greatly divided in this respect. Paradis (2004), for example, believes that implicit knowledge is made up of 'implicit computational procedures' whose nature we simply do not know. Furthermore, he argues, although there are several competing proposals in the literature, we have no criteria for selecting among them because the brain does not necessarily operate in the most 'elegant' or 'economical' way.

Wallach and Lebiere (2003) distinguish three broad theoretical approaches that aim at explaining the implicit mental structures that implicit learning generates. The first approach assumes the (unconscious) acquisition of rules that capture covariation patterns of physical stimuli, rather than recording details of a single episode. This is the position taken by Reber (1967, 1993,

2003), who envisioned some abstract mental representation of the rules that comprise implicit grammars. By contrast, other researchers favour more episodic theories that are based on the storage of intact exemplars rather than abstract rules, an approach that, as we saw in the last chapter, formed the basis of usage-based theories of language acquisition. A third position believes in the storage of only some fragments or chunks of the exemplars, and these segments are distributed in a parallel manner. This position follows the connectionist logic. Later in this chapter we are going to see more details of this broad division when we look at the closely related issues of explicit–implicit memory, the declarative–procedural dichotomy, and the interface of explicit and implicit knowledge.

Explicit versus implicit memory

It is widely accepted today in cognitive science that the human cognitive system contains several functionally and biologically distinct memory systems. The exact number of these systems is a contested issue and this is an area where a major restructuring of our knowledge is likely to happen during the next decade. In this book I discuss three different aspects of memory: first *explicit–implicit memory,* then the closely related *declarative–procedural memory system* as part of the declarative–procedural paradigm; and finally, in the next chapter, *working memory* within the framework of individual differences. These conceptual areas dominate contemporary memory research, each having its own substantial body of literature with too few attempts to synthesize the accumulated results. This is particularly surprising with regard to explicit–implicit versus declarative–procedural memory as these paradigms appear to cover very similar ground and the corresponding terms are, in fact, often used interchangeably. This compartmentalization tendency is an unfortunate characteristic of academic research in general, and as Reber's (1993: 109) summary below shows, it even applies to research on implicit learning and implicit memory:

> For over a decade the two research programs [on implicit learning and implicit memory] have, unfortunately, travelled parallel courses with precious little interaction. Indeed, if one were to construct a Venn diagram of the literature citations in these two related domains, the intersection would be very nearly the empty set . . . I am sure that there is some lesson in the sociology of science to be learnt here, and for whatever it is worth, I confess to having been as guilty as anyone else in contributing to this Balkanization of the field.

Definition of explicit and implicit memory

Although 'memory' is a widely used term in our everyday parlance referring to a mental storage place or capacity, it is usually defined in psychology with regard to the retrieval of information through memory tasks. This is well manifested in the standard definition of implicit and explicit memory by Schacter (1987: 501): 'Implicit memory is revealed when previous experiences facilitate performance on a task that does not require conscious or intentional recollection of those experiences; explicit memory is revealed when performance on a task requires conscious recollection of previous experiences.' What is usually omitted is Schacter's next sentence, which adds emphasis to the retrieval aspect: 'Note that these are *descriptive* concepts that are primarily concerned with a person's psychological experience at the time of retrieval' (emphasis in original).

Once we accept that memory as a psychological term is conceptualized in terms of *retrieval* rather than internal representation or structure (about which we know relatively little), it becomes clear why 'memory tasks' assume a special importance—after all, retrieval can be operationalized only through them. Perrig (2001: 7241) makes this link very clear:

> Thus, 'implicit memory' refers to memory effects that can be shown by implicit tasks or indirect tasks that, in contrast to explicit tasks, do not instruct the subjects to remember what happened in the past. Here, the terms 'implicit' and 'explicit' refer to different tasks, distinguished operationally by the instructions given to subjects at test.

And it is in this light that we can interpret Butler and Berry's (2001: 192) definition, whereby implicit memory is 'task performance that is not accompanied by conscious or intentional recollection'.

As is the case with explicit knowledge, scholars usually regard explicit memory as an unambiguous issue and focus most of their energies on exploring its implicit counterpart. Paradis's (2004: 9) view in this respect is not unusual: 'Implicit memory is much more fundamental and more pervasive than explicit memory...During the first 12 months of life, the child possesses only implicit memory, while explicit memory emerges only later.' I believe that this stance is correct—we usually have no problem understanding what explicit memory and explicit recollection involves: in N. Ellis's (2002*b*: 299) words, it refers to

> a conscious process of remembering a prior episodic experience; it is tapped by tasks like recall and recognition during which the individual is consciously aware of the knowledge held. Examples include your answers to *What did you have for breakfast?*, *What's your dog called?*, *Tell me the story of* It's a Wonderful Life, and *Who are you? Tell me* your *story.*

In contrast to the relatively straightforward nature of explicit memory, implicit memory is a contested issue. It is taken to be displayed when someone's behaviour reveals some unconscious memorial residue of an earlier experience. Priming tasks (discussed in Ch. 2) are good examples of this process. While the existence of implicit memories makes intuitive sense, the problem is that the methodology to identify them unambiguously has been the subject of heated debates in the literature. Butler and Berry (2001: 192), for example, argue that there is no genuine evidence regarding implicit memory in normal participants and suggest therefore that 'the term implicit memory might have outgrown its usefulness as an overall descriptor'. We should note, however, that they are talking about 'normal' patients only, because with amnesic patients research has produced some convincing support for the existence of implicit learning.

Amnesic patients have brain damage that causes problems with remembering: they cannot recognize people, cannot learn new names, and cannot recall previous experiences more than a few minutes after they have happened. Thus, their explicit memory is severely impaired. However, the surprising fact is that these patients retain the ability to learn novel skills or to exhibit sensitivity to past experiences of which they are not conscious (Cleeremans 2003; N. Ellis 2002*b*). Thus, they can show normal memory on implicit tests, which suggests that implicit memory is served by an independent cognitive system.

The declarative–procedural dichotomy

The declarative–procedural distinction is used with regard to knowledge and the memory that stores this knowledge. Declarative knowledge is often taken as a synonym for explicit knowledge and procedural knowledge for implicit knowledge, and indeed, in the following definition by Carlson (2003: 38) the terms could be replaced with their corresponding equivalents: 'Declarative knowledge is knowledge that can be explicitly expressed ("declared") or consulted, whereas procedural knowledge ("knowing how") can only be performed.' One difference in emphasis between the terms 'implicit' and 'procedural' is that, as the above definition also reflects, procedural knowledge/ memory is usually used in the context of skill learning and skill performance rather than rule learning.

We should recall Cleeremans' (2003) assertion referred to at the beginning of the discussion of the explicit–implicit dichotomy, namely that with the rapid development of the cognitive neurosciences many existing distinctions that were previously described in binary terms, such as the explicit–implicit or the declarative–procedural distinction, are now being increasingly reconceptualized in terms of graded characterizations. This is particularly true of the declarative–procedural memory dichotomy because current memory frameworks (described later in this chapter) distinguish between more memory types. For this reason, procedural memory has often been replaced recently by the term 'non-declarative memory', with 'procedural memory' proper referring only to one component of the non-declarative memory system (Ullman 2005). This quote by Reber and Squire (the latter scholar being arguably the best-known contemporary memory expert in cognitive psychology) illustrates the somewhat confusing state of terminology:

> Memory is not a single faculty but is composed of multiple separate abilities. One major distinction contrasts declarative (explicit)

memory, which supports conscious memory of facts and events, with nondeclarative (implicit) memory, which supports a range of phenomena including habit learning, simple conditioning, and priming. (Reber and Squire 1998: 248)

The declarative–procedural dichotomy is closely associated with the work of cognitive psychologist John Anderson and his colleagues and forms an integral part of Anderson's 'ACT-R' theory. I will describe this theory in detail below, but before I do so let us look at some more generic aspects of the declarative–procedural paradigm.

Declarative versus procedural knowledge

For all practical purposes, *declarative* and *procedural knowledge* correspond to explicit and implicit knowledge, respectively. The main difference is not really within content but in scientific approach. As we have seen, the conceptualization of explicit–implicit knowledge has grown out of research on explicit–implicit learning and is centred around the key issue of awareness/consciousness. In contrast, the 'knowing that' versus 'knowing how' dichotomy has been around in Western thinking for over a century and the corresponding declarative–procedural knowledge distinction was formalized in artificial intelligence research in the 1970s—see Squire 2004. We should note here that although the scope of the declarative–procedural paradigm is broad, it does not contain straightforward 'declarative learning' or 'procedural learning' constructs. Instead, the acquisition of knowledge in the declarative–procedural paradigm is usually discussed in relation to skill learning theory and automatization, which will be discussed in separate sections below.

Declarative versus procedural memory

A great deal of research over the past two decades has focused on what has been seen as two independent memory systems: *declarative memory* and *procedural memory*. As Squire (2007) summarizes, declarative memory is representational, and what is learnt can be expressed through conscious recollection. It involves the storage and retrieval of facts ('semantic knowledge') and events ('episodic knowledge'). In many ways, Squire points out, this is the kind of memory that is referred to when the term 'memory' is used in everyday language. According to Ullman (2004), an important feature of this memory system is that it allows for very rapid and flexible learning, sometimes even based on a single stimulus presentation (i.e. a single exposure to the information to be learnt).

In contrast, and similar to implicit memory (of which it is often used as a synonym), procedural memory is expressed through performance rather than conscious recollection. It involves the storage and retrieval of sensori-motor and cognitive habits, skills, and other types of sequences, which can be as complex as playing an instrument or a game. In many ways, this unconscious memory system reflects our experiences in interacting with the world, and it allows for gradual learning on an ongoing basis during multiple presentations of stimuli and responses (Ullman 2004). Schumann (2004*b*) highlights an important aspect of this memory system, namely that it is relatively inflexible and non-transferrable, that is, it is only available in contexts that are identical or very similar to the original learning situation (e.g. the ability to play one string instrument cannot be transferred effectively to playing another). This is compensated for by its robustness, manifested for example by the fact that procedural memory is preserved much more than declarative memory in the elderly or in people with dementia.

One important aspect of both declarative and procedural memory is that neuroanatomical studies have been fairly successful in identifying the brain areas where each memory system resides. Declarative memory appears to be primarily located in the medial temporal lobe, including the hippocampus, whereas procedural memory is usually associated with a network of more diffuse brain structures rooted in the frontal/basal-ganglia circuits. (For detailed discussions, see Crowell 2004; Lee 2004; Ullman 2004.) While the exact localization is still an ongoing effort (and we should also note the possible reservations about localization attempts discussed in Ch. 2), the important lesson from these studies is that they clearly dissociate the two systems from each other.

Beyond the declarative–procedural memory systems

Although the declarative–procedural dichotomy makes a lot of sense both empirically and intuitively, Squire (2007) explains that it became clear after the mid-1980s that this binary system is untenable. A number of new memory abilities were identified and neurobiologically validated by linking them to specific brain structures. This resulted in a general shift in perspective towards a framework of multiple memory systems. Declarative memory remained untouched (although it can be subdivided into event- and fact-related components), but procedural memory was replaced by the umbrella term 'non-declarative memory', referring to memory systems in charge of a range of learning functions. The exact number of the different systems in this category is still undecided but the main facets mentioned in the literature include memory for (1) skills and habits (which is procedural memory in the narrow sense), (2), priming and perceptual learning, (3) classical conditioning, and (4) non-associative learning (i.e. behavioural change brought by repeated presentation of one stimulus) (see Figure 4.1).

Anderson's ACT-R theory

The ACT-R (Adaptive Control of Thought–Rational) theory is an evolving conceptualization of the overall architecture of human cognition by John Anderson and his colleagues. (For a recent review, see Anderson *et al.* 2004; for a variety of information including a comprehensive list of downloadable

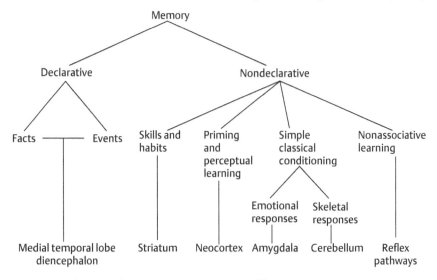

Figure 4.1 Squire's (2007: 341) taxonomy of long-term memory systems with the brain structures central to each

publications, see <http://act-r.psy.cmu.edu>.) The acronym refers to both the theoretical construct and a corresponding computer model that constitutes a hybrid model of symbolic elements linked to a non-symbolic learning network. A key feature of the system is that it distinguishes between a permanent procedural memory and a permanent declarative memory. As Wallach and Lebiere (2003) summarize, procedural knowledge is encoded in condition-action rules (productions), whereas the declarative structures used to store factual knowledge in declarative memory are conceived as chunks.

ACT-R has grown out of Anderson's earlier ACT theory, which represented a cognitive psychological approach based on the distinction between declarative and procedural knowledge since its inception in the mid-1970s. This idea was further developed in the ACT* theory in the early 1980s, by adding the concept of 'proceduralization', which was a specific proposal for how procedural knowledge derived from declarative knowledge—see below in detail. The ACT-R was introduced ten years later, shifting the emphasis from explicit instruction as the origin of the initial declarative knowledge to declarative memory for exemplars of how the procedures should be executed. The current version of the theory is the result of yet another major revision by Anderson *et al.* (2004), aiming at generating neural plausibility of the ACT-R model. Thus, Anderson's thinking has evolved considerably over the years and even the current version is admittedly little more than an ambitious work in progress that facilitates a better conception of the mind while acknowledging that 'No theory in the foreseeable future can hope to account for all of cognition' (p. 1057).

From our point of view, possibly the most important aspect of Anderson's theory is his elaboration of Fitts and Posner's (1967) original three-stage proposal of acquiring cognitive skills into a coherent description of the move from declarative to procedural knowledge in terms of three broad stages: (1) a conscious *cognitive* or *declarative* stage, where a declarative description of the procedure is learnt; (2) an *associative* or *procedural* stage, where the learner works on productions for performing the process; and (3) an *autonomous* or *automatic* stage, where execution of the skill becomes fully automatized. (For a review, see Anderson 2000b.) These three stages, which are now a standard part of general skill learning theory (see later for a more detailed account detail), are highly relevant from an SLA perspective because the developmental process describes, in effect, how people move from the use of explicit/declarative L2 knowledge (e.g. grammar rules and lexis) to automatized application of implicit/procedural knowledge (i.e. fluent language use). In the following section I will describe this progression within the broader theoretical context of examining the interface of explicit/declarative and implicit/procedural knowledge. This will be followed by a specific examination of how theoretical knowledge can be applied to the study of second language learning.

At the interface of explicit/declarative and implicit/procedural knowledge

I started out this chapter with the claim that the non-symbolic, connectionist theories described in Ch. 3 are of only limited relevance to SLA because they do not contain a sufficiently prominent explicit/declarative component that would explain the salient conscious learning part of SLA, let alone instructed SLA. Krashen's (1981, 1982, 1985) theory of second language acquisition/learning highlighted the significance of understanding of how explicit and implicit aspects of L2 proficiency interact almost 30 years ago and the complex issue of the explicit/declarative–implicit/procedural interface has been at the heart of nearly all the influential proposals about second language learning since then. As Nick Ellis (2005a) summarized in a special issue of *Studies in Second Language Acquisition* (27/2) devoted entirely to the topic of explicit and implicit language learning, 'The interface question has driven research in applied linguistics and SLA for the last 20 years' (p. 309).

A good starting point in exploring the psychological basis of the explicit–implicit interface is to review the classic theory of *skill learning*. This is a broad, generic model of how various skills move from an initial declarative stage to increased automaticity through being proceduralized. It is related to Anderson's (2000b) ACT-R theory as well as a number of other approaches to automatization and proceduralization, including Logan's (1988, 2005) instance learning theory. Following this, I will summarize contemporary thinking on automatization more generally, in terms of the cooperation of explicit and implicit learning processes. The theoretical propositions presented will, then, form the basis of the final part section of this chapter that looks at the theoretical underpinnings of SLA.

Skill learning theory

Practice makes perfect. Correcting the overstatement of a maxim: Almost always, practice brings improvement, and more practice brings more improvement.
(Newell and Rosenbloom 1981: 1)

According to Carlson (2003: 36), a *skill* refers to 'an acquired ability that has improved as a consequence of practice'. It is clear that 'ability' is not used here in the strict sense of the word because Carlson, along with other skill learning experts, adds that skills can not only be mental or cognitive (e.g. playing chess or solving a mathematical problem) but also physical or motor in nature (e.g. riding a bicycle). Thus, the term 'skill' refers to a rather mixed bag, which makes it difficult to decide to what extent lessons from skill learning theory can be generalized to learning language knowledge and language skills (which are, of course, ambiguous terms themselves). We may rightly wonder why such a broad and fuzzy term became the centre of an influential theoretical approach. The answer lies in a remarkable feature of skills, namely their improvement with practice (i.e. repeated performance of the same activity) from slow, deliberate, memory-intensive, error-prone performance on a task, to rapid, automatic, near-error-free performance (Johnson, Wang, and Zhang 2003). What is more, this pattern has been observed across a wide range of skills. In DeKeyser's (2007c: 97) words:

> The basic claim of skill acquisition theory is that the learning of a wide variety of skills shows a remarkable similarity in development from initial representation of knowledge through initial changes in behaviour to eventual fluent, spontaneous, largely effortless, and highly skilled behaviour, and that this set of phenomena can be accounted for by a set of basic principles common to the acquisition of all skills.

Thus, the uniform learning pattern forms the foundation of skill learning theory. In a way, it also defines the scope of phenomena covered by the term of 'skill': it can refer to any cognitive or physical capability that displays practice-related progression towards a largely automatic process. It is this aspect of skills that Johnson, Wang, and Zhang (2003: 30) highlight in their description: 'Skills are thought to consist largely of collections of automatic processes. Automatic processing often occurs without attention. It is often fast, effortless, stereotypic, autonomous, and unavailable to conscious awareness.'

Language teaching practitioners might be particularly pleased to see the word 'practice' above. This is a key issue in any L2 teaching methodology and yet since the demise of the audiolingual method with its behaviourist foundations, applied linguistic theory has had surprisingly little to say about it, even though textbooks for L2 learning/teaching have for the most part continued to include practice-based material. Its absence from applied linguistics discourse is probably accounted for by the fact that the field had no theoretical justification for it. (See the discussion in Larsen-Freeman 2003.) This situation is likely to change because cognitive theories of automatization and proceduralization—that is, methods to increase fluency—pay a great deal of attention to practice; in fact, one of the central issues in the overall question of the interface of explicit/declarative and implicit/procedural knowledge is exactly how we conceptualize and implement practice. This is why a recent volume on practice in SLA, edited by Robert DeKeyser (2007*b*), is a particularly welcome addition to the professional literature.

Power law of practice

A recognition that inspired a lot of subsequent research into skill learning was the observation that the practice-induced developmental pattern of cognitive and motor skills showed a remarkable regularity across tasks and situations, and could be described by a mathematical power function. This regularity has been referred to as the 'power law of practice' (or 'power law of learning') and it allowed for computing the decrease of performance speed or error rate as a mathematical function of the amount of practice (more specifically, the number of trials raised to some power). The diagram in Figure 4.2 shows a

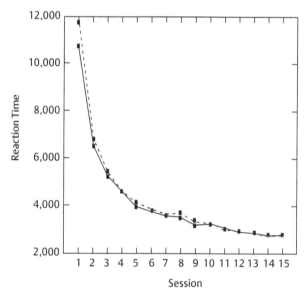

Figure 4.2 Typical power law curve of reaction time as a function of the number of trials (DeKeyser 1997: 205; solid and dashed lines indicate two conditions)

fairly typical learning curve: the practice effects are greatest at the beginning stages and then gradually decrease. Such negatively accelerating but never ending improvement has been repeatedly observed with a wide range of skills (Ritter and Schooler 2001).

DeKeyser (2007c) explains that the remarkable consistency of the rate and shape of the improvement curve across a variety of tasks has suggested to scholars that the power law of practice reflects the functioning of some fundamental underlying learning mechanisms. As Newell and Rosenbloom (1981: 3) summed this up in their seminal paper on the topic, 'A general regularity such as the log-log law might say something interesting about the basic mechanisms of turning knowledge into action.' This is a fair assumption, and indeed, there have been no influential learning theories over the past three decades that did not attempt to provide an explanation for what cognitive mechanisms cause the quantitative change pattern. (We will come back to this question below when we discuss the issue of automatization.)

Stages of skill learning

[V]irtually all interesting complex human skills are acquired in a characteristic fashion.
(Reber 1993: 16)

The regularity in the acquisition of diverse skills was first noted by Fitts (1964) and Fitts and Posner (1967), whose work was further developed by Anderson's ACT* theory. Accordingly, skill acquisition is thought to proceed through three characteristic stages. Fitts and Posner called these *cognitive*, *associative*, and *autonomous*, while Anderson used the terms *declarative*, *procedural*, and *automatic*. In practice both sets of descriptors are used and, indeed, in a general introduction to learning and memory, Anderson (2000a) himself presented skill learning theory in terms of Fitts and Posner's categories. In the following discussion, therefore, I will be referring to both sets.

The main thrust of the skill learning progression is a gradual move from the laboured, conscious, and overtly controlled declarative processes of the novice to the smooth, unconscious, and covertly controlled procedural processes of the expert (Reber 1993). This developmental pattern shows a remarkable similarity to the mastery of L2 skills, which is also characterized by progression of the initial performance that is slow and prone to errors towards fluent, competent, and error-free L2 use. Let us have a look at the three stages of skill learning theory in more detail.

Cognitive or declarative stage

The learning of specific skills always has a distinct starting point when we have to perform the particular skill for the first time. Scholars agree that this early stage typically requires some kind of explicit direction to provide relevant facts and guidelines about the skill so that the learner/trainee can develop a rough mental approximation of it that can be put to the test. The most effective method tends not to be to throw the learners into deep water to see if they sink or swim, but rather to prepare them for the task in a number of ways, most notably through verbal (or written) instruction or explanation, as well as by modelling the skill through a demonstration (perhaps with accompanying commentary), through examples, or by analogy to an existing skill (Carlson 2003; DeKeyser 2007c).

This initial encoding of the skill (called the *cognitive* or *declarative* phase) is generally believed to be mostly in the form of declarative knowledge, which the learner subsequently interprets and rehearses during the performance of the first trials. As everybody who remembers his/her first driving lessons knows, these first trials present a massive load to the working memory in terms of remembering the sequence of things to do and what to pay attention to, and the resulting performance is an error prone, arduous process that (thankfully) does not usually last longer than a few trials.

Associative or procedural stage

We saw above when discussing the power law of practice that the initial improvement in acquiring a skill is typically fast and the learning curve is steep—indeed, learners regularly amaze themselves by how quickly they can get from the 'which-pedal-is-the-accelerator?' stage to driving in real traffic. In a study on the automatization of skills in using an artificial language, DeKeyser (1997) found, for example, that his research participants completed the first skill learning phase (i.e. the cognitive/declarative phase) before the end of the first practice session (out of a total of 15 sessions). DeKeyser explains this speed with the availability of the relevant declarative knowledge that the learner could draw on, which in his study was provided prior to the practice sessions. This highlights the importance of explicit preparation and has obvious educational implications (to be discussed later).

The second, *associative/procedural* phase of the skill learning process—that is, when we start driving in real traffic with an instructor—can be described as a practice period. There is a shift from relying on declarative facts to procedural knowledge as the learner develops efficient procedures of performing the skill, often by skipping or compounding steps that were presented in the first phase. This gradual process is usually called 'proceduralization' (Anderson 2000a), and Anderson's ACT-R theory (e.g. Anderson *et al.* 2004) suggest that it involves the development of condition-action rules ('productions') that the learner will increasingly draw on instead of the initially acquired declarative knowledge. Juffs and DeKeyser (2003) explain that the creation and fine-tuning of such highly specialized rules occur when people repeatedly engage in the relevant behaviour while all the relevant knowledge is easily accessible in long-term memory. However, it is still subject to debate whether the qualitative transformation of the knowledge base that the learner draws on (i.e. the formation of production rules) is a direct conversion/replacement of declarative knowledge with procedural knowledge, or whether it involves the building up of a parallel procedural knowledge base that coexists with declarative knowledge side by side, thus allowing the learner to fall back to accessing declarative knowledge at certain times. Hulstijn (2002*a*), for example, argues that the most likely scenario is not that explicit knowledge actually transforms into implicit knowledge, but rather that a separate network is constructed of an implicit nature over the number of trials involved in training.

Autonomous or automatic stage

The final stage of the skill learning process—the *autonomous/automatic stage*—involves the continuous improvement in the performance of a skill that is already well established. The level of automaticity and fluency increases while cognitive involvement decreases, so much so that, as Johnson, Wang, and Zhang (2003) describe, learners often lose the ability to describe verbally how they do the task. Reaching this stage, however, requires a large amount of practice, and DeKeyser (2007*c*) warns us that even highly automatized behaviours are not 100 per cent error-free. For example, communication breakdowns of varying severity regularly happen both in our L1 and L2, requiring the use of a range of problem-solving mechanisms that are usually called 'communication strategies'. (See e.g. Dörnyei and Kormos 1998; Kormos 2006.) In SLA we also need to give account of the fact that in the vast majority of language learners the developmental process of at least some aspects of their emerging L2 skills terminates at some plateau level resulting in a fossilized state. This question will be further discussed in the next chapter when we look at age affects.

   The expertise produced by the *autonomous/automatic* stage has two key characteristics: first, as we will discuss in more detail in the next section on automatization, highly automated skills require fewer attentional resources, which means in effect that experts perform a large proportion of their established skills on auto-pilot. Second, the increasingly fine-tuned production rules become more and more skill-specific. As Carlson (2003) describes, even slight changes in the conditions or parameters of performing a skill might result in losing the benefits of practice. In contemporary education we often talk about 'transferrable skills', but skill learning theory actually predicts that the transferability of skills from task to task is quite narrow, even if the tasks are fairly similar. In the domain of language learning it has been well documented, for example, that skills in L2 comprehension do not transfer well to L2 production and even situational changes might seriously inhibit performance fluency. DeKeyser (2007*c*) argues that a solid declarative knowledge base can help learners through the difficult times when confronting new contexts of use.

Automatization

Skill learning theory offers a good inroad into understanding the development of fluent and error-free task execution skills, because the two foundations of this theory—the three-stage developmental pattern and the power law of practice—appear to be universally applicable. Therefore, any theory of automatization needs to account for these characteristics. The previous overview of skill learning theory also revealed a third feature that consistently emerges from the various accounts, the cooperation of the explicit and implicit systems during the process. Let us now have a closer look at the various theoretical proposals concerning this explicit–implicit interface in the course of automatization.

Definitions of automatization

'Automatization' (or 'automaticity') as a technical term has been used in different meanings in the literature. As Segalowitz and Hulstijn (2005) summarize, some of these meanings are based on broad and rather loose definitions, whereas other conceptualizations involve narrow and highly specific operationalizations. The broad definitions usually concentrate on one of three aspects of automatic behaviour: Logan (2005: 130) defines automatization as the 'power-function speedup in reaction time', Lee (2004: 44) states that automatization is 'another name for acquiring procedural memory', and Segalowitz and Hulstijn (2005) describe the generally understood essence of the concept as the 'absence of attentional control in the execution of a cognitive activity' (p. 371). While all these three aspects of automatized skill performance—speed, procedural knowledge use, absence of conscious attention—are intuitively convincing, Hulstijn (2002a) argues that increased speed is not a defining criterion if it only concerns a quantitative change in the execution of a programme; according to him, the hallmark of real automatization is a *qualitative change* in processing.

In agreement with this last view, N. Ellis (2005a) also concludes that the speeded-up retrieval of explicit, declarative knowledge that is due to improved access or to schematization and script-building (i.e. linking together explicit steps and retrieving them as a sequence) does not constitute genuinely automatized behaviour. Automatic processing, according to him, needs to occur *ballistically* (i.e. automatic in the sense that it cannot be stopped), outside explicit control. Thus, we should be able to perform an automatic behaviour without thinking about it, which requires the utilization of procedural knowledge. In accordance with this view, the main theoretical issue in psycholinguistics has been trying to explain the exact nature of the declarative-to-procedural shift.

The declarative-to-procedural shift

In Ch. 3 we looked at various implicit L1 acquisition processes such as segmenting speech and computing frequency statistics of its distributional characteristics. In these cases it was argued that no conscious, explicit knowledge is involved. However, when we talk about the acquisition and automatization of skills beyond infancy (including the learning of L2 skills), all the contemporary theories assume some interaction of declarative and procedural knowledge, with a move from predominantly declarative to predominantly procedural. As mentioned earlier, there are competing positions in operationalizing this shift and, more generally, the development of procedural knowledge. Let us review the three best-known stances in this respect. (For a detailed overview and discussion, see DeKeyser 2001.)

- *Proceduralization of declarative knowledge:* this approach, best represented by Anderson's ACT* and ACT-R theories (see above), assumes that mechanisms that are initially based on the retrieval of declarative knowledge become routinized with practice, which means that the declarative, factual rule sequences become chunked and stored as procedural routines. This process has been referred to as 'proceduralization'. Anderson and Fincham (1994) argue that although a major avenue to proceduralization is when the starting point is to store declarative representations of relevant examples, other avenues are also possible and, in fact, procedural knowledge can even be acquired without any initial declarative knowledge.
- *Building up parallel procedural knowledge:* a second proposal (see e.g. Hulstijn 2002a; Paradis 2004; Ullman 2005) maintains that because declarative and procedural knowledge are neuroanatomically independent, declarative rule knowledge cannot be converted into procedural knowledge. In other words, declarative rules cannot be automatized in the strict sense; instead, what we call 'automatization' is the gradual building up, through the implicit learning provided by extensive practice, of a separate procedural knowledge base that after a while takes over the processing of skills. Thus, the essence of the process is a shift from one mechanism to another, the replacement of the controlled application of explicit rules by the automatic use of implicit procedures. As Hulstijn (2002a) concludes, according to this view 'automatization is an incidental feature of implicit learning' (p. 211). Ullman (2005) reviews neuroimaging research that corroborates these claims. He concludes that due to its rapid learning capacity, the declarative memory system is expected to acquire knowledge initially, while the procedural system gradually learns the same or analogous knowledge. When the latter system is ready to take over, a shift takes place from declarative to procedural memory.
- *Building up a repertoire of episodic instances:* the third theoretical stance that has been influential in psycholinguistic explanations of automaticity over the past two decades is Logan's (1988, 2005) instance theory. It proposes that automatization is construed as the acquisition of a domain-specific knowledge base of separate representations, or *instances,* of each exposure to the task. Initially, a person performs an action following explicit rules. However, on every subsequent occasion the person is engaged in performing the particular skill, a new memory trace is formed corresponding to the action executed, and thus practice leads to the storage of an increasing number of these memorized instances. The significance of this ever-increasing memory base, according to Logan, is that in subsequent

exposures to the task, the learner will not compute the initial algorithm consciously but will rather retrieve one of the stored instances as a single step; the power law of practice is explained by the fact that the more episodic instances are stored in the memory, the quicker the learner's mind finds one to be retrieved. This is, therefore, an item-based theory of automatization, conceiving automaticity as a transition from algorithm-based performance to a memory function.

These three stances can give us a taste of the approaches scholars have taken to explain the declarative-to-procedural shift. (See DeKeyser 2001 for a discussion of some attempts in the literature to produce a synthesis.) As our understanding of the dynamics underlying learning and memory processes increases, we are likely to see major theoretical developments in this area in the near future. Johnson, Wang, and Zhang (2003), for example, review neurobiological investigations which suggest that there are at least four mechanisms that work together during the process of skill acquisition: separate subsystems are linked together, the size or the number of brain areas involved increases, initial processing components are replaced with more efficient components, and circuit changes occur in brain structures performing a task. Furthermore, Poldrack and Packard (2003) draw attention to the competition among multiple memory systems that are activated simultaneously and in parallel in various learning tasks, proposing that these systems may interact with each other. Thus, we can safely conclude that current explanations of skill automatization that suggest a relatively straightforward shift from declarative to procedural knowledge will become more complex in future revisions.

Initial attention and noticing

In skill learning theory and in the models of automatization, the starting point is the development of a declarative knowledge base. Does the same pattern apply to learning in general or can learning take place without any initial explicit component? As Baars (1997a) sums up, this is a notoriously difficult question to answer; but, he argues, the real question is not whether unconscious learning is possible but rather whether there is a positive correlation between consciousness and learning. That is, does conscious exposure in general lead to more knowledge? As he claims, the answer is an 'obvious and resounding yes' (p. 161). Other scholars are equally affirmative; for example, Logan, Taylor, and Etherton (1999: 179) states, 'What is learnt during automatization depends on what is attended to and how attention is deployed.'

Drawing on research findings with amnesiacs, N. Ellis (2002b, 2005a) comes to a similar conclusion. As he summarizes, amnesia is not a failure to notice but a failure to consolidate an explicit memory as a result of noticing. Thus, while amnesiacs show normal implicit memory operation in their perceptual and motor systems for pre-existing memory representations, their learning of new associations is very slow. This implies that new associations are best learnt explicitly and implicit learning comes into its own when tuning the strengths of the pre-existing representations and integrating them in the broader cognitive system. In N. Ellis's (2005*a*: 340) words, 'The input to our connectionist implicit learning systems comes via unitized explicit representations forged from prior attended processing.' We will come back to this question of conscious noticing when discussing the noticing hypothesis in SLA research at the end of this chapter.

Explicit versus implicit language learning

Having reviewed a number of powerful theories in this and the previous chapter, let us look at the lessons we can draw from these with regard to SLA theory (and Ch. 7 will address the practical implications). The discussion will inevitably start with Stephen Krashen's work and the famous/infamous interface debate. Then I will describe Ullman's theory of declarative–procedural language knowledge, followed by the related proposals regarding L2 skill learning and automatization, and an overview of Schmidt's noticing hypothesis. In the final section of this chapter I will provide a summary of the explicit–implicit interface in SLA.

Krashen and the various interface positions

Any psychological examination of SLA is likely to start with discussing the work of Stephen Krashen (1981, 1982, 2003), as his views on the distinct systems of second language acquisition and second language learning not only had a profound impact on the field of SLA but were also directly related to the explicit–implicit interface. In Krashen's view, conscious (i.e. explicit) learning was of secondary importance, and learnt knowledge acted only as a monitor or editor to make small corrections on the language output. The key role in the theory was assigned to natural (i.e. implicit) acquisition, which was responsible for both fluency and most of our accuracy. Krashen made a convincing case for the superiority of acquisition in his writings and presentations, and coined some powerful terms and metaphors (e.g. input hypothesis, comprehensible input, affective filter) that have become an integral part of the SLA jargon. However, although his psychological approach was refreshingly modern, he was unwilling to move on and consider any real changes to his proposals; this had a hugely polarizing effect on the field. His most debated subtheory was related to the interface of the learnt and acquired L2 knowledge, and as we will see below, this debate still has some relevance. Krashen himself championed a 'non-interface' position, with others allowing either a 'weak interface' or a 'strong interface' option between the two types of language knowledge. Let us look at these versions in some detail.

Non-interface position

As Rod Ellis (2005) describes, the *non-interface position* claims that explicit learning and implicit acquisition are independent language attainment mechanisms, and the resulting sets of language knowledge are stored in different parts of the brain—we have seen earlier that recent neuropsychological research has confirmed this view. In its pure form, this position rejects both the possibility of explicit knowledge transforming directly into implicit knowledge and the possibility of implicit knowledge becoming explicit. This led Krashen to claim that learners could not draw on their explicitly learnt knowledge for actual, fluent communication, and a logical consequence of this stance was his rejection of any form of explicit grammar teaching, This, as we can well imagine, considerably divided L2 practitioners and theoreticians worldwide.

   Although Krashen's work has been marginalized in applied linguistics over the past decade, the non-interface position still has some influential supporters. Jan Hulstijn and Michel Paradis, for example, belong to this camp as they believe in the independence of the explicit and implicit linguistic systems. However, modern conceptions of the non-interface position do not hold the extreme view that explicit L2 instruction (in the form of rule presentation or negative feedback) plays only a minimal role in the language acquisition process. Anybody who has learnt or taught a language as a school subject knows that this is simply not true in its strict form. Hulstijn (2002a: 209), for example, sums up his own view thus:

> whereas Krashen is sceptical about the practical usefulness of explicit L2
> knowledge, I consider explicit knowledge to be a worthwhile, sometimes
> indeed indispensable, form of knowledge to be used as a resource
> where and when implicit knowledge is not (yet) available.

Thus, applied linguists were faced with a real challenge in responding to Krashen. Although it was clear to many that simply knowing a grammar rule does not lead to fluent and error-free use of the particular grammatical regularity, they could also see that an extreme non-interface position offers a simplistic and inaccurate description of the language learning process. Subsequently, more and more people realized that the secret lay in the details and that some sort of a halfway position had to be achieved. The resulting proposals can be divided into a *weak* and a *strong interface position*.

Weak interface position

Proponents of the *weak interface position* have suggested several avenues whereby explicit language knowledge could be utilized in the learning process. R. Ellis (2005) points out that most of these proposals were theoretical, without any empirical backing, and because virtually everybody in the field held a view on the significance and nature of grammar teaching, the question inspired some spirited debates. One particularly influential view has been the claim that the knowledge of grammatical regularities and other forms of explicit linguistic information contributes *indirectly* to the acquisition of implicit knowledge by promoting certain processes in which implicit learning can occur (e.g. controlled practice) or by making certain features of the language salient. As N. Ellis (2005*a*: 325) argues, 'the degree of influence of metalinguistic information on the nature of that processing is so profound that claims of interface and interaction seem fully justified'.

The above quote would put N. Ellis in a different camp from Hulstijn, yet the essence of what the two scholars are suggesting is the same, namely that both the implicit and the explicit forms of mastering a language have their uses, and in order to get the full picture, we need to consider the two processes in concert. I will come back to discussing the various proposals of explicit–implicit interconnectedness at the end of this chapter.

Strong interface position

The *strong interface position* claims that explicit knowledge can be converted into implicit knowledge through practice; that is, learners can first learn a rule as a declarative fact and then transform it into an implicit representation—see R. Ellis 2005. Such a strong approach has been supported by highly competent second language learners (and many applied linguists fall into this category) who know from experience that they managed to internalize the vast amount of explicit information they were exposed to in their foreign language classes with only very limited communicative practice (if any). Successful L2 users coming out of self-study language programmes were also thought to be living proof that learning under explicit conditions can convert into acquisition.

As we have seen, the strong interface position also received support from Anderson's ACT theory, where the proceduralization of declarative knowledge is a central component, although even this theory is not completely clear about what qualifies as 'conversion of knowledge'. And given the neuroanatomical confirmation of the independence of the declarative and the procedural memory systems, Segalowitz and Hulstijn (2005) conclude that the strong interface position should be taken to mean that explicit knowledge forms a prerequisite for the generation of implicit knowledge rather than actually transforming it into implicit knowledge. In this sense, the strong hypothesis corresponds to the main principles of automatization and the noticing hypothesis in SLA (to be discussed below).

Ullman's declarative–procedural model

Michael Ullman and his Brain and Language Lab at Georgetown University in Washington DC has been pursuing a unique, focused agenda to investigate the neurocognition of both first and second language, using cutting-edge research methodological (e.g. neuroimaging) techniques. Ullman's research is rooted in Anderson's distinction of procedural and declarative memory (see earlier section) and he has proposed an ambitious theory that applies this distinction to L2 knowledge. (See e.g. Ullman 2001, 2004, 2005.)

The *declarative–procedural* (DP) model posits that the brain system under-lying declarative memory (located in the temporal lobe) also underlies the mental lexicon, that is, all arbitrary, idiosyncratic word-specific knowledge, including word meanings, word sounds, and abstract representations such as word categories. This system is complemented by a second, independent brain system (located in a network of frontal, basal-ganglia, parietal, and cerebellar structures), which subserves both procedural memory and gram-matical knowledge, that is, rule-based procedures that govern the regularities of language. Ullman (2001, 2004, 2005) presents an impressive amount of varied evidence to support these correspondences, including neurophysiolog-ical data from lesion studies and neuroimaging data (ERP, PET, and fMRI). Indeed, one of the main attractions of this theory is that the specific claims it makes lend themselves to empirical testing.

Thus, the DP model gives support to the existence of a dual language system, consisting of broadly conceived vocabulary and grammar. As Ullman explains, this dichotomy corresponds to the dual nature of idiosyncratic versus rule-based linguistic information: idiosyncratic information must be memorized and stored in some sort of mental lexicon, whereas the rules that underlie the sequential order and hierarchical relation of lexical items are stored as implicit algorithms. Although the DP model is primarily represen-tational rather than acquisitional, it allows for the comparison of different learner groups, such as novice and expert L2 learners, and thus it can inform SLA research. The available evidence so far indicates that novice L2 learners tend to rely on their declarative learning systems more than native speakers, which is explained by the short-term effectiveness of associative declara-tive memory. As Ullman (2005) points out, memorizing complex forms and even rules may be expected to lead to a fairly high degree of proficiency, but constructions that cannot be easily memorized (e.g. because they involve long-distance dependencies) pose problems. Sustained experience with the L2, however, leads to increased procedural learning, making the co-operation of the two memory systems more balanced. Thus, Ullman's overall proposal is in line with the broad declarative-to-procedural shift suggested by various skill acquisition and automatization theories.

Automatization and skill learning in a second language

The notion of automatization is not new in the field of SLA. Originally introduced by proponents of behaviourism and the audiolingual method (see DeKeyser 1997; N. Ellis 2002*a*), it was often mentioned in the litera-ture in the 1960s and 1970s. Indeed, the whole idea of habit-formation and 'overlearning' through the stimulus-response chain was centred around the enhancement of automaticity. The methodological manifestation of this early approach was a variety of language drills (both mechanical and communica-tive) that are still widely used in classroom practice. Over the last decade the concept has seen a revival as several studies addressed L2 automatization from a cognitive and psycholinguistic perspective. (For reviews, see DeKeyser 2001, 2007*a*, 2007*c*; Segalowitz and Hulstijn 2005.)

Automatization was also much discussed in applied linguistics under the disguise of 'fluency'. This concept, as Segalowitz (2007) explains, cuts across all areas and levels of analysis in SLA research, referring to those aspects of productive and receptive language ability that are characterized by 'fluidity (smoothness) of performance' (p. 181). The L2 fluency literature has been rich (e.g. Brumfit 1984; Fillmore 1979; Pawley and Syder 1983; Riggenbach 2000) and has also included psychologically based conceptualizations (e.g. Dewaele 2002; Larsen-Freeman 2006; Schmidt 1992; Skehan 1998; Skehan and Foster 2001). However, the concept of fluency has been specifically linked to automatization and skill learning only recently—see Segalowitz 2007.

The theoretical and practical significance of automatization and skill learning theory has by now been well documented in the SLA literature (see e.g. DeKeyser 2007*a*; N. Ellis 2005*a*; Juffs and DeKeyser 2003), very much along the same lines as in the psychological literature (reviewed earlier), but few actual empirical studies have been conducted in the area. (For exceptions, see DeKeyser 1997 and the studies in DeKeyser 2007*b*, especially Ranta and Lyster 2007; for reviews, see DeKeyser 2001; Segalowitz and Hulstijn 2005.) The available findings suggest that automatization of second language grammar rules follows the patterns documented in cognitive and experimental psychology, and the improvement of the performance rate with experience can be characterized by the power law of practice. Thus, it seems that grammatical knowledge can be automatized through the same broad mechanisms that are assumed to operate in other cognitive domains.

The question of L2 automatization and skill learning has obvious teaching methodological implications, regarding the effective integration of explicit and implicit learning methods and the scientific design of curricula. DeKeyser (2007*c*), for example, argues that one main reason for the shortcomings of language teaching in general, and in preparing students for maximum benefit from a stay abroad in particular, is skipping, reversing, or rushing crucial stages in the skill acquisition sequence because of our insufficient understanding of the theory. We are going to look at the practical issues in Ch. 7 in detail, but let me highlight here one theoretical point that may have a rather unexpected and unwanted classroom consequence: the narrow domain-specificity of cognitive skill training.

We saw earlier (when we discussed the stages of skill learning) that the more fine-tuned the implicit production rules become, the more skill- and context-specific they are. This means that even slight changes in the conditions of performing a skill might result in losing the benefits of practice. In other words, highly automatized skills are not very transferrable, which explains partly the huge intrapersonal contextual variation we can observe in many learners' language performance. Thus, for example, comprehension-related skills do not transfer well to L2 production (DeKeyser 1997). What this means in practice is that training effects do not generalize much beyond the specific rules and skills practised, and therefore 'for most structures, most skill uses, and most learners, access to the relevant explicitly learnt rules is not fully automatic' (DeKeyser and Juffs 2005: 445).

Schmidt's noticing hypothesis

Richard Schmidt's (1995, 2001) *noticing hypothesis* was the first psychologically orientated theory that succeeded in achieving mainstream status in SLA research. Its great popularity was due to the fact that it addressed two fundamental issues that applied linguistics had been grappling with: the role of explicit, conscious learning in the SLA process (particularly after Krashen's implicit-only view had been by and large rejected) and the explanation of why only a selected portion of input becomes intake during the learning process. At the heart of the noticing hypothesis is the claim that only those parts of the input become available for intake and effective processing that the learner notices; in Skehan's (1998: 48) words, 'Schmidt is claiming, in contrast to Krashen (1985), that a degree of awareness is important before material can be incorporated into a developing interlanguage system.' Thus, the noticing theory is in complete accordance with the 'explicit/declarative first, implicit/procedural second' trend that seems to have emerged in a number of diverse areas. But does it actually say more than merely establishing some broad prioritization for effective learning? In order to answer this question, we must look at the details.

Noticing and implicit learning

Let us examine the main claim of the noticing hypothesis first, namely that in order to learn some new information effectively, the learner needs to attend to it at the first encounter. This claim is generally accepted both by SLA researchers and cognitive psychologists, but we must realize that it leaves two questions open: (1) the claim is only true for the 'effective' learning of any new information—there are indications that some limited and certainly less effective learning can take place without conscious attention; and (2) what exactly do we mean by 'attending to' the new information? What aspects of the target are to be noticed for learning to take place? Both points will be discussed in some detail below.

Even with these two open issues, the above claim is powerful and has significant implications. As Schmidt (2001: 3) summarizes, 'There is no doubt that attended learning is far superior, and for all practical purposes, attention is necessary for all aspects of L2 learning.' Of course, this claim is only true if by 'learning' we mean the initial learning of new information, because we have seen that implicit learning has an important role in fine-tuning, integrating, and automatizing the newly learnt material. In N. Ellis's (2002*b*: 301) words, 'implicit learning is specialized for incremental cumulative change—the tuning of strengths of preexisting representations. New associations are best learnt explicitly'. Thus, the noticing hypothesis states, in effect, that effective implicit learning cannot happen without explicitly creating the initial mental representation of a new stimulus. Once, however, the initial conscious registration of a construction has occurred, there is scope for its implicit learning on every subsequent occasion of use, and this automatization process does not necessarily require the subsequent noticing of the particular target (N. Ellis 2005*a*).

What exactly needs to be noticed?

What aspects of the target language structures need to be noticed? The strong version of the noticing hypothesis claims that only those features of a target structure that are noticed will be learnt; that is, there are no freebies or spin-offs. This would mean that even if we notice the pragmatic significance of a formulaic expression, if we only focus on the pragmatic meaning, we may not get the intonation contour or the exact preposition in the middle of the phrase right. Schmidt (2001: 30) is very clear about this when he states that 'attention must be directed to whatever evidence is relevant for a particular learning domain, i.e. that attention must be specifically focused and not just global. Nothing is free.' This is, in fact, the position taken by several cognitive psychologists mentioned earlier when discussing the question of initial noticing in psychological theories.

   This claim is supported by Robinson (2003) in a detailed analysis of the role of attention in SLA. He argues that only the strong form of the noticing hypothesis can explain the frequently observed cases when even abundant exposure accompanied by focus on meaning only (such as in immersion classrooms) results in an imbalance between the high fluency of the learners' communicative skills and the significantly lower level of accuracy of their speech. As he summarizes, such learners failed to notice the communicatively redundant, perceptually non-salient, or infrequent forms in the input.

Are there exceptions to the noticing hypothesis?

While the noticing hypothesis describes a robust process, there appear to be exceptions to the learning-only-through-initial-noticing tenet. N. Ellis (2002*b*) describes experiments on artificial grammar learning that have shown that when two structures that have been noticed individually before occur regularly together in the same sequence, this co-occurrence can lead to implicit chunking, which is the central mechanism of the exemplar-based (or usage-based) theories of language acquisition described in the previous chapter. Paradis (2004) also acknowledges the possibility of unconscious learning in cases where we focus on one aspect of speech sequences while picking up something other than what is noticed, namely the covert implicit underlying structure. It is likely, however, that associations that are more complex than adjacency or first-order dependency will require conscious attention, but at the moment we do not know how various aspects of language differ in their attentional requirements (N. Ellis 2002*b*).

Schmidt (2001: 27) accepts that the strong form of the noticing hypothesis does not hold in some situations and that 'there can be representation and storage in memory of unattended novel stimuli, something frequently claimed but not convincingly demonstrated in the past'. He also mentions the possibility that because many features of language are too subtle and abstract to notice, global rather than specific attention to L2 input might be sufficient in their case. But, similar to N. Ellis (2002*a*, *b*, 2005*a*), he argues that in certain cases there are no exceptions to the requirement of attentional focus. Typical examples include cases when due to existing L1–L2 differences it is necessary to attend to new kinds of information or to suppress the automatic processing of other information. Schmidt concludes this discussion thus:

> The question of whether all learning from input requires attention to that input remains problematic, and conceptual issues and methodological problems have combined to make a definitive answer illusive, even after a century of psychological experimentation. If the issue is seen as one of intention or the voluntary orientation of attention onto stimuli, the answer seems to be that intention is not a general requirement. However, because goals and motivation are such important determinants of the focus on attention, paying deliberate attention to less salient or redundant aspects of L2 input may be a practical necessity. (p. 29)

In conclusion, while we cannot exclude cases where we learn language aspects that are not specifically attended to, it is universally accepted that specifically attending to aspects of the language input enhances the effectiveness of learning. Thus, as argued earlier, there is an undeniable positive correlation between consciousness and learning. In Schmidt's (2001: 3) words, 'There is no doubt that attended learning is far superior, and for all practical purposes, attention is necessary for all aspects of L2 learning.' This recognition has led over the past 15 years to the development of a number of different language teaching approaches that include an explicit component such as consciousness raising, input enhancement, processing instruction, focus on form, and the principled communicative approach. We will look at these in Ch. 7.

The explicit–implicit interface in SLA

The process of mastering a second language is undoubtedly a complex one, involving the dynamic interplay of many components. The field of SLA research has come a long way since the early and relatively unarticulated proposals by Krashen (1982). The theories described in this and the previous chapter outline a picture in which some powerful broad processes are at work during language learning, but it is clear that the secret lies in the details because it is the unique interaction of the various processes and conditions that shapes the individual progression pattern of L2 learners. Admittedly, we are still a long way from being able to explain, let alone predict, individual learning trajectories with precision, and we do not even know for certain the extent to which such predictions are possible—emergentism and dynamic systems theory would suggest that there is a definite limit to forecasting the details of a complex system such as SLA.

In this final section of our exploration of the psychological processes in language acquisition, I will sum up where we are currently and where we are going in SLA research. Although, as we saw in the last chapter, L1 acquisition is driven by implicit learning processes, when it comes to SLA, scholars are undivided in proposing that any realistic account of the process needs to include some sort of an integration of explicit and implicit learning and declarative and procedural knowledge/memory. So, the key issue in SLA is the explicit–implicit interface and this summary is centred around the main facets of this matter.

As we saw earlier, the first prominent appearance of the interface issue in applied linguistics was triggered by Krashen's (1982) uncompromising non-interface position, which was followed by an extensive debate amongst scholars representing different views on the explicit–implicit transition. With hindsight we can admit that contrasting the non-, weak, and strong interface positions had only limited use in furthering the field because a great deal of the debate remained at a very general—philosophical and terminological—level. Thus, although these arguments did create an interest in the matter and certainly motivated further research, what the field really needed was specific proposals about the nature of the mechanisms and processes that underlay the language learning enterprise. The last decade has seen a real breakthrough in SLA research in outlining potentially relevant implicit and explicit learning mechanisms; although most of them were originally proposed for L1 acquisition, SLA researchers have initiated a research programme with a real momentum to explore the dynamic interactions of the relevant processes and factors in L2 learning. In the following section I review these developments, focusing on three main themes: (1) the implicit learning enigma and the ambiguous nature of incidental learning; (2) the co-operation of explicit and implicit learning; and (3) how to make the most of explicit learning.

The implicit learning enigma

The 'implicit learning enigma' is succinctly summarized by DeKeyser and Juffs (2005: 441) as follows: 'Nobody doubts that implicitly acquired procedural knowledge would be useful; the main question is to what extent it exists.' There are many highly proficient L2 speakers who have mastered an L2 in a formal educational training programme and are aware of a great deal of the testable structural regularities of the L2 system, and yet even these learners do not consciously recall and apply all the various rules of pedagogic grammar in their spontaneous communication, which underscores the significance of implicitly learnt knowledge in communicative L2 use. In Hulstijn's (2007*b*: 787–8) words:

There are forms of cognition from which we can form conscious, explicit, knowledge. Linguists and psycholinguists have uncovered, empirically investigated, and documented an impressive amount of regularities in the knowledge and online processing of language. At school, in mother tongue and foreign-language classes, many students learn some of these regularities, couched in the terms of pedagogic grammars (e.g. 'Say a and an when the following word begins with a consonant or vowel, respectively'). However, adult native speakers do not consciously apply such rules when they speak or listen to others. It is safe to conclude that...fluent language use does not involve the rapid, serial application of explicit rules. Fluency emanates from a form of implicit cognition that is not open to conscious inspection.

Although there are exceptions when we do fill a gap by running a rule through our mind quickly (see below), the main trend is unambiguous: fluent speech is largely automatized in the sense that it draws on implicit language knowledge. In addition, fluency is not the only manifestation of implicit learning. Learners with sufficient experience with the L2 are aware of frequency effects of the language input—for example, they develop a sense of what is common or, more interestingly, what is rare; they also become competent using formulaic language and collocations, many (if not most) of which are not learnt explicitly. In sum, it is an undeniable fact that L2 proficiency involves a great deal of implicit knowledge.

The puzzle is, however, where this implicit knowledge comes from. We know where it comes from in our first language: from the implicit, usage-based processes that characterize infants' mother-tongue learning (with or without some innate basis, depending on the scholars' theoretical stance). The problem is that when we look at SLA, the processes that seem to work so effectively and effortlessly for infants (e.g. probabilistic learning) do not seem to exist, or if they do, they have a rather limited impact. And looking at this issue from the other end, learning mechanisms that we do commonly observe in second language learning seem to be completely absent in L1 acquisition and do not seem to be related to implicit learning. Thus, whether we like it or not, we cannot deny the truth of DeKeyser and Juffs's (2005: 444) conclusion: 'For classroom learners...or for adults, implicit learning is very limited; in the former case because of grossly insufficient time/input, for the latter because of restrictions on their implicit learning capacities.'

In the above quote, DeKeyser and Juffs (2005) mention two key factors that work against implicit learning: the issues of time and age. Indeed, successful implicit L2 learning may take an extremely long time through exposure to a very large amount of L2 input (Hulstijn 2002a), and even if we are fortunate to have an abundance of natural input, the final outcome may not be native-like (as is the case with many immersion students; see Ch. 7). Furthermore, DeKeyser and Juffs highlight the commonly held view that the inhibition of the effectiveness of implicit learning capacity is related somehow to the learner's chronological age. This assumption was supported by Paradis (2004) and Ullman (2005), who reviewed neuroimaging evidence that indicates that late L2 speakers rely more on declarative-memory-based processes and less on implicit linguistic knowledge. We will revisit these issues in more detail in Ch. 6 when discussing age effects on language acquisition.

Thus, implicit learning poses a real enigma in SLA: we know that it is there somewhere, because we can see its outcomes, but it is elusive and it does not seem to work very well for most people. Before we make an attempt to explore this puzzle any further, let us briefly look at how the implicit enigma is manifested in 'incidental learning', a process that is often taken as a synonym for implicit learning in SLA contexts.

The ambiguous nature of incidental learning

We saw earlier that incidental learning is often regarded as implicit when contrasted with intentional learning. Intentional learning refers to specific instructional tasks in which students are told that they would be tested at the end, whereas in incidental learning students engage in meaning-focused language use such as reading a book and pick up language as a spin-off of this task engagement. (For reviews, see Hulstijn 2003; Rieder 2003.) This might lead us to conclude that incidental language learning in general refers to the natural mastery of language through using it meaningfully, but this generalization is not the case for two reasons. First, the term has almost exclusively been used for receptive tasks (i.e. reading and listening) and did not include meaning-focused communicative oral practice; second, the term has almost always been used for vocabulary learning only.

I have argued earlier that the key process underlying vocabulary learning, form–meaning pairing, is an inherently explicit activity, because it produces explicit/declarative vocabulary knowledge (in the sense that it can be searched and recalled on demand). However, within this explicit learning domain, scholars have identified two alternative avenues of learning that differ strongly in the degree of their explicitness: the conscious memorization of vocabulary and the effortless acquisition of lexis as part of a task where our attention is meaning-focused. The term 'incidental learning' has been introduced to refer to this latter process, that is, to the non-explicit end of the vocabulary learning continuum. This explains its ambiguous nature: it refers to the implicit-like features of an explicit process, which is well reflected in Robinson's (2003: 641) characterization: 'Undoubtedly, while processing oral L2 input for meaning, as in naturalistic or immersion environments and during L2 reading, learners do unintentionally attend to, notice, and learn many vocabulary or grammatical and pragmatic features of the L2 (incidental learning).' It is admittedly easy to get confused here (e.g. what are we to make of 'unintentional noticing'?), and therefore we should not be surprised that we find a mixture of somewhat different meanings of the term in the literature.

Of course, if we examine vocabulary learning more closely, we find that it is a complex process that goes beyond what is typically simplified as 'form–meaning pairing'. Learning the depth and breadth of vocabulary are, for example, two separate aspects, and it also makes a huge difference whether we restrict vocabulary acquisition to learning the meaning of single words only (as is typically done) or whether we also include a wider range of lexical units such as expressions, idioms, collocations, and other types of formulaic sequences with conventionalized meaning. It could be argued that a broader, more elaborate conceptualization of vocabulary learning would involve salient implicit aspects (such as acquiring the common collocational contexts of lexical items), which might be seen as a justification for using 'incidental learning' in an implicit sense. However, once we embark on such a conceptual elaboration, it might be advisable to leave the rather crude and ambiguous incidental–intentional distinction behind and use the psychologically more valid implicit–explicit dichotomy. A good example of this latter approach is N. Ellis's (1994*a*) overview of the field, whose title reflects the intricate situation well: 'Vocabulary acquisition: The implicit ins and outs of explicit cognitive mediation.'

In a recent review of the L2 vocabulary learning literature, Schmitt (2008) summarized the main results of studies utilizing incidental learning. He found that although worthwhile vocabulary learning does occur from reading (the most common form of incidental learning), the 'pickup rate is relatively low, and it seems to be difficult to gain a productive level of mastery from just exposure'. Thus, he concluded that 'it is probably best not to rely upon incidental learning as the primary source of learning for new words. Rather, incidental learning seems to be better at enhancing knowledge of words which have already been met' (p. 348).

What Schmitt means by 'words which have already been met' at the end of this quote is an initial explicit encounter with the particular lexical unit, and therefore his conclusion suggests, in effect, that even when we talk about the 'semi-implicit' process of incidental learning, the best results can be achieved if we combine it with explicit learning. This conclusion is congruent with my general thesis so far and leads us to the next section that examines the possible co-operation of explicit and implicit learning.

The co-operation of explicit and implicit learning

Metalinguistic information connects with implicit learning, and they meet and interact in processing. It is a dynamic interface.
(N. Ellis 2005*a*: 325)

Given the inhibited function of implicit learning mechanisms in SLA, how can so many of us achieve a very high level of L2 proficiency, including native-like fluency? The answer is that we tend to be very good explicit learners and the explicit learning mechanisms co-operate somehow with the imperfect implicit system, thereby enhancing its functioning. The evidence we have today points to the general conclusion that we cannot develop sufficient implicit knowledge in an L2 without the effective functioning of our explicit learning mechanisms. This does not necessarily mean that explicit learning creates implicit knowledge or that the explicit knowledge is simply converted into an implicit currency. Rather, the key to L2 learning efficiency is the successful *co-operation* of the explicit and implicit learning systems. Crowell (2004) presents neurobiological evidence that the two systems (centred in the basal ganglia and the hippocampus) are interconnected and operate in a parallel manner, which outlines the neurobiological basis of this co-operation. Let us have a look at six different ways by which explicit learning mechanisms can support implicit L2 acquisition: (1) explicit registration of linguistic information allows implicit fine-tuning; (2) explicit practice creates implicit learning opportunities; (3) explicit knowledge channels implicit learning; (4) explicit rote learning can provide material for implicit processing; (5) explicit knowledge fills the gaps in implicit knowledge; (6) explicit learning increases the overall level of accuracy in implicit knowledge.

Explicit registration of linguistic information allows implicit fine-tuning

Implicit language learning can be seen as the consolidation, integration, and fine-tuning of linguistic information in the system, for example through chunking (see Ch. 7), tallying (i.e. computing frequency distributions), or detecting other underlying patterns. However, as we have seen earlier, most scholars believe that this process can only take off if the linguistic stimulus has been explicitly registered as a language representation—see for example, N. Ellis (2002*a*, 2007*c*). According to the noticing hypothesis, this can only take place if we consciously notice the particular stimulus.

Explicit practice creates implicit learning opportunities

Hulstijn (2002*a*) argues that because implicit learning is an unstoppable information processing mechanism, it will automatically accompany any explicit language practice the learners are engaged in during listening, reading, speaking, and writing activities. In this way, 'Learners who have chosen to try to master an L2 with the help of grammar rules, and are thus engaged in processing primary linguistic information...cannot prevent a process of implicit learning taking place simultaneously' (p. 208). Chapter 7 will present several explicit techniques that can promote implicit learning.

Explicit knowledge channels implicit learning

Not only does explicit practice provide implicit learning opportunities, but N. Ellis (2005*a*) adds that explicit, metalinguistic information can also serve as a powerful constraint upon the processing of subsequent forms, priming their conscious interpretations. That is, metaphorically speaking, explicit knowledge can create a conscious channel for the unconscious flow of implicit processing. Paradis (2004: 52–3) sees this indirect explicit-to-implicit chain that results in focused practice thus:

rule presentation and negative feedback contribute to the development of metalinguistic knowledge, which may in turn monitor the output of linguistic competence, thus allowing conscious self-correction, which results in further practice of the desired form. The repeated practicing of the target form may eventually lead to the internalization of the implicit computational procedures that result in the automatic comprehension and production of that form. It is not the instruction and resulting knowledge that affect competence, but the extra practice provided by the use of the corrected form.

Explicit rote learning can provide material for implicit processing

We saw at the beginning of this chapter that the study of implicit learning was instigated by a series of experiments by Reber (1967) in which people memorized meaningless letter strings that were generated by a simple pattern and then classified novel strings as following the same system of patterns or not. Evidence for implicit learning was provided by the better-than-chance classification results and the fact that the participants were unable to describe the rules in subsequent verbal reports. If we consider these experiments more closely, although they do point to the existence of implicit learning, this learning did not take place on its own but in tandem with the initial explicit memorization task. So, strictly speaking, Reber did not find evidence for implicit learning but for a successful combination of explicit and implicit learning.

Rote learning has been a traditionally explored activity in language education programmes worldwide, and Reber's (1967) experiments (as well as the many replications of these artificial grammar learning tasks) show that initially memorized knowledge can give rise to implicit processing and subsequent implicit knowledge. Unfortunately, I am not aware of any empirically validated knowledge about the optimal characteristics of the type and size of language to be memorized. (We will come back to discussing practical questions in Ch. 7.)

Explicit knowledge fills the gaps in implicit knowledge

It is a well-known fact that some language learners—according to DeKeyser and Juffs (2005), particularly the ones with high language aptitude and especially with a substantial working-memory capacity—are able to draw on explicit knowledge rather easily even during spontaneous communication to fill the gaps in their implicit/automatized language knowledge. Drawing on neuroimaging findings on practice-related changes in functional brain anatomy (e.g. Raichle *et al.* 1994), Paradis (2004) explains that when we have parallel explicit and implicit L2 knowledge, the faster implicit system tends to be used, which is in accordance with the competition view between parallel memory systems proposed, for example, by Poldrack and Packard (2003). However, if the implicit system is incomplete or impaired, the learner can consciously revert to the explicit system, thereby compensating for the existing gaps by using metalinguistic knowledge.

Paradis (2004) also highlights an interesting study by Hirschman (2000), in which children with a developmental language disorder—specific language impairment (SLI), which is characterized by deficiency in the use of complex sentences—were given metalinguistic training for over a year, resulting in an increase in the use of complex sentences to at least normal levels in the experimental groups. Thus, metalinguistic training could overcome even neurological deficits by 'providing a "metalinguistic bridge" via which information can bypass the damaged area' (Hirschman 2000: 251).

Explicit learning increases the overall level of accuracy
in implicit knowledge

This point is related to the previous one in that it concerns the capacity of explicit learning of metalinguistic knowledge to compensate for the shortcoming of implicit language learning, but it may be worth discussing it separately because the particular shortcoming—insufficient accuracy—does not concern any specific gaps but rather a whole facet of language proficiency. It has been a well-established finding for at least two decades that learners who acquire the L2 in ways that do not emphasize metalinguistic awareness (e.g. picking up the L2 in the host environment without formal instruction or studying in an L2 immersion school) will continue to have difficulty with basic structures, particularly with those that are neither salient nor have any significant communicative value (see Ch. 7; for a detailed analysis of the factors that make linguistic forms fall short of intake, see N. Ellis 2006*b*) and thus are likely to reach a fossilized end-state that is far short of native-like ability, particularly in terms of accuracy (N. Ellis 2008). In other words, implicit learning by itself tends not to generate flawless L2 competence, a point phrased by Lightbown and Spada (2006: 176):

> While there is good evidence that learners make considerable progress in both comprehension and production in comprehension-based programmes, we do not find support for the hypothesis that language acquisition will take care of itself if second language learners simply focus on meaning in comprehensible input. Comprehension-based approaches are most successful when they include guided attention to language features as a component of instruction.

Their recommendation, therefore, is to incorporate form-focused elements in any language teaching programme. Schmidt (2001) also highlights the learner's role in striving for accuracy by means of self-regulating attention. As he argues, because so many features of L2 input are infrequent, perceptually non-salient, and communicatively redundant, successful mastery of these features requires intentionally focused attention. Accordingly, he concludes, language learners who take a 'passive approach to learning, waiting patiently and depending on involuntary attentional processes to trigger automatic noticing, are likely to be slow and unsuccessful learners' (p. 24). Therefore, language teaching programmes need to include a featured awareness-raising component, highlighting the importance of 'metacognitive control strategies', which is part of self-motivation (Dörnyei 2001a). Of course, as in so many other areas, the secret lies in the details, that is, in finding the right balance of explicit–implicit treatment and in providing the right type of form-focused (i.e. metalinguistic) and motivational (i.e. metacognitive) training. This will be a focal issue in the discussion of instructed SLA in Ch. 7.

Factors affecting the explicit–implicit co-operation

We have seen above that there are several ways by which explicit and implicit learning methods can be combined to good effect. It is not difficult to predict that one of the main directions in SLA research over the next decade will involve the examination of the optimal balance and sequence of the explicit and implicit components. This optimal balance is likely to vary according to the characteristics of the learners, the learning situation, and the L2 area focused on. More specifically, scholars have suggested that the positive impact of the explicit learning component is contingent on the following factors (see DeKeyser and Juffs 2005; N. Ellis 2005a; R. Ellis 2005; Hulstijn 2002a; 2005; Lightbown and Spada 2006):

- learner characteristics (the learner's age, metalinguistic sophistication, prior educational experience, motivation, cognitive style, and language aptitude, especially working memory capacity; see Chs. 5 and 6);
- L2-L1 similarities and differences;
- characteristics of the target L2 structure/area (e.g. complexity, prototypicality, regularity, form- or meaning-based nature; see Ch. 7);
- characteristics of the available/accessible natural L2 input (e.g. overall amount and the frequency and salience with which the target L2 structures are represented in it; see Ch. 7);
- the length of time available for the learning process.

Thus, we cannot expect simple solutions or patterns, particularly in the light of the fact that these factors interact with each other. It is obvious that a great deal of further research is needed in these areas—DeKeyser (2001), for example points out that virtually no empirical research exists on the learning conditions that are conducive to automatization.

Summary

This chapter began with a discussion of consciousness and attention, and all the subsequent learning theories presented were related to these two issues. Following this, in the first part of the chapter, I provided an overview of the various facets of the declarative–procedural dichotomy. Scholars agree that communicatively useful L2 proficiency needs to be highly automatized and therefore it needs to be stored in some implicit form. Therefore, the main theoretical question addressed in the second part of the chapter concerned how such implicit L2 knowledge can be achieved. The most obvious avenue towards implicit L2 knowledge would be through implicit language learning—after all, this is the primary channel of first language acquisition for infants. The problem is, however, that when it comes to implicit language learning, we face a real enigma: there are obvious indications that it does have a role in SLA, but this role seems to be seriously limited and therefore implicit learning in itself does not deliver high-level L2 proficiency in the majority of cases. Instead, as scholars and practitioners would generally agree, the most effective path towards mastering an L2 is through a combination of explicit and implicit learning. DeKeyser and Juffs (2005: 442) sum this up very clearly:

> There is now converging evidence from studies in the laboratory, the classroom, and the natural L2 environment that the best way to develop implicit/procedural/automatized knowledge may not be to try to provide it directly, but instead to foster optimal conditions for its acquisition in the long run, and that means providing an explicit jump start.

The notion of 'incidental learning' also presented a puzzling situation. In L2 vocabulary studies this is often treated as the equivalent of implicit learning, even though it is not implicit in several respects. Yes, the parallel with implicit learning is unmistakable: if we master grammatical regularities without explicit teaching, by simply being exposed to meaning-focused L2 input, this would be an example of acquiring implicit grammar knowledge; however, the curious situation is that if the same thing happens to vocabulary, the resulting lexical knowledge is explicit in nature and therefore the process cannot really be described as implicit, which is why the new term 'incidental' was introduced for this specific process. This draws attention to the fundamental difference between the mastery of rules and the mastery of form–meaning pairing, and this area warrants further theoretical study in the future.

In sum, although our understanding of the psychological basis of SLA is far from being clear, one finding has emerged consistently in a number of different areas, namely that effective L2 learning needs to include an explicit component. It was reassuring to find that other recent reviewers of the field have come to the same conclusion; for example, N. Ellis (2005a: 307) stated that 'the weight of the subsequent findings demonstrates that language acquisition can be speeded by explicit instruction' and DeKeyser and Juffs (2005: 445) emphasized that 'the focus of the debate in applied linguistics should not be on the usefulness of implicit versus explicit learning or knowledge, but on ways to maximize explicit learning and the automatization of its product'.

Thus, we can set some obvious broad objectives for future SLA research, but the details still need to be worked out. The kinds of question that will need to be answered are not categorical such as the debate about the superiority of a non-, a weak, or a strong interface between explicit and implicit L2 knowledge, but much more fine-grained. This is well illustrated by the issues raised, for example, by Robinson (2003: 641):

> [I]s it more effective to proactively instruct learners in targeted features prior to communicative activities, via a brief rule explanation or metalinguistic summary (instructed learning)? Or is it better to adopt less communicatively intrusive techniques for focusing attention on form, by giving learners instructions to process for meaning (e.g. to read a news article in preparation for a debate) while drawing their attention, through underlining or highlighting, to targeted forms in the text (enhanced learning)?

The key questions Lightbown and Spada (2006: 180) list for the future are of a very similar type:

> How can classroom instruction provide the right balance of meaning-based and form-focused instruction? Which features of language will respond best to form-focused instruction, and which will be acquired without explicit focus if learners have adequate access to the language? Which learners will respond well to metalinguistic information and which will require some other way of focusing attention on language form? When is it best to draw learners' attention to form—before, after, or during communicative practice? How should corrective feedback be offered and when should learners be allowed to focus their attention on the content of their utterances?

In order to be able to answer questions such as these we need to make the psychological focus of SLA research sharper and more geared to examining the fine-grained details of the explicit–implicit interface. As mentioned above, for example, DeKeyser (2001) points out that there is very limited empirical research specifically examining automatization of L2 skills and there is also little research specifically examining the various options of co-operation between explicit and implicit learning processes. One reason for the insufficient amount of relevant research on implicit and explicit learning is, according to R. Ellis (2005), the lack of valid measures of L2 implicit and explicit knowledge. Developing a range of such measures is an obvious starting point and the instruments designed in Ellis's study are forward-pointing. Hulstijn's (2005: 137) summary fully supports this emphasis:

> For the moment, it appears that we should first be concerned with the empirical side of implicit and explicit learning and knowledge.... R. Ellis (2005) presents concrete proposals of how to operationalize implicit and explicit knowledge by means of various tests. We might disagree with his operationalizations or with his interpretation of the outcome of his factor analyses, but, regardless of future empirical or theoretical work, Ellis's paper signals a crucial moment in rendering theories of implicit and explicit knowledge and learning testable. It is not unlikely that the SLA

field will now enter a phase marked by questions of validity, reminiscent of the debate concerning the definition and testing of the notion of intelligence. We could soon witness discussions of construct-definition claims such as 'Implicit knowledge of a L2 is what task X measures.' I would welcome such discussions as part and parcel of normal science.

5

The learner in the language learning process I: the dynamic interplay of learner characteristics and the learning environment

A central problem of biology, not only for biological scientists but for the general public, is the question of the origin of similarities and differences between individual organisms. Why are some short and others tall, some fat and others thin, some prolific setters of seed and some nearly sterile, some clever and others dull, some successful and others failures? Every individual organism begins life as a single cell, a seed or fertilized egg, that is neither tall nor short, neither clever nor dull. Through a series of cell divisions, differentiations, and movements of tissues, an entire organism is formed that has a front and a back, an inside and an outside, and a collection of organs that interact with each other in a complex way. Changes in size, shape, and function occur continually throughout life until the moment of death.
(Lewontin 2000: 4)

People differ from each other in virtually every one of their attributes and every way of functioning. In other words, individual variation occurs around every central tendency in humans. In fact, one of the most important ways in which the social sciences differ from the natural sciences is exactly this human variability. The molecules of a cell, if treated identically, will always respond identically, whereas human behaviour—even that of identical twins—may vary significantly in response to a certain stimulus. Schumann (2004b) explains that this variation is already reflected in our brains: in spite of the usual treatment of neural structure in psychology as homogeneous and uniform, neurobiological research shows that brains are as unique as faces, both at the micro-level of neural structure and at the gross level of sulci and gyri. Schumann suggests that this neurobiological differentiation is responsible to a large extent for interindividual variation in mental and physical behaviour.

Interestingly, one of the very few mental operations in which people display a remarkable homogeneity concerns language, more specifically the acquisition of our L1. As pointed out in Ch. 2, virtually everybody without any language impairment will master their mother tongue at a native-speaker level regardless of personal abilities or environmental circumstances. However, as Shore (1995) argues, even this seeming homogeneity needs to be qualified, because there are obvious individual differences in the qualitative routes of language development and it is only the final outcome that appears to be relatively uniform. For example, Fenstermacher and Saudino (2006) have highlighted the fact that infants' early imitative behaviour—which is considered by many as one of the foundations of mother-tongue acquisition—demonstrates marked variability. We should also realize that the common statement that L1 acquisition is relatively homogeneous with regard to its final outcome largely concerns grammatical accuracy only because other areas of language competence—such as vocabulary size or pragmatic skills—display considerable interindividual differences.

While L1 acquisition is relatively free of substantial individual variation, the opposite is true of the learning of an L2. Here we can see dramatic person-to-person disparity in both the quality and the quantity of the attained L2 knowledge and skills. For this reason, the study of various learner characteristics—usually called *individual differences* (IDs)—such as language aptitude, motivation, and learning styles, have been prominent areas of applied linguistic investigations for the past 30 years. In 2005, I conducted a book-sized review of ID research in the L2 field (Dörnyei 2005), and although many people saw this book as challenging, or even provocative in places, it actually adopted a rather conservative stance: it intentionally set out to be 'a standard ID book, following the tradition of L2 scholars—particularly that of Peter Skehan and Peter Robinson—working in the individual differences paradigm' (p. xii), and although I concluded in the book that most IDs in the L2 field needed theoretical restructuring, I never questioned the existence of IDs in general or the suitability of addressing learner-based variation within an ID framework.

In the light of the growing recognition of the process-oriented and situated nature of IDs in general, I feel now that mere reforms may not be enough to bring the ID paradigm up to date. In this chapter, therefore, I will suggest that we need to take a radically new approach in order to understand the complexity of learner-based performance variation; I will propose that the learner's contribution to the learning process can be best understood within a dynamic systems theory paradigm. (For a review of DST, see Ch. 3.) As a preliminary, let me emphasize that when I argue that the concept of 'individual differences' may have outlived its time, I do not wish to imply that the significant correlational results between IDs and learning achievement (such as the massive correlations typically observed between language aptitude and L2 proficiency) that secured such a prominent place for ID research within the social sciences are invalid. They did (and still do) reflect some robust tendencies, but using the ID paradigm, I believe, is unlikely to get us much further in uncovering the true nature of these trends.

Thus, I start this chapter by describing what I call the 'individual differences myth' and the main problems with it. Then I discuss why dynamic systems theory can help us to overcome the various obstacles in examining learner characteristics. Finally, I propose a dynamic tripartite framework consisting of three interacting systems—cognitive, motivational, and emotional—that might be used to capture the variance in learner variation. In doing so, and in line with the rest of this book, I will focus on the main underlying processes and principles rather than the actual review of relevant ID research. Thus, I will not try to deal with all the various individual difference variables comprehensively in this chapter, but rather my focus will be on foregrounding a dynamic view of learner factors. For detailed summaries of the different strands of ID research, please refer to my book *The Psychology of the Language Learner* (Dörnyei 2005) and the references in it, as well as two recent volumes addressing key ID areas, by Robinson (forthcoming) on language aptitude and by Dörnyei and Ushioda (2009) on motivation.

The 'individual differences' paradigm: the myth and the problems

As summarized by Dörnyei (2005), ever since the early days of its existence the field of psychology has been trying to achieve two different and somewhat contradictory objectives: to understand the *general principles* of the human mind and to explore the *uniqueness* of the individual mind. The latter direction has formed an independent subdiscipline within the field that has traditionally been termed 'differential psychology' but recently more frequently referred to as 'individual difference research'. As the term suggests, *individual differences* (IDs) are characteristics or traits in respect of which individuals may be shown to differ from each other. That such human variation exists is not a question; we can observe it in various behavioural attributes, including global dimensions of human cognitive ability, interest, and personality, as well as more specific attributes related to our everyday functioning in the world (Lubinski and Webb 2003). The question is how we conceptualize the sources of this variation and the dynamic interaction amongst them.

Traditionally, IDs have been defined in the broadest sense as any attribute or personal characteristic that marks a person as a distinct and unique human being. While this makes sense, it is also clear that in order to avoid too large a list of variables that would qualify as IDs we need to set some further restrictions. Therefore, all scientific definitions of IDs assume the relevance of *stability*: differential psychology emphasizes individual variation from person to person only to the extent that those individualizing features exhibit continuity over time (De Raad 2000). Yet, even with this restriction the kinds and number of ways an individual can be different are extensive due to the innumerable interactions between heredity and environment that occur throughout one's lifespan. Therefore, individual difference research does not focus on mere idiosyncrasies, even when these are stable ones, but rather on broader dimensions that are applicable to everyone and that discriminate among people (Snow, Corno, and Jackson 1996). Thus, ID constructs refer to dimensions of enduring personal characteristics—or traits—that are assumed to apply to everybody and on which people differ by degree.

Individual differences have been well established in SLA research as a relatively straightforward concept: ID factors concern background learner variables that modify the general acquisitional processes. In many ways, they are typically thought of as the systematic part of the background 'noise' in SLA. Broadly speaking, *motivation* was seen to concern the affective characteristics of the learner, referring to the direction and magnitude of learning behaviour in terms of the learner's choice, intensity, and duration of learning. *Language aptitude* determined the cognitive dimension, referring to the capacity and quality of learning. *Learning styles* were seen to refer to the manner of learning, and *learning strategies* were somewhere in between motivation and learning styles by referring to the learner's proactiveness in selecting specific made-to-measure learning routes. Thus, the composite of these variables was seen to answer *why, how long, how hard, how well, how proactively*, and *in what way* the learner engages in the learning process.

What is wrong with this conceptualization of individual difference factors? It appears to be logical, comprehensive, and intuitively convincing. Indeed, as N. Ellis (2007*b*: 23) expressively put it, 'Cognitive factors such as attention, working memory, implicit categorization and tallying, interference, consciousness and explicit learning are the heart of SLA, as social, affective, and cultural motivations are its soul'. Thus, IDs are viewed as important mediating variables in the SLA process, explaining a significant proportion of learner variation in L2 attainment and performance. They act almost like filters or, to use another metaphor, ingredients of a chemical substance in which SLA burgeons. You describe the parameters of the filter/substance and you can make predictions about the rate of progress of learning.

This idyllic picture rests on at least four assumptions: (1) IDs exist in the sense that we can identify, define, and operationalize them in a rigorous scientific manner; (2) IDs are relatively stable attributes; (3) different IDs form relatively monolithic components that concern different aspects of human functioning and that are therefore only moderately related to each other; and (4) IDs are learner-internal, and thus relatively independent from the external factors of the environment. As we will see below, serious issues can be raised about each of these four assumptions.

Problems with the traditional conceptualization of ID factors

Let us start with some initial issues with the conceptualization of the five best-known ID factors in SLA—language aptitude, motivation, learning/cognitive styles, learning strategies, and anxiety—based on the reviews in Dörnyei (2005, 2006*a*).

- *Language aptitude*: although the composite measures yielded by language aptitude batteries consistently explain a significant amount of variance in learning achievement measures, the concept of 'language aptitude' has been increasingly seen as too broad an umbrella term, one that refers to an unspecified mixture of cognitive variables. For this reason, scholars investigating specific cognitive abilities, such as working memory (e.g. Miyake and Friedman 1998) or word recognition (e.g. Dufva and Voeten 1999), have tended to avoid using the term. Recent research (e.g. by Robinson 2007) has also shown that language aptitude is best viewed in a situated manner, taking in account the dynamic interplay between aptitude and context.

- *Motivation* is typically treated as an 'affective' variable and is thus contrasted with the cognitive variable of language aptitude. However, almost all influential contemporary motivation theories in psychology are cognitive in nature and affective (i.e. emotional) issues hardly ever feature on motivation research agendas. If this is so, how is motivation different from 'language aptitude', which is the collective term used to refer to cognitive factors? Furthermore, not unlike aptitude research, several recent studies have started to reconceptualize motivation as a process-oriented and situated construct that shows regular fluctuation, which is in contrast with the everyday meaning of motivation as a static attribute that is so often used by laypeople and scholars alike.

- *Learning styles:* the main problem with learning styles (or cognitive styles) is that even though the various style dimensions proposed in the literature seem to have an intuitive appeal, the concept of learning/cognitive styles has eluded any rigorous scientific definition. The picture that emerges in both the cognitive psychological and the SLA literature is that learning styles are 'halfway' products: they refer to learning mode preferences, but these can be of varying degree; they are related to learning strategies but are somewhat different from them as they fall midway between innate abilities and strategies; they appear to be situation-independent but they are not entirely free of situational influences; and some style dimensions (e.g. extroversion/introversion) are also listed as major components of personality. Indeed, learning styles appear to have very soft boundaries, making the category rather open-ended, regardless of the specific perspective we approach it from. For this reason, several scholars have abandoned using the term altogether.

- *Learning strategies* as such are not ID factors even in the traditional sense because rather than being learner attributes, they refer to idiosyncratic self-regulated behaviour, and a particular learning behaviour can be strategic for one learner and non-strategic for another. In order to tap into the stable trait underlying strategic learning, we need to shift our focus from the outcome to the learner's *self-regulating capacity*, that is, the extent of the learner's proactiveness.

- *Anxiety* is a curious variable because although its conceptualization is straightforward, there is a general uncertainty about the broader categorization of the concept: in some theories it refers to a motivational component (it is often included in motivation constructs in addition to, or as part of, self-confidence), in some others to a personality trait (it has been found to be the primary personality trait with the strongest correlation with student performance; see Matthews *et al.* 2000), and it is also often mentioned as one of the basic emotions—see MacIntyre (2002).

Problems with the traditional selection of ID factors

The five ID factors above have traditionally been regarded as the most important ones in SLA, but we must realize that this selection itself is also part of the 'individual differences myth' because there are at least three other personality facets—*emotions, interests*, and *general knowledge*—that would arguably qualify for being ID factors more than some of the traditional categories.

- *Emotions* such as fear, anger, distress, and joy are a salient part of our everyday lives, affecting both our thinking and our behaviours, yet they have been by and large neglected in L2 individual difference research (with the exception of anxiety; see MacIntyre 2002). This is all the more curious as the process of learning an L2 is known to be emotionally highly loaded. There are at least two main reasons for this omission. First, with the onset of the 'cognitive revolution' in psychology (from about the 1970s), emotions have been assigned a secondary role in psychological accounts, placing the emphasis on cognitive factors. Second, emotions are often thought of as transient states that do not qualify as trait-like ID factors. While it is true that feelings such as anger or fear are situation-dependent, Keltner and Ekman (2000) point out that (1) individual differences in emotion emerge in the first months of life; (2) they are quite stable during a person's development; and (3) the life histories of individuals prone to different emotions differ profoundly. Indeed, in an analysis of the various levels of emotions, Rosenberg (1998) argues that humans display stable predispositions towards certain types of emotional responding, and these 'affective traits' (as she calls them) constitute enduring aspects of our personalities. Such traits have also been referred to as 'temperamental traits', 'emotional biases', and 'trait emotional intelligence', and scholars are in general agreement that they exert a broad influence on behaviour, cognition, and motivation. This recognition motivated Dewaele's (2005: 377–8) spirited plea: 'I fervently believe that a stronger focus on physiological, psychological, affective, and emotional issues in SLA can provide crucial theoretical insights into L2 acquisition that are now missing.' In agreement with these considerations, I will come back to discussing the role of emotions in SLA later in this chapter when I propose an integrated framework of learner characteristics that include a prominent emotional dimension.
- *Interest* in the psychological literature is often used more broadly than, for example, the 'interest in foreign languages' category in Gardner's (1985) integrative motivation construct. It refers to a broad orientational dimension that has been found to be defined by six general interest themes: 'realistic'

(working with things and tools), 'investigative' (scientific pursuits), 'artistic' (aesthetic pursuits and self-expression), 'social' (contact with and helping people), 'enterprising' (buying, marketing, and selling), and 'conventional' (office practices and well-structured tasks) (Lubinski and Webb 2003). Some scholars have reduced these themes to two broad dimensions, 'people' versus 'things' and 'data' versus 'ideas', and the strength of the people/thing factor is evidenced by the fact that, as Lubinski and Webb (2003) describe, it displays some of the largest sex differences discovered by psychological science on a continuous dimension. Interests are heritable, are predictive of a broad spectrum of criteria in areas ranging from educational and vocational settings to activities in everyday life (hobbies and pastimes), and the concept appears to be theoretically more straightforward and temporarily more stable than several other ID factors.

- *General knowledge* or its L2 equivalent, L2 proficiency, refers to the amount of domain-specific knowledge that that person has acquired in the past. General knowledge has traditionally been included in models of intelligence; it is, for example, one of the key components of Cattell's well-known theory, referred to as 'crystallized intelligence' (g_c), forming the counterpart of 'fluid intelligence' (g_f), which is the domain-free reasoning, learning, and problem-solving aspect of intelligence. g_c is understood to result from the investment of fluid ability in broad educational experiences, that is, g_c is the result of applying g_f over time (Chamorro-Premuzic, Furnham, and Ackerman 2006). Because general knowledge has considerable predictive power in determining performance in school and the workplace—in fact, as Hunt (2005) summarizes, the highest correlates with performance measures have often been achieved by tests of crystallized intelligence—several IQ tests include some measurement of acquired information and learnt skills. The significance of domain knowledge has recently been recognized by its inclusion in, for example, Ackerman's influential PPIK model— Intelligence as Processes, Personality, Interests, and Knowledge. (See e.g. Ackerman and Kanfer 2004.) Interestingly, this framework also covers interest as defined above. In SLA, nobody would question that language performance is dependent of one's level of L2 proficiency, yet proficiency has not been considered a traditional ID factor. This is because it was not thought to be a trait, that is, a sufficiently stable part of the individual's personality structure. While this may be so, growing recognition that other established ID factors such as motivation are not stable over time either— and that even intelligence is learnt to a considerable degree—renders the exclusion of general knowledge somewhat arbitrary. (We will continue this discussion later when we look at the cognitive system in general.)

Two meanings of 'individual difference research'

The issues raised above indicate that the way traditional ID factors have been identified and defined is not consistent. However, at the heart of these inconsistencies lie some broader issues concerning IDs in general. Let us start examining these by looking at an anomaly that is hardly ever highlighted, yet that causes a great deal of misunderstanding, namely the fact that the term 'individual difference research' is used in two rather different meanings in the literature; one focuses on ID factors, the other looks at individual-level analysis in research.

Individual difference research as the study of IDs: the term 'individual difference research' used for describing the study of IDs is a misnomer in the sense that this research hardly ever concerns the individual proper. This research direction typically involves a quantitative, that is, group-based, research paradigm that focuses on variables along which people differ systematically. Ushioda (2009: 215) summarizes this very clearly: 'In essence, one might say that research on individual differences focuses not on differences between individuals, but on averages and aggregates that group together people who share certain characteristics, such as high intrinsic motivation or low self-efficacy.' It is interesting to note that originally this research direction had a different name in psychology—'differential psychology'—which provided a more accurate label.

Individual-level analysis: a very interesting recent trend in the social sciences, including applied linguistics, has been the call for more individual difference research in the sense of analysing individual cases rather than group-level data. Of course, the dichotomy of individual- versus group-level analysis has been salient in research methodology for several decades, with individual-level analysis usually falling under the category of qualitative research and group-level analysis under quantitative research. (See e.g. Dörnyei 2007b.) The unique feature of the new trend, however, is that it comes from scholars who would normally be aligned with the quantitative paradigm. This peculiarity is well reflected by the title of a position paper written by a group of distinguished cognitive- and neuropsychologists, Kosslyn *et al.* (2002): 'Bridging Psychology and Biology: The Analysis of Individuals in Groups'. This issue has already been addressed briefly at the end of Ch. 3 when I reviewed the various concerns with neuroimaging studies (under the heading 'Group versus individual level analysis'), because the controversial nature of group-based analysis becomes particularly prominent when neurobiological information about the brain is presented in a statistically averaged format, resulting in 'anatomical averaging'.

The problem with anatomical and any other type of statistical averaging is that it highlights a central tendency that may not be true of any particular person in the participant sample, and treats individual deviations from this as irrelevant noise. The key question is whether this noise is really negligible or whether some essential truths are revealed exactly by this noise. In biology, for example, minority patterns are often treated as highly significant—which is the basis of the detailed classification schemes of species—and in medicine, too, a finding that, say, 3 per cent of the population have two hearts, would not be considered irrelevant noise just because 97 per cent have one.

The other side of the coin is, though, that if we find in social psychology that 90 per cent of the responses to a questionnaire indicate prejudices against, say, an ethnic group, we would rightly claim that the observed population is racist as a whole, which would perhaps (but not necessarily) justify ignoring the responses coming from the remaining 10 per cent (i.e. treating them as noise). So, we can conclude that there are two coexisting yet contrasting scientific approaches with regard to the level of analysis—focusing on the central tendency versus paying increasing attention to the idiosyncratic deviations or 'noise'—and the new phenomenon of emphasizing individual-level analysis concerns a marked shift in areas where traditionally the former was the default towards highlighting the latter approach.

In Ch. 3, I described the new research paradigms of emergentism and dynamic systems theory. These approaches question, by definition, the assumed supremacy of any central tendencies or regularities; N. Ellis and Larsen-Freeman (2006: 564), for example, hold that 'What generalizations exist at the group level often fail at the individual level,' and these scholars further argue that from a dynamic systems perspective, individual variability should not be seen as merely noise but 'as a source of development as well as the specific moment in a developmental process'. This explains the call for an individual-level analysis in recent papers championing these modern research directions (e.g. de Bot, Lowie, and Verspoor 2007a; N. Ellis and Larsen-Freeman 2006; Larsen-Freeman 2006; van Geert and Steenbeek 2005b), thereby joining ranks with postmodernist researchers who have traditionally advocated individual-level approaches in applied linguistics. (For a discussion, see Dewaele 2005.) This converged position is well reflected in the conclusion of two leading experts on DST, van Geert and Steenbeek (2005a):

> It is our belief that a better understanding of the dynamics of the process of learning and teaching requires studies of socially situated individual processes, on the short-term time scale of a single lesson or scaffolding event as well as on the long-term time scale of the acquisition of skills and knowledge. (p. 127)

In cognitive neuroscience the prominence of individual-level analysis has been underscored by the recognition that there are parallel mental strategies or neural processes that can lead to the same outcome and, therefore, if we only consider pooled information gathered from participant samples, we could fail to detect the specific mechanisms that underlie mental functions. The realistic danger of this possibility was verified by Ganis, Thompson, and Kosslyn (2005) in an empirical study addressing this very issue. (See also Kosslyn *et al.* 2002; Thompson-Schill, Braver, and Jonides 2005; Parasuraman and Greenwood 2006.) By way of illustration, Kosslyn *et al.* (2002: 343) explained that 'individual differences in imagery are best understood in terms of a set of underlying processes, which are common to all people but which vary for any given individual'. In a similar vein, Thelen and Smith (1994) also argued that each human infant learns to reach for objects or learns to walk in its own distinct fashion, thus demonstrating the uniqueness of individual solutions to developmental challenges. Kosslyn *et al.*'s conclusion points to the need to combine the two approaches (which is reminiscent of the call for mixed methods approaches in recent research methodological texts; see Dörnyei 2007*b*):

> Neither group nor individual differences research alone is sufficient; researchers need to combine the two. Indeed, by combining the two, one may discover that the group results reflect the combination of several strategies, each of which draws on a different (or partially different) system. Thus, the group and individual differences findings mutually inform each other, with the synergy between them illuminating the complex relations between psychology and biology. (Kosslyn *et al.* 2002: 348)

Lack of stability and context-independence

> *The fact is that the effect of variables waxes and wanes. The many actors in the cast of language learning have different hours upon the stage, different prominences in different acts and scenes. The play evolves as goals and subgoals are set and met, strong motives once satisfied fade into history, forces gather then dissipate once the battle is done, a brief entrance can change fate from tragedy to farce, a kingdom may be lost all for the want of a horseshoe nail.*
> (N. Ellis and Larsen-Freeman 2006: 563)

One of the most prevailing sources of the 'individual differences myth' is the belief that IDs are relatively stable human attributes that are by and large free from any contextual influence. This is, in fact, the meaning that we typically convey in everyday parlance when we say that 'Dominic is bright' or 'Hilda is motivated'—both statements refer to a generalized state that applies to different contexts. Unfortunately, as has already been mentioned above with regard to language aptitude and motivation, the timeless and context-free stability of IDs is an illusion, because no matter how bright Dominic is, his cognitive effectiveness will vary from time to time and from situation to situation, and Hilda's motivation will show even greater ebbs and flows. Indeed, one of the main conclusions of my 2005 review of individual differences (Dörnyei 2005: 218) was that the most striking aspect of nearly all the recent ID literature had been the emerging theme of *context*:

> It appears that cutting-edge research in all these diverse areas has been addressing the same issue, that is, the situated nature of the ID factors in question. Scholars have come to reject the notion that the various traits are context-independent and absolute, and are now increasingly proposing new dynamic conceptualizations in which ID factors enter

into some interaction with the situational parameters rather than cutting across tasks and environments.

In their recent analysis of SLA, N. Ellis and Larsen-Freeman (2006: 563) came to a similar conclusion with regard to the temporal and situational context of L2 variables when they stated, 'To attribute causality to any one variable (or even a constellation of variables) without taking time and context into account is misguided.' In fact, even one of the most stable of all ID variables, fluid intelligence (i.e. general aptitude), undergoes variation in terms of its impact. As Chamorro-Premuzic, Furnham, and Ackerman (2006) summarize, this impact tends to decline as individuals progress through the educational system, and as acquired information and learnt skills take on a greater role. Aptitude has also been found to interact with learning conditions, which forms the basis of Cronbach's 'aptitude–treatment interaction' approach (see Corno *et al.* 2002), which has been successfully adapted to the study of SLA by Peter Robinson (2001, 2002*a*, 2002*b*, 2007).

Finally, a decisive argument for the environment-dependence of ID factors comes from genetic research. As we will see later in more detail, twin studies and molecular genetic research have provided evidence for what is usually thought to be one of the key doctrines of modern genetics, namely that DNA is both inherited and sensitive to environments; that is, what we are like is determined by the interaction of certain genes and the environment, not one over the other (Grigorenko 2007). To demonstrate the impact of the environment, let us take the most extreme case: the relationship of the IQ of identical twins. Schumann (2004*b*) points out that although, as expected, we find a substantial correlation, the explained variance is less than 75 per cent, and with identical twins who have been reared apart (i.e. do not share a common environment), the same percentage is around 70 per cent (Lubinski and Webb 2003). The degree of heritability of other ID variables is considerably less; according to Bouchard and McGue (2003), for example, genetic influences account for approximately 40–55 per cent of the variance in personality. Thus, it is now widely recognized that genetic instruction alone cannot explain the brain's complexity—environmental influences make the brains of even identical twins appreciably different (Modell 2003).

Multicomponential nature

We saw in the previous section that it is simply not true that traditionally conceived IDs are robust attributes that can be generalized across situations and time, since even genetically inherited characteristics interact with environmental factors, displaying an integrated impact. What makes the picture even more complicated, however, is the fact that most human attributes are multicomponential, made up of the dynamic interaction of several layers of constituents. Talking about cognitive abilities of various abstraction, Kosslyn and Smith (2000: 961–2) describe the various levels of human functioning very clearly:

> [W]e consider examples of cognitive abilities that are often characterized as higher brain functions, as distinct from lower brain functions. Functions like those involved in early perception and motor control are considered 'lower', while those involved in reasoning and problem solving are considered to be 'higher'. Lower functions often appear to rest on a relatively small collection of processes. And these processes perform a small number of specific operations, interact in straightforward ways, and operate in the same way over a wide range of different 'contents' (specific information). . . . In contrast, higher functions rely on relatively large numbers of processes, and these processes may themselves have complex internal structures. Moreover, their interactions are rarely straightforward, and their operations can vary for different contents. . . . Higher functions are often organized hierarchically, the more complex ones drawing on collections of more fundamental (and simpler) ones.

Extending Kosslyn and Smith's (2000) description beyond cognitive abilities to the whole spectrum of IDs, it is clear that concepts such as aptitude, motivation, or emotion are higher-order mental characteristics, subsuming a range of lower-level components and processes. In exploring this issue further, let us first examine the primary level of individual variation that is determined by our genetic inheritance, followed by a look at the other extreme, highly complex ID constellations. A particularly interesting question regarding this latter issue is how much the various IDs interact with each other at the level of their multiple components, that is, whether there are any 'hybrid' ID factors.

Genetics and ID research

> *The genetics of behaviour offers more opportunity for media sensationalism than any other branch of current science. Frequent news reports claim that researchers have discovered the 'gene for' such traits as aggression, intelligence, criminality, homosexuality, feminine intuition, and even bad luck. Such reports tend to suggest, usually incorrectly, that there is a direct correspondence between carrying a mutation in the gene and manifesting the trait or disorder.*
> (McGuffin, Riley, and Plomin 2001: 1232)

The importance of genetics for ID research lies in the assumption that the most basic differences amongst us—the primary IDs that are the lowest common denominators and as such are used as the building blocks of the more complex ID factors—are likely to be related to one's genetic make-up. Indeed, if such stable primary differences exist, they must be rooted somewhere in our genes and cannot be derived only from the ever-changing impact of the environment. Accordingly, there is indeed a widespread belief that genetic heritability makes a considerable difference; as Plomin, Kovas, and Haworth (2007) summarize, more than 90 per cent of teachers and parents reported in a study that they believed genetics to be at least as important as the environment for learning abilities and disabilities. In addition, we should also recall the statistics already cited that indicate that the average weighted heritability (i.e. proportion of phenotypic variance that is attributed to genetic variance) ranges from 45 to 70 per cent in the attributes that are likely to be most determined genetically. The problem is that this figure can be explained in two ways, emphasizing either the genetic stability or the environmental variability of IDs, as with the glass of wine that is half full or half empty.

Schumann's (2004*b*) summary of relevant brain research illustrates this halfway situation well. As he reports, research has shown that the total brain size or volume is the same in identical twins, which points to genetic control. However, it has also been established that the gyral patterns of brains are different, even in the case of identical twin pairs, and this variable architecture must therefore be the result of external, environmental phenomena. Modell (2003) interprets this situation as evidence that our brains develop in the light of our experiences: although the basic anatomy of the brain is likely to be constrained by genes, connectivity at the level of synapses is established by somatic selection during the individual's development.

The scientific study of the genetic sources of individual differences in human behaviour started in the late nineteenth and early twentieth centuries, when scholars showed that a number of human characteristics, including intelligence and personality, were highly heritable. Studies typically examined identical and fraternal twins to decide the extent of the heritability of a trait relative to the impact of external, environmental influences, which led to the 'nature versus nurture' debate. Research over the last decade took a dramatic turn because the completion of the 'Human Genome Project' opened up new avenues for genetic studies—usually referred to as 'molecular genetics' (see the end of Ch. 3 for a description)—to complement twin studies.

Begun formally in 1990, the Human Genome Project (<http://www.ornl.gov/sci/techresources/Human_Genome/project/about.shtml>) was a 13-year effort co-ordinated by United States government agencies to identify all the approximately 20,000–25,000 genes in human DNA and to determine the sequences of the three billion chemical base pairs that make up human DNA. These goals were successfully completed by 2003. The realization that any two humans are approximately 99.9 per cent the same at the genetic level (Hernandez and Blazer 2006) raised scholars' hopes that the ubiquitous genetic influences on individual differences amongst humans can be pinpointed by simply identifying the DNA base pairs that differ amongst us.

Although the current climate is characterized by optimism, Lewontin (2000) warns us that not all the information about protein structure is stored in the DNA sequence: the folding of polypeptides into proteins is not completely specified by their amino acid sequences. And, he points out, we simply do not yet know what the rules of protein folding are and no one has as yet succeeded in writing a computer program that can take the sequence of amino acids in a polypeptide and predict the folding of the molecule. 'Molecular biologists do not usually call attention to this ignorance about the determination of protein structure but instead repeat the mantra that DNA makes proteins' (p. 74).

Thus, the picture is not as straightforward as the media would like us to believe. Yet, there is no question that genes do act as the main building blocks of neurons and as such, our genes play a decisive role in determining how the human brain develops into the amazingly complex system that it is. Therefore, molecular genetics offers a great deal of potential for identifying genetic correlates to individual variation in cognitive functions, and efforts to identify genes that are associated with individual differences in elementary cognitive operations are already on the way with promising results. (See e.g. Parasuraman and Greenwood 2006.) The coming decade is likely to witness an explosion in research of this type, but before we have our hopes raised too high, we had better heed McGuffin, Riley, and Plomin's (2001) warning published in *Science Magazine*. These well-known scholars point out that most journalists, in common with most educated laypeople, tend to have a straightforward, single-gene view of genetics. However, single genes do not determine most human behaviours as the latter depend on an interplay between environmental factors and *multiple* genes. According to McGuffin and his colleagues, some of these patterns may turn out to be 'so complicated that they will never be detected' (p. 1249).

Generalist genes

In order to illustrate the potential complexity of the human genetic landscape and, at the same time, to show how interesting and relevant genetic research can be, let us look at a very recent finding by Robert Plomin's well-known research group at London University, the identification of 'generalist genes'—see for example, Plomin, Kovas, and Haworth (2007). According to Plomin and his colleagues, one of the most important recent findings from quantitative genetic research has been the observation that the same set of genes is largely responsible for genetic influence across a broad area of academic abilities. In other words, it was found that most genes associated with a particular learning ability (e.g. reading) will also be associated with other learning abilities (e.g. mathematics), and the observed genetic overlap is surprisingly substantial even between relatively distant domains such as English and mathematics. Moreover, as Plomin *et al.* emphasize, some genes associated with learning abilities and disabilities in general appear to have an even broader impact, encompassing other cognitive abilities such as memory and spatial ability; they can display genetic correlations greater than 0.50 and often near 1.0 across diverse cognitive abilities. These genes have been called *generalist genes* to highlight their pervasive influence. The only caveat is that these are still only virtual genes, derived from statistical analyses of multivariate results of twin studies, and are therefore yet to be physically identified. If this can be done, it will 'greatly accelerate research on general mechanisms at all levels of analysis from genes to brain to behaviour' (p. 11).

Link between IDs of different nature

Although it would be nice to be able to identify genetically the primary ID factors (as with primary colours) that are then combined to form complex ID functioning patterns (the whole colour spectrum), this has not happened yet and may not happen at all in such a simplistic linear form. If generalist genes are indeed identified, for example, that would totally change our view of how human cognitive functions are genetically underpinned. In any case, the ID variables that SLA research has been interested in—such as language aptitude and motivation—are complex, higher-order attributes, resulting from the integrated operation of several subcomponents and subprocesses.

The interesting fact is that once we take such a multicomponential view, we cannot fail to realize that many (if not most) learner characteristics mentioned in the literature involve at one level or another the co-operation of components of a very different nature (e.g. motivational factors involve cognitive constituents). A good example of such a mixture is Laufer and Hulstijn's (2001) proposed construct of 'involvement' for L2 vocabulary learning, which consists of two cognitive components (search and evaluation) and a motivational component (need). In another study, Dörnyei and Tseng (forthcoming) examined motivational task processing and provided empirical validation for a circular process in which signals from the appraisal system concerning task execution trigger the need to activate relevant action control strategies, which in turn further facilitate the execution process. Thus, a process that is primarily motivational in nature relies heavily on a cognitive appraisal component. The inclusion of appraisal in broader constructs is not unique in this example because, as we will see below, most theoretical conceptualizations of emotion contain a cognitive appraisal component that is responsible for the evaluation of the situation that evokes an emotional response (Lewis 2005).

A further example of the combined operation of mixed components is the much-publicized phenomenon of 'flow' (Csikszentmihalyi 1990). This is an experiential state with a particularly intense involvement in an activity, to the extent that people may even lose self-consciousness and track of time amidst their absorption. In an empirical study, Egbert (2003) found that the task conditions under which flow can occur can be organized along four dimensions: (1) there is a perceived balance of task challenge and participant skills during the task; (2) the task offers opportunities for intense concentration and the participants' attention is focused on the pursuit of clear task goals; (3) the participants find the task intrinsically interesting or authentic; and (4) the participants perceive a sense of control over the task process and outcomes. Here again we find a fusion of cognitive and motivational constituents. (See also Guastello, Johnson, and Rieke 1999.)

A final illustration of the integration of diverse components is my 'L2 Motivational Self System' (Dörnyei 2005, 2009; see separate section below for details), in which one of the key components, the 'Ideal L2 Self' is related to the learner's vision; this in turn is linked to the visuospatial component of the working memory, which is increasingly seen as the main construct underlying language aptitude (see below). Thus, individual differences in motivation are related to individual differences in the aptitude to form visual images (Modell 2003), which has been confirmed within an SLA context by Al-Shehri (2009). In many ways, the cognitive–motivational overlap is quite a common observation—after all, as I mentioned at the beginning of this chapter, the most currently dominant motivation theories in psychology are cognitive in nature—so much so that Schumann (2004*b*: 3) concluded:

> Additionally, the chapter indicates that motivation is not independent of cognition (as it is frequently treated in SLA research), but instead it is part of cognition, and therefore, there can be no 'cognitive' approaches to SLA that do not include motivation.

Interim summary: the dynamic nature of individual difference factors

Broadly speaking, the 'individual differences myth' claims that while the main trajectory of SLA (when aggregated at a group level) is determined by language acquisitional processes, relatively stable and monolithic learner attributes—called individual differences—cause systematic deviations from the overall trend. However, the previous sections have presented arguments and illustrations that, when we look more closely, individual learner characteristics are seen to be very different from the meaning we give them in everyday parlance and traditional professional discourse: They are not stable but show salient temporal and situational variation, and they are not monolithic but are complex constellations made up of different parts that interact with each other and the environment synchronically and diachronically. Simple cause–effect relationships are unable to do justice to these multi-level interactions and the temporal changes. For example, the motivation to complete this book was constantly affected by my changing appraisal of how well the writing was going; how well our university library was resourced; how many other social and academic activities competed for my free time; how intellectually demanding the researching of a particular section was and, as a result, how confident or (sometimes) disempowered I felt; which part of the day it was; how well my children were behaving; and how near I was getting to the end of my sabbatical period—to name but a few salient influences. These and other relevant factors resulted in varying minute-to-minute motivational constellations that sustained (or failed to sustain) the act of typing on the keyboard. As a result, I experienced productive stretches and lean periods; desperate searches for excuses to take a break or excuses to exempt myself from family programmes so that I could put in a few more hours of work when it was going well; the desire to stay up late some nights and to go to bed early some others; and in the end, this book got written!

It is clear that in such a complex web of relevant factors the mutual influences among the elements are non-linear, which, as we saw in Ch. 3, simply means that a change in one element does not produce a proportional change in other elements, let alone in the resultant outcome. Various combinations are associated with different levels of influence and therefore even a slight alteration of one condition can bring about a disproportionate change in the state of other elements (Vallacher and Nowak 1999). It is also clear that such a complex situation is not a unique state of affairs relevant only to writing academic books: a careful analysis of many (if not most) real-life learning/ achievement situations will reveal that individual variation is determined by several components, most of which are likely to be composite factors themselves, and most of which will have their own independent trajectories over time. The interactions of these components with each other and the environment, then, can reach such a complexity that is, for most practical purposes, equivalent to unpredictability. It is in this light that we can fully appreciate the truth in N. Ellis and Larsen-Freeman's (2006: 560–1) summary:

> There are many agencies and variables that underpin language phenomena, even as apparently simple a phenomenon as that of cross-linguistic lexical intrusions. Language is complex. Learners are complex. These variables interact over time in a nonlinear fashion, modulating and mediating each other, sometimes attenuating each other, sometimes amplifying each other in positive feedback relationships to the point where their combined weight exceeds the tipping point, which results in a change of state.

What is the lesson from all these considerations with regard to individual differences? I have come to believe that the key area where the traditional ID view must be reformed is the need to accept that individual variation is not so much a function of the strength of any individual determinant (e.g. aptitude or motivation) as the way by which the complex system of all the relevant factors works together. Larsen-Freeman (2006: 615–16) summarizes this clearly when she states that 'children differ in language learning skill not because of domain-specific knowledge that they either have or don't have, but because of variations in how and when the pieces of the process were put together during learning'.

Having come this far, I believe that we cannot fail to notice that the above conclusion and, more generally, the arguments in the previous sections have been increasingly in line with the key tenets of dynamic systems theory and the closely related theory of emergentism as described in Ch. 3. I would suggest therefore that individual learner variation can be fruitfully described in terms of the operation of a complex dynamic system in the sense that high-level mental attributes and functions are determined by a complex set of interconnected components that continuously evolve over time. The value of each component keeps changing depending on the overall state of the system and in response to external influences, making ID factors dynamic variables in the DST sense (Vallacher and Nowak 1999). Therefore, the logical next step is to attempt to reframe individual differences from a dynamic systems perspective.

Individual differences and dynamic systems theory

[We should be] adopting a genuine time and change perspective, rather than paying only lip service to the process character of all mental functioning and going on happily to study static verbal state concepts; and...using a real systems approach rather than using 'system' as a metaphor for what are really categories.
(Scherer 1995: 5)

My shift to adopting a dynamic systems perspective for the study of individual differences has been gradual, but I can recall one particular trigger that made me rethink my views of ID factors: This happened when I read N. Ellis and Larsen-Freeman's (2006) position paper on 'Language Emergence: Implications for Applied Linguistics', which introduced a special issue on Language Emergence in the journal *Applied Linguistics* (27/4). In this paper the authors quoted a description of motivation by Peter Skehan and myself (Dörnyei and Skehan 2003: 617) as an example of an emergentist approach:

> During the lengthy process of mastering certain subject matters, motivation does not remain constant, but is associated with a dynamically changing and evolving mental process, characterized by constant (re) appraisal and balancing of the various internal and external influences that the individual is exposed to. Indeed, even within the duration of a single course of instruction, most learners experience a fluctuation of their enthusiasm/commitment, sometimes on a day-to-day basis.

N. Ellis and Larsen-Freeman (2006: 563) then concluded that 'Motivation is less a trait than fluid play, an ever-changing one that emerges from the processes of interaction of many agents, internal and external, in the ever-changing complex world of the learner.' This was an accurate summary of my thinking, and within the context of their paper and the whole special issue of *Applied Linguistics* our conceptualization did indeed seem fully emergentist in nature. And yet, when I was developing my process-oriented approach to motivation (Dörnyei 2000, 2001a; Dörnyei and Ottó 1998) I had never for a moment considered the possibility that my views could be compatible with emergentism. After all, I thought, although I was reframing motivation as a dynamically changing cumulative arousal in a person, I was still working within a process-oriented paradigm that was characterized by linear cause–effect relations. In retrospect, however, I can see that the model I was proposing had multiple, parallel, and interacting cause–effect relationships, accompanied by several circular feedback loops, making the validity of the overall linear nature highly questionable. Thus, it was really a matter of time before I realized that such a patchwork of interwoven cause–effect relationships would not do the complexity of the motivation system justice and therefore a more radical reformulation was needed.

It seems to me that the process I went through—from a process-oriented to a dynamic systems perspective—is not an altogether unique path. I was interested to see, for example, that the thinking of one of the leading emotion researchers, Klaus Scherer, seems to have gone through a similar transformation, arriving at the same conclusion. Originally interested in the componential structure of emotions (for a review, see Scherer 2001), Scherer became acutely aware of the changing nature of these components over time. Therefore, he called for the abandoning of 'static state concepts' (Scherer 1995: 5) and suggested instead that scholars 'move from a domain oriented approach to a process oriented approach' (p. 5). However, the interlinking of different functional systems, involving cognitive, affective, and motivational aspects, pushed his conceptualization one step further:

> Unfortunately, neither our conceptual nor our methodological tool kits are adapted to dealing with systems of the degree of complexity exhibited by emotion processes. There is little hope of 'repairing' our concepts and methods in a piecemeal fashion in order to do justice to the phenomenon under study. Rather, we need a complete revolution in our thinking about the nature of emotion, comparable to other paradigm shifts in the history of science. In particular, we need to move from thinking in terms of discrete boxes, labels, or even neural programs to a nonlinear dynamic systems perspective of emotion. (Scherer 2000: 77–80)

A dynamic systems approach seems attractive in that it is able to accommodate several of the issues concerning IDs listed earlier, namely their lack of stability, their context-dependence, their multicomponent nature, and their multiple interactions with each other and the environment, resulting in non-linear dynamics. However, in order for the revised theory to be really usable, a crucial point needs to be addressed. It seems clear that drawing on DST can help us to account for the dynamic nature of learner characteristics; however, past empirical results have revealed significant correlations between various ID variables and learner behaviour/achievement, attesting to substantial linear predictability in the system. How can DST explain these systematic and consistent tendencies? Or, more generally: even though our various personality characteristics show dynamic changes, there is also a great deal of stability—how can these conflicting tendencies be reconciled?

Reconciliation of personality stability and dynamism

It was argued in the discussion of DST in Ch. 3 that even in highly complex systems that display a great deal of variation and change over time, there are times of seeming stability, to the extent that the system can be seen as static or fossilized. It is my belief that the reason why correlation-based studies of IDs have often produced highly significant results in the past is that these investigations tapped into such stable tendencies. So, the question is: how can we explain these non-dynamic, settled states within a DST framework?

In a thorough overview of the dynamic foundations of individual variation, Nowak, Vallacher, and Zochowski (2005) summarize the issue of the coexisting human tendencies of stability and dynamism thus: 'The notion of personality implies some form of stability in thought, emotion, and action. At the same time, human experience is inherently dynamic and constantly evolving in response to external circumstances and events' (p. 378). Put in another way, 'The proclivity for intrinsic dynamics cannot be denied, but neither can the tendency for psychological systems to demonstrate stability and resistance to change' (p. 353). Nowak and his colleagues, along with other scholars, believe that the key to resolving such conflicting tendencies lies in the concept of *attractors,* because from a DST perspective, any regulation is a function of the various attractors and attractor states in the system.

Individual differences as attractors

We saw in Ch. 3 that attractor states are preferred states towards which the system gravitates, a little bit like a beach ball that settles temporarily in a hollow in the ground before being blown further by the fresh sea wind. Such stable states are predictable and they occur when there are powerful attractors in place. In contrast, unstable phases are characterized by weak, changing, or multiple attractors. In this light, we can draw an obvious parallel between certain higher-order ID variables and attractors: for example, a strong goal, incentive, talent, or interest will definitely act as a stabilizing force, similarly to a deep hollow for a beach ball.

Thelen and Smith (1994) explain that some attractor states can be so stable that they look as though they are inevitable. However, the authors point out that these equilibrium states are none the less changeable and dynamic and can be moved from their preferred positions by large pushes:

> We will argue here that many configurations in action and cognition, and in development, that act like permanent programs or structures are stable attractors whose stability limits may indeed be shifted under appropriate circumstances. That is to say, many mental constructs and movement configurations, object permanence and walking, for example, are attractors of such strength and stability that only the most severe perturbations can disrupt them. They look as though they are wired in. (p. 61)

In sum, the dynamic systems perspective suggests that no seemingly stable mental configurations are absolute but are the result of a dynamic system settling into a preferred pattern in an attractor state, and ID variables act as potentially powerful attractors. In a system with potent attractors, a wide range of starting points (initial states) will eventually converge on a much smaller set of states; that is, despite differences at the outset in people's thoughts, feelings, or motives, the process unfolds in the unifying direction of the attractor. This process, according to Nowak, Vallacher, and Zochowski (2005), restricts intra-individual variation and thus promotes the emergence of systematic inter-individual differences (i.e. ID factors).

The stability of attractor states

How stable is an attractor state? In other words, how predictable—and consequently, measurable—is the impact of ID factors conceptualized as attractors? If we think of the beach ball analogy, two determinants of stability are obvious: (1) the depth of the hollow in the ground in which the ball rests, that is, the strength of the attractor; and (2) the strength of the wind, that is, the amplitude of the combined effect of internal and external factors that keep 'shaking up' the system, thus attempting to move it out of its stable pattern. If the overall turbulence is low, the system will hover around the governing attractor (Nowak *et al.* 2005) because there is enough power in it to counterbalance the disrupting forces and reinstate the system at its attractor. If the turmoil becomes too strong and there is a sudden gust of wind on the beach, which in human terms can be, for example, extreme stress or a powerful new arousal, even strong attractors become unstable and the system may be unable to achieve any coherent mode of functioning. We can easily think of situations when seemingly sensible and stable people suddenly 'lose it' and start acting irrationally.

There is a third factor that impacts on the stability of the beach ball: the overall shape of the terrain. If the hollow the ball has settled in is at the bottom of a valley, even if it is moved out of it temporarily by a gust of wind, it will gravitate back to it in time. Or, to take another scenario, there might be more than one attractor on the terrain, pulling the ball in different directions, and the final destination of the ball will be influenced by the bumps and dips in the ground. These broader properties of the terrain have been discussed under the term 'basins of attractor'.

Basins of attractor and multiple attractors

The *basin of attractor* (or simply 'attractor basin') refers to an attractor's region of attraction in the sense that all trajectories that enter the basin move towards that attractor (Carver and Scheier 1999). With regard to individual differences, the basin of attractor indicates the breadth of an attractor construct, that is, the subcomponents and their values that the construct subsumes. Nowak, Vallacher, and Zochowski (2005) explain that within a given basin, even quite different initial states, values, and constellations will promote a trajectory that eventually converges on the stable state associated with the attractor. As we have seen earlier, individual difference factors often have wide basins, including components of a different nature (e.g. cognitive, motivational, and emotional). Attractors are obviously more predictable if they have a wide basin associated with diverse components and values—a highly optimistic person, for example, might react to neutral or even moderately bad news positively, or a person with strong self-efficacy will not lose his/her motivation in the face of failure.

Real-life situations are usually characterized by the coexistence of multiple attractors with their own basins that may overlap; if our metaphorical ball bounces into these overlapping areas, we can anticipate instability. An example would be a person with mixed loyalties, torn between two tendencies or responses, and in such cases seemingly small differences in circumstances will tip the balance one way or another—of course, the same effect can be caused by the absence of a single powerful or dominant attractor (e.g. in a person who lacks any principles, ambitions, or salient self-concept). In general, human behaviour is captured well by the metaphor of a rugged landscape with many different attractor basins. Our movement might seem erratic at the micro-level but if we know the main attractors, the long-term trajectory is predictable to some extent when aggregated across time (Carver and Scheier 1999).

Sources of attractors

How do attractors come into being? Nowak *et al.* (2005) emphasize two main sources: the synchronization of individuals' internal states in social interaction, and the self-organization of thoughts and feelings with respect to a higher-order property (e.g. a goal or self-concept). Examples of the first include social learning, modelling, and being exposed to instruction, whereas internal processes are associated with self-analysis, reflections about past successes/failures, various appraisal mechanisms, and imaginations about alternative or future states. Of course, the two sources are dynamically related, a relationship expressively described by Thelen and Smith (1994: 320):

> From an initial bias, a diffuse attractor landscape with a few deep wells, infants, through their repeated experience producing and perceiving emotional states and their associated activities, come to acquire a more complex, differentiated set of stable basins of attraction. Along the way, some associations are lost, while others are diverted to new social situations. In this way, the social and cultural expectations become part and parcel of the felt emotions and of the activities that communicate those felt emotions to others. These activities, again, may be thought of as layered and completely intersecting with the landscapes of motivation and cognition.

The proposed framework of learner-based variance in SLA

We saw earlier that, given the complex and interlocking nature of higher-order cognitive human functioning, individual differences in these mental functions involve a blended operation of cognitive, affective, and motivational components. 'Indeed, the differences among motivation, affect, and cognition become paper thin' (Mayer, Chabot, and Carlsmith 1997: 32). The following sections will offer several concrete illustrations of various integrations of these three factors. This convergence becomes even more obvious if we take a neuropsychological perspective, because—quite frankly—at the level of neural networks it is difficult to maintain the traditional separation of functions. This is very clearly expressed by Lewis (2005: 194) in his discussion of cognition and emotion (and we should note that his conception of emotions already subsumes motivation):

> A DS [dynamic systems] analysis of the neurobiology of emotion then demonstrates, in precise and concrete terms, that cognition and emotion were never two distinct systems at all. They are not distinct at the level of interacting parts, nor at the level of the wholes to which these interactions give rise.... Although it remains useful to differentiate cognition and emotion for many research agendas, a neuroscientific analysis finds them to be different aspects of a unitary phenomenon in which interpretation and relevance emerge together.

Lewis is an emotion researcher, so it might be argued that his view is biased by the wish to reinstate the significance of emotions in an era of cognitive psychology. However, we find the same conclusion in the writings of leading cognitive psychologists in the introduction of an edited volume that is entirely devoted to outlining a new integrated perspective on intellectual functioning and development by bringing together motivation, emotion, and cognition (Dai and Sternberg 2004: 29):

> In this introduction chapter, we attempt to make a case that intellectual functioning and development never occur as solely cognitive events but involve motivation and emotion, or the whole person vis-à-vis adaptive pressures and challenges. Going beyond cognitivism does not imply that motivational and emotional issues are more important than or as important as cognitive processes and mechanisms. Rather, our point is that without taking into consideration the motivational and emotional aspects of intellectual functioning and development, we cannot even properly understand the cognitive processes involved. Reducing intellectual functioning and development to merely cognitive matters is simply no longer tenable both on theoretical grounds and in light of empirical evidence.

Several chapters in this anthology, written by eminent cognitive and motivational psychologists (e.g. Dweck, Mangels, and Good 2004; Linnenbrink and Pintrich 2004; Matthews and Zeidner 2004) reiterate the theme that studying cognition in isolation from motivation and affect cannot yield a valid picture of the workings of the mind.

In the light of all these considerations, can there be any justification for proposing any macro-structuring principles to individual variation in human mental functions (such as cognitive or motivational functions)? I believe that there is one perspective from which the main function types can be separated: the *phenomenological* (i.e. experiential) view. I would suggest that different functional dimensions refer to different types of phenomenally conscious episodes and are therefore distinguishable. In short, they can be differentiated because they 'feel' different: if we want something, we have the distinct experience of 'wanting' it and we can even grade this experience in terms of its strength (e.g. 'I can hardly wait...' or 'I really-really-really want it!'). People typically have no problem with distinguishing this motivational experience from emotional experiences such as feeling happy or sad or angry. Finally, our thoughts have also been traditionally kept as a distinct experiential category, which is revealed in phrases such as 'cold intellect', capturing a key feature of cognition, namely that it has no valence (i.e. it is not gradable in terms of intensity either in the positive or negative directions). Thus, I propose that people can phenomenally separate three areas of mental functioning, *cognition*, *motivation*, and *affect* (or emotions), which warrants their use as primary organizing principles of learner-based characteristics.

Interestingly, scholars have traditionally divided mental processes along this tripartite structure. Scherer (1995) explains that already Plato proposed that the human soul contained three components: *cognition* (corresponding to thought and reason and associated with the ruling class of philosophers, kings, and statesmen), *emotion/passion* (corresponding to anger or spirited higher-ideal emotions and associated with the warrior class), and *conation/ motivation* (associated with impulses, cravings, and desires and associated with the lower classes). This division into 'an appetitive part that produces various irrational desires, a spirited part that produces anger and other feelings, and a reasoning part that permits reflection and rationality' (Parrott 2004: 7) has traditionally been referred to as the 'trilogy of mind', reflecting three interrelated but conceptually distinct mental systems. (For a detailed analysis, see Mayer, Chabot, and Carlsmith 1997.) In the following, I will first describe the three systems separately, and then discuss their interaction with each other and the environment.

The cognitive system

For the last four decades the terms 'cognition' and 'cognitive' have been of central prominence in various disciplines in the social sciences referring to a range of slightly different meanings. With regard to mental functioning, cognition is associated with knowing and knowledge representation, memory, attention, learning, information processing, abstract thinking, appraisal, judging, reasoning, problem-solving, decision-making, etc. Thus, the cognitive system is broad in its scope, and in fact there has been a tendency in psychology over the past two decades to try to 'cognitize' every conscious mental operation, including those related to motivation and affect.

Most laypeople would associate cognition with intelligence, and especially with the famous IQ (Intelligence Quotient)—in this case the folk wisdom carries a great deal of truth. Without any doubt, at the heart of the scientific study of cognition lies the general cognitive factor '*g*' (which can be seen as the scientific equivalent of the commonsense concept of intelligence or IQ). Ever since Spearman introduced the notion of 'general intelligence' at the very beginning of the twentieth century (in 1904), this concept has been the most researched and best-known psychological factor not only in individual difference research but arguably in experimental psychology in general. Scholars have always known that there is 'life beyond *g*', that is, not all the human abilities are covered by this factor, but recent theorizing has taken a full circle and there is a general consensus amongst contemporary aptitude researchers that *g* is at the apex of a hierarchical structure of a system of aptitudes. (For a review, see Lubinski 2004.) There is also broad agreement that objective measures of *g* can be obtained by factor analysing multiple correlated abilities (e.g. mathematical reasoning, spatial visualization, and verbal ability, to mention the best-known second-order factors). As Bouchard and McGue (2003: 10) conclude, 'the *g* factors derived from different well-chosen arrays of tests, often specified by a competing theory, are so highly correlated that they are essentially identical'. In what is probably the most comprehensive survey of empirical research on cognitive abilities, Carroll (1993) studied—and in many cases reanalysed—more than 400 different datasets and concluded that *g* accounted for approximately 50 per cent of the overall variance (although there was variation from study to study).

What is *g*?

In the light of this consistent picture, it is surprising that nobody really knows what *g* is. The original insight by Spearman simply confirmed the general observation that if someone is highly developed in one intellectual ability, the person is likely to be, on average, highly developed in other intellectual abilities as well (Garlick 2002). So *g* is the general factor that is common to all cognitive functions and, in measurement contexts, to all tests of intellectual ability. Genetic research has also confirmed (e.g. Plomin, Kovas, and Haworth 2007) that diverse cognitive abilities consistently display genetic correlations greater than 0.50 and often near 1.0 with each other, and a substantial amount (but not all) of the genetic variance in academic performance is attributable to *g*.

How can we verbally describe g? As Lubinski (2004) summarizes, some scholars have equated it with the 'ability to learn', while others have associated it with a broader and deeper capability for making sense of our surroundings. There is also a strong view that *g* is not a theoretically driven construct but merely a mathematical artefact. Oberauer *et al.* (2005), for example, assert: 'By definition, *g* is conceptually opaque—it is the common variance of a set of tasks that happened to be constructed and used by intelligence researchers over a century. It reflects no explicit theoretical concept' (p. 64). This latter view is supported by Garlick (2002), who argues that such a broad and relatively stable attribute appears to be inconsistent with current findings in cognitive neuroscience, according to which different intellectual abilities are based on different neural circuits, and which emphasize the emergence of neural connections in response to environmental stimuli. Brody (2005) also points out that although the heritability of general intelligence implies genetic links—see the 'generalist gene hypothesis' discussed earlier—not many of the specific genes responsible for this intelligence factor have been identified, and neither has it been established how heritable dispositions interact with the social structures that influence social outcomes.

Thus, we find in the literature an uneasy theoretical limbo with regard to the interpretation of *g*, as well as an apparent clash between the robust findings of psychometric intelligence research and genetics on the one hand and cognitive neuroscience on the other. One solution to this dilemma has been proposed by Garlick (2002): his theory equates *g* with the axonal and dendritic plasticity of the neural system, that is, with the capacity of the central nervous system to exercise major connectional changes between neurons in response to environmental stimuli and experience. Thus, according to this view, *g* is not directly related to general intelligence but rather to the neurobiological conditions that are needed for intelligence to develop. This makes sense: individual differences in how people can adapt their neural circuits to the environment would indeed result in a broad impact on various neural circuits, changing their processing characteristics, thereby causing overlapping strengths and weaknesses across different abilities.

General knowledge

We have already seen earlier that some theories of intelligence (e.g. that of Cattell) include *general knowledge* (or 'crystallized intelligence') as a key component of the cognitive system, conceived as the result of applying general intelligence over time. Unlike general (or 'fluid') intelligence, it continues to develop throughout most of the life span, explaining why we become wiser with age. As a result, its capacity to predict academic success increases after people reach young adulthood (Ackerman and Kanfer 2004; Chamorro-Premuzic, Furnham, and Ackerman 2006). Hunt (2005), for example, reminds us that the tests that appear to be the highest correlates of performance in school and the workplace are tests of crystallized intelligence, that is, tests of the ability to apply previously acquired information and problem-solving methods to the current problem. His conclusion is straightforward: 'Knowledge counts' (p. 21). And most applied linguists would agree: language proficiency counts.

Including general knowledge in the cognitive system raises the broader question of how ability and achievement indices should be related to each other. Lubinski (2004) cites the conclusion of an American Psychological Association task force in the mid-1970s, which suggested that achievement and aptitude or ability tests do not differ in kind, only in degree. This is an interesting point that we will come back to below when we look at cognition from a dynamic systems perspective.

Working memory

Working memory (WM) is a popular concept in contemporary cognitive psychology. It refers to the 'temporary storage and manipulation of information that is assumed to be necessary for a wide range of complex cognitive activities' (Baddeley 2003: 189); thus, it underpins our capacity for thinking and has important specific implications for language processing. The overall capacity of working memory can be expressed in terms of the *working memory span*. This has proved to be a robust predictor of a wide range of complex cognitive skills and it is highly correlated with performance on the type of reasoning tasks that form the basis of standard tests of intelligence. It is measured by instruments and procedures whereby participants are typically required to combine some sort of (1) processing and (2) storage of information in a dynamic and simultaneous manner; thus, the assessment goes beyond traditional memory tests such as digit or word span measures. One important finding in the measurement of working memory capacity has been its limited nature. Even individuals with a developed WM capacity cannot keep in it more than seven unrelated verbal items and about four visual ones (Baars 1997*a*). This is closely linked to the general bottleneck nature of conscious attention relative to our unconscious processing capacity described in Chs. 2 and 4.

How is the construct of 'working memory' structured? In 1974 Baddeley and Hitch proposed that it could be divided into several distinct subsystems—for a review, see Baddeley (2003):

1 The *phonological loop* is the specialized verbal component of working memory, concerned with the temporary storage of verbal and acoustic information. The stored material is subject to rapid decay (over approximately two seconds) but the loss of information can be offset by 'subvocal rehearsal', which reactivates the decaying representations and which can also translate visual information into phonological form.

2 The *visuospatial sketchpad* is the visual equivalent of the phonological loop, responsible for integrating spatial, visual, and kinesthetic information into a unified representation, which can be temporarily stored and manipulated. This system is involved, for example, in everyday reading tasks but its functioning has been less studied than that of the phonological loop. Baddeley suggests, however, that similarly to the phonological loop, the visuospatial sketchpad also has a storage and a processing component (the latter termed the 'inner scribe') which can, for example, translate verbal information into an image-based code.

3 The *central executive* is the most important and least understood aspect of working memory, responsible for its attentional control. It constitutes the supervisory attentional system that allocates attentional resources and regulates the selection, initiation, and termination of processing routines

(e.g. encoding, storing, and retrieving). Thus, it receives, co-ordinates, and integrates information from the subsystems of the visuospatial sketchpad and the phonological loop as well as from long-term memory to carry out complex cognitive tasks such as future planning, decision-making, mathematical calculations, and reasoning. It is also involved in reading and comprehension, and—interestingly—in trouble-shooting in situations in which the automatic processes run into difficulty, which links it to the use of communication strategies (cf. Dörnyei and Kormos 1998). The central executive is of particular relevance to our discussion because the executive processes are thought to be the principal factors determining individual differences in 'working memory span' (Baddeley 2003; Daneman and Carpenter 1980).

4 The *episodic buffer* has recently been added to the working memory construct to constitute a storage counterpart of the central executive, which is now seen purely as a control system without any storage capacity. The episodic buffer combines information from different sources and modalities into a single, multifaceted code, or 'episode'—hence the 'episodic' part of the label. It is assumed to underpin the capacity for conscious awareness.

How is working memory related to intelligence? This question was the subject of a lively exchange in the 2005 volume of *Psychological Bulletin*. It started with a paper by Ackerman, Beier, and Boyle (2005) questioning the popular view that WM and *g* were identical, or nearly identical, constructs, from an ID perspective. To test the claim that general intelligence equals WM capacity, the authors conducted a meta-analysis of 86 samples that related WM to *g* and found that 'WM is a factor that has as much contribution to the general factor of intelligence as the content and reasoning factors do, but in this context it has little more common variance than Spatial ability has with *g*, and has less common variance than Reasoning does with *g*' (p. 44). In response, Oberauer *et al.* (2005) reanalysed the data using a slightly different method and found much higher correlations between WM and *g*, and a reanalysis of part of the sample by Kane, Hambrick, and Conway (2005) also resulted in higher coefficients. In spite of these disagreements about the magnitude of the correlations, all the parties agreed that WM and *g* were different constructs.

If working memory and general intelligence are not isomorphic, then what exactly is WM? To start with, the concept is a latent, inferred construct, which has been produced after decades of systematic observations in experimental psychology. The theory associated with the work of Baddeley and his colleagues (for a review, see e.g. Baddeley 2003) involves a theoretical construct that is proposed to exist in order for the observed experimental findings to make sense. Baars (2007b: 8), however, warns us that the current construct is not ultimate and that it is quite possible that future research will produce an even more attractive way of interpreting the research evidence. Indeed, in a validation study Chein, Ravizza, and Fiez (2003) did not succeed in establishing neuroanatomical correlates for Baddeley's construct. On the other hand, we must also acknowledge that theoretical constructs such as Baddeley's working memory are very useful in summarizing existing knowledge and facilitating hypothesis formation. Oberauer *et al.* (2005) emphasize that 'working memory capacity' forms a bridge between research on individual differences in abilities and cognitive science, including experimental cognitive psychology, and formal modelling of cognitive processes. They even go as far as to claim that 'investigating WMC, and its relationship with intelligence, is psychology's best hope to date to understand intelligence' (p. 64).

Cognition and dynamic systems theory

At first glance general intelligence is a robust, stable, and pervasive human attribute, constituting the prototype of any ID factor conceived in the traditional sense. Yet, even a person's cognitive capacity is best interpreted in a dynamic systems framework for a number of reasons:

- *General intelligence as a powerful attractor:* cognitive abilities are related to *g*, which acts very much like a powerful attractor: it does not seem to have a meaning of its own but is rather a general force of gravity affecting the whole landscape of specific cognitive abilities, which can be seen as a broad attractor basin.
- *The role of general knowledge:* the systemic nature of cognition is also evidenced by the important role that general knowledge (i.e. crystallized intelligence) plays in predicting performance. It was stated above that performance in a dynamic system is erratic at the micro-level but if the system is governed by an attractor, the long-term trajectory of the system is predictable to some extent when aggregated across time (Carver and Scheier 1999). General knowledge is the result of applying general intelligence over time and is therefore a good example of such an aggregate. It can also be seen as the product of the interaction between intelligence and the environment. Thus, it is in accordance with the dynamic systems perspective of cognition that general knowledge should be aligned with the main attractor—indeed, we saw that achievement and aptitude tests do not differ in kind, only in degree.
- *The changing role of fluid and crystallized intelligence:* we saw above that there is a gradual shift from fluid to crystallized intelligence over time in terms of being the dominant predictive index of performance. This shows that the overall cognitive system is not static but is in an ongoing (slow) process of change.
- *The interaction of cognition with motivation and emotion:* it was already argued earlier (and will be discussed in more detail below) that various cognitive functions interact with motivational and emotional processes, forming complex relationships within a system. As a result, cognition cannot be characterized as a linear computational sequence between input and output functions but rather as a dynamic process of self-organization with only partial predictability from moment to moment (Lewis 2005).

Thus, as Lewis summarizes, the cognitive system reconfigures itself by achieving states of higher order through the synchronization of their constituents, both in real time, in response to disturbances and interferences, and in development, through experience-dependent change. Examples of the higher-order states are schemas, expectancies, beliefs, and appraisals, while the developmental aspects are reflected, for example, by the emergence of novel skills and habits. Lubinski and Webb (2003) report an interesting longitudinal study in which the developmental trajectories of three different types of profoundly gifted individuals were compared over a period of 10 years. The three groups consisted of students who were (1) high on mathematical reasoning and relatively low on verbal reasoning; (2) high on verbal reasoning and relatively low on mathematical reasoning; and (3) high on both abilities. As could be expected, the abilities acted as strong attractors for long-term development, and differential interests were apparent in the three groups in their choice of favourite courses in high school and college, as well as in the awards and other accomplishments they achieved: high-math individuals tended to succeed in areas of science and technology, whereas high-verbal individuals tended to succeed in the humanities and arts.

The cognitive system in SLA

The general tendency when talking about the cognitive aspects of learner differences in SLA is to focus on 'language aptitude', which is usually defined in a broad way, highlighting the natural giftedness or talent for learning an L2. Thus, language aptitude is usually treated in the same manner in applied linguistics as general intelligence in psychology, and the similarities are also evident in that in actual practice 'language aptitude' is equated with the scores of language aptitude tests, in a way similar to the close association of intelligence with the results yielded by intelligence tests in psychology. The highest correlations between any self-report learner measure and L2 learning achievement have consistently been achieved by language aptitude, explaining around 25 per cent of the variance, and this figure is almost identical to the figure reported by Sternberg (2002) with regard to the impact of intelligence in general school performance.

In my 2005 overview of the field (Dörnyei 2005), I concluded that contemporary language aptitude research is moving beyond the aptitude testing traditionally associated with the work of John Carroll (e.g. 1973, 1981, 1990) and with the best-known battery, the Modern Language Aptitude Test (MLAT; Carroll and Sapon 1959), and is focusing more and more on the role of specific cognitive factors and processes such as working memory or word recognition. Scholars have also been reframing language aptitude in a situated manner, examining the dynamic interplay between aptitude and context, and such contextually sensitive measures of language aptitude have opened up new possibilities for integrating aptitude research into mainstream SLA studies by linking cognitive abilities to specific acquisitional processes (e.g. Robinson 2001, 2002*a*, 2002*b*, 2007; Skehan 1998, 2002). The study of working memory is believed to have a great deal of potential for our future understanding of the cognitive system in SLA, but we should also note Robinson's (2002*a*) caution that working memory capacity alone cannot be equated with language aptitude; this is in line with the findings concerning the relationship of working memory with general intelligence in psychology (reported earlier).

Besides language aptitude, the cognitive system in SLA covers several other established areas. (For reviews, see DeKeyser and Juffs 2005; Dörnyei 2005, 2006*a*.) *Learning/cognitive styles*—that is, the individual's preferred and habitual modes of perceiving, remembering, organizing, processing, and representing information—have been a much-studied topic, along with *learning strategies* and the recent reconfiguration of this line of research, *self-regulation*. Scholars have also studied other cognitive aspects such as *learner beliefs*, and even the study of motivation has included salient cognitive themes, most notably appraisals, expectations, and attributions. Thus, the variety of cognitive contributors to SLA is rich and the gradual establishment of a systemic approach has been well reflected by the emphasis on studying aptitude measures in combination with other ID variables in various trait complexes (see later in more detail), while also examining the interaction of these complexes with instructional and situational variables. As DeKeyser and Juffs (2005: 446) conclude:

> The future of aptitude research in the L2 domain probably lies in the study of these interactions between (components of) aptitude and learning contexts, instructional treatments, age of learning, and stages of acquisition, not only because such research gives a more accurate empirical picture of reality and a better ability to predict success or failure than studies on any of these variables can separately, but also because establishing such interaction effects tells us more about what elementary cognitive mechanisms underlie aptitude, and what cognitive processes take place under various conditions of learning than mere correlational aptitude research or mere experimental research on treatments.

The dynamics systems approach advocated above is in line with this conclusion and offers a theoretical framework and a set of useful organizational tools to handle this dynamic interrelationship in a principled manner.

The motivational system

The issue of intentionality in complex systems is, of course, a slippery one.
(Kelso 1995: 138)

I have argued earlier that the validity of the motivational system hinges largely on its phenomenally salient nature: motivation refers to a cumulative arousal, or want, that we are aware of. Although there is a plethora of factors, conditions, motives, etc. that can affect behaviour, these work as a system whose outcome is tangible for the individual at any moment in time. The resultant of the relevant forces is in a process of continuous change, displaying frequent and often irrational fluctuation (e.g. motivational ups and downs during a language course or even during a single lesson), but also larger, more predictable trajectories (e.g. more general dispositions or commitments), which is in accordance with a dynamic systems perspective. In fact, unlike cognitive aspects where the apparent stability of attributes such as *g* might create the illusion that those cognitive variables are system-independent, the field of motivation research has been moving steadily towards a process-oriented conceptualization for the past decade. For example, in an authoritative summary of motivation in education, Pintrich and Schunk (1996: 4) state: 'Motivation is the process whereby goal-directed activity is instigated and sustained,' and Garcia (1999: 231) points out that 'as noted in chapter 1 of any Introduction to Motivation text, one of the prime characteristics of motivation is that it ebbs and flows'.

Within the study of SLA, motivation research was initially dominated by a macro-social-psychological perspective advocated by Robert Gardner and his Canadian associates (e.g. Clément and Gardner 2001; Gardner 1985, 2001; Gardner and Lambert 1959, 1972), examining the general motivational dispositions of whole language communities. While at this societal level the changing nature of motivation was not prominent, as soon as the 'educational shift' in L2 motivation research moved the research focus in the 1990s to the micro-level of learning environments such as language classrooms, it became evident that motivational evolution cannot be ignored. (See e.g. Ushioda 1996; Williams and Burden 1997.) During this period my own research interest also turned towards exploring the temporal progression of L2 motivation, and this effort resulted in an elaborate Process Model of L2 Motivation (Dörnyei 2000, 2001*b*; Dörnyei and Ottó 1998). Within the broad framework of a flow diagram, this model contained an intricate net of cause–effect relationships accompanied by feedback loops, and therefore—as I mentioned earlier—it was really only a matter of time before I had to realize that such a patchwork of interwoven cause–effect relationships would not do the complexity of the system justice and therefore a more radical change was needed.

The necessary change, I believe, is the implementation of the principles of dynamic systems theory in conceiving L2 motivation. The main difference of this new approach does not lie in a radically new conceptualization of the actual motives that affect behaviour or the nature of these motives but rather in the conceptualization of their relationship to behaviour. Traditionally, we have thought of motives as exerting a linear effect on action, which was then captured quantitatively by means of correlation-based analyses (i.e. correlation, factor analysis, or structural equation modelling). However, motives interpreted as attractors do not necessarily have a linear relationship with ongoing action. Their pull or push is interfered with by a multitude of other pulls and pushes, and the relative power of a particular pull/push will be amplified or mitigated by particular constellations of environmental and temporal factors. This means, for example, that what was insignificant a short while ago might assume fleeting or enduring power now, depending on the circumstances. This dynamic conception requires a new approach to examining motivated behavioural trajectories: rather than trying to impose ready-made theoretical paradigms on the motivational sources of behaviour, we need to look for situated, environmentally relevant basins of attractors, and the stability of the system will be dependent not only on the power of the attractors but also on the number of the existing attractor basins in the person's life space.

Rather than provide a detailed review of L2 motivation research (see Dörnyei 2005; MacIntyre 2002; Ushioda 2007), I describe in what follows two different conceptualizations of motivation with systemic properties. The first one is Lewin's classic 'field theory' from the 1940s, which shares a surprising amount in common with a DST conception and which therefore shows that a dynamic approach is inherent in the study of motivation. The second construct is the 'L2 Motivational Self System' that I proposed in 2005, and which, I believe, follows closely the dynamic and phenomenologically salient criteria of the overall motivational system.

Lewin's field theory

Kurt Lewin was one of the most influential psychologists of the twentieth century, whose work is seen as the precursor of several areas of social psychology, including the whole field of group dynamics. He is also the initiator of encounter groups in psychotherapy and of action research in research methodology, and it was his empirical study that originally introduced the tripartite construct of democratic, autocratic, and laissez-faire leadership styles in educational and organizational psychology. While I have been familiar with Lewin's work in these areas, it was Thelen and Smith (1994) who drew my attention to Lewin's motivation theory, the 'field theory', 'whose behavioural dynamics foreshadowed contemporary dynamic systems by over half a century' (p. 313).

Influenced by Gestalt psychology, Lewin (1943, 1952) was a true systems theorist and his construct of the 'field', which is the 'life space' of the individual, considered the individual embedded within his/her environment. Thus, the field includes internal 'forces' such as needs, goals, and cognitive structure, as well as external events and processes that have direct effects upon individual behaviour. In the Introduction of his edited work, Lewin's colleague, Dorwin Cartwright (1952: p. xii), emphasized:

> Many of Lewin's contributions to the understanding of human behaviour consisted of showing that a wider and wider realm of determinants must be treated as part of a single, interdependent field and that phenomena traditionally parcelled out to separate 'disciplines' must be treated in a single coherent system of constructs.

According to Cartwright (1952), in the last few months before his untimely death in 1947, Lewin was coming to reframe motivation to highlight determinants such as group membership, personal ability, economic and political resources, and social channels, which are exactly the kind of interdependent ingredients of motivation that are seen to make up a socially sensitive complex system. Within this constellation of personal traits, cognition, and environmental influences, the meaning of any component is only identifiable in relation to the other components and the whole state of the system, and behaviour is the cumulative function of the whole life space. In addition, Lewin also extended the field to have temporal facets, and, as the following extract demonstrates, his views are closely related to the motivational self-system described in the next section:

> [T]he psychological field which exists at a given time contains also the views of that individual about his future and past. The individual sees not only his present situation; he has certain expectations, wishes, fears, daydreams for his future. His views about his own past and that of the rest of the physical and social world are often incorrect, but nevertheless constitute, in his life space, the 'reality-level' of the past. In addition, a wish-level in regard to the past can frequently be observed. The discrepancy between the structure of this wish- or irreality-level of the psychological past and the reality-level plays an important role for the phenomenon of guilt. The structure of the psychological future is closely related, for instance, to hope and planning. (Lewin 1943: 302–3)

The L2 motivational self system

Humans are social animals, but they are also noteworthy for being self-aware. Indeed, the capacity for self-reflection, and especially for self-concept formation, distinguishes humans from virtually every other species. Research on this unique feature of human psychology has demonstrated that the self is more than an epiphenomenon, but rather functions as an important platform for the regulation of thought, emotion, action, and interpersonal relations.
(Nowak *et al.* 2005: 368)

In 2005, I proposed a reconfiguration of L2 motivation as part of the individual's self-system (Dörnyei 2005). The new construct—the 'L2 Motivational Self System'—attempts to synthesize a number of influential approaches in the field (e.g. Gardner 1985; Noels 2003; Ushioda 2001) and at the same time broadens the scope of L2 motivation theory to make it applicable in diverse language learning environments in the current, increasingly globalized world. (For a detailed description, see Dörnyei 2009.) My theory drew on psychological research on 'possible selves' and 'future self-guides'. The concept of *possible selves* was introduced by Markus and Nurius (1986), representing the individuals' ideas of what they *might* become, what they *would like* to become, and what they are *afraid of* becoming. More specifically, Markus and Nurius distinguished between three main types of possible selves: (1) 'ideal selves that we would very much like to become'; (2) 'selves that we could become'; and (3) 'selves we are afraid of becoming' (p. 954).

The novelty of the possible self concept lies in the fact that it concerns how people conceptualize their as yet unrealized potential and as such, it also draws on hopes, wishes, and fantasies. In this sense, possible selves act as 'self-guides', reflecting a dynamic, forward-pointing conception that can explain how someone is moved from the present towards the future. At the heart of this movement is the complex interplay of current and imaginative self-identities and its impact on purposive behaviour. Markus's (2006: p. xi) summary also highlights the potential of the theory to integrate emotional, cognitive, and contextual factors:

> Our excitement with the notion of possible selves had multiple sources. Focusing on possible selves gave us license to speculate about the remarkable power of imagination in human life. We also had room to think about the importance of the self-structure as a dynamic interpretive matrix for thought, feeling, and action, and to begin to theorize about the role of sociocultural contexts in behaviour.

While I always believed in the importance of taking the language learner's whole personality into account when we examine learner characteristics, the main attraction of Markus's theory was its phenomenological validity (which is, of course, the key tenet in the current definition of the motivational system within a dynamic systems approach to individual differences): possible selves involve tangible images and senses. As Markus and Nurius (1986) emphasize, they are represented in the same imaginary and semantic way as the here-and-now self, that is, they are a *reality* for the individual: people can 'see' and 'hear' a possible self. Markus and Ruvolo (1989) argue that it is a major advantage to frame future goals in this way because this representation seems to capture some elements of what people actually experience when they are engaged in goal-directed behaviour. As the authors state, by focusing on possible selves we are 'phenomenologically very close to the actual thoughts and feelings that individuals experience as they are in the process of motivated behaviour and instrumental action' (p. 217). In other words, the imagery and sensual components of possible selves approximate what people actually experience when they are engaged in motivated or goal-directed behaviour. Thus, possible selves can be seen, according to Markus and Ruvolo (1989: 217), as the resultant of the various motivational factors (e.g. expectancies, attributions, value beliefs) 'that is psychologically experienced and that is a durable aspect of consciousness'.

Future self-guides: ideal and ought selves

Possible selves are often referred to as 'future self-guides', but strictly speaking, not every type of possible self has this guiding function. For example, the expected, 'could-become' self refers to a default situation and therefore it does not really guide but rather predicts the likely future scenario. In contrast, the ideal self has a definite guiding function in setting to-be-reached standards and, in a negative way, the feared self also regulates behaviour by guiding the individual *away* from something. It does not need much justification that from the point of view of acting as academic self-guides, the learner's ideal self is particularly important; this is an area that has been the subject of a great deal of research by Tory Higgins and his associates (e.g. Higgins 1987, 1998; Higgins, Klein, and Strauman 1985; Higgins *et al.* 1994).

The two key components of Higgins's (1987; Higgins, Klein, and Strauman 1985) self-theory are the 'ideal self' and the 'ought self'. The *ideal self* refers to the representation of the attributes that someone would ideally like to possess (i.e. representation of hopes, aspirations, or wishes), while the *ought self* refers to the representation of attributes that one believes one ought to possess (i.e. representation of someone's sense of duties, obligations, or moral responsibilities) and that therefore may bear little resemblance to desires or wishes. While this is a straightforward and intuitively convincing dichotomy, two points need to be mentioned regarding it.

First, Boyatzis and Akrivou (2006) highlight a potential source of confusion in the distinction between the ideal and the ought selves concerning the level of internalization of the ought self. They argue that because various reference groups (which every individual belongs to) affect the individual by anticipatory socialization or value induction, it is not always straightforward to decide at times of social pressure whether an ideal-like self-state represents one's genuine dreams or has been compromised by the desire of role conformity. Indeed, group norms, as their name suggests, impose a normative function on group members and because we are social beings, most of us adhere to some extent to these norms—see Dörnyei (2007a). This means that there is a pressure to internalize our ought selves to some extent, resulting in various degrees of integration.

Second, the ought self raises one more issue. In Higgins's (1987; Higgins, Klein, and Strauman 1985) original conceptualization it referred only to positive reference points (i.e. the person whom I believe I ought to be), but Higgins (1996) suggests that this meaning may be extended to include negative reference points (i.e. the person I don't want to be), similar to Markus and Nurius's (1986) feared self. This is an important issue that we will come back to when we look at the theory from a dynamic systems perspective.

The motivational function of possible selves and future self-guides

For Markus the main motivational power of possible selves lies in the imagery component, that is, in 'self-relevant imagery'. (See Ruvolo and Markus 1992.) Indeed, the imagination has been known to be related to motivation since the ancient Greeks. Aristotle, for example, claimed that 'There's no desiring without imagination' (Modell 2003: 108) and, as McMahon (1973) explains, Aristotle defined the image in the soul as the prime motivating force in human action; he believed that when an image of something to be pursued or avoided was present in imagination, the soul was moved in the same manner as if the objects of desire were materially present. Interestingly, contemporary research on mental imagery confirms the assumption that humans respond to mental images similarly to visual ones. Kosslyn *et al.* (2002), for example, report on neuroimaging studies that indicated that visual mental imagery and visual perception activated about two thirds of the same brain areas. (For a recent summary of relevant research, see Kosslyn, Thompson, and Ganis 2006.) These results provide a neuropsychological basis for Markus and Ruvolo's (1989: 213) claim that 'imaging one's own actions through the construction of elaborated possible selves achieving the desired goal may thus directly facilitate the translation of goals into intentions and instrumental actions'; a similar idea has been expressed by Wenger (1998: 176) when he described the concept of 'imagination':

> My use of the concept of imagination refers to a process of expanding our self by transcending our time and space and creating new images of the world and ourselves. Imagination in this sense is looking at an apple seed and seeing a tree. It is playing scales on a piano, and envisioning a concert hall.

The motivating power of mental imagery has also been well documented in the field of sport psychology. Inspired by Paivio's (1985) influential model of cognitive functions of imagery in human performance, hundreds of studies have examined the relationship between mental imagery and sport performance, and as Gregg and Hall (2006) summarize, it has been generally concluded that imagery is an effective performance enhancement technique. As a result, virtually every successful athlete in the world applies some sort of imagery enhancement technique during their training.

Let us now look at how Higgins (1987; Higgins, Klein, and Strauman 1985) described the motivational capacity of future self-guides. Interestingly, he followed a more cognitive approach than Markus and did not refer to the imagery component. Instead, he saw the source of motivation in the comparison of actual (i.e. current) and future selves and formulated a broader *self-discrepancy theory* to describe the impact of any possible mismatch. The theory postulates that people are motivated to reach a condition where their self-concept matches their personally relevant self-guides. In other words, motivation involves the desire to reduce the discrepancy between one's actual self and the projected behavioural standards of the ideal/ought selves. Future self-guides provide incentive, direction, and impetus for action, and sufficient discrepancy between these and the actual self initiates distinctive self-regulatory strategies with the aim of reducing the discrepancy. In sum, future self-guides represent points of comparisons to be reconciled through behaviour (Hoyle and Sherrill 2006).

Conditions for the motivating capacity of the ideal and ought selves

Although the above description of possible selves theory points to the conclusion that future self-guides motivate action by triggering the execution of self-regulatory mechanisms, several studies have found that this does not always happen automatically (e.g. Oyserman, Bybee, and Terry 2006; Yowell 2002). Past research suggests that the following conditions can enhance or hinder the motivational impact of the ideal and ought selves:

- *Availability of an elaborate and vivid future self-image:* the primary and obvious prerequisite for the motivational capacity of future self-guides is that they *need to exist*. It has been observed that people differ in how easily they can generate a successful possible self (Ruvolo and Markus 1992), which may explain the absence of sufficient motivation in many people. Furthermore, even if the self-image does exist, it may not have a sufficient degree of elaborateness and vividness to be effective. It has been found that the more elaborate the possible self in terms of imaginative, visual, and other content elements, the more motivational power it has. People display significant individual differences in the vividness of their mental imagery (Richardson 1994) and a possible self with insufficient specificity and detail may not be able to stir up the necessary motivational response.
- *Perceived plausibility:* Ruvolo and Markus (1992: 96) argue that it is the individual's 'specific representations of what is possible for the self that embody and give rise to generalized feelings of efficacy, competence, control, or optimism, and that provide the means by which these global constructs have their powerful impact on behaviour'. In other words, possible selves are only effective insomuch as the individual does indeed perceive them as *possible*, that is, realistic within the person's individual circumstances. Ackerman and Wolman (2007: 76) emphasize in a similar vein that self-estimates of ability are closely related to 'trait complexes that are composed of personality, motivation, interests, and experiences' as they jointly determine how 'individuals make relevant decisions about which activities to attempt and which to avoid, for perceived lack of ability'.
- *Harmony between the ideal and the ought selves:* because the ought self is closely related to peer-group norms and other normative pressures (e.g. ethnic community expectations), learners' (and especially adolescents') ought selves are likely to contain certain peer-induced views about academic attainment (e.g. low-achieving expectations that are often called the 'norm of mediocrity') that are in conflict with the individual's ideal self. Thus, an important condition for effective future self-guides is that they should feel congruent with important social identities, that is, that the ideal and the ought selves should be in harmony.
- *Necessary activation/priming:* even if the learner does have a well-developed and plausible ideal/ought self-image, this may not always be active in the working memory. Hoyle and Sherrill (2006) argue that possible selves become relevant for behaviour only when they are recruited into the working self-concept and for this to happen they need to be activated. This priming of the self-image can be triggered by various reminders and

self-relevant events, and they can also be deliberately invoked by the individual in response to an event or situation.

• *Accompanying procedural strategies:* in order to translate self-guide-induced arousal into action, people need to have a roadmap of tasks and strategies to follow to approximate the ideal self. For example, it is obviously not enough for an Olympic athlete merely to imagine herself walking into the Olympic stadium or stepping onto the podium if she has no coach or training plan. For this reason, along with many others, Oyserman, Bybee, and Terry (2006) argue that future self-guides are only effective if they are accompanied by a set of specific predeveloped and plausible action plans and self-regulatory strategies, which are cued automatically by the image. According to Miller and Brickman (2004), it is this system of specific proximal subgoals, or goal-focused strategies, that distinguishes reality-based future goals from empty dreams and fantasies.

• *Offset by feared self:* Oyserman and Markus (1990) have argued that a desired possible self will have maximal motivational effectiveness when it is offset or balanced by a counteracting feared possible self in the same domain. Thus, for best effect the negative consequences of not achieving a desired end-state need to be elaborated and made cognitively available to individuals. In a similar vein, Hoyle and Sherrill (2006) also stress that the motivation conferred by balanced possible selves is additive, involving both approach and avoid tendencies, and is therefore greater than the motivation conferred by the hoped-for or feared self alone.

The L2 motivational self system

In accordance with the theoretical considerations described above, I have proposed (Dörnyei 2005) that the L2 Motivational Self System should have a component associated with the ideal self and another with the ought self. However, I also felt that we needed to add a third major constituent, which was associated with the direct impact of the students' learning environment. After all, one of the main achievements of the 'educational shift' of motivation research in the 1990s was the recognition of the motivational impact of the main components of the classroom learning situation, such as the teacher, the curriculum, and the learner group. (For reviews, see Dörnyei 1994, 2001b; Ushioda 2003.) For some language learners the initial motivation to learn a language does not come from internally or externally generated self-images but rather from successful engagement with the actual language learning process (e.g. because they discover that they are good at it). Thus, the L2 Motivational Self System is made up of the following three components:

• *Ideal L2 Self*, which is the L2-specific facet of one's ideal self: if the person we would like to become speaks an L2, the ideal L2 self is a powerful motivator to learn the L2 because of the desire to reduce the discrepancy between our actual and ideal selves. Traditional integrative and internalized instrumental motives would typically belong to this component.

- *Ought-to L2 Self*, which concerns the attributes that one believes one ought to possess to meet expectations and to avoid possible negative outcomes. This dimension corresponds to Higgins's ought self and thus to the more extrinsic (i.e. less internalized) types of instrumental motives.
- *L2 Learning Experience*, which concerns situated, 'executive' motives related to the immediate learning environment and experience (e.g. the impact of the teacher, the curriculum, the peer group, or the experience of success). This component is conceptualized at a different level from the two self-guides and future research will, it is hoped, elaborate on the self-aspects of this bottom-up process.

Motivation and dynamic systems theory

Even though we claim to know the laws that govern the behavior of matter, such laws don't tell us anything at all about how or why we reach for a cup of coffee or walk down the street.
(Kelso 1995: p. xi)

A recurring claim in the previous sections was that motivational factors work in concert with cognitive factors (and as we will see below, also with emotional ones) as they interact with the environment. This combined operation was evidenced in Lewin's field theory, and also in several of the conditions that are necessary for self-guide-induced arousal to be translated into action. For example, the ideal self needs to be substantiated by the appraisal of its plausibility in the light of contextual circumstances and the self-evaluation of ability. Also, the ideal self needs to be in harmony with the students' ought self (or social identity) and it needs to be accompanied by relevant procedural knowledge and goal-specific schemata. Indeed, higher-order human mental functions such as motivation inevitably involve a combination of diverse factors, and therefore a dynamics systems approach offers a useful way of examining their combined effect and changing relationship.

I have argued above that one attraction of the possible self-based approach to conceptualizing motivation is the phenomenological validity of the proposed constructs. The various self-guides can be seen as powerful attractors that co-ordinate a range of pulling and pushing forces whose origin is both internal and external to the learner, resulting in a cumulative arousal that the learner is aware of. The L2 Motivational Self System outlines a motivational landscape with three possible attractor basins, one centred around the internal desires of the learner, the second around the motivational regulations of social pressures exercised by significant or authoritative people in the learner's environment, and the third around the actual experience of being engaged in the learning process. It is my belief that the existence of any one of these attractor basins alone is sufficient to provide the necessary modulating and co-ordinating influence on the direction, vigour, and persistence of behaviour to reach at least a working knowledge of the L2, but if the three systems are in harmony, that will have an increased, cumulative effect.

The emotional system

*Emotions are quintessentially psychological phenomena. They provide
life with its joys and sorrows, its energy, and in this sense, emotions
are fundamental to what it means to be human. Their place within
psychology, then, seems obvious and central, almost unquestionable. Yet,
oddly enough, the scientific study of emotion has not been consistently
present throughout the history of modern psychology.*
(Rosenberg and Fredrickson 1998: 243)

Everybody knows that emotions play an important role in our lives, yet
'affect'—the way by which emotions are often referred to in the research
literature—has been a rather neglected topic in psychology. Everybody knows
that classrooms are venues for a great deal of emotional turmoil, yet affect
has been an almost completely neglected topic in educational psychology.
Everybody knows that the study of a second language can be an emotionally
rather taxing experience, yet affect has been an almost completely neglected
topic in applied linguistics. And finally, everybody knows that emotions are
frequent sources of action—for example, when we act out of fear or anger
or happiness—and yet affect has been an almost completely neglected topic
in motivation research. Why? What is it about affect that has failed to
inspire, or has even inhibited, researchers to make it the subject of systematic
investigations?

Rosenberg and Fredrickson (1998) list a number of possible reasons for this
puzzling situation. First of all, behaviourism, one of the dominant directions
in psychology during the twentieth century, largely ignored affect because it
was not an objectively observable phenomenon. Furthermore, we may add,
the currently dominant psychological direction, cognitive psychology, has
not embraced affect either—after all, cognition and affect have been long
seen as separate paradigms. A further reason for the neglect is purely methodological: emotions are highly subjective and hard to measure in a reliable
manner, which may have discouraged researchers. Rosenberg and Fredrickson mention yet another thought-provoking point: with the advances and
growing specialization of psychology in the twentieth century, specific subdisciplinary boundaries were formed, separating distinct areas of study, and
affect did not fit neatly into any of these established subfields. Buck (2005:
198) is right when he concludes that emotion is 'remarkable in its relevance
to phenomena at widely different levels of analysis, literally from atoms,
molecules, and genes to social, cultural, and historical phenomena', but this
diversity backfired for a long period. The study of affect required the crossing
and blurring of subdisciplinary boundaries, which did not really happen until
the end of the twentieth century.

A further major obstacle to examining emotions in their own right is that
they are so closely intertwined with cognitive processes—most notably with
cognitive appraisal—that it is easy to believe that there is no meaningful way

to separate them. For example, Carver (2005: 199) is very clear about the intertwining nature of cognitive and emotional processes:

> I am among those inclined to ignore the assumption that appraisal and emotion are distinct functions. How can appraising an event as having adverse implications for the self not imply negative affect? How can negative affect exist apart from registering (at some level, not necessarily conscious) that an event has adverse implications for the self? These seem two sides of the same coin.

As with so many things in academia, the cognition–affect interlock is rooted in ancient Greek philosophy; this time not in Plato's thinking but in that of his best student, Aristotle. According to him, emotions were types of judgement or evaluations of events, and as Oatley (2000) points out, this functionalist view of linking emotions to appraisals was a forerunner to much contemporary thinking in cognitive psychology. Interestingly, in spite of this functional convergence, Carver (2005) himself still maintains that emotion should not be rendered just another class of cognition because, as he states, this class of experience is distinctly different from others, for example in the fact that it has graded valence or because of its link to physiological changes in the body. We will come back to the emotion–cognition interrelationship in more detail below.

Finally, the most unexpected discovery one is likely to make when reading the literature on emotion is the fact that most experts do not even accept that emotions coincide with personal feelings or, more scientifically, that they can be defined as phenomenally salient mental phenomena. Prinz (2005: 9) summarizes this as follows:

> From the very first philosophical musings about the emotions to the present day it has been popular to insist that emotions are not feelings. This position is so enshrined that it might be regarded as the Fundamental Axiom of emotion research.... On one approach, feelings are merely necessary, but not sufficient components of emotions. On another approach, feelings are contingent components. On a third approach, feelings aren't components at all; they are just ways of detecting emotions.

Even this brief overview demonstrates that emotion research is not for the faint-hearted: emotions for many are not affective but cognitive phenomena and are not even directly related to feelings—in other words, for many and for various reasons, emotions are not really emotions. Luckily, Lewis (2005: 182) reassures us that all is not lost because 'Many investigators believe that the affective feeling of emotion is a critical aspect of its motivational and adaptive properties.' Thank goodness for that, though this conception moves emotions a bit too close to the other extreme—to motivation, a relationship that will also be discussed later in detail.

Thus, it is no accident that in the introduction to a recent anthology entirely devoted to emotion in education, Schutz and Pekrun (2007) explain that until recently there has been virtually no inquiry on emotions in educational contexts apart from two notable exceptions, the study of affect in attribution theory—for an overview, see Weiner (2007)—and research on test anxiety—see Zeidner (2007). As a result, we know very little about the role of pleasant emotions, such as enjoyment, happiness, hope, surprise, anticipation, or pride, and unpleasant emotions (other than anxiety), such as anger, fear, sadness, hopelessness, disgust, shame, guilt, or boredom. This explains Linnenbrink and Pintrich's (2004: 84) call: 'Therefore, we urge other researchers to consider how mood and emotions relate to cognitive processing on a variety of educational tasks'. Because of the highly anxiety-provoking nature of SLA, applied linguists have conducted a great deal of research on anxiety, but apart from that the general trend of neglect has applied to our field, too. We must note here a notable exception to this trend, John Schumann's (1990, 1994, 1997, 1999, 2001) systematic work on the neurobiology of affect.

Defining emotions

I may have been too flippant in the previous introduction because, to be fair, emotions are hard to define and the term refers to a wide range of phenomena that have little in common. Although there is little doubt that basic feelings such as anger and sadness are emotions, Parrott (2004: 6) points out correctly that there is less agreement about whether to include 'moods (depression, irritability), long-term emotions (love that continues for years), dispositions (benevolence, cantankerousness), motivational feelings (hunger, sexual arousal), cognitive feelings (confusion, déjà vu), and "calm" emotions (sympathy, satisfaction)'. Most researchers would define emotions as brief, rapid responses involving physiological, experiential, and behavioural activity (Keltner and Ekman 2000), and the bodily phenomenology is often underscored: after all, what can be more salient indices of a phenomenon than racing hearts, tensing muscles, sweating palms, or hyperventilation. Prinz (2005: 23), for example, defines emotions as 'perceptions of bodily changes' and as he explains, 'when those perceptions are conscious, emotions are feelings'. The problem is, however, that along with others, Prinz further argues that unconscious emotions are also possible, that is, 'Some emotions aren't felt.' In order to grasp the experiential essence of emotions, Russell (2005) introduces the concept of 'Core Affect', which he considers the emotional quality of any conscious state. It is the 'neurophysiological state always accessible as simply feeling good or bad, energized or enervated, even if it is not always the focus of attention' (p. 26).

Thus, the conscious versus unconscious experiential nature of emotions is an obstacle to producing a straightforward definition; so, too, is the fact that although there exist discrete language labels referring to steady emotional states, these need to be offset by the recognition that emotional processes are also of a dynamic, continuously fluctuating nature (Scherer 2000). Thus, emotional processes are best thought of as processes that unfold in time. However, a proper description of this process requires the specification of a variety of components, starting with the evaluative perception (i.e. appraisal) of stimulus events that usually initiate any emotional episode, followed by the various forms of arousal and subjective feelings, and finally also including the impact of emotional reactions on one's thinking, behaviour, and physiology, and more generally, on one's social interactions. Different emotional theories focus on various aspects of this process, which explains why they inevitably highlight different features of the concept.

The third source of difficulty in producing a clear-cut definition of emotion is that emotional experiences or states can vary considerably in their duration and pervasiveness. Prolonged dwellings in emotional states are common as indicated by the special label that is used to refer to these by laypeople and experts alike: 'mood'. Most scholars agree with the commonsense charac-terization that moods are more enduring and have less specific causes than emotions, but it is not clear where and how to draw the boundary between the two. Furthermore, moods are not the most enduring phenomena on the emo-tional continuum because we can also observe 'emotional traits' in people (Rosenberg 1998). These refer to stable ways or predispositions to emotional responding, and as Rosenberg explains, they operate by setting the threshold for the occurrence of particular emotional states.

Emotional traits have been called by a variety of names—for example, affective styles, temperamental traits, emotional biases or habits, and general preferences of sentiment. All these terms try to capture the consistency they bring into the ebb and flow of emotional experience by exerting an organi-zational influence on the intensity and quality of the affective states. In fact, Keltner and Ekman (2000) argue that individual differences in emotion emerge as early as in the first months of life and are quite stable during development; indeed, the life histories of individuals prone to different emotions (e.g. anger or happiness) differ profoundly. In a recent study, Dewaele, Petrides, and Furnham (forthcoming) examined the impact of 'trait emotional intelligence' on SLA and found that people who were characterized by a high level of this trait could regulate their emotional reactions—more specifically, their communicative and foreign language anxiety—over time and manage stress better than people with low emotional intelligence.

Emotion and cognition

Curiously, most of the approaches in contemporary emotion research are within the confines of cognitive psychology and the central problem for emotion theory is how emotion interacts with cognition (Lewis 2005). It has been well documented that there is a two-way interaction between the two systems, with cognitive processes influencing emotions and vice versa. Phelps (2005), for example, describes how the cognitive awareness of the emotional significance of events and the conscious application of emotion regulation strategies can influence amygdala function and emotional expression, and how emotions—via the amygdala—influence cognition by modulating atten-tion and perception. As she concludes, the neural systems of emotion and cognition are both independent and interdependent, and therefore a compre-hensive understanding requires a consideration of the complex interactions between the two systems. In this respect, theories can roughly be divided into two types, the first examining the role that cognition—and primarily appraisals—play in giving rise to emotions, the other taking the opposite approach by emphasizing the primacy of affect and elaborating on the cognitive consequences and functions of emotions:

- *Emotion and appraisals:* appraisal theory is the most developed and coherent approach to the study of the cognition–emotion interface. Its focus is on the specific perceptions, evaluations, and interpretations that elicit a particular emotional state. Drawing on Scherer's work, Schumann (1997; Schumann and Wood 2004) specified five primary stimulus appraisal dimensions: *novelty* (degree of unexpectedness/familiarity), *pleasantness* (attractiveness), *goal/need significance* (whether the stimulus is instrumental in satisfying needs or achieving goals), *coping potential* (whether the individual expects to be able to cope with the event), and *self and social image* (whether the event is compatible with social norms and the individual's self-concept). These compute the emotional relevance of stimulus events in relation to information stored in a special 'value memory' module, thereby giving rise to an emotional response and generating emotional states. Thus, appraisal involves a cognitive evaluative and interpretative function that is seen as an antecedent of affect in most emotion theories.
- *Cognitive functions of emotions:* while it is easy to see how cognition can give rise to emotion (e.g. thoughts can lead to anger), it is perhaps less obvious to many that our thinking—and especially our attention—is also guided by emotion towards perceptions, interpretations, memories, goals, and plans that are relevant to the specific emotion (Lewis and Todd 2005). Yet, the observation that affect (e.g. happiness or anxiety) can bias or constrain our thinking, planning, and judgements is common and it has been found that our emotional state can influences even the memories we retrieve or our perceptions at a particular point of time.

Emotion and motivation

Emotions are fundamentally important motivators.
(MacIntyre, Mackinnon, and Clément 2009: 47)

A striking feature of the literature on emotion is that the concept of emotion is often broadened to such an extent that it subsumes, either explicitly or implicitly, motivation. For example, Lewis (2005) lists four indispensable features of emotion—arousal, action tendencies, attentional orientation, and affective feeling—the first three of which would be part of any standard conception of motivation. This quote from Lewis and Todd (2005: 215) leaves no doubt about these authors' view that emotions have motivational qualities because they are closely associated with intentions:

Even positive emotional states such as interest, attraction, and excitement are goal-related and they propel action as much as do fear and anger.

In fact, intentions are the emotional thrust of goal pursuit. If the goal can be attained right away, action takes its course and the emotions that directed it disappear quickly, often before we know they were ever present. We swat the mosquito, shout to a friend, pick up an interesting object, kick off our shoes, or avoid the unpleasant image on page three of the newspaper.

Scherer (2001) also argues that a comprehensive picture of emotions needs to include 'behaviour preparation' or 'action tendencies' because they can both change ongoing goal-directed behaviour and produce action tendencies that are specifically adapted to dealing with the environmental stimulus that has elicited the emotional response. Schumann and Wood (2004) provide a neurobiological description of how appraisals generate emotions such as joy, happiness, fear, anger, and shame, and how these emotions lead to action tendencies, such as the readiness to undertake mental or motor behaviours in relation to stimulus. This is in line with Lewis and Todd's (2005: 211) conclusion that 'the biological function of emotion is to impel appropriate behaviour, given past learning and present circumstances, by steering attention toward useful options for acting on the world and urging one to pursue them'. We should note that by assuming a sequence of *appraisal → emotional response → motivated action tendency,* scholars link cognition, emotion, and motivation in an interrelated cycle. We will look at the interaction of the three systems in a separate section below.

Emotions and dynamic systems theory

As outlined above, in past research emotion has been seen either as an outcome (of cognitive appraisals) or an antecedent (of motivated action tendencies and cognitive/attentional modifications). The reality, however, is that this is not an either/or situation because emotion functions in both roles simultaneously in an ongoing manner. That is, emotion needs to be seen within the framework of a 'dynamic time course of constantly changing affective tuning of organisms as based on continuous evaluative monitoring of their environment' (Scherer 2000: 70). The picture we have here is very similar to the dynamics of motivation described earlier, namely a reciprocal, multiple, and recursive pattern of causality that can be best captured within a dynamic systems paradigm. In this perspective, we cannot talk about any antecedents or consequences within distinct cause–effect relationships but rather about emerging outcomes of interactions among constituent systems underlying appraisal, emotion, and motivation.

Scherer (2000) so clearly summarizes that the fundamental problem of any emotion theory is to explain within a single model three seemingly contrasting paradoxes: (1) both the dynamic, continuously fluctuating nature of emotion processes and the existence of discrete language labels referring to steady states; (2) both the psychobiological nature of emotion and its cultural constitution and significance; (3) both the phenomenological distinctiveness and the intricate interweaving of cognition and emotion (and we can also add: motivation). Conceptualizing emotions within dynamic systems theory helps to achieve these diverse goals because the theory accounts for the dynamic interactions and fluctuations while also explaining the various aspects of undeniable stability (e.g. emotional states, moods, traits, as well as cultural trends) by associating them with attractor states.

The interaction of cognition, motivation, affect, and the environment

> *Cognition, consciousness, experience, embodiment, brain, self, and human interaction, society, culture, and history are all inextricably intertwined in rich, complex, and dynamic ways in language.*
> (N. Ellis and Robinson 2008: 3)

The thesis of the previous sections has been twofold: although a neuropsychological view of the networked neural architectures of the brain supports an integrated approach to conceptualizing higher-order mental functions, on a phenomenological basis it is possible, and I believe useful, to separate three subsystems within the human mind: cognition, affect, and motivation. However, it has become clear to many scholars that the three systems have continuous, dynamic interaction with each other and cannot exist in isolation from one another. As Buck (2005: 198) put it, 'In their fully articulated forms, emotions imply cognitions imply motives imply emotions, and so on.'

It is not easy to think of the human mind in such an integrated way; the natural tendency is to isolate the most relevant subsystem and try to establish its impact on the phenomenon in focus. The problem, as Lubinski and Webb (2003) conclude, is that examining dispositional attributes individually is often challenging and unfruitful, because the manner in which each operates depends on the full constellation of personal characteristics. Even people with similar ID patterns can travel very different paths as a result of some difference in a personality constituent that is seemingly irrelevant or of secondary importance; this is exactly what dynamic systems theory would expect. Therefore, it is my belief that the best way ahead is to identify higher-level amalgams or constellations of cognition, affect, and motivation that are relatively stable (i.e. are governed by a powerful attractor) and which act as 'wholes'. DST would expect that the self-organization of the various constituents will achieve such stabilized wholes, and, indeed, we do find some excellent candidates in the literature for such higher-level states or structures that cut across the cognition-affect-motivation trilogy of mind. Two prominent examples include Ackerman's *trait complexes* and the *future self-guides (ideal and ought selves)* discussed earlier:

- *Ackerman's trait complexes:* educational psychologists have been suggesting for a while that although isolated ID factors and personality traits are often shown to have a substantial impact on learning outcomes, certain optimal combinations of such traits are likely to have more predictive power than traits in isolation. (See Corno *et al.* 2002.) The best-known work to date along these lines is Phillip Ackerman and his colleagues' conceptualization of 'trait complexes' (e.g. Ackerman 2003, 2005; Ackerman and Heggestad 1997; Ackerman and Kanfer 2004). Ackerman and his associates have identified four broad trait complexes, called 'social', 'clerical/conventional', 'science/math', and 'intellectual/cultural'. They are made up of various combinations of cognitive abilities, personality dimensions, and interests, and function as 'wholes' in affecting the direction and intensity of the investment of cognitive effort and the type of knowledge/expertise acquired during adulthood. Interestingly, Ackerman (2005) stresses that these complexes are only the beginning, because they represent 'only a small sampling of underlying cognitive, affective, and conative communalities' (p. 104). Future, more principled research might be able to extend the current conceptualizations and may add new ability trait operationalizations. Ackerman mentions 'emotional intelligence' as a likely candidate for the latter. (For more information on emotional intelligence, see Dewaele, Petrides, and Furnham forthcoming.)

• *Future self-guides (ideal and ought selves):* as Markus (2006) points out in her review of the genesis of possible selves research, one of the main attractions of the new approach was that the self-structure could be seen as a 'dynamic interpretive matrix for thought, feeling and action, and to begin to theorize about the role of sociocultural contexts in behaviour' (p. xi). Although I discussed possible selves and future self-guides under the motivation heading, in concluding that section I argued that future self-guides can be seen as broad attractor basins subsuming a variety of components. Indeed, MacIntyre, Mackinnon, and Clément (2009: 47) point out that without a strong tie to the learner's emotional system, possible selves exist as 'cold cognition, and therefore lack motivational potency'. As they explain, 'When emotion is a prominent feature of a possible self, including a strong sense of fear, hope, or even obligation, a clear path exists by which to influence motivation and action.' A further constituent of this cognition-emotion-motivation amalgam is the salient imagery component, resulting in a potentially very powerful constellation that encompasses the whole spectrum of the human mind, from our thoughts to our senses.

The interaction between learner characteristics and the environment

Since at least the 1930s, deep thinkers as diverse as Allport (1937) and Lewin (1951) have argued that invidious comparisons miss the point because behavior is a function of an interaction between the person and the situation. By the 1980s this recognition had deteriorated into a truism. Nowadays, everybody is an interactionist.
(Funder 2006: 22)

So far the emphasis has been on the integrated functioning of the three main constituent systems making up the human mind: cognition, motivation, and affect. However, humans are social beings and therefore no learning is independent of environmental influences. More generally, to reiterate Dai and Sternberg's (2004: 29) assertion, 'Reducing intellectual functioning and development to merely cognitive matters is simply no longer tenable both on theoretical grounds and in light of empirical evidence.' This is particularly true when we talk about language, which is, besides its cognitive faculty, also the main channel of social organization. In the words of N. Ellis and Larsen-Freeman (2006: 573):

> Language is socially constructed. Language use, social roles, language learning, and conscious experience are all socially situated, negotiated, scaffolded, and guided. They emerge in the dynamic play of social intercourse. Our expectations, systematized and automatized by prior experience, provide the thesis, our model of language, and we speak accordingly.

Thus, language acquisition cannot be separated from the social arena in which it takes place, and, accordingly, the past decade has seen a surge of social theories in SLA research, well illustrated by a recent Focus Issue of *The Modern Language Journal* (Lafford 2007). (For good summaries of the cognitive-social debate in SLA, see Larsen-Freeman 2007*b*; Zuengler and Miller 2006.) This is a welcome phenomenon because, as we have seen earlier in this chapter and also in Ch. 3, dynamic systems theory takes a socially grounded approach in which neither the internal development of the organism nor the impact of the environment is given priority in explaining behaviour and its change. As Larsen-Freeman and Cameron (2008) emphasize, the context is part of the system and its complexity, which means that the internal faculties of the agent (i.e. learner) and the various aspects of the environment are all contributors to the complex system of forces that make up the life space of SLA. Equilibrium in this sense means a smooth, ongoing adaptation to contextual changes.

In the light of the above, the question is how we operationalize the social world around us, that is, how we identify and select the relevant environmental factors that need to be integrated in a particular research paradigm. This is not an easy or straightforward task; in a recent paper devoted to the analysis of the person-situation-behaviour triad, Funder (2006: 27) has emphasized that

> it is difficult to pin down just how situations are important, in part because of the common but unilluminating practice of assigning 'the situation' responsibility for all the behavioral variance not accounted for by a particular personality trait, *without* specifying what aspects of the situation are psychologically essential. There is a good deal of confusion concerning how situations should be conceptualized.

There are radically different ways of operationalizing the social world around us; for example, social psychology—which is by definition the socially most sensitive area of psychology—has been divided by the fundamental dilemma of how much to zoom in on the social world, that is, (1) whether to take a more individualistic and micro-perspective-based approach and consider the complexity of the social environment through the individual's eyes, as it is reflected in the individual's mental processes and the resulting attitudes, beliefs, and values (e.g. in social cognition theory), following the 'beauty is in the eye of the beholder' analogy; or (2) whether to adopt a societal perspective that focuses on broad social processes and macrocontextual factors, such as sociocultural norms, intergroup relations, acculturation/assimilation processes, and interethnic conflicts (as is done in social identity theory). Thus, similar to the many types and sizes of optical lenses used to transmit and focus light for diverse purposes, our research lenses can also be massively varied, magnifying different aspects of the environment.

In SLA research there have been several initiatives to situate research and thus capture environmental effects, for example in classroom ethnography (e.g. Harklau 2005; Toohey 2008; van Lier 1988; Watson-Gegeo 1997); the microanalysis of classroom discourse (e.g. Zuengler and Mori 2002); the interaction hypothesis (e.g. Gass 2003; Gass and Mackey 2006, 2007; Mackey and Polio forthcoming); the group dynamics of language learning and teaching (e.g. Dörnyei and Murphey 2003; Ehrman and Dörnyei 1998); sociocultural theory (e.g. Lantolf and Thorne 2006); and language socialization (e.g. Schieffelin and Ochs 1986; Watson-Gegeo 2004; Zuengler and Cole 2005). In fact, even the general issues of language instruction and how language input becomes intake concern the interaction of the learner and the environment.

Within the study of L2 individual differences, the most developed line of research in integrating environmental aspects has been Peter Robinson's (2001, 2002*b*, 2007) 'aptitude–treatment interaction' approach, which concerns the ways by which mental abilities interact with learning conditions. This is a forward-pointing attempt to describe concrete sets of cognitive demands that can be associated with some basic learning types/tasks, and then to identify specific aptitude complexes to match these cognitive processing conditions. Traditional L2 motivation research was dominated by Gardner and Lambert's (1959, 1972) macro-perspective, which emphasized the motivational disposition of whole communities. The educational shift in the 1990s, however, refocused the research lens and brought about a more fine-tuned and situated analysis of motivation as it operates in actual learning situations (such as language classrooms), characterized by a microperspective. In my recent proposal of the L2 Motivational Self System (described earlier), two of the three main components of the construct are directly related to social/contextual factors: the Ought-to L2 Self concerns the internalization of the views of authority figures, peers, and other significant others in the learner's environment, while the L2 Learning Experience component taps into the learner's appraisal of his/her experiences in the immediate learning context.

In sum, the significance of contextual influences has become a hot topic in several fields within the social sciences and, accordingly, conceptualizing situated constructs and research paradigms is the dominant tendency in virtually all contemporary SLA research. The challenge, then, is to adopt a dynamic perspective that allows us to consider simultaneously the ongoing multiple influences between environmental and learner factors in all their componential complexity, as well as the emerging changes in both the learner *and* the environment as a result of this development. This latter aspect is critical because, as Ushioda (2009) points out, context is generally defined in motivation research (and we may add, in individual difference research in general) as an independent background variable, or a static backdrop, which is theorized to influence motivation, but over which the learner has no control. Such a conceptualization, Ushioda argues, sustains the basic Cartesian dualism between the mental and the material worlds, between the inner life of the individual and the surrounding culture and society. A truly dynamic systems approach will need to bridge this gap between the inner mental world of the individual and the surrounding social environment. We need an approach that is similar to Ushioda's 'person-in-context relational view', which she has summarized thus:

> Let me summarize then what I mean by a person-in-context relational view of motivation. I mean a focus on real persons, rather than on learners as theoretical abstractions; a focus on the agency of the individual person as a thinking, feeling human being, with an identity, a personality, a unique history and background, a person with goals, motives and intention; a focus on the interaction between this self-reflective intentional agent, and the fluid and complex system of social relations, activities, experiences and multiple micro- and macro-contexts in which the person is embedded, moves, and is inherently part of. My argument is that we need to take a relational (rather than linear) view of these multiple contextual elements, and view motivation as an organic process that emerges through the complex system of interrelations. (p. 220)

Summary

Within academic settings and events, each student may be thought of as a self-organizing system that acts and reacts to both external and internal informational signals. These processes may explain the unique, individual facets of students' learning-related cognitions, emotions, motivations, and behaviours.
(Turner and Waugh 2007: 128)

This chapter started with the argument that the traditional notion of individual difference factors, conceived as stable and monolithic learner characteristics that act as modifying filters in the SLA process, is untenable because it ignores the multicomponential nature of these higher-order attributes and because the constituent components continuously interact with each other and the environment, thereby changing and causing change, and subsequently displaying highly complex developmental patterns. Having said that, these complex systems are also often characterized by enduring periods of stability and predictability, which may be seen as contradictory to the dynamic systems perspective adopted throughout the chapter. This, however, is not necessarily the case: if there are powerful attractors governing a dynamic system, the self-organizing capacity of the system causes the constellation to gravitate towards relatively stable attractor states, and as the process unfolds in the direction of the attractor, a wide range of starting points will eventually converge on a much smaller set of states. This process restricts intra-individual variation (i.e. makes a person more consistent and predictable) and thus promotes the emergence of seemingly stable inter-individual differences. However, it was emphasized that these equilibrium states are none the less changeable and dynamic and can—and in most cases will at some point—be moved from their preferred positions by some large push (or even by some small push, as the butterfly wings flapping in the butterfly effect; see Ch. 3).

A further problem about traditionally conceived individual difference variables is that the selection of potentially relevant factors has been somewhat haphazard. For example, in the past applied linguists have for various reasons typically ignored emotions, interests, and domain-specific knowledge (i.e. L2 proficiency), even though these factors have been shown to have a powerful impact on learning behaviour and outcomes. The selection ambiguity, however, is related to a broader issue concerning the identification of specific components of the system. If we look at the language learner as an organism characterized by system dynamics, the likely scenario is that the main attractors governing the system will be certain higher-order combinations of attributes that act as integrated wholes. This would suggest that identifying 'pure' individual difference factors has only limited value both from a theoretical and a practical point of view. Having said that, I believe that there is one organizing framework that may be useful in maintaining some order in this rather complicated set-up, the traditional 'trilogy of mind' made up of cognition, motivation, and affect, which, I argued, are phenomenologically distinct and can be seen as three underlying systems that interact with each other in forming broad attractor basins such as trait complexes or future self-guides, both of which cut across the three systems.

While I hope that this chapter has lent some appeal to a dynamic systems approach to individual difference research, let me address an issue that was originally raised by Carver and Scheier (1999): isn't the DST approach merely a descriptive model without any real explanatory power? Although we can certainly 'explain away' any dynamic movement–stability fluctuation by bringing in concepts such as emergence, self-organization, and attractor states, does this new conceptual system and terminology really help us to understand and predict the details of the learners' behaviour? That is, is the attractor landscape a useful model rather than being simply an appealing metaphor?

I would love to give a straightforward answer but the truth is that the jury is still out on this question. Personally I find it immensely helpful that DST offers a conceptual vocabulary to deal with complex interactions and non-linear changes. A further asset is the theoretical framework that can accommodate the interaction of diverse variables and interlocking temporal changes at various levels. This dynamic perspective feels much more valid than the traditional conceptualization of discrete factors and simple linear causality—in fact, one powerful argument in favour of DST is that we have tried the alternatives and they have been found lacking. There are, however, some obvious 'Yes, buts...'. At the moment it is not clear to me how this dynamic approach can be translated into actual research designs because we do not seem to have the necessary toolkit. Given that we are talking about a paradigm shift, this initial uncertainty may be seen as natural, yet it is still an uncertainty. In any case, Thelen and Smith's (1994: 342) conclusion about DST in developmental psychology in general certainly applies to SLA contexts as well:

> Finally, taken together, we believe a dynamic approach liberates developmental researchers from the tyranny of group-by-age comparisons and legitimizes alternative study designs. In particular, we encourage dense, multidimensional longitudinal studies using a few subjects where we can learn, not necessarily how all children effect some developmental transition, but in detail, how a few children do it. Such designs require extraordinary rigor, creativity, and dedication and would ideally be conducted by a multidisciplinary group in order to integrate dynamics at several levels of analysis. Such studies are an essential step in integrating dynamics over levels and time scales.

In sum, I believe most scholars would agree with Linnenbrink and Pintrich's (2004: 83) recommendation that 'future research tackle the complex issue of integrating affect, cognitive processing, and motivation into one model for learning in school'. As they explain, 'The integration and expansion of these models not only will better reflect the reality of student learning, but also may have important implications for the improvement of instruction.' Personally, the only way I can see such an integration happening is through a dynamic systems approach—there just do not seem to be any viable alternative ways. Thus, I agree with van Geert (2008: 197) that 'an understanding of dynamic systems is crucial if we want to go beyond the static or structural relationships between properties or variables and wish to understand the mechanism of development and learning as it applies to individuals'. And I also share Thelen and Smith's (1994: 341) experience:

> Once we began to view development from a dynamic and selectionist approach, we found the ideas so powerful that we could never go back to other ways of thinking. Every paper we read, every talk we heard, every new bit of data from our labs took on new meaning. We planned experiments differently and interpreted old experiments from a fresh perspective. Some questions motivating developmental research no longer seemed important; other, wholly new areas of inquiry begged for further work.

6

The learner in the language learning process II: the learner's age and the Critical Period Hypothesis

Almost everybody has a view of the role of age in language learning, and, curiously enough, most of these views are wrong. Strictly speaking, the age issue concerns one fundamental question (which is actually three): does human language learning capacity change with age, and if so, how and why? One would expect research to be able to produce a relatively straightforward answer to this question; after all, age—be it the learner's chronological age or the age of starting to learn the L2—is one of the few learner characteristics that can be easily assessed in an objective and reliable manner—all we need to do is ask the participants—and therefore it would appear to be a straightforward task to compare learners of different age groups in terms of their language learning capacity and achievement.

Thus, one would be justified in expecting some solid scientific research results with regard to the age issue, but the reality is very different: the study of age effects has produced many unforeseen obstacles and complications, and although scholarly work on age-related issues and the 'Critical Period Hypothesis'—which is the most common label under which age effects are discussed (see below)—can now fill a small library, there is still a great deal of disagreement and misunderstanding about the question. In fact, as Hyltenstam and Abrahamsson (2003) point out, the existence of a critical period for language acquisition has been one of the most widely debated issues in SLA research: while everybody agrees that the learner's age does influence the SLA process, scholars have not been able to establish the exact pattern or nature of age-related change, let alone identify the specific causes and mediators of the process.

If we think about it, however, the lack of a consensus in age-related SLA research is not at all surprising. We saw in the previous chapter that higher-order mental functions are determined by a dynamic interplay between various learner characteristics and environmental factors, and along with others I have argued that if we consider this complex system as it develops in real time, the interference of the various time-related trajectories makes the picture even more complicated. Seen from such a dynamic systems perspective, age-related effects concern the culmination of a number of power-ful temporal processes—biological ageing and maturation, general cognitive development, multiple L2 skill development—which are accompanied, depending on the context of learning, by strong additional acculturational and/or instructional influences. Furthermore, the outcome of the enterprise—attained L2 proficiency—is not a monolithic factor but is made up of various components (often described as the constituents of the learner's communica-tive competence) that have different developmental trajectories. Given that all these processes and factors are interlocked with the individual difference systems discussed in the previous chapter (i.e. cognition, affect, and motiva-tion), we can safely conclude that the age issue involves the most complex system dynamics in the whole SLA domain. In the light of this, we cannot realistically anticipate any easy answers here.

For the sake of illustrating the intricacy of the matter, let us take my own case as a learner of English as a foreign language: after studying English for almost 40 years and having lived in the UK for over ten years, I still have a recognizable Hungarian accent and my 10-year-old son takes great delight in correcting the mistakes I make in English. Yet, at the same time my academic writing skills are better in English than in Hungarian (which is my L1) and are native-like by most standards. How then would I be classified in a quan-titative critical period investigation in terms of my age-related parameters? A study would need to consider, as a minimum:

1 the age of onset of my learning English (9)
2 the age of moving to the UK (37)
3 the different developmental levels of the various facets of my attained English proficiency.

Furthermore, besides these basic biographical and proficiency-related data, a number of additional descriptors of my language learning history/situation would be necessary to obtain a comprehensive picture:

4 I initially studied English in a formal school context and only moved to the host environment at an adult age.
5 My wife is a native speaker of English and at home we predominantly use English (and did so even before we moved as a family to the UK).
6 When we were still living in Hungary, I spent ten years working in an envi-ronment (a department of English) where English was the language of most professional transactions, including teaching and staff meetings, and already during this period a great deal of our friends were native speakers of English.

Given this complex background, I would not be surprised if I was excluded from a participant sample for an age-related study because it would be diffi-cult to pigeon-hole me in any of the main categories. The problem is, however, that so many language learners can be characterized by a comparably intri-cate set of background characteristics—let us just consider, for example, the extremely varied circumstances of immigrants in terms of their living and working conditions, residential neighbourhoods, or social networks—yet past quantitative studies on age effects have usually addressed only a relatively small selection of these. This in itself may well be a source of inconsistent findings in this area.

While it is relatively easy to find supportive arguments for the inherent complexity of age-related research, the curious fact is that one of the main attractions of this research direction over the past five decades has been the observation of a number of straightforward and powerful general trends. The most popular such observation, acknowledged by many scholars and laypeople alike, is the 'younger is better' principle, referring to the common belief that the earlier we start learning an L2, the more likely it is that we will be successful. Although using such folk theories as a starting point may seem like an obvious inroad into understanding certain core issues of SLA, in actual practice such seemingly straightforward and robust paradigms can work as intricate 'honey traps', because scholars who are initially attracted to them will soon start losing their firm foothold in the quagmire of details. Indeed, we find in the literature many partially supported but vehemently defended views and heated debates in which scholars interpret the same set of evidence in strikingly different ways. There are certainly no dull moments in researching the critical period! Let us start making sense of the topic by asking a seemingly daft question: is the age issue really about age?

Is the age issue really about age?

My main disposition of the age issue has been determined by two contrasting tenets, 'the younger the better' and 'the older the better':

- *The younger the better:* it is one of the most prevailing beliefs in both the applied linguistics profession and the lay public that language learning is easier when one is young. Nobody would question that in a family that emigrates to a new country whose language they do not know, 5-year-old Jimmy's chances of attaining native-like L2 proficiency will be far better than those of his 30-year-old father, who in turn is likely to do better than 60-year-old Grandma Peggy.
- *The older the better:* anybody who has taught a foreign language to different age groups knows that a 5-year-old pupil is likely to make much less progress in a language course within a school context than a more mature learner of 15 or 30 (or even 60) years of age.

I believe that both tenets have some truth in them, so the question is: how can we resolve this contradiction? The answer lies in the fact that each tenet is true in a certain learning environment. In naturalistic language learning environments (e.g. learning a language in the host environment with plenty of direct and indirect contact with the language community, hence 'naturalistic SLA') we find many examples of young learners doing better than their older counterparts. In contrast, in formal school learning contexts (i.e. when the L2 is a school subject and the pupils have very limited, if any, direct contact with members of the L2 community, hence 'formal language learning') young learners typically do far worse than their teenage counterparts. We are going to examine these issues later in detail, but the point for now is that what is usually (and conveniently) classified under the 'age' rubric is not simply a temporal issue but rather involves an interplay of age and environment.

A further complicating factor is that age-related issues by definition concern the learning of an L2 rather than an L1, and one approach to defining the optimal window of language learning opportunity (i.e. 'critical' or 'sensitive period'; see below) in naturalistic SLA is by specifying it as the period during which the process of L2 learning is similar to the mastery of one's L1, leading to (near-)native-like L2 proficiency. A quote from a recent book-length summary of *Language Development and Age* by Herschensohn (2007: 1–2) offers a good illustration of this approach:

> Certainly, the difference between learning a first language as a child and a second language as an adult is dramatic enough to warrant the idea that there is a crucial chronological threshold which, when crossed, marks an irreversible deterioration of language learning ability.

Thus, the 'age issue' is also inextricably tied to the comparison of L1 and L2 acquisition (a huge area in itself) and it often uses the problematic concept of 'native-speaker proficiency' as the ultimate criterion level.

Finally, not even the temporal dimension underlying the age issue is straight-forward because it subsumes biological ageing and maturation, the general cognitive development of children as they grow into adults, and the different developmental trajectories of various L2 skill and competencies. These multiple factors, in turn, interact with the cognitive, affective, and motivational systems of learner characteristics discussed in the previous chapter (e.g. certain age/context combinations may favour certain types of learner). Thus, a comprehensive discussion of the age issue is never purely about age but also concerns a number of other important areas—quite frankly, we would be hard pressed to find a potentially more complex theme in SLA than the issue of age effects.

Critical period—sensitive period

Much of the literature on age effects appears under the rubric of the *critical period* (CP) or the *Critical Period Hypothesis* (CPH). As we will see below, the exact meaning of the CP shows some variation from author to author, but all the different conceptualizations specify a period in a child's life when L2 learning happens smoothly and almost inevitably, resulting in native-like or near-native-like proficiency. As a preliminary, we must note that several scholars have questioned whether a strong version of the CPH is applicable to SLA. This is why the term 'sensitive period' has been introduced in the literature to denote a softer version. Let us have a closer look at these concepts first and then examine the extent to which they are applicable to L1 and L2 acquisition.

Definitions of critical and sensitive periods

The concept of a *critical period* as a technical term originates in embryology and biology, where it was observed that certain developmental events can happen only in a limited period that has a specific closure, after which the organism in question has 'missed its chance'. Such missed opportunities, then, lead to a significant change in the behaviour or further growth of the particular organism. Thus, the CP concerns developmental phases when timing is crucial for the organism. The most popular illustration of the CP is the 'imprinting' phenomenon observed by Konrad Lorenz in the first half of the twentieth century. He demonstrated that incubator-hatched baby geese accept the first moving thing they perceive around them as their mother, and if during the brief critical bonding period (about 36 hours) it is a human who is around the goslings, this person will be irreversibly regarded as the mother goose. Further research discovered that such developmentally crucial periods may be found widely dispersed in animal and human neurobiology and behaviour, and the concept has been applied profitably to explaining developmental issues in a variety of fields (Bornstein 1989).

In a detailed analysis, Knudsen (2004) distinguished two types of developmentally decisive periods, 'sensitive periods' and 'critical periods': a *sensitive period* refers to any duration of time when the neuronal connections within the brain are particularly susceptible to environmental input, that is, when the brain displays a heightened sensitivity towards a particular type of stimulus, and if the stimulus occurs, this leads to learning with powerful and durable effects. The *critical period* is a special case of sensitive periods when the brain *must* receive certain stimulation or input in order to continue to function normally, and exposure to the stimulus, or the lack of it, leads to irreversible consequences:

> Experience exerts a profound influence on the brain and, therefore, on behaviour. When the effect of experience on the brain is particularly strong during a limited period in development, this period is referred to as a sensitive period. Such periods allow experience to instruct neural circuits to process or represent information in a way that is adaptive for the individual. When experience provides information that is essential for normal development and alters performance permanently, such sensitive periods are referred to as critical periods. (p. 1412)

The term 'critical' is appropriate in the sense that the specific developmental event can take place only within a sharply defined fixed period, whereas the developmental phase is said to be 'sensitive' only if the susceptibility in question does not diminish completely afterwards but only decreases in intensity. Thus, the terminus that follows a plateau of peak sensitivity is a crucial feature of a strict definition of a CP in distinguishing it from a sensitive period (Herschensohn 2007).

It is easy to see why the critical period metaphor has been so attractive to psychologists and applied linguists in describing language development: the 'younger is better' belief can easily be turned into the claim that there is a sensitive period for language learning, and if we believe that the automatic acquisition from mere exposure diminishes after a certain age, this might qualify for the special case of a critical period. However, as we will see below, not every scholar agrees that these analogies are a good representation of age-related effects in SLA. For example, Birdsong (2005: 109) argues that 'an analysis of end-state SLA research reveals little congruence with geometric and temporal features of critical periods. In particular, there is no apparent period within which age effects are observed; rather, they persist indefinitely.' Thus, a more detailed analysis is warranted; let us start this by looking at L1 acquisition.

Is there a critical period for first language acquisition?

It is not easy to examine the existence of a critical period in first language acquisition because virtually every infant is exposed to language from the moment he or she is born and therefore we have no direct evidence of what would happen if the start of the process were delayed. For this reason, the scholars who are renowned for first putting the critical period in language acquisition on the wider research agenda, Penfield and Roberts (1959) and Lenneberg (1967), had to rely largely on indirect psycholinguistic evidence when they speculated about the neurobiological basis of children's advantages in language learning.

More direct insights could be obtained from the few documented cases of 'feral children', that is, children who have grown up is total isolation, without receiving any language input. The most famous such child is Genie, a 13½-year-old girl discovered in the Los Angeles area in 1970. From the age of 20 months until her discovery, Genie was confined to a potty chair and a caged crib in an isolated bedroom by her psychologically unstable (depressed) father, who thought that the girl was severely retarded and who beat her up when she made any noise. As a result, she learnt to suppress all sound production and acquired no language: she knew only about 20 words and a few short phrases such as 'stopit' and 'nomore'. After she was found, intensive efforts were made to teach Genie language with little success: although the extent of her final mastery of English is still debated (see Jones 1995 for a critical analysis), she was clearly very far from native-speaking norms both in her grammar and vocabulary size. Unfortunately, an isolated case like Genie's cannot be considered reliable because we simply do not know how much her linguistic deficiencies were caused by her initial mental condition—her father was told when Genie was 20 months old that the girl was developmentally disabled and possibly mildly retarded, which triggered her confinement—or by the subsequent psychological damage of spending over ten years in isolation and deprivation.

Thus, I agree with Muñoz (2006) that data coming from feral children cannot constitute valid evidence for a firm conclusion regarding the critical period for language acquisition. Luckily, there is a second source of relevant information that offers more valid insights into this matter: developmental data about deaf children learning a sign language, such as the American Sign Language (ASL). Over the past 15 years Rachel Mayberry and her colleagues (e.g. Mayberry 1998, 2006; Mayberry and Lock 2003; Mayberry, Lock, and Kazmi 2002; for a recent review, see Mayberry 2007) have conducted a series of studies examining profoundly deaf children who started to learn a sign language as their L1 well after their births. This unique research situation is due to the fact that the majority of deaf infants (with the exception of cases where the parents themselves use sign language) are not exposed to a sign language until older ages, often after enrolling in some special school. In a series of controlled studies, Mayberry and her colleagues compared the language development of (1) native signers, that is, children who learnt ASL as their L1 from their deaf parents; (2) non-native signers, who learnt ASL as an L2 between the ages of 9 and 13, after they lost their hearing due to some viral infection; (3) 'delayed' signers, who learnt ASL as an L1 between the ages of 9 and 13 in specialist schools; and (4) control groups of normal hearing children.

The series of experiments compared, in different combinations, several aspects of the children's L1 and L2 development, the most relevant to our current theme being the comparison of the grammatical skills of hearing and deaf individuals who learnt English at similar ages but who had three contrasting types of language experience in early childhood: (1) early acquisition of a spoken language from birth; (2) early acquisition of a sign language from birth; and (3) little or no language acquisition during early childhood. The results showed unambiguously that the group with no early language was unable to acquire English grammar well even after many years of daily usage. Mayberry and Lock (2003) concluded that the observed differences were clearly due to a paucity of accessible and detailed linguistic input in early life rather than deafness, as evidenced by the high performance of the language group that was born profoundly deaf but experienced accessible language early. This summary of the scholars' findings in *Nature Magazine* clearly points to the existence of a critical period for first language acquisition:

> Our results show that the ability to learn language arises from a synergy
> between early brain development and language experience, and is
> seriously compromised when language is not experienced during early
> life. This is consistent with current knowledge about how experience
> affects visual development in animals and humans, and about learning
> and brain development in animals. The timing of the initial language

experience during human development strongly influences the capacity
to learn language throughout life, regardless of the sensori-motor form of
the early experience. (Mayberry, Lock, and Kazmi 2002: 38)

Interestingly, as Mayberry (2006) explains, delayed L1 learning affects not
only the ultimate attainment in L1 but also the outcome of L2 learning cross-
modally. That is, whereas early L1 learners of sign languages often show
near-native levels of L2 proficiency (e.g. in reading or lip-reading), delayed
L1 learners typically show low levels of ultimate L2 language proficiency.
This points to a strong relationship between the age when the L1 is learnt and
the ultimate L2 learning outcome, which suggests that missing the L1 critical
period has irreversible consequences for *any* subsequent language learning
experiences.

Is there a critical period for SLA?

Before we start answering this question, let me make two preliminary points:
first, because of the almost uniform success rate of L1 acquisition across languages, countries, and ethnic groups, there is not much point in talking about
maturational constraints with regard to the mastery of our mother tongue
(unless in special groups such as the deaf children described above), and
therefore most discussion about the 'critical period in language acquisition'
actually concerns L2 rather than L1 acquisition, whether it is explicitly stated
or not. Second, most discussion about the 'critical period in language acquisition' actually concerns learning that takes place in naturalistic SLA contexts
rather than formal learning: curiously, few authors seem to acknowledge that
very little of what is usually said about the CP is true in formal language
learning contexts and even fewer scholars offer any real explanation of the
causes of the typical reverse trend—namely, 'the older is better'—in formal
learning.

The basic tenet of the CPH is that in naturalistic language learning environments there is a circumscribed developmental period—similar to the
imprinting in goslings mentioned earlier—during which SLA is virtually
guaranteed and after which native-like mastery of an L2 is not achievable.
The strict version of CP would therefore mean that there is a specific cut-off
point before which everybody inevitably attains native-like L2 abilities and
after which nobody does. Thus, there should be a discontinuity in the slope of
the L2 attainment around the terminus of the CP, and after the cut-off point
there should be a gradual decrease in the degree of attained proficiency.

It is clear to most scholars that SLA does not meet these strict criteria for
a critical period on several grounds, particularly the lack of a sharp terminus and the extremely noisy empirical data with too many exceptions from
any generalizations. (For recent reviews, see DeKeyser and Larson-Hall
2005; Birdsong 2006; Herschensohn 2007; Nikolov and Djigunović 2006;
Singleton and Ryan 2004.) Yet, some researchers believe that if we take a less

rigid approach and focus on the essence of the CPH—namely, that at a certain phase in most children's lives appropriate language input will lead to native-like proficiency whereas the absence of the right input at the right time 'closes the door' forever in most people and only allows the attainment of limited L2 proficiency later—we can still talk about a (limited) CP effect. With regard to the actual time when the 'door closes', practically every age has been mentioned in the literature between 5 and 13 (puberty) and sometimes even later, up to 16–18.

DeKeyser (2000) makes an interesting point in defence of the CPH: he believes that as long as we narrow down its scope and consider in our analysis only the *implicit* learning of abstract structures, we can talk about a definite critical period:

> As long as L2 competence is assessed without regard for the learning mechanisms that produced it, it may appear that there is merely an optimal age for language learning, in the sense that there is a sizable negative correlation between age of acquisition and ultimate attainment. If the Critical Period Hypothesis is constrained, however, to implicit learning mechanisms, then it appears that there is more than just a sizable correlation: Early age confers an absolute, not a statistical, advantage— that is, there may very well be no exceptions to the age effect. Somewhere between the ages of 6–7 and 16–17, everybody loses the mental equipment required for the implicit induction of the abstract patterns underlying a human language, and the critical period really deserves its name. (p. 518)

As DeKeyser and Larson-Hall (2005) point out, this approach is in line with Lenneberg (1967) original observation that initiated subsequent thinking about the CPH, namely that 'automatic acquisition from mere exposure to a given language seems to disappear after this age' (p. 176). While DeKeyser's proposal is certainly appealing, we saw in Ch. 4 that adult SLA also involves some degree of implicit learning, which makes the case for a CP-based implicit–explicit switch less straightforward. Yet, several scholars agree with DeKeyser's view that the qualitative disparity between adult (i.e. post-CP) and child language acquisition suggests that somewhere along the line there is bound to be a break that is caused by maturational constraints (e.g. Hyltenstam and Abrahamsson 2003; Ioup 2005).

In contrast to the support for a limited CP notion outlined above, some researchers have taken the view that any proposed boundaries for superior learning capacity are too fluid and amount to a gradual offset at best, which, along with the numerous exceptions (e.g. adult L2 learners who manage to achieve native-like proficiency—see below) to the strict either/or categorization of a true CP as defined in biology, make it inappropriate to use the technical term 'critical period' in the case of SLA (see Birdsong 2005). One solution for salvaging the essence of the CPH has been to regard the heightened capacity for early learning in naturalistic SLA as being associated with a 'sensitive period' (Knudsen 2004). While this view allows for the existence of exceptions because it does not consider it critical, only highly advantageous, to start learning the L2 in the specified bounded period, it still assumes the existence of such a favoured period. This has been a stumbling block in CP research for several scholars, because studies have repeatedly found that age causes a gradual decline in language attainment rather than an attainment curve with a sharp discontinuity at the terminus of the period. For this reason, it has been argued, any mention of a 'period' is inappropriate and the linear relationship between age of onset of language learning (usually referred to as 'age of onset of acquisition' or AoA) and L2 attainment can be best captured by the more general term 'age effect'. Thus, the literature contains contrasting views proposed by well-respected scholars. I will begin to explore the reasons for this division by addressing three relevant issues: (1) non-native-like young learners and native-like adult learners, (2) multiple critical periods, and (3) the methodological difficulty of pooling data in quantitative CP research. Following this I will argue that age effects constitute a dynamic process that can be best understood through the lens of dynamic systems theory. I will conclude the chapter by providing a summary of the most important sources of age-related effects both in naturalistic SLA and formal learning contexts.

Non-native-like young learners and native-like adult learners

We find two groups of learners with such atypical language attainment characteristics that they have been seen to pose a real challenge to the CPH. On the one hand some learners who are young enough by any account to be considered within the CP still fail to master the L2 to a native-like level. On the other hand there are adult learners whose AoA is so late (e.g. learners in their twenties) that it simply has to be after the offset of the CP and yet who succeed in acquiring native-like proficiency. There are documented examples of both types of learner and they are normally cited as powerful evidence against the CPH. A recent example for young L2 learners whose L1-influence on pronunciation could still be detected after a long period in the host environment has been provided by Flege *et al.* (2006); in another recent investigation, Jia and Fuse (2007) found that none of the ten immigrant children whose development they followed over a five-year period in the United States managed to master the regular past tense -ed suffix at a minimum 80 per cent accuracy level, even though the youngest were 5 and 6 years old at the time of their arrival and all the children participated in mainstream schooling with additional English tuition. These examples illustrate Hyltenstam and Abrahamsson's (2003) conclusion:

> An important apparent difference from the first language context is that nativelike proficiency in a second language is not inevitable, even with

AOs in early childhood. Several studies note enduring non-native features in the ultimate attainment even of some very young starters. (p. 545)

In contrast to the relatively few studies that have identified early-starter L2 learners who should have, but have not, achieved native-like proficiency, documentation of the other CP-defeating extreme, native-like adult L2 learners, has received considerably more attention in the literature. In the light of the accumulated evidence there is little doubt that some late starters can master an L2 to an extent that they would be regarded by most people as native speakers of the particular language. Amazingly, some of these remarkable success stories are not even restricted to naturalistic SLA environments but occur in formal school contexts, with the learner studying the L2 only as a school subject. A personal friend of ours, for example, learnt English in Communist East Germany, where for obvious reasons even indirect contact with the language (e.g. English-speaking films or TV programmes) was extremely limited, let alone direct contact with native English speakers, and yet his English—including his accent—is astoundingly native-like. In fact, my wife—a native speaker of British English—sometimes mentioned to me that it was almost eerie to speak to him because of the dissonance between his native-like L2 command and his rather patchy cultural background knowledge. It was a bit like talking to a native speaker of American English who did not have a clue who the Simpsons were.

The plentiful anecdotal evidence about successful adult L2 learners has also been backed up by a decent body of empirical research over the years, and as Birdsong (2006) summarizes, these studies suggest that although native-likeness in late SLA is not typical, neither is it exceedingly rare. Common figures of the proportion of post-pubertal learners who reach a native-like level range between 5 and 10 per cent of learners in naturalistic learning environments (for a recent analysis, see Birdsong 2007), which is definitely large enough to qualify as something more than merely a few fluke cases. Thus, this summary by Bongaerts (2005: 261) seems to be well-founded:

> In sum, what these studies seem to have shown is that (1) native-like levels can be attained in a variety of linguistic domains, by individuals who begin to learn an L2 at ages beyond (sometimes well beyond) a purported critical period and that (2) the possibility of attaining native-likeness beyond the critical period is not restricted to native speakers of languages that are typologically closely related to the second language to be acquired.

At this point we must, however, note two important points that might qualify the 'adults-can-also-do-it' claim: first, Birdsong (2007) observed that the most successful late learners in his study had received phonetic training and were also very highly motivated to improve their L2 pronunciation, a finding that, as he reports, has also emerged in other studies (and is also true of our German friend, who is an English language teacher trainer by profession).

If this result is generalizable, it would indicate that even fully successful adult SLA differs from L1 acquisition in that it is not inevitable or automatic but requires certain conditions to be met. Second, it appears that if we dig deep enough, we might find chinks in the L2 armour of even the most successful expert adult L2 learners. There are several ways of assessing the native-like-ness of an L2 speaker, ranging from standard evaluative measures such as native-speaker judgement of L2 pronunciation, oral and written production tasks, and grammaticality judgements, to more sophisticated probes such as examining subtle phonetic differences in voice onset time or intonation contour. At the most refined end of the spectrum one might employ neuroim-aging techniques. It seems that even if standard measures identify someone to belong within the native-speaking range of performance—usually within two standard deviations of the mean rating obtained for a native-speaking norm group—more elaborate techniques can still detect subtle deviations from the native norm. For example, Perani *et al.* (2003) found a different brain activa-tion pattern when Spanish–Catalan bilinguals used their first and their second language, even though in the examined sample all the participants started to learn the L2 at the age of 3 and used both languages regularly, thus qualify-ing as being balanced bilinguals. It is in this light that we can understand Hyltenstam and Abrahamsson's (2001: 157) claim that 'published studies have still not identified a single adult learner who is indistinguishable from a native speaker in all relevant aspects of the L2'.

Thus, although folk wisdom holds that what looks like a duck and sounds like a duck *is* a duck, this does not necessarily apply to expert L2 learners. Or does it? How small a sign of non-native-likeness, asks Birdsong (2006), can be taken as a proof that L2 learning mechanisms are rendered defective by ageing? Could it be that some of the subtle departures from the monolingual norms are not due to a supposedly deficient acquisition process but are rather 'artefacts of the nature of bilingualism, wherein each language affects the other and neither is identical to that of a monolingual' (p. 22)? After all, there is evidence (see e.g. Obler and Gjerlow 1999) that even in the most balanced bilinguals who mastered both their languages simultaneously as L1s, very detailed linguistic scrutiny can expose certain deviations from a monolingual comparison group. It can be argued, therefore, that multilinguals do not use their languages in the same way as monolinguals. In de Bot's (2008a: 122–3) words:

> They are multilingual because they use more than one language, and for the functions for which monolinguals have only one code, multilinguals have two or more. Provided that they use multiple languages, the amount and type of use of each individual language will be different from that of monolingual native speakers.

Multiple critical periods

Whenever we use terms such as 'language mastery' or 'attained L2 profi-ciency', we indirectly imply that we are talking about a homogeneous, uniform entity. Of course, we all know that this is not so and L2 proficiency can be broken down into a number of constituent components that can be at different developmental levels from each other. Several scholars have suggested that since the different components of language—phonology, morphology, syntax, lexicon, pragmatics—are acquired relatively independently of each other, their development might follow different timetables, pointing to the possible existence of multiple critical periods for a person (e.g. Birdsong 2006; Herschensohn 2007; Seliger 1978). Knudsen (2004) also argues that language depends on a wide range of specialized sensory, motor, and cognitive skills that involve many neural networks and structures, and these circuits are shaped differently by experience. Indeed, some linguistic areas such as pragmatic knowledge and vocabulary size might show a continuous growth throughout the lifespan, whereas the hierarchy of neural circuits that underlies phonetic skills appears to be subject to CP effects.

In an often cited study of 240 Korean immigrants to the United States, Flege *et al.* (1999) found that age constrains the learning of L2 phonology to a greater extent than it does the learning of L2 morphosyntax. Observing that phonology/pronunciation/accent has a unique age-related position in SLA is, in fact, not an uncommon result in the literature. Scovel (2006) argues vigorously that the reason for the special susceptibility of pronunciation to maturation constraints is that speaking is the only overtly neuromuscular linguistic skill: it requires the intricate programming and timing of neuromuscular movement to produce native-like speech, and the mastery of this skill is qualitatively different from that of other aspects of language. A particularly convincing point Scovel makes to support this claim is that pronunciation is the only area where even very advanced L2 users cannot correct their performance once it has been brought to their attention that this performance deviates from native-like norms; with a grammar mistake or a pragmatic error advanced learners can usually make immediate repairs and thus approach native-like standards but, personally, no matter how hard I try to make some of my English sounds sound more English, they just don't seem to cut the mustard (so, to the great amusement of my family, when I call our local takeaway restaurant to order some food, all I have to say is 'Hello' and they immediately respond, 'Hello, Mr. Dörnyei').

Methodological difficulty of pooling data in quantitative CP research

Let us accept for a moment that there is indeed a critical period for attaining native-like proficiency in a new language. Even if this is so, would the terminus of this period be the same age for everybody? The chances are that it would not. With a complex and dynamic process such as learning an L2 we can expect temporal interferences by a host of internal and external variables, making the CP shorter for some and longer for others. After all, even though—as we saw in Ch. 1—L1 acquisition tends to follow a surprisingly uniform temporal pattern, we have all heard of children who deviated considerably from this (e.g. started to speak much later than their peers), and therefore, it is not unreasonable to assume that the diversity of individual developmental timelines might be even greater with regard to the learning of an L2. Accordingly, the offset of the CP can, hypothetically, range from as early as 4–5 to as late as 11–12 years of age (or even later).

How would this diversity show up in the kind of aggregated group study that is usually conducted by CP researchers? Such studies tend to be cross-sectional surveys where immigrants to a country are assessed in terms of the arrival time to the country, which is taken as the age of onset of language learning (AoA), and their language proficiency, which is taken as the ultimate level of language attainment. If we plot the attainment scores against AoA in a graph, we would find a uniformly high (i.e. native-like) attainment level for everybody who arrived before the earliest possible CP terminus—in our hypothetical example this would be under 4–5 years of age. Because the CP for some people ends at this point, when we move on along the timeline— say to the AoA of 6 years of age—we would already start finding people who could not master native-like proficiency because they arrived in the host environment after the closure of their CP door. Their lower-than-native-like proficiency level would dampen the aggregate group-proficiency level, result- ing in a decline in the attainment line. The further we proceed along the AoA line, the more people we will find with less-than-native-like ultimate attain- ment, lowering the aggregate attainment score even further. This decline would not stop at the point when the last critical period in our hypotheti- cal sample is terminated (i.e. at the AoA of 11–12), because several factors such as cognitive ageing, social factors, or decreased overall commitment (see below for more detail) would still cause a decreasing tendency, favouring younger adult learners to older ones.

In sum, even in a situation when we assume the existence of a CP in its strictest sense, a typical quantitative CP study would show a more-or-less consistent, linear decline in attainment (perhaps with a brief initial peak) with the increase of AoA—and certainly a significant negative correlation between attainment and AoA—simply because subjects with different CP offset times are pooled in a joint database and the AoA values of these subjects represent, in effect, scores measured on different scales depending on the subjects' individual variation in the length of their critical period. (From a psychometric perspective, this situation can be compared to com- puting, say, the mean attitude score of a group of people of whom some responded on a 9-point scale, others on a 3-point scale.) The obtained declining pattern is a very common result found in quantitative CP studies, but due to the methodological difficulty of pooling group-based data, the interpretation of the pattern is ambiguous: it could in theory indicate the existence of a CP in the strictest sense, as in the above example, but if the study did not sample enough learners with very young AoA, there may not be a sufficiently prominent discontinuity in the declining tendency to indicate the terminus of a CP, which could be used as evidence *against* the CPH. (For a detailed discussion of the various attainment patterns, see Birdsong 2006.)

A dynamic systems perspective on the Critical Period Hypothesis

We saw in the previous chapters that dynamic systems theory concerns systems with multiple interconnected components that have independent developmental trajectories over time. In such complex systems there is a constant dynamic interference amongst the various system parts as they change and are changed, and as they interact with the environment. As pointed out earlier, shaped by the interaction of a host of internal and external factors and conditions, our parallel chronological, biological, and cognitive ageing/ development can be seen as the most complex system dynamics in the whole SLA domain, characterized by a great deal of seemingly unpredictable individual-level variation. Indeed, looking at past CP research, we do find a lot of noise in the results and there are rather few studies that produced attainment curves that unambiguously supported the existence of a critical period. As Birdsong (2005) summarizes, the available behavioural evidence suggests that age effects in SLA do not operate within a well-defined temporal period, and the 'occasional nonlinearities in the age function do not reliably map onto predicted developmental and geometric patterns of declining sensitivity' (p. 119).

The absence of any robust trends and patterns is fully congruent with a dynamic systems perspective, because a basic premise of DST is that in complex systems nothing is permanent or absolute, and even seemingly solid equilibrium states are changeable as they can be moved from their preferred positions by a large enough push. A good illustration of this principle is that—as I have already mentioned and will discuss later in more detail—even such a powerful and widely accepted/observed regularity as the 'younger-is-better' tendency is not only cancelled out but is completely reversed under certain environmental conditions (by changing the learning context from naturalistic SLA to formal school learning). Of course, nobody doubts that in naturalistic SLA some powerful age-related attractors operate that benefit young learners and override a great deal of individual-level variation, but it is also clear that their influence is significantly different from the absolute temporal effects observed in CP phenomena in biology (for example in the imprinting of the goslings).

From a dynamic systems perspective, even the term 'sensitive period' is questionable, because it still implies a uniform and generalizable developmental pattern of a high plateau followed by a decline. How does this apply, for example, to the expert adult learners discussed above? Is the sensitive period extended in their case, or do they achieve their remarkable L2 success during an 'insensitive' period? And how do we know that there is only one sensitive period in a person's development? Does a sensitive period have more sensitive and less sensitive phases? If so, what causes the desensitization and in what way is the desensitized sensitive phase different from the insensitive one? Questions such as this abound and without properly considering them the term 'sensitive period' is, in effect, a mere synonym for the broad 'younger-is-better' tenet.

I believe that from a DST point of view these terminological issues are far less important than trying to specify the range of relevant attractors and attractor basins, as well as identifying certain optimal combinations of variables that promote L2 attainment. The significance of such variable patterns, or learner-environment combinations, has been highlighted by several scholars recently. Moyer (2004: 138), for example, stated:

> I have argued that multiple factors, in combination with one another, may account for age effects to a statistically significant degree. Age of exposure, like length of residence, may give us little indication of the underlying mechanisms responsible for attainment; instead, depending on the individual case, it may be more of an indication of cumulative experience, including constraints on the language learning process from several fronts. Those initiating language acquisition after puberty may be subject to an especially complex combination of influences from social, psychological and cognitive realms.

In their conclusion to their book-length overview of the age factor in language acquisition, Singleton and Ryan (2004: 227) express very similar beliefs when they suggest that 'the various age-related phenomena isolated by language acquisition research probably result from the interaction of a multiplicity of causes and that different phenomena may have different combinations of causes'. Importantly, and as I have argued above, they do not question the potential significance of certain neurobiological changes in the brain, only 'the notion that age effects are exclusively a matter of neurological predetermination, that they are associated with absolute, well-defined maturational limits and that they are particular to language'.

In sum, I would not like to trivialize the claim that a critical/sensitive period is a common and immensely powerful phenomenon. There are too many examples of the fact that some doors do close at some point with regard to L2 attainment. Having said that, I would like to shift the emphasis to the fact that multiple processes and multiple factors are at work in both constraining and promoting SLA, and their emergent outcome cannot be taken for granted in an absolute way that the CP logic would dictate. As we will see below, for example, the available evidence (empirical and anecdotal alike) suggests that there is no critical period involved in learning an L2 within formal school contexts—in fact, a young age can become a distinct disadvantage there. Furthermore, even in naturalistic SLA environments the combination of various internal and external factors can generate a considerable amount of unpredictability of the ultimate attainment levels, which is exactly what we would expect of a complex system regardless of the strength of the dominant attractors. In the rest of this chapter, therefore, I will take stock of the range of potential attractors so that we have a clearer picture of the attractor basins associated with age effects.

The age effect and its possible sources

> *It would appear that L2A [second language acquisition] is out of the*
> *running as a strict critical period phenomenon, yet the deterioration of*
> *language learning ability so evident to casual observers begs an explanation.*
> (Herschensohn 2007: 140)

Age matters in language learning but it is not quite clear how. The relevant literature contains a variety of different explanations and diverse lists of proposed age factors, making it rather difficult for the uninitiated reader to decide whom to believe. Addressing this question, Birdsong (2006) advises that we take the initial position that all the identified factors and mechanisms that are not at odds with empirical findings are potentially exerting some impact on the acquisition process. Following this advice, after a brief description of the 'younger-is-better' principle in naturalistic SLA and the 'older-is-better' principle in formal learning, I will review the main sources of the age effects separately in the two types of learning contexts.

The younger the better

One of the most pervasive beliefs about SLA is that language learning is easier at a younger age and, thus, the younger the better. This view is accepted by most non-specialists and specialists alike; for example, Kuhl (2000: 11855) states, 'There is no doubt that children learn language more naturally and efficiently than adults,' and N. Ellis (2005b: 5) also concludes, 'It is an incontrovertible fact that ultimate second language attainment is less successful in older than younger learners.' As a result, educational authorities all over the world are in the process of trying to bring forward the starting age of language instruction in primary schools (see Nikolov and Djigunović 2006).

The problem with the 'younger-is-better' view is that it only applies in optimal naturalistic SLA contexts, that is, when the learner is immersed in the host environment and has regular and rich interactions with a variety of native speakers. For a young immigrant child who starts primary school in the new country at the age of 5–6, such optimal conditions are often automatically provided by the school experience. However, for an adult immigrant whose main social network involves people from his/her own ethnolinguistic group, and who has few if any native-speaking colleagues at work, the learning conditions are far from ideal. Neither are they optimal for a foreign language learner whose contact with the L2 might be restricted to two or three language classes a week within a school context. In such cases a young age may not be an advantage. As mentioned before, most of the age-effect literature concerns speakers who engage in naturalistic SLA and authors also take it for granted that this context can, by definition, provide the learner with sufficient L2 input. We shall see later when we review social factors that this assumption is unwarranted in several contexts (e.g. where immigrants live in ethnolinguistic clusters).

Having voiced these initial caveats, there is a massive body of evidence that in naturalistic SLA a person's ultimate L2 attainment is negatively correlated with the age of onset of acquisition, which is typically taken to be the arrival in the L2 community. This strong tendency has been observed for a variety of aspects of L2 proficiency, from pronunciation to grammatical knowledge and accuracy, using a wide variety of testing formats. Of course, correlation does not mean causation, which is further coupled with the methodological difficulties in using aggregated group-data concerning AoA discussed earlier. On the other hand, the consistency and strength of the relationship between AoA and language attainment found in past research suggest that there is a powerful underlying age-related tendency involved.

The older the better

> *With very few exceptions ... the L2 learning context has not been included as an important factor in the discussion of the CPH, and findings from second language learning in naturalistic contexts have been generalized to foreign language learning in instructed contexts.*
> (Muñoz 2006: 6)

The 'younger-is-better' view is so deeply engraved in the public mind that it has been generalized to contexts where the principle does not hold at all. The most prominent such context is learning an L2 as a school subject; here not only is younger not better but, as mentioned before, the opposite seems to be true.

The first indications that formal learning contexts might present a radically different pattern of age effects came from Canada. Here it was found that those anglophone children in French immersion settings who entered the immersion programme relatively late (around the age of 9–11 or even later) soon caught up with the early immersion students, who start the immersion programme in kindergarten or when entering primary school. Information coming from non-immersion language programmes has also confirmed that in school settings older students tend to make considerably better progress than their younger peers, particularly in acquiring morphosyntactic and lexical aspects of the second language and sometimes also in acquiring phonological aspects. (For overviews, see Harley and Wang 1997; Herschensohn 2007; Lightbown and Spada 2006; Nikolov and Djigunović 2006.)

One possible way of reconciling these findings with the popular 'younger-is-better' principle was to suggest that younger children learn 'better' in educational settings only in the sense of going further rather than going faster. This idea, voiced by several authors over the past 30 years, has been based on speculation rather than empirical data, as acknowledged by Singleton and Ryan (2004: 223): 'Extrapolating from the naturalistic studies, one may plausibly argue that early formal instruction in an L2 is likely to yield advantages after rather longer periods of time than have so far been studied.' However, in the light of recent research in Spain (described below), we can conclude that no matter how plausible these speculations may have been, they are likely to be incorrect, as in formal school learning the younger does not seem to be better in any way.

Over the last few years two carefully designed and documented longitudinal investigations have been carried out in Spain in order to examine the 'older-is-better' issue. (For concise summaries, see García Mayo and García Lecumberri 2003; Nikolov and Djigunovič 2006.) Examining three groups of Basque learners of English—attending fifth year of primary school, second year of secondary school, and fifth year of secondary school—who had all been exposed to 600 hours of instruction, Cenoz (2003) reported that the oldest group obtained the highest level of English proficiency, followed by the intermediate group, and finally the youngest group. The only area where the youngest learners proved to be superior to their older peers was their attitudinal/motivational disposition. The second study investigating Catalan learners of English—the Barcelona Age Factor (BAF) Project (see Muñoz 2006)—produced very similar findings. Several groups of learners (total N = 1,928) with different AoA were examined three times, after 200 hours, 416 hours, and 726 hours of instruction. The results unambiguously confirmed that older learners of a foreign language progressed faster than younger learners. Furthermore, Muñoz also concluded that even after longer periods of time, younger starters did not outperform later starters, and the extensive span and size of this investigation makes this finding particularly robust.

These results have serious implications for formulating language teaching policies. They serve as strong evidence that in formal learning contexts younger is not better but worse. Accordingly, recent initiatives that attempt to push forward the starting age of learning a foreign language as a school subject in many countries of the world are misguided and potentially counterproductive. Thus, I am in full agreement with Lightbown and Spada (2006), who conclude that older learners are likely to be able to make better use of the limited time they have access to L2 instruction:

> When the goal is basic communicative ability for all students in an educational system, and when it is assumed that the child's native language will remain the primary language, it may be more efficient to begin second or foreign language teaching later. When learners receive only a few hours of instruction per week, learners who start later (for example, at age ten, eleven, or twelve) often catch up with those who began earlier. Some second or foreign language programmes that begin with very young learners but offer only minimal contact with the language do not lead to much progress.

Sources of the age effect in formal school learning contexts

Explanations of the superior L2 learning capacity of older children in educational settings usually centre around three interrelated issues: (1) the cognitive maturity and superior literacy of older learners, (2) a shift from implicit to explicit learning, and (3) quantitative and qualitative aspects of the typical L2 instruction.

- *Cognitive maturity and superior literacy:* one obvious reason why older language learners might be more efficient than their younger peers is their greater cognitive maturity, which enables them to make the most of educational tasks. This cognitive maturity involves their enhanced metalinguistic knowledge, their larger repertoire of various learning techniques and problem-solving skills, and their increased capacity to deal with abstract concepts such as grammatical rules. In addition, older is also better for becoming literate, and literacy is a powerful means towards success in instructed SLA.
- *Explicit–implicit divide:* we have already looked at DeKeyser's argument about the shift in L2 learners' learning mechanisms from the inherently implicit learning that characterizes L1 acquisition to a primarily explicit-based learning, which appears to be the foundation of most skill learning processes in adults. As will be elaborated below, typical formal teaching in educational settings caters for explicit learning, which young learners are simply not ready for. While this is certainly a contributing factor, the 'older-is-better' trend has also been found in full immersion programmes where the conditions for implicit learning are as good as they can get in school contexts (although still far inferior to the conditions offered by full immersion in the host environment).
- *Quantity of instruction:* the most obvious difference between naturalistic and formal language learning contexts is the amount of language input that is available to the learner. Just to illustrate the enormous gap between the two environments, in educational contexts 600 hours of learning history is regarded as fairly substantial and can usually be achieved only over several years, whereas the same amount of language input can easily be obtained in a period of two months immersed in the host environment. The limiting effects of insufficient instruction have been explicitly underscored by Lightbown and Spada (2006: 186–7):

One or two hours a week—even for seven or eight years—will not produce advanced second language speakers. This 'drip-feed' approach often leads to frustration as learners feel that they have been studying 'for years' without making much progress. Sadly, they are sometimes right about this.

It could, then, well be the case that older learners are more efficient because they are better equipped to cope with the poverty of L2 input than their younger peers.

- *Quality of instruction:* several scholars emphasize the fact that it is not only the quantity of language instruction that is usually lacking in formal learning but also the *quality* of the language input and learning experience the learners are exposed to. Different age groups need different types of input and practice opportunities, and although my personal experience is that the dominant language teaching methodology tends to be rather ineffective worldwide, there is no doubt that younger learners usually have a worse deal than their older peers. In order to capitalize on their implicit learning capacity, they should be engaged in tasks that offer hands-on, meaningful activities and an abundance of rich naturalistic-like input that they can access (songs and games are obvious activities for the youngest age group), yet language programmes organized along these lines are rare. On the other hand, young learners benefit little from explicit rules and tasks that require inductive/deductive reasoning skills and abstract thinking, and which tend to make up the bulk of the standard L2 instruction all over the world. (For a recent review, see Nikolov and Djigunovič 2006.)

Sources of the age effect in naturalistic SLA contexts

There has been a considerable amount of research conducted in the past to examine the reasons for the widely observed 'younger-is-better' phenomenon in naturalistic SLA contexts. As a result, a wide range of factors has been proposed that can be divided in six broad categories: (1) *biographical variables*; (2) *biological factors*; (3) *the implicit–explicit shift*; (4) *learner characteristics*; (5) *social factors*; and (6) *L1 influences*. It is important to note, however, Flege *et al.*'s (2006) warning that our current state of knowledge does not allow us to choose from among these competing explanations because they co-vary. That is, some of the assumed sources of age effects are closely linked—and hence interfere—with each other, which is in accordance with a dynamic systems perspective. An example given by Flege *et al.* concerns the widely observed inverse relationship between two central factors: the immigrants' AoA and their percentage L2 use. As a result of this correlation, Flege and his colleagues argue that a stronger foreign accent for late as opposed to early bilinguals might be equally attributed to diminished neural plasticity and to less L2 input.

Biographical variables

Let us start with the three main biographical variables—*age of onset of acquisition* (AoA), *length of residence* (LoR), and *age of exposure* (AoE)—even though it is clear that these are only broad indices that need to be linked up with mediating factors to arrive at real explanations.

Age of onset of acquisition: in most studies AoA is taken to be the immigrant's arrival—that is, immersion—in the L2 community. The obvious problem with this conceptualization is that many immigrants do not arrive in the host country with zero L2 proficiency and if this is the case then the 'L2 baggage' they may bring with them can interfere with any subsequent L2 learning. In spite of this, as Birdsong (2006) summarizes, the results of more than two dozen empirical studies converge on identifying a strong negative correlation between AoA and ultimate L2 attainment in naturalistic SLA, most notably in the areas of morphosyntax and pronunciation. (For reviews, see Birdsong 2005, 2006; DeKeyser and Larson-Hall 2005; Singleton 2005; Singleton and Ryan 2004.) This general pattern of lower ultimate attainment being associated with rising onset ages is, in fact, one of the most robust tendencies identified in SLA research to date, and currently we do not know of any better predictors of ultimate attainment than AoA.

While AoA is indeed a reliable predictor of ultimate L2 attainment, it is a rather general index that reflects a number of possible overlapping sources of age effects. Although AoA obviously indicates how early the onset of SLA was, in a cross-sectional survey it is also an index of the length of exposure to the L2 because people who arrived earlier have, by definition, been staying in the host environment longer. AoA is also an indirect index of how much schooling the person has been subject to in the host environment and indicates, too, how developed and established the individual's L1 was when he/she became immersed in the L2 context. In addition, earlier arrival can also be associated with a better integration into the host community and more native speakers in one's social network, and we could keep adding to the list of potentially confounding factors. The point to note is that when we compare the L2 proficiency of two people with different AoA, the observed difference cannot be automatically attributed to the earlier start. In statistical terms, even if we find a significant correlation between AoA and ultimate attainment, we must not forget that correlation does *not* mean causation.

Length of residence (LoR): LoR refers to the amount of time spent immersed in the L2 context. One would logically expect that the longer an immigrant spends in the host community, the better his/her L2 proficiency becomes, but this is not necessarily so. It seems that most people reach a certain plateau after a while and any residence beyond this plateau does not substantially increase the learners' attained proficiency level. For example, Flege *et al.* (2006) assessed the degree of foreign accent of a learner sample at two different points in time, with a 1.2-year interval between them, and found no measurable change over this time span. In another study investigating learners with high LoR, DeKeyser (2000) computed correlations between the participants' LoR and L2 proficiency. The coefficient was 0.00, which made DeKeyser conclude that 'length of residence no longer plays a role past the first 10 years' (p. 514).

Age of exposure (AoE): besides AoA and LoR, Birdsong (2006) mentions a third biographical variable, AoE, which is often distinct from AoA. It refers to the first encounter with the L2, either in a formal schooling environment or during a trip to a country where the L2 is spoken, or sometimes through some extended contact with relatives or friends who are L2 speakers. This factor is rarely taken into account in CP studies in spite of the fact that it is closely associated with the 'L2 baggage' that many immigrants bring to the host environment.

Biological factors

In examining the undeniable significance of a young age in naturalistic SLA, the first explanations scholars usually consider is a biological one, concerning some irreversible change in the neurostructure of the brain that is assumed to take place at a certain point, thereby 'closing a door' and directing SLA onto alternative and usually less effective paths. Lenneberg's (1967) pioneering ideas concerning the CPH certainly revolved around such an explanation and his proposal was that our capacity to acquire language naturally and effortlessly stops when the lateralization of the two hemispheres of the brain becomes firmly established, which happens for most people around puberty. Thus, Lenneberg believed that the terminus of CP is 'related to a loss of adaptability and inability for reorganization in the brain, particularly with respect to the topographical extent of neurophysiological processes' (p. 179), and he also noted that similar infantile plasticity with eventual irreversible topographical representation in the brain has been demonstrated for many higher mammals.

While Lenneberg (1967) drew on results of aphasia research, particularly on the fact that the prognosis for complete language recovery for children with brain damage rapidly deteriorates with advancing age after the early teens, he also admitted that the specific neurophysiological correlates of speech and language were 'completely unknown' and therefore he emphasized that drawing parallels between certain changes in structural and physiological substrates and the limited language capacity was only a suggestion. Although Lenneberg's proposal has inspired a great deal of related research over the past 40 years, it is still the case that we do not have an unambiguous link between neurobiological changes in the brain and any limitations in SLA capacity (Herschensohn 2007). The most frequently mentioned factor in this respect has been the decreasing plasticity of the brain; for example, MacWhinney (2001*a*: 86) states, 'This declining plasticity of the brain is at the root of the difficulties that older adults have in acquiring full competence in L2. This slow decline in flexibility is often discussed in terms of the theory of critical periods.' Yet, the evidence usually cited to support the plasticity argument is a reference to Lenneberg's work (or to the even earlier research by Penfield and Roberts 1959), which, as we have seen above, is less than conclusive. Furthermore, neuroimaging studies that point to a difference between L1 and L2 language activity are also inconclusive in that even if they successfully identify a marked difference in the activation patterns, this is not linked to impaired learning potential.

Birdsong (2006) conducted a review of research on cognitive ageing that affects our mental capacity in general, including language skills. As he summarizes, studies on the ageing brain reveal that several cognitive functions that are associated with language acquisition and processing are steadily compromised by age, including associative and working memory and processing speed. These losses begin in early adulthood and continue in a linear manner throughout a person's lifespan. The resulting negative effects, Birdsong argues, are likely to affect L2 acquisition more than operations involving our mother tongue because of the inferior level of automatization in the former. While such a decline is inevitable, it is clearly just one piece in a more complex puzzle, not solely responsible for language-related age effects.

In conclusion, if there is a definite neurobiological correlate of the 'younger-is-better' trend in naturalistic SLA, it has not yet been found. I do not think that anyone would seriously question the overall validity of the general observation that acquiring a new language through mere exposure becomes successively more difficult (but not impossible), and if there is indeed such a maturational constraint, it is likely to have specific neurobiological correlates that, it is hoped, will be identified in future research. The deaf studies reported earlier with regard to the existence of a critical period of L1 learning do point to the existence of certain fundamental neurobiological changes affecting the language acquisition process, and if this is indeed the case, these neurobiological factors will also affect SLA. Yet, it is my belief that even such biological factors will not constitute a strong enough attractor (or repeller) in the dynamics of our cognitive system that cannot be overridden by certain combinations of other variables.

The implicit–explicit shift

An interesting cognitive theory of age effects (briefly mentioned before) proposes that the decreasing language learning capacity in naturalistic SLA is due to the declining role of implicit learning and memory in the language acquisition process, and a parallel increase in the role of explicit learning and memory. (See e.g. DeKeyser 2000; DeKeyser and Juffs 2005; Paradis 2004; Ullman 2005.) The plausibility of this argument is supported by the wide agreement that learners 'process their late-learnt second language differently than their native language and the resulting performance is rarely (if ever) the same' (Paradis 2004: 60). A lot has been written in the literature questioning the existence of 'the native speaker', yet I believe that he/she *does* exist in the sense that there is something altogether different experientially about knowing/using an L1 and an L2. I have given the following personal illustration of this experience in a recent essay (Dörnyei 2006b):

> Because I probably write more and better in academic English than many NSs [native speakers], some people might say that I am a NS in this respect. However, the fact is I am not—I am keenly aware all the time that I am working in a second language. Even more interestingly, I find it very difficult to write academic texts in my mother tongue, and still I can sense a qualitative difference between producing polished L2 and clumsy L1 writing: When I write in the second language I know and feel that I am doing a good job as a NNS [non-native speaker], whereas with L1 written work I know and feel that I am doing a bad job as a NS. There is no mistaking the two.

A particular strength of the implicit–explicit shift hypothesis is that it can account for the contrasting age effects in naturalistic SLA and formal school learning: in the former, the dominating learning mechanism is implicit and therefore the younger we are the more we can capitalize on this; in the latter, however, the limited amount of L2 exposure and the cognitively structured input typically favours explicit learning and therefore we can benefit from this language environment more at an older age when the implicit–explicit shift is well on the way and has thus prepared us for utilizing explicit learning mechanisms.

Although it is often assumed that it is the loss of the implicit learning ability that 'forces late second-language learners to rely on explicit learning, which results in the use of a cognitive system different from that which supports the native language' (Paradis 2004: 59), the truth is that we do not know what causes the apparent implicit–explicit shift. One could also argue, for example, that rather than regarding implicit learning as the culprit whose mysterious disappearance creates a limbo that needs to be filled by explicit mechanisms, it is the growing cognitive maturity of adolescents that impedes implicit SLA, which makes implicit learning the expelled victim. A further question is to what extent implicit learning ceases to operate in post-infant language acquisition. We saw in Ch. 4, for example, that proceduralization plays an important role even in adult SLA, which underscores the implicit dimension of learning.

Learner characteristics

Much of the research on the critical period hypothesis has focused on the attainment of nativelike levels of proficiency for L2 learners and yet this is not the objective for most L2 learners.
(Tomlinson 2007: 6)

Almost every researcher analysing age effects highlights the importance of learner characteristics in SLA, in contrast with the inevitability of L1 acquisition. Of course, the latter 'inevitability' might be due to at least two very different causes: on the one hand, it can indicate that children learn their L1 *regardless of* any variation in their cognitive, emotional, and motivational systems; on the other hand, the invariable L1 acquisition success can also be due to the fact that the desire to become a fully participating member of the social community—which requires language skills as a prerequisite—generates such a strong desire to learn the L1 in the infant that it overrides any other learner variation. We know that little children feel very strongly motivated to accommodate to their surroundings language-wise; for example, if their family relocates to a new part of the country where people speak with a different accent, children manage to change their accent rapidly and dramatically so that they do not stand out from their peers at school. It may well be the case that a substantial source of age effects is the gradual weakening of such elementary desires. This view is compatible with Birdsong's (2007) observation, mentioned earlier, that most successful late learners in his study had attended phonetic training and were also very highly motivated to improve their L2 pronunciation: exceptional commitment can lead to native-like L2 competence even at later stages of life. This was confirmed by Nikolov and Djigunović's (2006: 239) study, in which the authors concluded that 'all the post-puberty learners who were frequently mistaken for native speakers definitely strived for unaccented proficiency, similarly to participants in previous studies'. As they further explained, for many of these successful adult L2 learners 'the target language was either part of their profession or they had very strong integrative motivation to become bona fide residents of L2 society'.

Thus, a learner-characteristics-based explanation of age effects includes the tenet that maturation brings about a change in the intensity and direction of several language-related learner characteristics—see for example Moyer (2004). The primary overarching desire to integrate fully into one's speech community that characterizes L1 acquisition is softened and diluted with age as well as by the fact that one already speaks a language and has various ties with the community that uses it. Thus, I believe that Tomlinson (2007: 4) makes an important point when he emphasizes that 'Most L2 acquirers never need to attain native-like levels of language use.' It is also often mentioned (e.g. Saville-Troike 2006) that young children tend to have fewer inhibitions than their older peers, let alone adult learners, and they are therefore more willing to plunge into any language learning experience, especially if it happens in the literal or metaphorical playground. Similarly, it can be (and has been) argued that young children have a weaker group identity, which helps them to integrate more in a host community and identify with its members.

Sociocultural factors and the language preference switch

The ease with which younger children acquire native-like L2 proficiency in naturalistic SLA has also been explained by what we can call 'sociocultural' factors that describe various aspects of the social and cultural environment immigrant children become integrated into. Such factors are associated with schooling, friendship patterns, and other social networks, cultural habits including media input, and various practices related to L1 maintenance. The broad argument is that different ages of arrival in the host country set immigrant children on different social contingency paths in terms of their friendship networks and various cultural practices, as a result of which early arrivals are exposed to a significantly richer L2 environment than late arrivals. Such systematic environmental differences lead to significant consequences in terms of long-term L1 attainment, reflected for example in the fact that young children often switch their language preference from L1 to L2, whereas older children maintain their L1 preference (Jia and Aaronson 2003; Jia and Fuse 2007).

Thus, at the heart of the sociocultural argument is the recognition that immigrants of different age groups differ in the social and cultural practices and preferences they develop in their new environment, and this difference is systematic across cohorts. This raises fundamental questions about the covert implication in various neurobiological and cognitive arguments concerning age effects that children with different AoA follow a roughly similar language socialization course—usually referred to as 'immersion in the L2 community'—with the only main discrepancy being the age at which they are exposed to the new language. Instead, as Moyer (2004) summarizes, early exposure predisposes children to a greater variety of contact sources and practice opportunities, leading to 'greater confidence and sense of self in the language' (p. 140). Stevens (1999) also emphasizes the fact that because language acquisition is a social process, it requires exposure to the language as well as opportunities to practice receptive and active skills as part of communicative and social interaction. Yet, she argues that most cross-sectional surveys underestimate the importance of 'the dynamic and irreducibly social processes that may intertwine increasing English skills with increasing participation in social settings' (p. 575). Her overall conclusion echoes the argument outlined above:

> [T]he timing of immigration within the life-course sets immigrants onto certain life-course trajectories. For example, immigrants who enter the country earlier in life are more likely to go school in the U.S., and are more likely to marry a native-born American, than those who enter the country at older ages. (p. 574)

A study of 240 Korean immigrants to the United States by Flege, Yeni-Komshian, and Liu (1999) partially confirmed the social claim: the researchers found that as the AoA of the children increased, their foreign accents grew stronger and their scores on tests of English morphosyntax decreased steadily. However, when confounding variables such as the length of schooling in the United States and their L1–L2 use percentage were controlled, the effect of AoA on the grammaticality judgement test scores (but not on foreign accent) became non-significant. Consequently, Flege *et al.* concluded that 'the observed decrease in morphosyntax scores was not the result of passing a maturationally defined critical period' (p. 78). The authors also identified a number of sociocultural factors that significantly contributed to the long-term attainment of both pronunciation and grammar, such as the motivation to integrate, the percentage use of L1 and L2, and the media input in the L2 (e.g. movies, videos, TV, and radio). At the same time, we must note that the variance these variables explained in this study was less than 10 per cent of the variance explained by AoA, and therefore although Flege *et al.*'s investigation raised some important issues, it did not provide sufficiently decisive evidence to support the significance of social factors. Indeed, the field in general has been divided on this issue, which is well illustrated, for example, by a spirited exchange between Marinova-Todd, Marshall, and Snow (2000, 2001) and Hyltenstam and Abrahamsson (2001) in *TESOL Quarterly*.

Further light on the social processes involved in the L2 acquisition of Asian immigrants in the United States has been shed by two intriguing studies by Jia, Aaronson, and Wu (2002) and Jia and Aaronson (2003). In the first study the researchers focused on the curious fact that while L2 proficiency decreases with the increase of AoA, L1 proficiency appears to increase at the same time. Thus, the relative levels of L1 and L2 proficiency have opposite patterns among younger and older arrivals. This suggested that sometime after their arrival to the United States younger arrivals tend to switch their dominant language from L1 to English, whereas older arrivals tend to maintain the L1 as their dominant language. Jia *et al.* believed that this shift of preference was socially motivated, and this assumption was supported by the fact that in their study the English proficiency of the participants' mothers was found to be a significant predictor of the participants' L2 proficiency.

In order to understand the details of the preference shift, Jia and Aaronson (2003) conducted a follow-up longitudinal study examining the language development of ten Chinese children who immigrated to the United States between the ages of 5 and 16 over a period of three years. All ten participants were in mainstream English classes from the beginning and also attended English as a second language classes for 1–3 years. The investigation revealed three striking tendencies:

- *Friends:* first, although younger and older arrivals had almost the same total number of friends in each year, younger arrivals as a group dramatically increased the average number of L2-speaking friends over the three-year period examined (from 1.8 to 6.2), while the number of their L1-speaking friends remained at a low level (decreased from 1.0 to 0.5). In contrast, older arrivals as a group had low numbers of L2-speaking friends (an increase from 0.1 to 2.3) but consistently high numbers of L1-speaking friends (an increase from 4.3 to 5.5).
- *Leisure reading:* it was found that younger arrivals read significantly more books and newspapers in the L2 than the older participants. For young arrivals, reading in their L1 decreased to close to zero as they forgot the Chinese characters they learnt. In contrast, late arrivals continued to do most of their leisure reading in Chinese.
- *Cultural preferences:* perhaps because they had had fewer native culture experiences, younger children were more curious about the broader popular American peer culture, such as baseball games and TV shows. Older children preferred to interact with peers from their own culture, and discussed with them familiar Chinese movies and songs, and shared CDs and information related to their favourite Chinese celebrities.

Jia and Aaronson (2003) acknowledged that some of the trends in peer preferences were not related to the participants' immigrant status. Younger children in general tend to develop friendships based on concrete activities and thus choose playmates who are close by, regardless of their ethnic background—with immigrant children, of course, such a free mixing requires English as the lingua franca. In contrast, older children tend to view friendship in terms of similar interests and cultural identities, as well as mutual consideration and understanding. Therefore, they choose friends based on similarities in race, ethnicity, gender, and social class—with immigrant children this means making friends with those of the same cultural background and speaking their L1 with one another. Jia and Aaronson's study thus illustrates clearly how their different AoA set children on different ethnolinguistic and sociocultural trajectories, which then significantly affected the level of their L2 use and attainment.

In a follow-up study, Jia and Fuse (2007) analysed the acquisition of English grammatical morphemes by the same children five years after their arrival. They conducted a growth-curve analysis, which indicated that 'when L2 environment, measured concurrently with L2 morphological proficiency, was incorporated into the analysis together with AoA, L2 environment won out as a significant predictor over AoA' (p. 1296). More specifically, when they partialled out the effects of the environmental factors mentioned above, the independent contribution of AoA became insignificant. Thus, the authors concluded that 'AoA effects can be largely attributed to differences in language environment associated with age' (p. 1296).

L1 Influences: 'entrenchment' and 'native language neural commitment' (NLNC)

We have already covered four major potential sources of age effects: neurobiological and cognitive changes in the brain, and factors associated with the learner and the learning environment. This list seems to be comprehensive and yet there is a final key element in the equation that might be behind age effects in acquiring an L2: the first language knowledge that L2 learners already possess by definition. The general idea is that learners with later AoA have far more experience with their native tongue than very young children, which suggests a possible cause for any age effect, namely that the more established one's mother tongue, the more difficult it becomes to attain a new language. Several scholars believe that this is indeed the case and some intriguing theories have been offered to support this claim.

The inverse relationship between L1 and L2 proficiency in naturalistic SLA contexts has been noticed and documented by many. Flege, for example, has proposed more than once that as the L1 sound system develops during childhood, its influence on L2 pronunciation grows stronger (for a review, see Flege *et al.* 2006), and in their study described above, Jia, Aaronson, and Wu (2002) also point out the common trend in CP studies that long-term L2 proficiency decreases but long-term L1 proficiency increases with increasing AoA. N. Ellis (2007c) explains this general observation by the fact that the processing habits developed during L1 acquisition pose an obstacle to overcome for SLA. The two most coherent theories concerning the details of such interfering processing habits have been Brian MacWhinney's 'entrenchment' theory and Patricia Kuhl's 'native language neural commitment' (NLNC) theory.

Entrenchment: the central theme in MacWhinney's (2004, 2006, 2008) theory of entrenchment is that age effects are attributed to the competition between an entrenched L1 and a weak and parasitic L2. In MacWhinney's new unified model of language acquisition (see Ch. 3) the notion of entrenchment forms an integral part of the construct as it emphasizes the extent to which repeated use of L1 leads to its ongoing entrenchment in different linguistic areas, with the strongest entrenchment effect occurring in output phonology (i.e. pronunciation) and the least entrenchment occurring in the area of lexicon, where new learning continues to take place throughout a person's lifespan. The operationalization of entrenchment is offered by MacWhinney within the context of 'self-organizing maps' (see Ch. 3 for a description), which are a special type of computational model. Although the idea of entrenchment is appealing, currently few specific details are given on its operation, and—as is the case with computational models in general—it is not straightforward to decide how much neurobiological validity these computational networks have.

Native language neural commitment (NLNC): Kuhl's NLNC theory (Kuhl 2000, 2004; Kuhl *et al.* 2005) shares some similarities with MacWhinney's entrenchment theory, but it has grown out of a completely different disciplinary area: brain research, especially in speech and hearing sciences. Interestingly, the experimental basis of Kuhl's approach with little children made her views accessible not only for the academic community but also for the media. (Some of the TV coverage is available on Kuhl's website at Washington University's Institute for Learning and Brain Sciences.) According to the NLNC theory, infant L1 learning produces dedicated neural networks that code the patterns of native-language speech. As we saw in Ch. 3, the process of L1 acquisition involves the infants' parsing the speech stream that makes up the auditory world around them and the detection of statistical and prosodic regularities in the aural stimulus, which in turn leads to phonetic and word learning. As a result of repeated input, infants commit neural networks to the specific regularities of their native language and these learnt patterns promote subsequent L1 acquisition. Thus, the theory predicts that the more established one's native language neural commitment (NLNC), the easier it is for the infant to proceed further with the mastery of the L1. On the other hand, because languages differ in their specific prosodic and statistical patterns, it also follows from the NLNC hypothesis that once neural networks become dedicated to the L1 code, this will hinder the learning of new patterns associated with an L2. In sum, L1-specific NLNC is assumed to correlate positively with future L1 acquisition and negatively with L2 acquisition.

Kuhl *et al.* (2005) provide convincing empirical evidence for the hypothesis. They tested 7-month-old American infants on two phonetic contrasts: a native English contrast (/ta/, /pa/), and a non-native Mandarin Chinese fricative–affricate contrast at a place of articulation that does not occur in English. In a creatively designed experiment infants were first trained to turn towards a loudspeaker on their left when they detected a change from the repeating background sound to the target sound. Then, they were exposed to a total of 30 trials and the 'hits' and 'misses' (in terms of turning to the loudspeaker at the right time or not) were recorded. As predicted, a signif-icant negative correlation was obtained between the scores for the native and non-native contrasts ($r = -.48$). Furthermore, the contrast scores also predicted later language development: early L1 phonetic discrimination was positively correlated with word production at 18 months ($r = .50$), sentence complexity at 24 months ($r = .42$), and mean length of the longest three utterances at 24 months ($r = .49$), while correlations with early non-native-language phonetic discrimination produced negative coefficients. Thus, the results suggested that the trajectory of language development from 7 months to 30 months depends on infants' native versus non-native abilities. As Kuhl *et al.* stated, other studies from their laboratory had consistently produced the same pattern.

Based on their results, Kuhl *et al.* (2005) concluded that for L1 acquisition to ensue, the initial state of equipotentiality must give way to NLNC. This, in turn, furthers language development and reduces the capacity to respond to non-native contrasts and to subsequent learning based on non-native contrasts. An interesting aspect of the results that is not elaborated on or explained by the authors is that children seem to vary in how firmly NLNC has been established in them. This would suggest that even though there is a powerful neurobiological process in operation, additional factors cause individual-level variation in the outcome. This is exactly what a dynamic systems account would predict and, indeed, Kuhl *et al.* conclude that their theory 'seems to be consistent with dynamic systems views of develop-ment' (p. 258).

In sum, the assumption held by several scholars that the infant's growing L1 proficiency affects somehow any subsequent L2 learning—acting as a kind of language residue or sediment—has received some theoretical and empirical confirmation. However, while various entrenchment theories are undoubtedly attractive, DeKeyser (personal communication) points out that Mayberry's studies on sign-language acquisition (reviewed earlier) indicate that age effects are just as pronounced in L1 acquisition as in SLA, where, of course, there is no previous language sediment holding up the flow of lan-guage acquisition. This again points to the conclusion that we are unlikely to find a single 'magic formula' to solve the age mystery.

Summary

What is quite clear from the foregoing discussion is that there are very few simple truths concerning the role of age in language acquisition.
(Singleton and Ryan 2004: 226)

This chapter has presented a complex picture of age effects and it is prob-ably clear to most readers by now (if it wasn't before) that the rich but at the same time inconclusive material allows for several different interpreta-tions. Scholars agree universally that age matters, but opinions differ on the exact sources and consequences of the age factor. What we are facing is the longitudinal development of a highly complex system—the human learner—as it acquires a highly complex mental function—communication—and as it interacts with a highly complex linguistic and social environment. This kind of set-up lends itself to analysis from a dynamic systems perspective, and indeed, the typically observed language attainment outcome exhibits a great deal of non-linear variation, to the extent that a younger starting age of language acquisition can either be an advantage or a hindrance depending on the properties of the environment. In other words, there is no single decisive age factor, but many, all interacting with each other, and even if in a certain situation one factor tends to dominate, the others relate to it in varying degrees of dependency, causing a certain amount of interference.

Applying a dynamic systems approach does not mean that there are no predictable aspects of the system behaviour. DST suggests that if a complex system is governed by powerful attractors, we can expect certain regularities and stability as the process unfolds in the unifying direction of the attractor. The equilibrium, however, is never absolute, and on this basis the very strict connotations of a critical period in the biological sense do not seem to describe the dynamics of age effects adequately. Having said that, we must also acknowledge the fact that there is sufficient available evidence for the occurrence of certain potent neurobiological inhibitions or constraints as childhood progresses and therefore it is understandable why some people consider the impact of these processes reminiscent of a perhaps softer version of the CPH. One of the most revealing lines of research in this respect has been the studies of deaf children learning sign languages in a delayed manner, pointing to the existence of an L1 CP phenomenon. However, before we draw some far-reaching conclusions from these findings regarding SLA, we must also consider the undeniable fact that in formal school contexts the younger is not only not better but is often worse.

I would suggest that the reason why the understanding of age effects appears to defy efforts to produce unambiguous principles and tenets is that we are facing a complex system with multiple powerful attractors that can form a number of compelling combinations: neurobiological and cognitive processes take place in the brain; social trajectories are activated by different ages of arrival in immigrant situations; and strong interferences are to be expected both from our L1 system and our personal characteristics. There is an undeniable success rate of L2 learning for very young immigrant children, but this may be due to the co-ordinated impact of at least three powerful factors that work in concert: the fact that 'early arrivals are within a sensitive time window, have a richer L2 environment, and experience less interference from their L1' (Jia and Fuse 2007: 1281). I cannot help thinking that even the universal inevitability of success in L1 acquisition might be the result of the combination of several factors in the sense that if one factor fails, another kicks in. After all, there are individual differences in the rate and style of L1 development (see, e.g. Shore 1995) and while everybody achieves a native-like 'common denominator', the truth is that this denominator is restricted to some limited aspects of the L1 proficiency and that there are marked differences in native speakers' overall ultimate L1 attainment.

Throughout the writing of this chapter I have had the distinct feeling that some important discoveries are still to come in this area and therefore attempts to explain away the holes in our knowledge at this stage in order to produce a coherent account may be premature. Consequently, I am in agreement with Flege *et al.* (2006: 155) that 'It is not possible at present to choose from among these competing explanations of age effects.' Yet, I believe that there is at least one key question that we *can* answer with some confidence: what is the best age to start learning a second language? The answer is twofold: in naturalistic SLA environments such as immigrant situations, younger is definitely better for a variety of reasons even if it does not guarantee native-like ultimate attainment. On the other hand, in formal educational contexts where the L2 is learnt primarily as a school subject with only a limited amount of direct contact with L2 speakers, starting before the age of about 11 will mainly have attitudinal rather than linguistic benefits. I would like to stress that this is not at all a partisan view and that Scovel's (2006: 44) conclusion about the all too common 'earlier is better' view in educational settings is shared by most scholars in the field:

> It is most unfortunate that the mammoth educational changes that have been effected to introduce English [as a foreign language] at lower and earlier levels of education by ministries of education and other supposedly responsible institutions have been based on misrepresentations of SLA research and on unsubstantiated intuitions.

On the other hand, being a motivation researcher myself, I would not like to play down the significance of the potential attitudinal gains of starting L2 learning at an early age—planting the seeds of loving foreign languages and cultures early is likely to pay considerable dividends later. However, in the reality of primary school contexts worldwide we find huge problems with the actual language instruction of young children, ranging from inadequate methodologies and insufficiently trained teachers to the lack of proper transition between primary and secondary school courses. (See Nikolov and Djigunovič 2006.) These problems too frequently quench children's initial positive disposition, thus making one wonder whether it was really worth the effort.

7

The psychology of instructed second language acquisition

The field of second language acquisition research, since its inception, has been inextricably intertwined with pedagogical concerns.
(Han 2008*b*: p. xi)

Most scholars who decide to devote their working career to studying second language acquisition have a keen interest in the practical implications of their research; Han (2008*b*) is so right when she points out that for many, if not all, SLA researchers the ultimate goal is to develop insights and instructional strategies that will eventually improve the efficacy and efficiency of L2 learning. This has also been true of me, and it was this interest to bring about improvement in the area of language instruction that motivated the writing of this book in the first place. Therefore, this last chapter on 'instructed SLA'—which is an academic label for classroom language learning and teaching—is in many ways the logical finale of our long journey of exploration.

To start with, please allow me to state the obvious: this chapter cannot offer a systematic overview of language teaching methodology—it is a complex business with a long history and a very rich variety. Instead, it is intended to offer some valid, scientifically tested pointers and principles that can inform future developments in language instruction. I do not want to pretend that SLA research has succeeded in answering all the questions practitioners may have, not even the main ones; in fact, I have no doubt that with regard to L2 teaching methodological issues, the accumulated wisdom of best practices in the teaching profession considerably exceeds the significance of the findings of empirical investigations to date. Thus, I would genuinely like to avoid the common situation that Widdowson (2003: 112) describes here:

It is interesting to note . . . that linguists apparently think it entirely reasonable to castigate language teachers for the way they represent language on the grounds that it does not measure up to their descriptions. . . . Linguists have few inhibitions about pointing out the limitations of pedagogic versions of language, but bridle at any suggestion that their own versions might be limited from a pedagogic point of view, putting such suggestion down to ignorance and complacency.

Yet, I also believe that in the almost unlimited variety of options and potentials of creative language teaching methodology, any solid cornerstone that scholarly work can offer is an invaluable reference point. When I started out as a practising language teacher almost three decades ago, I remember how eagerly I was searching for such firm points of orientation (which is why I became an applied linguist). In looking for empirical signposts for our pedagogy, we should recognize that the 'accumulated wisdom of best practices' referred to above has often been based on systematic enquiry by applied linguists of differing persuasions into the nature and use of language, following a primarily (educational) linguistic approach. Given the psychological angle of this book, these research orientations fall largely outside the scope of the following overview. Yet I have no doubt that we can only make best practice better if we find ways of integrating the whole spectrum of previous and ongoing research approaches. As Widdowson (1978: p. ix) astutely remarked over thirty years ago, 'We do not progress very far in our pedagogy by simply replacing abstract isolates of a linguistic kind by those of a cognitive or behavioural kind.' A constructive synthesis will be a formidable task and I sincerely hope that the following psychological take on established topics such as communicative language teaching or the role of accuracy and fluency will contribute to moving the field forward—our brains certainly have the capacity to do much better than the current average learning performance, so our task is to figure out how to access this cerebral potential.

In the following, I first reiterate the core dilemma in instructed SLA: the uneasy relationship between implicit and explicit learning. Then I examine three iconic teaching approaches—*grammar-translation, the audiolingual method,* and *communicative language teaching*—because these embody three alternative avenues to acquiring an L2 and, as such, form the basis of most contemporary 'post-method' teaching practices. Following this, in the second part of the chapter I analyse three cardinal issues of instructed SLA research that are at the heart of any current developments in the field: (1) *focus on form and form-focused instruction*; (2) *fluency and automatization*; and (3) *formulaic language*.

Let me add a final, terminological point before we start. The applied linguistics literature has often distinguished the meaning of certain words that everyday parlance would consider synonyms, such as language 'learning' and 'acquisition', or teacher 'training' and 'development' (and even 'teacher education'). Unless otherwise stated, I will use such words in their everyday generic sense; for example 'language teaching' and 'language instruction' will be interchangeable throughout this chapter.

Implicit versus explicit learning in instructed SLA

It is almost a commonplace nowadays to point out that over the past century language teaching methodology has followed a fluctuating pattern, alternating between emphasis on the explicit teaching of linguistic features such as grammar and vocabulary and the promotion of communicative fluency in a more implicit manner. While the truth of such a statement is dependent on what we actually mean by 'grammar', 'vocabulary', and 'fluency', let alone 'explicit' or 'implicit' teaching, there is no doubt that one of the fundamental issues of SLA theory and practice is how directly and systematically the various components of the L2 code—and most notably grammar rules and lexis—need to be dealt with in language classrooms. (The term 'explicit teaching' will be used in this chapter to refer to any consciously applied teaching practice that elicits explicit learning.)

The ongoing hesitation about the degree of explicitness required in L2 instruction would be highly unusual in many (if not most) other academic subjects. After all, in biology, for example, we do not agonize over whether we should describe certain plants or animals overtly in the textbooks or, instead, send out the learners to the jungle to become familiar with these first through some outdoor experience. Similarly, few people would doubt that mathematical rules ought to be introduced first and practised later. Language, however, is very different because, as we saw briefly in Chs. 1 and 3, the main model for all of us—the mastery of our mother tongue—predominantly involves implicit processes without any explicit teaching: children acquire the complex system of their L1 through engaging in natural and meaningful communication with their parents and other caretakers; in fact, this process is so implicit that even after successfully completing it, most native speakers are at a loss when asked to explain, or even describe, the rules of the acquired system.

Thus, the implicit L1 acquisition process is a universally shared experience and as such, people consider it 'natural' (which is why the type of SLA that happens in a similarly spontaneous and effortless manner is often called 'naturalistic SLA'); in Klein's (2001: 13768) words, 'Linguists and laymen alike tend to consider children's way to their mother tongue to be the most important type of language acquisition.' So, if we have a universal model of how nature teaches us languages, isn't it the obvious conclusion that we ought to model any subsequent L2 learning enterprise after this? That is, is explicit instruction necessary for L2 learning at all? This question touches upon the core issue of the SLA process.

Is explicit instruction necessary for L2 learning?

Post-critical period SLA is notorious for its difficulty, high degree of variation, and often very poor outcome. The primary aim of L2 instruction is to ameliorate, if not solve, these problems.
(Doughty 2003: 256)

The well-known American saying states, 'If it ain't broke, don't fix it'; therefore, why don't we simply rely on the tried-and-tested implicit L1 learning mechanisms without necessarily introducing an explicit teaching component for L2 learning? The problem, as explained in Ch. 4, is that implicit learning, which does such a great job in generating native-speaking L1 proficiency in infants, does not seem to work efficiently when we want to master an L2 at a later stage in our lives. Chapter 6 looked at some of the reasons for this anomaly, but the main point to note for the present discussion is that—alas!—untutored learning through simple exposure to natural language input does not seem to lead to sufficient progress in L2 attainment for most school learners. In consequence, the overall consensus in the profession is that the ineffectiveness of implicit learning mechanisms makes it necessary for us to draw on the additional resources of various explicit learning procedures. N. Ellis (2007c: 26) summarizes this issue:

> As with other implicit modules, when automatic capabilities fail, there follows a call for recruiting additional collaborative conscious support: We only think about walking when we stumble, about driving when a child runs into the road, and about language when communication breaks down. In unpredictable conditions, the capacity of consciousness to organize existing knowledge in new ways is indispensable.

There are two strong sources of evidence available to illustrate and support the above claim: (1) experiences in educational contexts—particularly in immersion programmes—that provide optimal conditions for implicit learning; and (2) reviews of empirical studies that specifically compared implicit and explicit instruction.

Immersion programmes and communicative classrooms offering 'naturalistic' SLA conditions

The first powerful indications that implicit learning might not work in instructed SLA came from Canadian immersion programmes, where students not only participate in L2 teaching but also study some (or most) of their academic subjects in the L2. Arguably, immersion classrooms offer the best possible context for implicit language instruction within educational frameworks, given the amount of meaning-focused language input the students are exposed to and the amount of time spent functioning in the second language (Doughty 2003). This is undoubtedly the most communicative language context educators have ever been able to conceive and therefore the outcomes of these programmes are hugely important for considering the potentials of instructed SLA.

Studies evaluating the effectiveness of immersion classrooms (for summaries, see e.g. de Bot, Lowie, and Verspoor 2005; Doughty 2003; Lightbown and Spada 2006; Ranta and Lyster 2007; Spada and Lightbown 2008) converge on two broad conclusions: on the one hand, the overall academic achievement of immersion students matches that of their peers in regular L1 programmes, indicating that they become fully functional in the L2 environment; on the other hand, as Ranta and Lyster (2007: 143) summarize, their L2 production skills retain obvious marks of non-nativeness in terms of 'grammatical structure and nonidiomatic...lexical choices and prag- matic expression'. Even more surprisingly, the authors continue, when meeting native L2-speaking peers, immersion students 'often encounter real difficulties in making themselves understood'. Although I believe that this latter, extreme situation only arises occasionally, when students try to communicate highly sophisticated messages, the mere fact that it is men- tioned in the literature as a possible outcome indicates that in spite of their effectiveness, immersion programmes are not the ultimate solution to instructed SLA.

Lightbown and Spada (2006) further add that non-target-like grammatical and pragmatic competencies are also characteristic of other communicative, non-interventionist programmes that intentionally ignore the explicit teach- ing of linguistic structures. They thus conclude, 'we do not find support for the hypothesis that language acquisition will take care of itself if second lan- guage learners simply focus on meaning in comprehensible input' (p. 176). It seems, therefore, that although the mere use of an L2 in a functional and meaningful way in an interaction-rich environment may result in high-level communicative skills, it often fails to produce, even under the best possi- ble circumstances, a degree of language competence that is indistinguishable from that of the members of the L2 speech community. And even though the aim of instructed SLA is rarely the achievement of complete conformity to native-like language competence, it is the principle that matters here: even such optimal communicative environments cannot lead to success without the support of explicit learning mechanisms.

Laboratory and classroom investigations comparing implicit and explicit learning

The shortcomings of implicit learning that emerged in immersion and other communicative L2 programmes were corroborated by the findings of focused research studies that compared the effectiveness of explicit and implicit learning both in laboratory and classroom settings. In a highly influential meta-analysis of the 49 most rigorous relevant investigations identified in the literature, Norris and Ortega (2000) examined the effectiveness of L2 instruc- tion and demonstrated a significant advantage of explicit types of L2 instruction over implicit types. They summarized their main findings thus:

> On average, instruction that incorporates explicit (including deductive and inductive) techniques leads to more substantial effects than implicit instruction (with average effect sizes differing by 0.59 standard deviation units), and this is a probabilistically trustworthy difference....the current state of empirical findings indicates that explicit instruction is more effective than implicit instruction. (pp. 500–1)

In a review of the cognitive aspects of L2 learning, DeKeyser and Juffs (2005: 442) came to the same conclusion when they stated that 'the advantage of explicit over implicit instruction is the most clearly documented method effect in the empirical literature on types of instruction'.

Thus, all the available evidence points to the conclusion that mere exposure to L2 input accompanied by communicative practice is not sufficient to help school learners to become either completely proficient or accurate in the second language. Consequently, we need explicit learning procedures—such as focus on form (see below) or controlled practice—to push learners beyond communicatively effective language toward target-like second language ability (Doughty and Williams 1998). This recognition led de Bot, Lowie, and Verspoor (2005: 84) to conclude, 'The question therefore no longer is whether some explicit teaching is helpful, but what type of explicit teaching is the most effective.' Let me stress here at the same time that the search for ways of reintegrating explicit learning processes in the theory of instructed SLA does not mean that we should regard them as replacements of implicit learning. Instead, as we saw at the end of Ch. 4 (and will see again later), the real challenge is to maximize the *co-operation* of explicit and implicit learning.

Three past approaches to L2 instruction

[L]anguage teaching is a field where fads and heroes have come and gone in a manner fairly consistent with the kinds of changes that occur in youth culture.
(Celce-Murcia 2001: 3)

The teaching of foreign languages is a massive worldwide enterprise with a great deal of diversity. Countries, regions, school types, and target languages display immense variation in the actual process of what goes on in the language classroom, and in the light of this heterogeneity it is questionable whether we can talk about any uniform trends, approaches, or methods to characterize the teaching practice of certain periods. A good example is communicative language teaching (CLT); even though, according to Gatbonton and Segalowitz (2005), most language teachers today claim to follow a communicative approach, genuinely communicative classrooms still seem to be in the minority. This indicates that even when the majority of the teaching profession accepts, in theory, the importance of a methodological development, it may be little more than mere lip-service in view of the actual practice on the ground. Accordingly, I am not going to attempt to draw up here a psychological profile of the evolution of L2 instruction. (For summaries, see Howatt 2004; Larsen-Freeman 2000; Richards and Rodgers 2001.) Yet, it is a useful analytical task to look at three iconic teaching methods—grammar-translation, audiolingual method, and communicative language teaching—in their stereotypical, or idealized, pure forms. These three distinct approaches embody certain core assumptions about the goal of L2 instruction and the theoretical foundations of the process. Thus, although these three psychological sketches may not have too much to do with the (often unglamorous)

reality of actual classroom practice, they describe three alternative conceptions of language teaching practice. Contrasting them can lead to valuable
psychological insights into L2 instruction in general.

The grammar-translation method

The grammar-translation method can be viewed and interpreted in several
different ways, particularly because the label is often used nowadays as an
umbrella term to refer to any teaching practice that does not have any communicative aspirations. Strictly speaking, grammar-translation originally
involved a very traditional way of teaching Latin in nineteenth-century
Germany, which explains why this method was not concerned with developing productive L2 competence in the learners. As Richards and Rodgers
(2001: 5) rightly summarize, the goal of foreign language study in this approach
is to learn the L2 'in order to read its literature or in order to benefit from the
mental discipline and intellectual development that result from foreign language study'. My impression is, however, that the contemporary widespread
use of this approach has little to do with any desire for mental discipline or
access to literary texts. Rather, the pervasiveness of the method is, I believe,
due to the fact that (1) this is a very safe and easy-to-implement teaching
approach in situations where large class sizes predominate and where the
teachers' huge workload and often insufficient L2 communicative competence push them to rely heavily on textbooks; and (2) this approach can be
easily assessed by discrete-point (multiple-choice) tests. Indeed, following the
grammar-translation method requires relatively little preparation on the part
of the teachers, the well-established and highly structured classroom activities (e.g. 'read-and-translate') can be delivered without fluent use of the L2,
and the well-defined teacher and student roles fit neatly into the traditional
teacher-fronted instructional practice that is characteristic of the teaching of
most subject matters in much of the world.

From a psychological point of view, the grammar-translation method is surprisingly interesting. It represents an almost pure manifestation of an explicit
teaching approach, with hardly any pretence of, or ambition for, any implicit
learning components. The instruction is largely in the L1, with an emphasis
on learning *about* the L2 rather than the L2 itself; and the overt goal is to
generate a great deal of metacognitive knowledge by focusing on rules and
regularities, particularly on grammatical parsing. The explicit nature of the
method is further augmented by the extensive memorization of vocabulary
lists and verb conjugation tables. In sum, the ultimate aim of the instruction is
to produce explicit knowledge that allows students to translate L2 sentences
into their L1 and to successfully pass grammar and vocabulary tests.

N. Ellis (2007c) points out that the explicit grammar-translation teaching
method was motivated by the belief that perception and awareness of language rules necessarily precede their use, but regrettably it almost always gets
stuck at the awareness raising stage without moving on to tackle L2 use. As

a consequence, the concepts of L2 communicative competence and fluency do not feature in any aspect of the approach. No wonder, therefore, that in spite of its influence worldwide, virtually no L2 experts would claim that grammar-translation is conducive to developing productive language skills.

The audiolingual method

[I]f audiolingualism is indeed a 'translation' of Skinner's operant psychology to second language pedagogy, it has to be, at the very least, labelled a 'gross mistranslation'.
(Castagnaro 2006: 520)

During World War II, the United States army had an urgent need for personnel with active communicative skills for military purposes. Because of the obvious inadequacy of grammar-translation to generate communicative competence, linguists and L2 experts were commissioned to develop a new method that would result in the ability to use the L2 fluently in real-life situations. The outcome of this effort was the *audiolingual method*. Teacher trainees are usually taught that this was the first language teaching method with an explicit scientific research base that drew on structural linguistics (Bloomfield) and behaviourist psychology (Skinner), and that the method dominated language teaching in the 1950s and 1960s. The best-known language teaching tasks originating in this method (still used today) are various grammar drills and dialogue teaching techniques, with the latter involving the presentation of new vocabulary and structures through dialogues, which are then learnt through imitation and repetition. More detailed discussions of audiolingualism usually zoom in on the behaviourist foundations of the method, highlighting the principal belief that language learning is the acquisition of a set of correct *language habits;* habit formation involves repetition and rote learning to the extent that students should 'over-learn' a range of stimulus–response chains, that is, develop automatized responses.

In an interesting recent article, Castagnaro (2006) points out that the superficial association of behaviourism with the audiolingual method may not hold, because, for example, in spite of popular belief, the term 'habit' did not come from behaviourism at all but was a contribution of structural linguist Bloomfield. In fact, Castagnaro points out, Skinner himself has often criticized the term as non-technical and misleading in that it ignored context and relevant environmental contingencies, which were key elements of Skinner's operant conditioning theory. In other words, the mechanical stimulus—response—reinforcement sequence (i.e. drill and practice) that is often associated with the audiolingual method strips away the functional dimension from Skinner's behaviourist views; paradoxically, operant conditioning is better represented by the communicative drills introduced in the 1970s.

The 'habit' issue is not the only surprise offered by a closer look at audiolingualism. In a detailed rediscovery of the significance of the work of Lado

(1957, 1964), who was the main theoretician of the audiolingual era, N. Ellis (2002*a*) highlights the fact that some of Lado's ideas were genuinely modern and 'surprisingly reminiscent of cognitive linguistic approaches' (p. 176) in their emphasis on frequency of stimulus and emergent grammar. As he summarizes, for Lado, language acquisition was the learning of patterns of expression, content, and their association, which is in harmony with the principles of usage-based acquisition theories discussed in Ch. 3. Tomasello (2003), for example, points out that the cognitive revitalization of the key behaviourist concepts of 'frequency' and 'entrenchment' has turned out to be of great significance in understanding how constructions are acquired, cognitively represented, and used by speakers. Furthermore, and coming back to Lado's theory, it was also compatible with skill learning theories discussed in cognitive psychology (see Ch. 4 and a separate section later in this chapter) in its emphasis on the shift from attentional to unconscious processing through automatization. Thus, the audiolingual method made a principled effort to operationalize the promotion of implicit learning processes in classroom activities in order to develop productive, communicative language skills in the learners.

So, if audiolingualism was associated with such modern ideas, why did it fall from favour? N. Ellis (2002*a*) mentions two main reasons. The first is the decline in behaviourist theories of language acquisition after Chomsky's (1959) famous and highly influential critique of Skinner's (1957) *Verbal Behavior*. The second concerns the actual, and rather misguided, implementations of the theories in audiolingual practice. Motivated by the belief that practice makes perfect, learning in the classroom was conceived to take place by imitating and repeating the same structures time after time (Mitchell and Myles 2004). This focus on meaningless pattern drilling produced bizarre textbook-based exercises and generated the overall image of mindless mechanical language production. In N. Ellis's (2002*a*: 177) words, 'The ALM [audiolingual method] was a blinkered and limited implementation of theories of frequency and habit in language learning.' Furthermore, the audiolingual dialogue teaching technique, based on repetition and memorization, also compared rather unfavourably with the emerging meaningful and creative role-play activities advocated by communicative language teaching. We have to note here that, ironically, neither the infamous 'mimicry-memorization' technique, nor the audiolingual dialogue practices were based on Skinner's or Lado's ideas but were introduced earlier by structuralist linguists Bloomfield and Fries (Castagnaro 2006).

Communicative language teaching

> *The communicative approach is, of course, very much in vogue at present. As with all matters of fashion, the problem is that popular approbation tends to conceal the need for critical examination.*
> Widdowson (1978: p. ix)

Communicative language teaching (CLT) has become a real buzzword; as mentioned earlier, most contemporary L2 teachers would claim that they follow CLT, even if this might not actually be the case (Gatbonton and Segalowitz 2005). Thus, it seems that the communicative reform movement that was launched in the 1970s has finally achieved worldwide recognition. (For recent overviews, see Savignon 2005; Spada 2007.) Curiously, however, while everything in the teaching profession seems to be turning 'communicative', in applied linguistics the term is rapidly disappearing as it is being replaced by the new concept of 'task-based learning' or 'task-based language teaching' (TBLT). I will come back to this phenomenon at the end of this section.

So what is CLT about? The name is a give-away: the central theme of the approach is to underscore the importance of meaningful communication and usable communicative skills in L2 instruction. In the words of one of the founders of the approach, Sandra Savignon (1990: 210), the primary focus in CLT was 'the elaboration and implementation of programs and methodologies that promote the development of L2 functional competence through learner participation in communicative events'. In this sense, therefore, CLT pursued very similar goals to those of the audiolingual method, which is interesting given that CLT is often seen as a reaction to audiolingualism. The reason for this seeming contradiction lies in the very different ways by which the two approaches intended to build up an implicit knowledge base in the learners. In contrast to the key audiolingual techniques of automatization through drilling and memorization, CLT methodology was centred around the learner's participatory experience in meaningful L2 interaction in (often simulated) communicative situations, which underscored the significance of less structured and more creative language tasks. For this reason, the learning of scripted dialogues was replaced by games, problem-solving tasks, and unscripted situational role-plays, and pattern drilling was either completely abandoned or replaced by 'communicative drills'. Regarding the latter, Lightbown (2008) points out that the term may sound like an oxymoron to many SLA researchers and teachers, yet such controlled communicative practice tasks can be designed in the sense that although they make repeated use of a small sample of utterances, they do so in situations where the learners have to choose the utterance that fits the specific meaning *they* want to convey. (For an illustration of communicative drilling, see Gatbonton and Segalowitz's ACCESS approach described in a separate section at the end of this chapter.)

A second difference between audiolingual and communicative attempts at developing productive L2 competence concerned the fact that while audiolingualism was associated with a specific learning theory—behaviourism—the communicative reform was centred around the radical renewal of the linguistic course content without any systematic psychological conception of learning to accompany it (Widdowson personal communication). Thus, while communicative syllabuses were informed by Austin (1962) and Searle's (1969) speech act theory, Hymes's (1972) model of communicative competence and its application to L2 proficiency by Canale and Swain (1980; Canale

1983), as well as Halliday's (1985) systemic functional grammar, the only learning-specific principle that was available for CLT materials developers and practitioners was the broad guideline to develop the learners' communicative competence through their active participation in seeking situational meaning. The imbalance between innovation in linguistic content and learning method was already expressed by Brumfit (1979: 187) in the early days of CLT development:

> There has been a widespread assumption that communicative teaching should not simply be a matter of the specification of the elements in a course, but that it should involve a profound change in the methodology. Yet it is noteworthy that most discussion has been based on long-standing procedures, such as use of group and pair work, simulation and role-play exercises, and other techniques which have been used, though possibly more in the second than the foreign language situation, for many years.

Partly because of the vagueness of the 'seeking situational meaning' tenet, since the genesis of CLT in the early 1970s in the UK and the United States its proponents have developed a very wide range of variants that were only loosely related to each other. Thus, Richards and Rodgers (2001: 155) rightly point out about CLT that 'There is no single text or authority on it, nor any single model that is universally accepted as authoritative.' As one extreme, for example, people often associate CLT with a strictly-no-grammar approach, whereas some of the founders of CLT were quite keen to emphasize a salient structural component. In one of the earliest communicative manifestos, Henry Widdowson (1972: 15) stated, for example, that 'we might characterize the recommended approach as one which combines situational presentation with structural practice'. And in an influential early British teaching methodology book on the topic, Littlewood's (1981: 1) starting sentence was as follows: 'One of the most characteristic features of communicative language teaching is that it pays systematic attention to functional as well as structural aspects of language, combining these into a more fully communicative view.' This view was echoed in more detail by Morrow (1981: 61):

> The crucial feature of a communicative method will be that it operates with stretches of language above the sentence level, and operates with real language in real situations. Interestingly, this principle may lead to procedures which are themselves either synthetic or analytic. A synthetic procedure would involve students in learning forms individually and then practising how to combine them; an analytic procedure would introduce complete interactions of texts and focus for learning purposes on the way these are constructed.... A communicative method is likely to make use of both.

In spite of the emphasis of the leading theorists of the CLT movement that 'the new importance attached to function should not be bought at the expense of form' (Cook 2000: 189), the emerging view of typical communicative classroom was that it approximates to a naturalistic SLA environment as closely as possible, thereby providing plenty of authentic input to feed the students' implicit learning processes without necessarily involving conscious attention to rules. Unfortunately, as we saw earlier in this chapter, relying on a purely implicit learning approach has turned out to be less than successful in SLA in general and therefore the past decade has seen a transformation of our idealized CLT image. In her summary of this shift, Spada (2007: 271) explained that 'most second language educators agree that CLT is undergoing a transformation—one that includes increased recognition of and attention to language form within exclusively or primarily meaning-oriented CLT approaches to second language instruction'. It was in this vein that in 1997 Marianne Celce-Murcia, Sarah Thurrell, and I suggested (Celce-Murcia, Dörnyei, and Thurrell 1997, see also 1998) that CLT had arrived at a new phase that we termed 'principled communicative language teaching':

> In sum, we believe that CLT has arrived at a turning point: Explicit, direct elements are gaining significance in teaching communicative abilities and skills. The emerging new approach can be described as a principled communicative approach; by bridging the gap between current research on aspects of communicative competence and actual communicative classroom practice, this approach has the potential to synthesize direct, knowledge-oriented and indirect, skill-oriented teaching approaches. Therefore, rather than being a complete departure from the original, indirect practice of CLT, it extends and further develops CLT methodology. (Celce-Murcia *et al.* 1997: 147–8)

As we emphasized, the increasing directness of the emerging principled CLT could not be equated with a back-to-grammar tendency. Rather, it involved an attempt to extend the systematic treatment of language issues traditionally restricted to sentence-bound rules (i.e. grammar) to the explicit development of other knowledge areas and skills necessary for efficient communication. In retrospect, the emerging transition we were talking about took an interesting turn: the term 'communicative language teaching' became virtually abandoned both by methodologists and researchers who were working on advancing the field; the former relaunched the communicative principles under the banner of 'task-based language teaching' (TBLT), while the main research attention shifted to the 'focus on form' paradigm. Let us briefly look at TBLT below and examine focus on form later in this chapter when discussing current issues in L2 learning and teaching.

Task-based language teaching (TBLT)

In his book-length overview of task-based language learning and teaching, R. Ellis (2003) states that TBLT is a version of CLT, and I am in full agreement with this position: there is nothing in the various conceptions of TBLT that would be in disaccord with any traditional CLT principles—which, of course, raises the obvious question of why a growing number of theoreticians have decided to replace CLT with the new term. One of the central driving forces for the change was the desire to generate a tighter, more research-able paradigm than the rather open-ended conceptual domain of CLT. Spada (2007), for example, pointed out the existence of a widespread feeling in the profession that because there have been so many different interpretations and implementations of CLT since it was introduced in the 1970s, it was no longer seen by many as a useful concept and should probably be discarded. In this respect the study of *language learning tasks* offers a viable alternative direc-tion, because by focusing on tasks, we are able to break down the complex, prolonged learning process into discrete segments with clear-cut bounda-ries, thereby creating distinct behavioural units that have a well-definable profile in terms of the L2 input/output and the language operations involved (Dörnyei 2002).

Thus, tasks lend themselves to being seen as the primary instructional vari-ables, or building blocks, of communicative language learning; as Samuda and Bygate (2008) explain in their recent comprehensive monograph on L2 tasks, 'TBLT refers to contexts where tasks are the central unit of instruc-tion: they "drive" classroom activity, they define curriculum and syllabuses and they determine modes of assessment' (p. 58). In this light it is under-standable why the term 'task-based language teaching' has been endorsed widely: it underscores the new, more principled approach to instructed SLA and thus offers an attractive label to represent the transformed nature of CLT. This point is clearly expressed by one of the most influential task researchers, Peter Skehan, in this justification of the labelling change from CLT to TBLT (Skehan 2007: 290):

> Although [the term communicative language teaching] is still very widely used, a task-based approach to language teaching is more associated with (a) an acceptance that a Focus-on-Form is essential; (b) the belief that it is not enough to explore the creativity and engagement of tasks, rather they need to be related to acquisition and language development; and (c) the belief that tasks and the conditions under which tasks are implemented also need to be researched and claims about them subjected to testing.

On the other hand, we must also acknowledge that this transition from CLT to TBLT is not unproblematic because CLT has also been based on tasks as central organizational units right from its genesis and, as we saw above, the form-focused element was also present already in the early CLT theoreticians' writings. No wonder therefore that Samuda and Bygate (2008: 58) conclude, 'Even after two decades, TBLT...continues to be extremely controversial and has attracted a number of highly vocal critics and detractors.'

Current issues in L2 learning and teaching

The three L2 teaching methods described in the previous section—grammar translation, audiolingualism, and CLT—represent three very different approaches to generating L2 knowledge and skill: broadly speaking, grammar translation emphasized the significance of explicit knowledge, audiolingualism concentrated on automatizing language skills through rote learning and drilling, and CLT shifted the focus to implicit learning through participation in meaningful communication. In their pure forms all the three approaches were found lacking, but, as we will see below, the main themes of these approaches still dominate the theoretical advances in the study of instructed SLA. The big difference is that contemporary SLA researchers no longer believe in the existence or the desirability of pure teaching methods (see e.g. Kumaravadivelu 1994, 2006; Long 1991) and, therefore, in the current, 'post-method' era of language instruction the main question is not 'which method is the best?' but rather 'which combination of ingredients is the best?' It has been widely recognized that different learning environments require different mixtures of various teaching components to achieve maximum effectiveness. Therefore, the primary concern of contemporary theoreticians is to explore the main ingredients underlying the various situated best practices in order to allow teachers to be 'cautiously eclectic in making enlightened choices of teaching practices' (Brown 1994: 73). In my view, three key issues lie at the heart of the most forward-pointing discussions in the literature: (1) *focus on form* and *form-focused instruction*; (2) *fluency* and *automatization*; and (3) *formulaic language*.

Focus on form and form-focused instruction

> [R]eaders will inevitably come to see that there is not, as yet, and probably never will be, any single solution to the intriguing problem of how to implement focus on form in communicative classrooms.
> (Doughty and Williams 1998: 11)

I would not be surprised if people who are not familiar with the evolution of SLA theory found the frequently used term 'focus on form' uninformative, if not confusing, particularly if they were told that the term is often contrasted with a rather different concept, 'focus on forms' (Long 1991). What exactly does 'form' mean—the form of what? How does 'form' differ from 'forms'? Is form-focused instruction related to 'form' or 'forms'? And more generally, how do we 'focus' on this unspecified form? As we will see below, there is no single definitive answer to these questions because scholars with different theoretical stances use these terms somewhat differently to indicate variations in content or approach. Yet, in spite of these ambiguities, 'focus on form' (often abbreviated as FonF or FoF) and the instructional approach associated with it, form-focused instruction (often abbreviated as FFI) have become key themes in SLA theory over the past decade. (For recent reviews, see N. Ellis 2008; Fotos and Nassaji 2007; Williams 2005.) What explains this popularity?

The content of the term 'form(s)' becomes clearer if we look at the following definition of language by Larsen-Freeman (2003: 142): 'Language is a dynamic process of pattern formation by which humans use linguistic forms to make meaning in context-appropriate ways.' This definition is consistent with other contemporary approaches in that it highlights two key dimensions of language: 'form' (or 'linguistic form') and 'meaning'. In this sense, the term 'form' broadly refers to the formal properties of language, many of which used to be included in the grammatical and discourse competencies of communicative competence (e.g. Celce-Murcia, Dörnyei, and Thurrell 1995). It is no accident, however, that in this latest development in SLA theory the term 'grammar' has been carefully avoided. As we saw in the previous section, after the grammar-translation method's exclusive emphasis on the explicit knowledge of the formal properties of language, there was a strong backlash against grammar teaching, so much so that Krashen's (1982) influential theory—that has come to be referred to as the 'non-interface' position—excluded any consciously learnt (grammatical) knowledge from contributing to the L2 competence that underlies fluent, communicative language use—see Ch. 4. During the past decade, the emergence of a more principled communicative approach indicated that the pendulum had changed direction again, but it did not swing all the way back to explicit, sentence-bound grammar instruction. Instead, the new concern with the structural system of language retained a strong communicative quality and it is this emerging integrated approach that came to be labelled 'focus on form'.

In order to distinguish this new position (i.e. focus on form) from traditional grammar teaching, Long (1991) referred to the latter as 'focus on forms'. However, the similarity of the two terms—differing only in a single letter—is a recipe for confusion and therefore I will avoid using 'focus on forms' in the remainder of this chapter. With regard to the final question of how 'form-focused instruction' comes into the picture, because of its communicative emphasis it certainly concerns focus on 'form' rather than 'forms'. Some scholars specialized in this area would look at FFI and FonF as two different strands and distinguish the substance they cover and the pedagogical interventions they use, but my feeling is that this distinction may not prevail in the long run. Instead, it might be more useful to take the terms at their face value to refer to two related aspects of the same approach, with FonF being used when talking about the theoretical principles and psycholinguistic underpinnings of the approach, and FFI when discussing the pedagogical applications of these.

Thus, focus on form expresses a halfway position between a concern for situational meaning and the linguistic features of the language code; that is, it denotes a primarily meaning-focused instruction in which some degree of attention is paid to form. As Doughty and Williams (1998) explain, the main FonF principle is that the learner's engagement in seeking situational meaning is a prerequisite before attention to linguistic form can be expected to be effective. Originally, Long (1991) defined FonF as *reactive*, that is, limited to spontaneous classroom events where the teacher responded to a difficulty that arose while students engaged in communicative practice, with no advance planning. However, as Spada and Lightbown (2008) summarize, more recent interpretations of FonF have also included instructional techniques in which teachers anticipated a certain difficulty and designed a communicative activity so that it would target that feature through feedback and other pedagogical interventions. Furthermore, these authors argue that one type of form-focused instruction—which they refer to as 'isolated FFI'—involves the focus on form in tasks that are separate from any actual communicative use of the L2 but occur as part of a broad communicative programme *in preparation for* or *after* a communicative activity. In short, the original reactive character of FonF has been extended over the years to also include *proactive* and *pre-emptive* interventions.

   Thus, although FFI 'has come to mean different things to those who have adopted the term' (Williams 2005: 671), it in effect amounts to a (new) type of grammar instruction embedded within a communicative approach, an idea that is not incompatible with the principled communicative approach described earlier. We saw at the beginning of this chapter that because of the observed shortcomings of implicit learning processes in instructed SLA, the main challenge for contemporary SLA theory is to find ways to maximize the effectiveness of explicit learning. Focus on form is fully compatible with this position and, in fact, the vagueness and open-endedness of the terms 'focus' and 'form' are useful in allowing for the inclusion of a variety of alternative approaches and techniques under the form-focused umbrella.

Types of form-focused instruction

So, if the concepts of FonF and FFI are rather vague and have been interpreted in somewhat different ways, what exactly has the 'focus on form' movement contributed to our understanding of the relationship between explicit and implicit instruction? I believe that its most beneficial role has been to set a clear agenda for furthering the theory of instructed SLA along the explicit–implicit learning interface. By avoiding previous jargon with unwanted loading (such as 'grammar' or 'CLT'), FonF has drawn attention to the key question of how this interface can be conceived of and implemented in actual classroom practice. In response to this challenge, several alternative but not necessarily competing methodological options have been proposed over the past two decades. One of the main proponents of the approach, Rod Ellis, has drawn up the following comprehensive framework of the various form-focused options, distinguishing four macro-options—for a review, see R. Ellis (2008: 879–80):

- *Input-based options* involve the manipulation of the language input that learners are exposed to or are required to process. The main types of this macro-option are *input flooding* (i.e. providing input that contains an artificially increased number of examples of the target structure), *enhanced input* (i.e. input in which the target feature is made salient to the learners in some way, for example by highlighting it visually in a text), and *structured input* (i.e. input that the learner is forced to process in order to be able to provide a required follow-up response).

- *Explicit options* involve instruction that can be direct (i.e. learners are provided with metalinguistic descriptions of the target feature, e.g. in deductive instruction) or indirect (i.e. learners are provided with data illustrating the target feature and are required to 'discover' the rule for themselves, for example, in inductive instruction).
- *Production options* involve instruction geared at enabling and inducing learners to produce utterances containing the target structure. According to R. Ellis (2008), this type can be further subdivided in terms of whether it involves text-manipulation (e.g. fill-in-the-blank exercises) or text-creation.
- *Corrective feedback options* involve either implicit feedback (e.g. recasts or clarification requests) or explicit correction (e.g. metalinguistic explanation or elicitation), and we can also distinguish between feedback that is input-providing (e.g. recasts or metalinguistic explanation) or output-prompting (e.g. requests for clarification or elicitation).

R. Ellis's (2008) taxonomy offers a practical classification of the techniques that already exist. What about developing new options? Can we offer any theoretical guidelines or organizing principles to facilitate the design of new FonF approaches? I believe that a fruitful way forward in this respect is to draw on what we know about the possible co-operation of explicit and implicit learning. At the end of Ch. 4, I concluded that past research has highlighted six different avenues to this cooperation: (1) explicit registration of linguistic information allows implicit fine-tuning; (2) explicit practice creates implicit learning opportunities; (3) explicit knowledge channels implicit learning; (4) explicit rote learning can provide material for implicit processing; (5) explicit knowledge fills the gaps in implicit knowledge; (6) explicit learning increases the overall level of accuracy in implicit knowledge. These options can be taken as broad templates for specifying the cognitive content of FonF tasks in future materials development projects. It would be a worthwhile project and a good starting point for further research to take stock of the wide array of findings and recommendations in the FonF literature and group them according to the above six types of explicit–implicit cooperation.

Factors determining the effectiveness of various FonF approaches

Given the variety of existing approaches in form-focused instruction, we need to examine which of these is preferable to or more effective than others. Past studies addressing this question are in agreement that the answer depends on a whole range of factors such as the target linguistic form, the curriculum, the characteristics of the learners, the dynamics of the language class, and the instructional style of the teacher, amongst others. Chapter 3 introduced the main features of dynamic systems theory, and this perspective would suggest that the completion of a language task is best understood within a dynamic framework where relatively small and seemingly irrelevant components of the system—such as the misbehaviour of a single child—might make a substantial difference in the task behaviour of the whole learner group and may even tip the balance from success to failure. Yet, we saw in the discussion of individual differences in Ch. 5 that even in such multicomponential dynamic systems it is worth trying to identify powerful attractors because, if they are in operation, the behaviour of the system becomes to some extent predictable. The three factors that have received arguably the most attention in the FonF literature concern the nature of (1) the difficulty and salience of the *target structure*; (2) the *metacognitive rule* available to explain the target structure; and (3) the amount and timing of the *form-focused intervention*. Let us look at these briefly; as a preliminary, however, we should note that the existing research on these complex issues is far from being conclusive and therefore the following points are only intended to illustrate the scope of the issues.

- *The difficulty and salience of the target structure:* there is no doubt that some linguistic features require more focused treatment than others, and some structures respond better to FonF treatment than others. A fundamental variable in this respect is the degree of difficulty of the target structures in question. Existing analyses of this matter (e.g. DeKeyser 2005; N. Ellis 2007c; Han 2008a; Juffs and DeKeyser 2003; Spada and Lightbown 2008) have revisited and underscored several old themes in error analysis and contrastive analysis that require special attention; examples include the difficulty caused by misleading L2 similarities to the L1 or the problematic nature of linguistic areas where the second language offers fewer options than the first language because learners cannot be expected to notice the absence of L1 parallels. It has also been found that explicit instruction is particularly effective with simple/straightforward regularities or with more complex material that contains only a limited number of variables and salient critical features (N. Ellis 2007c). DeKeyser (2005) adds that even if the linguistic form itself is not particularly problematic, a structure can still be difficult if the link between form and meaning is not transparent. Furthermore, certain linguistic cues (e.g. some aspects of morphology) may have such low salience in terms of sentence meaning that they are easily overlooked by learners as their misuse is unlikely to cause any communication breakdown (Spada and Lightbown 2008). Talking about recasts, Long (2007: 112) summarizes this very clearly:

  the issue of classes of problematic target features more or less susceptible to treatment via implicit negative feedback is a particularly important topic for those concerned with both language acquisition and language instruction. It is quite possible that future research will support what current findings already suggest: Recasts or other delicate, unobtrusive forms of corrective feedback work satisfactorily for some linguistic targets (e.g. meaning-bearing items) better than others, but that more explicit, more intrusive intervention is required for communicatively redundant, acoustically nonsalient forms.

- *The nature of the available metacognitive rule:* experienced teachers are well aware of the fact that metacognitive explanations only work if the learners can be told a fairly straightforward story, that is, if there are some simple and powerful rules available for explanation. Complex and fuzzy rules are of no help and if we only have those, it might be better to leave the issue to be mastered through implicit learning (Juffs and DeKeyser 2003). Hulstijn (2007*b*) adds to this the consideration that because humans can handle only a limited amount of explicit knowledge at a time, explicit rules must be as short and simple as possible. Therefore, he argues, in order to help learners to implement the rules consciously, complex rules must be broken down into simple rules of thumb. In my own teaching practice I favoured a hybrid procedure whereby I presented a simple and robust rule to explain the core regularity of a phenomenon and then left the exceptions and subtheories to gradually 'take care of themselves', through a mixture of implicit (incidental) learning and occasional low-level corrective feedback on my part.
- *The amount and timing of the FonF intervention:* Lightbown and Spada (2006) point out that in order to implement a specific FonF intervention in the classroom, L2 teachers must have clear answers to very specific questions concerning timing, such as when it is best to highlight the target form: before, after, or during communicative practice? In this respect, Leow (2007) stresses the fact that providing explicit grammatical information at strategic points during input processing may enhance the learners' capacity to elicit generalizable knowledge from a limited set of input data. But how can we define these strategic points and how much grammatical information is necessary for good effect? A related question is how much metalinguistic explanation should accompany any corrective feedback in general. Knowing the right amount is particularly important in the light of the observation that there is an inverse relationship between generating error-focused and communicative mindsets in the learners. Therefore, as DeKeyser (2007*b*) summarizes, one of the key questions in this area is how strongly form-focused activities should be integrated into the curriculum without reverting to a structural syllabus.

In sum, research on form-focused instruction has generated a substantial body of insights, but the jury is still out on the main question as to whether the painstaking research efforts of the past decade have been—or indeed can be—worthwhile in providing sufficiently useful guidelines that teachers can follow in their everyday classroom practice. As R. Ellis (2008) concludes, while there are certain macro-distinctions, these always involve a number of possible micro-options, which makes it difficult to synthesize and generalize the obtained results. Looking at this question from a dynamic systems perspective, unless we can identify some truly generalizable and potent attractors, the complexity of the system(s) involved will override any real hope of predictability and teachers will be left to their own devices to make things work (which has been, to a large extent, the traditional situation). Whether or not such attractors exist in form-focused instruction is still an open question that will need to be decided by future research. In Mackey's (2007: 87) words:

> To date, there is no claim that one or more of the interactional processes, including comprehensible input, feedback, and modified output, work better than any of the others, although it is possible that these processes may be differentially effective for various aspects of language, learner characteristics, contexts, and task demands. Indeed, interactional processes may work in concert or in unique ways.

Fluency and automatization

Form-focused instruction has been primarily concerned with linguistic accuracy and the knowledge of grammatical structures, but everybody who has ever tried to speak in a foreign language knows that the accurate use of linguistic form is not the only, and often not even the most serious, concern with regard to communicative effectiveness. In many respects L2 *fluency* is equally, if not more, important. In the psychological literature 'fluency' is usually treated under the labels of 'automaticity/automatization' (see Ch. 4), whereas in linguistic research the term has often been conceptualized in a broader manner than merely focusing on the level of automatization. Therefore, I will first look at the various definitions of fluency, and then explore the pedagogical implications of automatization and skill learning.

Definitions of fluency

The primary meaning of fluency in linguistics is associated with the temporal aspect of oral language production, referring to a non-hesitant flow of continuous speech with few pauses and interruptions. This meaning was indeed the first definition that Fillmore (1979) provided in his seminal paper on the topic. However, he then also added three further possible defining aspects of fluency: the ability to talk in a coherent and reasoned manner, the ability to speak appropriately in different contexts, and being creative and imaginative in using the language. Furthermore, Fillmore also pointed out that fluency is closely related to lexical knowledge, because fluent speech is dependent among other things on the speaker's knowledge of fixed linguistic forms; the speaker's mastery of vocabulary items that are relevant to particular semantic domains; the knowledge of formulaic expressions and their appropriate contexts; and the control of a number of processes for creating new expressions. The link between fluency and formulaic language was elaborated on by Pawley and Syder's (1983) classic paper on 'native-like selection and native-like fluency', and we will come back to this question in the next section.

In applied linguistics, one of the best and most often cited definitions of fluency has been offered by Lennon (2000: 26), who defined it as 'the rapid, smooth, accurate, lucid, and efficient translation of thought or communicative intention into language under the temporal constraints of online processing'. It is clear that although this definition does touch upon several related conceptual links, the emphasis is on the rapid and smooth delivery of language, which is the meaning typically associated with the term in everyday parlance.

In the psychological literature fluency is discussed under the broader concept of 'automaticity/automatization', and the promotion of fluency is usually subsumed under 'skill learning theory' (to be discussed below). We saw in Ch. 4 that the term 'automatization' has been used in at least four different meanings in the literature: (1) speed of processing, (2) availability of relevant procedural memory, (3) absence of attentional control, and (4) ballistic (i.e. unstoppable) processing. Segalowitz (2003: 383) provides a very clear description of the main psychological sense of the term, which echoes some of the main linguistic aspects mentioned earlier:

> [T]he term automatic has a number of different technical meanings. Nevertheless, psychologists generally use the term in a sense similar to what is meant in ordinary language when we say, for example, that an automatic shift car changes gears without deliberate intervention by the driver, in contrast to a standard shift car which requires the driver to perform a manual operation. Thus, when we perform aspects of a task automatically, we perform them without experiencing the need to invest additional effort and attention (or at least with significantly less effort and attention). When the activity does become automatic in this sense, we often also find that performance has become relatively immune to disruption by potentially interfering events, such as external sights, sounds, concurrently performed tasks, intruding thoughts, or the like. Also, performance appears to be more efficient; it is faster, more accurate, and more stable.

Interestingly, from a psychological perspective 'speed' may not be a defining feature of automaticity because fast processing is not necessarily automatic. We saw in Ch. 4 that several scholars believe that if increased speed reflects a mere quantitative change in the execution of a task without a qualitative change in processing, it is not truly a manifestation of automatic processing in the sense that it is not linked to increased proceduralization.

Automatization and skill learning

Automaticity figures as an important issue in nearly all theories of cognitive skill acquisition including treatments of first language performance and in many discussions of second language acquisition.
(Segalowitz 2003: 394)

A central issue in instructed SLA is how we can promote fluency in L2 speech. Translated into psychological terms, the question is how L2 skills can be automatized. Enabling learners to produce fluent speech was one of the key objectives of the endless drilling in audiolingualism in order to develop automatic stimulus–reaction chains. By shifting the focus to meaningfulness, CLT abandoned this aspiration and, as Segalowitz and Hulstijn (2005) conclude, the openness of typical CLT activities did not provide sufficient repetitive, controlled practice opportunities for automatization to occur. Therefore, while most of the discussions about post-CLT—or principled CLT—methodologies concentrate on the focus-on-form issue, an equally important concern should be finding communicative ways of designing instructional techniques that lead to automaticity. The key question in this respect is this (Segalowitz and Hulstijn 2005): once language learners have been exposed to new linguistic information, what must they do to be able to achieve later automatic access to that information? This is an area where the psychological literature of skill acquisition can offer a great many practical insights and suggestions. (For a recent overview, see DeKeyser 2007c.)

Skill learning theory (discussed in detail in Ch. 4) boils down to the following basic sequence: 'Automatization requires procedural knowledge. Proceduralization requires declarative knowledge and slow deliberate practice. The acquisition of declarative knowledge of a kind that can be proceduralized requires the judicious use of rules and examples' (DeKeyser 2007c: 107). Therefore and in accord with the phases of the skill learning process discussed in Ch. 4, a systematically designed fluency-building task will include an initial *declarative input stage* and subsequent *extended practice;* the practice stage can be further divided into *controlled practice* (corresponding to the associative/procedural stage of skill learning) and additional *open-ended practice* (corresponding to the autonomous/automatic stage of skill learning). This 'declarative input → controlled practice → open-ended practice' sequence is reminiscent of the well-known methodological progression of presentation—practice—production (PPP; for a discussion, see Widdowson 2003: ch. 9), and this similarity is good and bad news at the same time. It is good news because—as I stated in the introduction of this chapter—the accumulated practical expertise of language teaching methodology currently exceeds the amount of relevant research-based evidence both in terms of quantity and quality, and therefore the convergence of a theoretical approach with established classroom procedures is a mark of validity. The bad news is that merely catching up with classroom practice can easily be seen as reinventing the wheel rather than pushing the field forward. Of course, as in almost everything concerning classroom teaching, the secret lies in the details, so let us have a closer look at the three stages.

Declarative input stage

Skill learning theory is very clear about the need for the initial encoding of the skill, prior to any practice sessions, in the form of declarative knowledge.

Then, during the performances of the first trials, the learner interprets and rehearses this knowledge. In a recent paper, Ranta and Lyster (2007) proposed a three-phase instructional sequence that was motivated by cognitive skill learning theory. In their sequence the declarative input stage is referred to as the 'awareness phase', which expresses the essence of the cognitive encoding well. They argued that there is no reason to limit this awareness stage to deductive, metalinguistic instruction (such as the upfront presentation of grammar rules); instead, inductive tasks that encourage students to notice the gap between what they say and the corresponding target-language forms are likely to be more motivating. Indeed, the declarative input stage allows for the use of a wide range of FonF activities as long as by the end of it the students have been presented with a combination of abstract rules and concrete examples.

Controlled practice

The essence of the controlled practice stage (corresponding to the associative/procedural stage in skill learning theory; see Ch. 4) is to facilitate a shift in the students from relying on declarative rules to procedural knowledge by developing efficient procedures of performing the skill. This can take place through repetition within a narrow context, which is what drills are all about. Therefore, the key to the effectiveness of this stage is to design interesting drills that are not demotivating. Several motivational strategies can be used for this purpose—see Dörnyei (2001*a*); for example:

- creating variation through modulating the speed, volume, or emotional content of how certain patterns or utterances are repeated;
- designing 'communicative drills' in which the content of the task is made psychologically authentic by means of personalization, intriguing through the activation of imagination and fantasy, or engaging through drawing on motives of the youth culture;
- combining communicative drills with role-play performance;
- disguising the drill in games, songs, or chants;
- utilizing CALL programmes (i.e. language teaching software), which are often strong on creative and yet structured practice activities.

Segalowitz and Hulstijn (2005) emphasize that when devising controlled practice tasks, it is important to select activities that do not require the allocation of much attention to the higher levels of information (e.g. unfamiliar input, too varied content), thereby allowing learners to pay attention to information at the particular lower levels that the automatization process targets. Furthermore, we should also note that the label 'controlled' does not only signify that we need to keep the context of the task narrow to ensure an inherently repetitive engagement with the activity in question, but also that the students' performance needs to be monitored and, if need be, corrected by appropriate feedback. These requirements lead to a seeming contradiction: can we elicit highly decontextualized, repetitive, and strictly monitored content while maintaining at the same time the meaningfulness and authenticity of a communicative approach? It is my experience that achieving a satisfactory trade-off is possible, which is well illustrated by the creative automatization tasks of Gatbonton and Segalowitz (1988, 2005) that will be discussed in the next section on formulaic language.

Finally, a peculiar feature of the proceduralization process in controlled practice is that it leads to highly task-specific skills. For example, a study by DeKeyser (1997) showed that when productive skills were automatized, the acquired expertise did not transfer seamlessly to comprehension tasks focusing on the same target features. In fact, even smaller changes in the conditions or parameters of performing a skill might result in losing the benefits of practice. Therefore, in a later phase of the controlled practice stage—and already leading into the subsequent open practice—we may start consciously varying some key parameters or conditions of the automatized skill or task.

Open-ended practice

The final stage of the skill-learning process—open-ended practice (corresponding to the autonomous/automatic stage in skill-learning theory)—involves the continuous improvement in the performance of a skill that is already well established. According to DeKeyser (2007a), this is the most problematic of the three stages of skill acquisition in instructed SLA, because language classrooms are usually unable to provide the learner with the large amount of practice time that is needed for the completion of the automatization process. It is also difficult to decide how open the open-ended practice should be, that is, how systematically and how frequently we need to recycle target structures that have already been through the first two phases. Finally, as mentioned above, the increasingly fine-tuned production rules that are developed as a result of systematic practice become more and more skill- and situation-specific, and currently we do not know what the best strategy is to broaden the applicability range of such highly task-specific skills. Lightbown (2008) argues that widening the range of situations, practice modes, and processing types in which target features are encountered increases the likelihood that the learning conditions will match the conditions of language use, thereby increasing the number of retrieval routes for accessing the learned material.

Perhaps because of these uncertainties, in their three-phase instructional sequence Ranta and Lyster (2007) deviated somewhat from Anderson's ACT-R theory (described in Ch. 4) that forms the basis of most skill-learning approaches when devising the third phase: instead of merely focusing on the quantity of relevant practice, they decided to centre this phase around teacher feedback on student performance in open-ended communicative activities (e.g. in content-based instruction). In the Ranta–Lyster model feedback is designed in such a way that it prompts learners to self-repair, and the authors argue that the modified output that such feedback generates constitutes proper practice and therefore contributes to the proceduralization process.

Rote learning

An age-old technique that has been used to master the ability of fluent speech is *rote learning* L2 texts such as dialogues, songs, or chants. This technique was widely employed in audiolingualism as part of dialogue teaching, but curiously, ever since the audiolingual method fell from favour, it has been virtually ignored by applied linguists (but not by methodologists, as evidenced, for example, by the huge success of Carolyn Graham's 1978 *Jazz Chants* and its sequels). One interesting recent theoretical approach to reinstate rote learning, repetition, and recitation as enjoyable learning strategies has been Guy Cook's (2000) call for utilizing the creative potentials of 'language play' in instructed SLA. As Cook argues, the fascination with the creative manipulation of linguistic form is evident in children's nursery rhymes, but repetitive and rhythmic language which is markedly play-like as well as rhythmic jingles and plays on words are also salient in more serious adult discourses such as ceremonies, advertisements, jokes, poems, films, or political slogans. His following conclusion is fully in line with the thesis of this chapter:

> If we accept the role of conscious and deliberate learning rather than only passive acquisition, then the use of a form-focused, strikingly unusual example (no matter whether attested elsewhere or invented for the purpose) can have a strong mnemonic motivation, and be recalled as a model for a structure or contextualized use of an item of vocabulary when needed. The genres of language play also frequently involve or provoke authentic spontaneous repetition, rote learning, and recitation. These activities should not, then, be regarded as unauthentic. (p. 199)

In the previous section, I discussed one approach to developing procedural knowledge that is based on Anderson's skill-learning theory. This is clearly one of the most influential theoretical explanations of the process of automatization, but as we saw in Ch. 4, a powerful alternative approach to generating procedural knowledge has also been proposed in cognitive psychology: Logan's (1988, 2005) instance theory. This approach suggests that increased automaticity is the function of a growing repertoire of memorized bits of domain-specific knowledge (labelled 'instances'). Once the repertoire of memorized instances has been built up, the learner does not have to rely on following rules but can retrieve a relevant stored instance as a single step. This is, therefore, an exemplar/item-based theory of automatization, conceiving automaticity as a transition from rule-based performance to a memory function, and as such highlights the significance of committing instances of language to memory, for example by rote learning.

Further support for the potential role of rote learning in SLA comes from an interesting methodological innovation by Gatbonton and Segalowitz (1988, 2005) that involves the 'creative automatization' of formulaic phrases and utterances rather than of grammar rules. This method will be discussed later in this chapter in detail, but let me note here the researchers' claim that one reason for the lack of any real success in past attempts to achieve automatized fluency (e.g. in audiolingualism) was the fact that the techniques employed were 'geared toward the mastery of specific structures or rules, not of utterances as such' (Gatbonton and Segalowitz 1988: 477). In other words, the authors argue that because the repetitive practice element in these automatization techniques was directed at grammatical rules and functions rather than at lexis, the activities did not produce the expected outcome. Accordingly, Gatbonton and Segalowitz's proposed technique focuses on item automatization rather than rule automatization, and as such, can be seen as a type of a communicative rote learning task.

Suggestopedia and accelerated learning

I said before that rote learning has not been considered a scientifically sound learning technique over the past three decades, but this is not entirely true. Lozanov's (1979, 2005) innovative language teaching method of *suggestopedia* is centred around memorizing a great amount of L2 material in a relatively short period of time by bringing the learner into a pleasantly relaxed, yet receptive state of mind. (For reviews, see Larsen-Freeman 2000; Norman 2006; Richards and Rodgers 2001.) In fact, suggestopedia is only one of several learning avenues subsumed by the umbrella term 'accelerated learning' (see e.g. Rose and Nicholl 1998), which all seek to present information in novel ways that activate a much larger proportion of the learners' brain capacity than is usually exploited for the purpose of (language) learning.

A particularly interesting accelerated learning approach in the 1980s was the experimentation with *biofeedback* (e.g. Peper 1979; Rosenbaum 1989) to help learners reach the 'alpha state'—a relaxed and receptive state of mind characterized by the dominance of alpha brain waves (8–12 Hz)—by means of electronic instrumentation that amplifies various biological signals of the body of which we are normally unaware (e.g. breathing rhythm, heartbeat, muscle tension, brain waves, skin temperature, skin moisture, blood pressure, etc.) and then converts these to visual or auditory signals that are fed back to the individual. In this way, subconscious information is brought to the conscious level, which has been found to increase the ability to control several of the body's involuntary functions. For example, in a method developed in Germany—the SITA Learning System (also called Relaxopedia in some other countries)—the learner puts on a mask with attached earphones, which is connected to an electronic device that includes a cassette recorder. A sensor below the learner's nose registers the breathing rate and, in synchrony with the breathing rhythm, a pleasant visual image appears before the closed eyes and a gentle sound is heard through the earphones. These two biofeedback signals help the learner to relax completely. A microprocessor in the control unit monitors the feedback received from the mask and when the breathing pattern indicates complete relaxation, a cassette containing a recorded learning programme is automatically switched on.

Such accelerated learning methods have often been on the periphery of respectable scholarship, but the few studies that assessed their effectiveness tended to report spectacular intakes of declarative knowledge (usually in terms of the mastery of huge amounts of lexis). Although they seem to have disappeared during the past 15 years from the L2 teaching scene, their potential for establishing a more direct channel of inputting declarative knowledge remains interesting, particularly in the light of automatization theories that can provide theoretical templates for processing the accumulated explicit knowledge to achieve proceduralized (i.e. usable) L2 skills.

Formulaic language

> *Of the various fundamental and mysterious processes involved in the use of human language, one of the most fundamental and most mysterious is the process of conventionalization, that is, the process by which members of a community somehow come to share the sound-meaning pairings that constitute their means of verbal communication ...*
> (Ferguson 1994: 15)

Although applied linguists have been aware of the significance of formulaic language such as lexical phrases, idioms, and conventionalized expressions (hence *formulaic sequences*) for several decades (see e.g. Nattinger and DeCarrico 1992; Pawley and Syder 1983), it is fair to say that formulaic sequences have truly been discovered only during the past ten years. In this section I cannot offer a comprehensive overview of the relevant research (for summaries, see Biber, Conrad, and Cortes 2003; Schmitt 2004; Wray 2002, 2008); instead, I will focus only on the psychological aspects of acquiring formulaic language—particularly on the theory of 'chunking'—and then on the teaching of formulaic sequences.

To start with, we need to realize that there is something fundamental about formulaic sequences. Widdowson (1989: 135), for example, argued two decades ago that 'communicative competence is not a matter of knowing rules ... It is much more a matter of knowing a stock of partially pre-assembled patterns, formulaic frameworks', and indeed many would agree with him that competent speakers of a language are in command of thousands (if not tens of thousands) of language chunks, and use them as basic building blocks in their speech and writing. In his well-known 'idiom principle', Sinclair (1991: 112) also underscores the important role idioms (i.e. formulaic sequences) play in discourse. As he concludes, 'The overwhelming nature of this evidence leads us to elevate the principle of idiom from being a rather minor feature, compared with grammar, to being at least as important as grammar in the explanation of how meaning arises in text.'

Formulaic sequences are also the ultimate manifestations of the 'mysterious' conventionalization process mentioned by Ferguson (1994) in the quote at the beginning of this section. Addressing this issue, Larsen-Freeman and Cameron (2008) point out that, although the knowledge of linguistic rules and lexical items would allow speakers to produce an infinite number of novel, well-formed utterances, 'in practice they do nothing of the sort. Instead, they cobble together the constructions they have registered earlier' (p. 100). Indeed, the authors add, the 'fluency and familiarity of native-like language can be explained by the fact that it is generally not composed of wholly novel combinations of words but rather of sequences that are "sedimented" from human speech interaction' (ibid.). This proposed link between formulaic language competence and automatized, fluent language production has been mentioned more than once in the previous sections. It has traditionally been accounted for by the fact that formulaic sequences are stored in the memory as single units and therefore their retrieval is cognitively relatively undemanding, This in turn allows the speaker to attend to other aspects of communication and to plan larger pieces of discourse, which would naturally facilitate fluent language production under real-time conditions. We are going to come back to this claim below when we look at the process of chunking.

Chunking

In an analysis of 'chunking' in SLA, N. Ellis (2003: 68) explains that formulaic sequences can be considered 'lexical chunks which result from memorizing the sequence of frequent collocations'. Although the term 'chunk' may sound somewhat informal in this context, it is in fact an important technical term in psychology, introduced at the genesis of cognitive science in Miller's (1956) famous article on 'The magical number seven' (mentioned in Ch. 1). In this paper, Miller examined the limited capacity of human short-term memory and made the observation that the maximum number of independent information units—or *chunks*—this memory could store was 7 ± 2. The intriguing feature of these chunks was, however, that the number stayed roughly constant regardless of how big they were. This means, for example, that if we combine two chunks and remember it as one unit (as we often do with, say, telephone numbers), this frees up spare capacity to remember another chunk.

Over the past 50 years chunking has become a central theme in cognitive science, related to many processes of perception, learning, and cognition. As Gobet *et al.* (2001) summarize, the relevant literature can be divided into two broad areas. The first, *goal-oriented chunking*, conceptualizes chunking as a deliberate, purposeful process under the individual's strategic control—this type includes the mnemonic mechanisms Miller (1956) discussed in his paper. The second type of chunking, *perceptual chunking*, concerns automatic and unconscious perceptual processes that are, for example, involved in implicit learning. MacWhinney (2001*b*) also stresses that the term 'chunk' has been utilized in three different functional areas: perception, production, and memory. Although the three areas are clearly interrelated, the nature of the chunks in them—for example, perceptual chunks, motoric chunks, or memory chunks—differs, which may lead to confusion.

Motor sequence learning

An area of chunking research that has been thriving since the early 1950s is the study of the learning of sequential responses in motor behaviour, such as, for example, pressing the keys when playing the piano. It was found in many experiments (see e.g. Koch and Hoffmann 2000; Sakai, Kitaguchi, and Hikosaka 2003) that in spite of the linear nature of the elementary movements that make up such sequences, people learn the sequence as a series of chunks, that is, they spontaneously divide the whole series into segments and memorize clusters of the moves as single units. This becomes obvious if there is a break or interruption in the sequence chain within the boundaries of a unit, making the subsequent elements inaccessible—this is evidenced when we cannot continue from where we stopped without going back to a natural starting point (to a chunk boundary) and rerun the sequence. The chunks in such sequence chains are hierarchical, that is, one larger unit can be built up of several sub-units.

In the light of the obvious relevance of these findings to the learning of formulaic sequences (to be discussed below), it is important to examine how the specific chunks emerge. The first point to note is that chunking is a naturally and spontaneously occurring process (i.e. one does not have to decide to 'do some chunking' for it to happen). Second, past studies have shown that there is considerable individual-level variation in how different people organize the same sequence chain into a number of different chunks and unique chunk patterns. (See Sakai *et al.* 2003.) However, Koch and Hoffmann (2000) also found that the internal relations, characteristics, and patterns of the sequence chain have an influence on the formation of chunks, resulting in what the authors called 'relational chunking'. Thus, the emerging chunking pattern can potentially be manipulated externally by generating sequences that tend to 'hang together' by means of repetition or with the insertion of temporal delay between elements.

Chunking as a general learning mechanism

Motor sequence learning experiments provide powerful illustrations of the existence of chunking mechanisms, but this is not the only area where chunking plays a role. Already Miller (1956) suspected that the chunking process he observed was likely to turn out to be 'a very general and important one for psychology' (p. 93). As he added, chunking is 'an extremely powerful weapon for increasing the amount of information that we can deal with. In one form or another we use receding [i.e. chunking] constantly in our daily behaviour' (p. 95). Subsequent research has borne out Miller's prediction because chunking has been found to be a basic associative learning process that can occur in every representational system (N. Ellis 2001). In one of the most famous studies in this respect, Servan-Schreiber and Anderson (1990) proposed a competitive chunking model to account for artificial grammar learning based on statistical dependencies between successive units or substrings. Chunking is also one of the main learning mechanisms for converting declarative knowledge into procedural knowledge in the automatization process by compiling multiple cognitive processing steps for achieving a goal into a single production rule (Johnson, Wang, and Zhang 2003). Thus, chunking can be seen as a general learning mechanism that has a great deal of direct and indirect relevance to SLA.

Chunking in language acquisition

Language is inherently sequential in nature, with any stretches of discourse—speech streams or written texts—organized into sequential patterns. For this reason, N. Ellis (2001) argues that language acquisition is essentially a sequence learning problem. The close association between language and chunking theory is well illustrated in the following extract from Servan-Schreiber and Anderson's (1990: 593) paper, in which they use linguistic metaphors—including the term 'phrase chunk'—to describe the task of learning a long string of meaningless letters:

> In the process of memorizing the string, the subject has created five chunks. These chunks are organized in a hierarchy at the bottom of which are *elementary* chunks, which are the letters themselves. At the next level up are the *word* chunks, which are made of those elementary chunks. At the top of the hierarchy are the *sentence* chunks, which encode a full stimulus. In between the word and sentence levels are any number of hierarchically organized levels of *phrase* chunks.

Thus, chunking theory might be useful in explaining several levels of language organization, including how strings of sounds are parsed into words, but here I address only the issue of formulaic, multi-word sequences. In this regard, the primary question is how they are formed, that is, how and why co-occurring items get bound up in an entrenched formula that can subsequently be retrieved as a single unit from the memory. Talking about sequence learning in general, Higham (1997) points out that the common theme of all chunk models is that the chunking performance can be predicted by some metric derived from the frequency with which certain features occur within the stimuli. Therefore, it does not come as a surprise that frequency distribution is seen as the driving force of language chunking, as evidenced by Bybee and Hopper's (2001: 3) summary:

> The frequency with which certain items and strings of items are used has a profound influence on the way language is broken up into chunks in memory storage, the way such chunks are related to other stored material and the ease with which they are accessed.

This emphasis on frequency is compatible with Ferguson's (1994) claim about the fundamental tendency for human language to become conventionalized at various levels: in recurring contexts and in recurring situations, people tend to use a limited range of utterances, and this repetitive input, in turn, triggers the inherent human cognitive mechanism of learning through chunking. Accordingly, we would expect to find formulaic sequences to convey common discourse and communicative functions and this is indeed true in both cases.

Unfortunately, frequency itself may not provide the full answer because not every frequently co-occurring string of words forms a chunked whole on the one hand, and not every formulaic sequence is all that frequent on the other. Thus, there is undoubtedly a dynamic relationship between the frequency of certain patterns and their semantic content, which would also explain to some extent how some formulaic sequences are completely fixed whereas others, labelled 'templates' by Gobet (2005), contain open slots. Furthermore, in a recent paper, MacWhinney (2008) points out that although chunking is certainly an important process, it cannot by itself produce full fluency because there are simply too many possible chunks to learn. Instead, fluency should be seen as the flexible online combination and integration of chunks and other linguistic units, which, according to MacWhinney, requires the extension of the original conception of chunking that regarded the process merely as a memory device.

Teaching formulaic sequences

> *[A]lthough many have written about the expected benefits of teaching formulaic utterances, few have actually proposed how to accomplish this.*
> (Gatbonton and Segalowitz 2005: 342)

Given the significance of formulaic sequences in L2 proficiency, the question of their teachability ought to have a prominent place in the study of instructed SLA. Regrettably, there has been very little research in this area to date; for example, in a comprehensive overview of research on instructed L2 vocabulary learning, Schmitt (2008) decided not to include the learning and teaching of formulaic language (although he was well aware of the importance of formulaic sequences as he himself had edited a book on this topic in 2004), because there was simply not enough relevant material to report on (personal communication). Taguchi (2007) also highlighted the insufficient amount of empirical study of the systematic training of chunks in different types of drills and exercises.

What explains this neglect of any pedagogic research in this area? I do not think that it is the result of the profession's ignorance of the significance of formulaic language in general, because in research circles its importance has been widely acknowledged over the past 30 years. For example, in Wong-Fillmore's (1979) seminal study of five Mexican children's acquisition of English in the United States, three of the eight key strategies that were identified as facilitating the learning process directly involved formulaic language; and in the early 1990s Nattinger and DeCarrico's (1992) book on lexical phrases was awarded the prestigious Duke of Edinburgh Prize. In a similar vein, the teaching of expressions and idioms has traditionally been a featured area of materials development amongst L2 practitioners resulting in dozens of 'expressions-for-L2-learners' types of texts. I even co-authored one of these many years ago (Dörnyei and Thurrell 1990), and Lewis's (1993, 1997) well-known 'lexical approach' has also placed an importance on the teaching of various phrases and collocations. Rather, the main obstacle to giving formulaic sequences their due importance in L2 research has been the difficulty of defining and operationalizing this rather elusive language phenomenon at the level of precision that is required to serve as an effective theoretical foundation to build on.

Indeed, it is symptomatic of the tentative nature of research that we do not even have a universally accepted label for conventionalized phrases, and while everybody would accept that an expression such as 'kick the bucket' is a formulaic sequence that needs to be taught as such, many (if not the majority) of the multi-word lexical items that could potentially qualify for the formulaic sequence category are not so clearly distinguishable. How shall we treat, for example, 'lexicalized sentence stems' (Pawley and Syder 1983) or 'slot-and-frame patterns' (N. Ellis 2003), that is, variable or discontinuous frames? And what about common everyday utterance phrases such as 'I love you, Mum' or 'Let's get out of here!' that are surely not put together word-by-word by the speakers? Without any defining rule of what is formulaic and what is not, the category becomes too open-ended for materials designers and language teachers to start developing systematic programmes around it.

Recently, however, things have started to change: the past decade has brought about a renewed vigour in studying formulaic language and some important studies have also been published on the classroom practice of promoting chunks and formulaic sequences (e.g. Boers *et al.* 2006; Gatbonton and Segalowitz 2005; Taguchi 2007). Taguchi summarizes the overall message of this line of research thus:

> In summary, previous findings have documented that classroom practice of target-like chunks can prepare learners for the creative production of forms and the subsequent development of L2 competence. The findings imply that chunk learning through contextualized, meaningful drills can promote language development. (p. 437)

In one of the few principled investigations of the effectiveness of formulaic language training, Boers *et al.* (2006) set out to implement a 'phrasal methodology' primarily by raising the learners' awareness about the pervasiveness of formulaic sequences in authentic L2 (English as a foreign language) texts, thereby helping students to notice them and, in the long run, to develop a new 'mindset'. This approach was in line of Lewis's (1993) recommendation on how to teach formulaic sequences as part of his lexical approach. Boers *et al.* found that the awareness-raising method worked: in a quasi-experimental study consisting of 22 hours of special formulaic training embedded in a language course over an eight-month period, the experimental group displayed significant gains over the control group in terms of their fluency and their use of formulaic sequences.

Taguchi's (2007) aims were similar to those of Boers *et al.* (2006), but she adopted a very different, more direct approach. Allocating 15 minutes of each L2 class for a period of 10 weeks (with four classes per week) to the promotion of formulaic language competence, she developed a dialogue-based teaching programme of grammatical chunks (semi-fixed grammatical patterns), consisting of an initial video presentation of the target dialogue, followed by choral and pair repetition of the text and rule explanation. Students then underwent structured drilling of the chunks within a communicative context, and finally they memorized and performed short dialogues that included the target sequences. These presentations were graded and they counted 10 per cent against the learners' final course grade. The results indicated a substantial development, with the range and number of the chunks performed by the students doubling over the training period.

Gatbonton and Segalowitz's ACCESS

The most principled attempt over the past two decades to develop a coherent approach for the promotion of formulaic sequences has been made by Gatbonton and Segalowitz (1988, 2005). The proposed methodology is called ACCESS, standing for Automatization in Communicative Contexts of Essential Speech Segments, and it attempts to offer a principled adaptation of communicative language teaching that aims to generate fluency by drawing on the theories of automatization and formulaic language. Thus, ACCESS covers in a way a great deal of the material presented in this chapter.

'Essential speech segments' in the name of the approach refer to formulaic utterances, and their central position in the approach was motivated by the analysis of the insufficient effectiveness of traditional CLT to develop automatized L2 skills. Gatbonton and Segalowitz (1988) argued that most CLT methods did not provide sufficient repetitive practice to promote automatization, and even the variants that placed an emphasis on communicative drills tended to focus on language structures rather than phrases, and thus generated only a few tokens of each utterance, which was not enough to automatize them. If this was indeed the case, then the logical remedy would be to shift the emphasis from rule automatization to item automatization, which is exactly what ACCESS was designed to achieve. The method, then, can be seen as a principled task sequence for the communicative drilling of formulaic sequences.

ACCESS lessons have three phases—a Creative Automatization Phase, a Language Consolidation Phase, and a Free Communication Phase. The key component is the first phase: this is where the formulaic sequences are presented and practised, while the follow-up phases are aimed at consolidating the knowledge. According to the authors, in order to ensure that the Creative Automatization Phase promotes the learning, use, and practice of formulaic utterances, the main task in this phase must meet three criteria: it must be *genuinely communicative*, *inherently repetitive*, and *functionally formulaic*. Thus, the challenge for task design is to generate a communicative language-use situation that focuses on a salient communicative function and that requires the repeated meaningful use of a limited number of formulaic phrases. This is not easy but with some creativity—hence the name of the first phase of ACCESS—it is 'quite possible to capitalize upon the advantages of the communicatively oriented learning setting to explicitly promote automatization' (Gatbonton and Segalowitz 1988: 478; examples are also provided in Gatbonton and Segalowitz 2005). One example of such a task is a group activity in which students need to elicit or report information from/to many people, in individual, face-to-face communication, using a grid as a prop, for example (Segalowitz and Hulstijn 2005).

The purpose of the Language Consolidation Phase is to provide additional, intensive practice of any problematic utterances identified during the earlier phase, while the final Free Communication Phase is designed to promote the use of the targeted formulaic sequences in a more open context by providing students with opportunities to speak freely about issues related to the module's theme. This latter phase is in contrast to the initial creative automatization component in that the relative narrowness of the communicative topic that was initially imposed to ensure the necessary target-specific repetitive focus is broadened here to allow learners to explore the whole range of the topic and thus to extend the use of the automatized phrases to a more varied context.

Gatbonton and Segalowitz's work is noteworthy because, in my view, it represents the most principled integration of contemporary L2 teaching methodology and cutting-edge applied linguistic research. ACCESS is interesting in itself, but its significance also lies in the broader fact that it can be seen as a methodological template for a new, more systematic approach to communicative language teaching. The authors (Gatbonton and Segalowitz 2005: 339) summarize this template thus:

> ACCESS differs from these CLT methodologies because the communication component itself both initiates and sustains automatization, thus overcoming the alleged incompatibility between communication and automatization. This is accomplished in ACCESS by situating automatization in context (genuine communication criterion), by eliciting and subjecting to automatization a critical mass of utterances (functional-formulaicity criterion), and by repeatedly eliciting and practising many tokens of each targeted utterance (inherent repetitiveness criterion).

Summary

[O]ptimal L2 practice in the foreign language classroom should be interactive, meaningful, and with a built-in focus on selective aspects of the language code that are integral to the very nature of that practice.
(Ortega 2007a: 198)

I started out this chapter by stating that, for the time being, the accumulated wisdom of best practices in the L2 teaching profession exceeds the methodological significance of the findings of empirical investigations, and this is particularly true of the psychologically oriented research that is the subject of this book. (For a very detailed recent account of linguistically and pedagogically oriented research, see R. Ellis 2008.) The material reviewed in this chapter has admittedly often failed to offer the level of detail and elaboration that classroom practitioners would need in order to be able to implement the proposed ideas. Yet, I also pointed out at the beginning that any solid principles that scholarly research can offer are invaluable reference points for classroom practitioners, and I believe that some of the insights emerging from the material covered in this chapter are sufficiently solid and far-reaching to orientate and inspire future developments in the field.

It was argued throughout the chapter that from a psychological perspective, the real challenge of instructed SLA is to specify the nature of the optimal co-operation between explicit and implicit learning processes. Regrettably, the effortless, unstoppable, and successful-by-default implicit learning process that is characteristic of first language acquisition does not seem to be taking care of instructed SLA and therefore mere exposure to L2 input, even if accompanied by some broad communicative practice, is insufficient to help school learners to become completely proficient or fluent in the L2. Consequently, we need to complement implicit learning with explicit learning procedures—such as focus on form, principled skill acquisition tasks, and focused instruction of formulaic language—in order to push the learners beyond communicatively effective language towards target-like second language ability. The previous overview of relevant research in these areas demonstrated that applied linguists are increasingly aware of both the theoretical and pedagogical significance of the main issues involved, and we have seen that the past decade has generated some important research output to inform instructed SLA. At the same time, it is fair to say that we still need a great deal of work before SLA researchers will be in a position to offer detailed advice to language practitioners on what sort of classroom activities to conduct and how.

Although this book has not covered language teacher development, there is a robust implication for teacher education that emerges from the discussion of the significance of explicit learning in instructed SLA. As Simon Murison-Bowie (personal communication) points out, in order to become an instructor of any skill (including language skills), one needs to develop the kind of explicit, declarative knowledge of the performance of the skill that will need to be presented to learners in an explicit manner to complement their implicit learning. In language teaching terms this would imply that it is not enough to be fully competent in the L2—as native speakers are—without being cognizant of the underlying rules and regulations. Thus, while skill automatization involves a move from predominantly declarative to predominantly procedural knowledge, the training of instructors requires a reverse process.

To conclude, let me reiterate six key—and somewhat overlapping—principles that are, I believe, in accordance with the state of the art of our research knowledge of instructed SLA:

1 Instructed SLA should be meaning-focused and personally engaging as a whole. However, similar to the training of musicians or athletes, it should also include controlled practice activities to promote the automatization of L2 skills. The purpose of this practice should be clearly explained to the learners and the content/format should be made as motivating and meaningful as possible within the tasks' inherent constraints.

2 To provide jump starts for subsequent proceduralization and automatization, instructed SLA should contain explicit initial input components. This declarative input can be offered in several creative ways, including the potential utilization of accelerated learning techniques that attempt to put the mind in a receptive state and then open up a direct input channel to it. Another important source of the internalization of declarative knowledge is rote-learning.

3 While maintaining an overall meaning-oriented approach, instructed SLA should also pay attention to the formal/structural aspects of the L2 that determine accuracy and appropriateness at the linguistic, discourse, and pragmatic levels. The hallmark of good teaching is finding the optimal balance between meaning-based and form-focused activities in the dynamic classroom context.

4 Instructed SLA should include the teaching of formulaic sequences as a featured component. There should be sufficient awareness raising of the significance and pervasiveness of formulaic language, and selected phrases should be practiced and recycled intensively.

5 Instructed SLA should offer learners extensive exposure to large amounts of L2 input that can feed the learners' implicit learning mechanisms. In order to make the most of this exposure, learners should be given some explicit preparation in terms of pre-task activities (e.g. pre-reading/listening/watching tasks or explanations of some salient aspects of the material) to prime them for maximum intake.

6 Instructed SLA should offer learners ample opportunities to participate in genuine L2 interaction. For best effect, such communicative practice should always have a specific formal or functional focus, and should always be associated with target phrases to practice.

In sum, the essence of the principled communicative approach I am advocating is the creative integration of meaningful communication with relevant declarative input and the automatization of both linguistic rules and lexical items. In instructed SLA, the more is not the merrier if it is not focused.

Afterword

When I decided to do a Ph.D. in Applied Linguistics in Hungary in 1985, I was told that there was no academic discipline called 'applied linguistics'. But surely, I pleaded, the theory of second language learning is an important theoretical question, worthy of scientific investigation. Yes it is, was the answer, but the relevant discipline to study it is not 'applied linguistics' but rather 'psycholinguistics'. This is how I ended up doing my Ph.D. in Psycholinguistics, even though my main research topic, the role of motivation in language learning, had little to do with that discipline.

When I was about to be promoted to full Professor in the UK in 2004, I was asked what my title should be (in the UK a professorship is always linked to a specific subject). 'Professor of Applied Linguistics', I replied. However, because my department already had a Professor of Applied Linguistics (Mike McCarthy) and we were also in the process of advertising for a second professorship in the area, I was asked to choose another label. This is how I became 'Professor of Psycholinguistics', even though my main research topic, the role of motivation in language learning, had little to do with that discipline.

Thus, I have spent the past two decades of my working life classified as a psycholinguist even though I wasn't one. Then came this book and with it the hope that I would finally find out what I have been over all these years. Looking back, I am actually quite pleased with what I have found: psycholinguistics is a vibrant and fascinating (and very scholarly!) discipline and, therefore, being a psycholinguist is undoubtedly cool.

Regrettably, just as I thought that I had finally succeeded in appropriating my psycholinguistic persona, the term 'psycholinguistics' started to fade away and evolve into a new emerging discipline that can be broadly labelled 'cognitive second language neuroscience'. Which, of course, means that my quest for a professional identity is to continue! I suspect that I am not alone in this state of disorientation—most second language researchers will have been affected by the ongoing academic paradigm shift (termed 'psycho-blitzkrieg' in the Preface). Perhaps one way of making a virtue of this highly uncomfortable situation is to claim that 'it is the journey that matters not the getting there'. And to conclude on a positive note, let me cite a Dutch proverb that I have found on the Internet: 'He who is outside his door already has the hard part of his journey behind him.' (Unfortunately, several Dutch friends and colleagues insist that this proverb does not exist in Dutch.)

References

Abutalebi, J., and D. Green 2007. 'Bilingual language production: The neurocognition of language representation and control'. *Journal of Neurolinguistics* 20: 242–75.
—— S. F. Cappa, and D. Perani 2005. 'What can functional neuroimaging tell us about the bilingual brain?' in J. F. Kroll and A. M. B. De Groot (eds.): *Handbook of Bilingualism: Psycholinguistic Approaches*. Oxford: Oxford University Press, 497–515.
Achard, M., and S. Niemeier (eds.) 2004. *Cognitive Linguistics, Second Language Acquisition, and Foreign Language Teaching* Berlin: Mouton de Gruyter.
Ackerman, P. L. 2003. 'Aptitude complexes and trait complexes'. *Educational Psychologist* 38/2: 85–93.
—— 2005. 'Personality, trait complexes and adult intelligence' in A. Eliasz, S. E. Hampson, and B. De Raad (eds.): *Advances in Personality Psychology*. Hove: Psychology Press, ii. 91–112.
—— and E. D. Heggestad 1997. 'Intelligence, personality, and interests: Evidence for overlapping traits'. *Psychological Bulletin* 121/2: 219–45.
—— and R. Kanfer 2004. 'Cognitive, affective, and conative aspects of adult intellect within a typical and maximal performance framework' in D. Y. Dai and R. J. Sternberg (eds.): *Motivation, Emotion, and Cognition: Integrative Perspectives on Intellectual Functioning and Development*. Mahwah, NJ: Lawrence Erlbaum, 119–41.
—— and S. D. Wolman 2007. 'Determinants and validity of self-estimates of abilities and self-concept measures'. *Journal of Experimental Psychology: Applied* 13/2: 57–78.
—— M. E. Beier, and M. O. Boyle 2005. 'Working memory and intelligence: The same or different constructs?' *Psychological Bulletin* 131/1: 30–60.
Ahlsén, E. 2006. *Introduction to Neurolinguistics*. Amsterdam: John Benjamins.
Allport, G. W. 1937. *Personality: A Psychological Interpretation*. New York: Holt Rinehart & Winston.
Al-Shehri, A. S. 2009. 'Motivation and vision: The relation between the Ideal L2 Self, imagination and visual style' in Dörnyei and Ushioda (2009: 164–71).
Altmann, G. T. M. 2006. 'History of psycholinguistics' in K. Brown (ed.): *The Encyclopedia of Language and Linguistics*, 2nd edn. Oxford: Elsevier, 257–65.
Anderson, J. R. 2000a. *Cognitive Psychology and Its Implications*, 5th edn. New York: Worth.
—— 2000b. *Learning and Memory: An Integrated Approach*, 2nd edn. Hoboken, NJ: John Wiley & Sons.
—— and J. M. Fincham 1994. 'Acquisition of procedural skills from examples'. *Journal of Experimental Psychology: Learning, Memory, and Cognition* 20/6: 1322–40.
—— D. Bothell, M. D. Byrne, S. Douglass, C. Lebiere, and Y. Qin 2004. 'An integrated theory of the mind'. *Psychological Review* 111/4: 1036–60.
Austin, J. L. 1962. *How to Do Things with Words*. Oxford: Clarendon.
Baars, B. J. 1997a. *In the Theater of Consciousness*. New York: Oxford University Press.
—— 1997b. 'In the theatre of consciousness: Global Workspace theory, a rigorous scientific theory of consciousness'. *Journal of Consciousness Studies* 4/4: 292–309.
—— 2007a. 'Language' in Baars and Gage (2007a: 317–42).
—— 2007b. 'Mind and brain' in Baars and Gage (2007a: 1–29).
—— and N. M. Gage 2007a. B. J. Baars and N. M. Gage (eds.): *Cognition, Brain, and Consciousness: Introduction to Cognitive Neuroscience*. London: Academic Press.
Baars, B. J. and N. M. Gage 2007b. 'Preface' in Baars and Gage (2007a: pp. xiii–xv).

Baddeley, A. D. 2003. 'Working memory and language: An overview'. *Journal of Communication Disorders* 36: 189–208.

Berko Gleason, J. 2005. 'The development of language: An overview and a preview' in J. Berko Gleason (ed.): *The Development of Language*, 6th edn. Boston: Pearson, 1–38.

—— and N. Bernstein Ratner (eds.) 1998. *Psycholinguistics*, 2nd edn. Fort Worth: Harcourt Brace.

Bialystok, E. 2005. 'Consequences of bilingualism for cognitive development' in J. F. Kroll and A. M. B. De Groot (eds.): *Handbook of Bilingualism: Psycholinguistic Approaches*. Oxford: Oxford University Press, 417–32.

—— 2007. 'Language acquisition and bilingualism: Consequences for a multilingual society'. *Applied Psycholinguistics* 28: 393–7.

—— F. I. M. Craik, and M. Freedman 2007. 'Bilingualism as a protection against the onset of symptoms of dementia'. *Neuropsychologia* 45: 459–64.

—— —— and J. Ryan 2006. 'Executive control in a modified antisaccade task: Effects of aging and bilingualism'. *Journal of Experimental Psychology: Learning, Memory, and Cognition* 32/6: 1341–54.

—— —— R. Klein, and M. Viswanathan 2004. 'Bilingualism, aging, and cognitive control: Evidence from the Simon task'. *Psychology and Aging* 19/2: 290–303.

Biber, D., S. Conrad, and V. Cortes 2003. 'Lexical bundles in speech and writing: An initial taxonomy' in A. Wilson, P. Rayson, and T. McEnery (eds.): *Corpus Linguistics by the Lune: A Festschrift for Geoffrey Leech*. Frankfurt: Peter Lang, 71–92.

Billingsley, R. L., P. G. Simos, E. M. Castillo, F. Maestú, S. Sarkari, J. I. Breier, and A. C. Papanicolaou 2003. 'Functional brain imaging of language: Criteria for scientific merit and supporting data from magnetic source imaging'. *Journal of Neurolinguistics* 16: 255–75.

Birdsong, D. 2005. 'Interpreting age affects in second language acquisition' in J. F. Kroll and A. M. B. De Groot (eds.): *Handbook of Bilingualism: Psycholinguistic Approaches*. Oxford: Oxford University Press, 109–37.

—— 2006. 'Age and second language acquisition and processing: A selective overview' in M. Gullberg and P. Indefrey (eds.): *The Cognitive Neuroscience of Second Language Acquisition*. Malden, Mass.: Blackwell, 9–49.

—— 2007. 'Nativelike pronunciation among late learners of French as a second language' in O.-S. Bohn and M. J. Munro (eds.): *Language Experience in Second Language Learning*. Amsterdam: John Benjamins, 99–116.

Bloom, P. 2006, June. 'Seduced by the flickering lights of the brain'. *Seed Magazine* <http://seedmagazine.com/news/2006/06/seduced_by_the_flickering_ligh.php>, accessed 22 August 2008.

Bod, R. 2003. 'Exemplar-based syntax: How to get productivity from examples'. *Linguistic Review* 23/3: 291–320.

—— J. Hay, and S. Jannedy 2003a. 'Introduction' in eid. (eds.): *Probabilistic Linguistic*. Cambridge, Mass.: MIT, 1–10.

—— —— —— 2003b. 'Preface' in eid. (eds.): *Probabilistic Linguistic*. Cambridge, Mass.: MIT, pp. vii–viii.

Boers, F., J. Eyckmans, J. Kappel, H. Stengers, and M. Demecheleer 2006. 'Formulaic sequences and perceived oral proficiency: putting a Lexical Approach to the test'. *Language Teaching Research* 10/3: 245–61.

Bohannon, J. N., and J. D. Bonvillian 2005. 'Theoretical approaches to language acquisition' in J. Berko Gleason (ed.) *The Development of Language*, 6th edn. Boston: Pearson, 230–91.

Bongaerts, T. 2005. 'Introduction: Ultimate attainment and the critical period hypothesis for second language acquisition'. *IRAL* 43: 259–67.

Bornstein, M. H. 1989. 'Sensitive periods in development: Structural characteristics and causal interpretations'. *Psychological Bulletin* 105/2: 179–97.

Bouchard, T. J., and M. McGue 2003. 'Genetic and environmental influences on human psychological differences'. *Journal of Neurobiology* 54/1: 4–45.

Boyatzis, R. E., and **K. Akrivou** 2006. 'The ideal self as the driver of intentional change'. *Journal of Management Development* 25/7: 624–42.

Brody, N. 2005. 'Phenotypes and genotypes of personality and intelligence: Similarities and differences' in A. Eliasz, S. E. Hampson, and B. De Raad (eds.) *Advances in Personality Psychology*. Hove: Psychology Press, ii. 113–38.

Brown, H. D. 1994. *Teaching by Principles*. Englewood Cliffs, NJ: Prentice Hall.

Brumfit, C. J. 1979. ' "Communicative" language teaching:. An educational Perspective' in C. J. Brumfit (ed.): *The Communicative Approach to Language Teaching*. Oxford: Oxford University Press, 183–91.

—— 1984. *Communicative Methodology in Language Teaching: The Roles of Fluency and Accuracy*. Cambridge: Cambridge University Press.

Buck, R. 2005. 'Adding ingredients to the self-organizing dynamic system stew: Motivation, communication, and higher-level emotions—and don't forget the genes!' *Behavioral and Brain Science* 28/2: 197–8.

Butler, L. T., and D. C. Berry 2001. 'Implicit memory: Intention and awareness revisited'. *Trends in Cognitive Sciences* 5/5: 192–7.

Bybee, J. 2002. 'Phonological evidence for exemplar storage of multiword sequences'. *Studies in Second Language Acquisition* 24: 215–21.

—— 2007. *Frequency of Use and the Organization of Language*. Oxford: Oxford University Press.

—— and **P. Hopper** (eds.) 2001a. *Frequency and the Emergence of Linguistic Structure*. Amsterdam: John Benjamins.

—— —— 2001b. 'Introduction to frequency and the emergence of linguistic structure' in Bybee and Hopper (2001a: 1–24).

Byrne, D. 2002. *Interpreting Quantitative Data*. London: Sage.

Cameron, L. 2003. *Metaphor in Educational Discourse*. London: Continuum.

Cameron, L., and **D. Larsen-Freeman** 2007. 'Complex systems and applied linguistics'. *International Journal of Applied Linguistics* 17/2: 226–40.

Canale, M. 1983. 'From communicative competence to communicative language pedagogy' in J. C. Richards and R. W. Schmidt (eds.): *Language and Communication*. Harlow: Longman, 2–27.

Canale, M., and **M. Swain** 1980. 'Theoretical bases of communicative approaches to second language teaching and testing'. *Applied Linguistics* 1: 1–47.

Carlson, R. A. 2003. 'Skill learning' in L. Nadel (ed.): *Encyclopedia of Cognitive Science*. London: Nature Publishing, iv. 36–42.

Carroll, J. B. 1973. 'Implications of aptitude test research and psycholinguistic theory for foreign language teaching'. *International Journal of Psycholinguistics* 2: 5–14.

—— 1981. 'Twenty-five years of research in foreign language aptitude' in K. C. Diller (ed.): *Individual Differences and Universals in Language Learning Aptitude*. Rowley, Mass.: Newbury House, 83–118.

—— 1990. 'Cognitive abilities in foreign language aptitude: Then and now' in T. Parry and C. Stansfield (eds.): *Language Aptitude Reconsidered*. Englewood Cliffs, NJ: Prentice-Hall Regents, 11–29.

—— 1993. *Human Cognitive Abilities: A Survey of Factor-Analytic Studies*. Cambridge: Cambridge University Press.

—— and **S. Sapon** 1959. *The Modern Language Aptitude Test*. San Antonio, Tex.: Psychological Corporation.

Cartwright, D. 1952. 'Forward' in D. Cartwright (ed.): *Field Theory in Social Science: Selected Theoretical Papers by Kurt Lewin*. London: Tavistock, pp. vii–xv.

Carver, C. S. 2005. 'Emotion theory is about more than affect and cognition: Taking triggers and actions into account'. *Behavioral and Brain Science* 28/2: 198–9.

—— and **M. F. Scheier** 1999. 'Themes and issues in the self-regulation of behavior' in R. S. J. Wyer (ed.): *Perspectives on Behavioral Self-Regulation*. Mahwah, NJ: Lawrence Erlbaum, 1–105.

Castagnaro, P. J. 2006. 'Audiolingual method and behaviorism: From misunderstanding to myth'. *Applied Linguistics* 27/3: 519–26.

Celce-Murcia, M. 2001. 'Language teaching approaches: An overview' in M. Celce-Murcia (ed.): *Teaching English as a Second or Foreign Language*, 3rd edn. Boston: Heinle & Heinle, 3–11.

—————— M., Z. Dörnyei, and S. Thurrell 1995. 'Communicative competence: A pedagogically motivated model with content specifications'. *Issues in Applied Linguistics* 6: 5–35.

—————— 1997. 'Direct approaches in L2 instruction: A turning point in communicative language teaching?' *TESOL Quarterly* 31: 141–52.

—————— 1998. 'On directness in communicative language teaching'. *TESOL Quarterly* 32: 116–19.

Cenoz, J. 2003. 'The influence of age on the acquisition of English: General proficiency, attitudes and code-mixing' in M. P. García Mayo and M. L. García Lecumberri (eds.): *Age and the Acquisition of English as a Foreign Language*. Clevedon: Multilingual Matters, pp. 77–93.

Chamorro-Premuzic, T., A. Furnham, and P. L. Ackerman 2006. 'Ability and personality correlates of general knowledge'. *Personality and Individual Differences* 41: 419–29.

Chater, N., and C. D. Manning 2006. 'Probabilistic models of language processing and acquisition'. *Trends in Cognitive Sciences* 10/7: 335–44.

—— J. B. Tennebaum, and A. Yuille (eds.) 2006. 'Probabilistic models of cognition', Special Issue. *Trends in Cognitive Sciences* 10/7.

Chein, J. M., S. M. Ravizza, and J. A. Fiez 2003. 'Using neuroimaging to evaluate models of working memory and their implications for language processing'. *Journal of Neurolinguistics* 16: 315–39.

Chi, M. T. H., and S. Ohlsson 2005. 'Complex declarative learning' in K. J. Holyoak and R. G. Morrison (eds.): *The Cambridge Handbook of Thinking and Reasoning*. Cambridge: Cambridge University Press, 371–99.

Chomsky, N. 1959. 'Review of the book *Verbal Behavior*'. *Language* 35: 26–58.

—— 1965. *Aspects of the Theory of Syntax*. Cambridge. Mass.: MIT.

Cleeremans, A. 2003. 'Implicit learning models' in L. Nadel (ed.): *Encyclopedia of Cognitive Science*. London: Nature Publishing, ii. 491–9.

—— A. Destrebecqz, and M. Boyer 1998. 'Implicit learning: News from the front'. *Trends in Cognitive Sciences* 2/10: 406–16.

Clément, R., and R. C. Gardner 2001. 'Second language mastery' in H. Giles and W. P. Robinson (eds.): *The New Handbook of Language and Social Psychology*, 2nd edn. London: Wiley, 489–504.

Coltheart, M. 2006. 'What has functional neuroimaging told us about the mind (so far)?' *Cortex* 42: 323–31.

Cook, G. 2000. *Language Play, Language Learning*. Oxford: Oxford University Press.

Corder, S. P. 1967. 'The significance of learners' errors'. *International Review of Applied Linguistics* 5: 161–9.

Corning, P. A. 2002. 'A venerable concept in search of a theory'. *Complexity* 7/6: 18–30.

Corno, L., L. J. Cronbach, H. Kupermintz, D. F. Lohman, E. B. Mandinach, A. W. Porteus, and J. E. Talbert 2002. *Remaking the Concept of Aptitude: Extending the Legacy of Richard E. Snow*. Mahwah, NJ: Lawrence Erlbaum.

Crain, S., and R. Thornton 2006. 'Acquisition of syntax and semantics' in M. J. Traxler and M. A. Gernsbacher (eds.): *Handbook of Psycholinguistics*, 2nd edn. London: Academic Press, 1073–110.

Croft, W., and D. A. Cruse 2004. *Cognitive Linguistics*. Cambridge: Cambridge University Press.

Crowell, S. E. 2004. 'The neurobiology of declarative memory' in J. H. Schumann, S. E. Crowell, N. E. Jones, N. Lee, S. A. Schuchert, and L. A. Wood (eds.): *The Neurobiology of Learning: Perspectives from Second Language Acquisition*. Mahwah, NJ: Lawrence Erlbaum, 75–109.

Csikszentmihalyi, M. 1990. *Flow: The Psychology of Optimal Experience*. New York: Harper & Row.

Dai, D. Y., and R. J. Sternberg 2004. 'Beyond cognitivism: Toward an integrated understanding of intellectual functioning and development' in D. Y. Dai and R. J. Sternberg (eds.): *Motivation, Emotion, and Cognition: Integrative Perspectives on Intellectual Functioning and Development*. Mahwah, NJ: Lawrence Erlbaum, 3–38.

Daneman, M., and P. A. Carpenter 1980. 'Individual differences in working memory and reading'. *Journal of Verbal Learning and Verbal Behavior* 19: 450–66.

Davies, M. 2001. 'Knowledge (explicit and implicit): Philosophical aspects' in N. J. Smelser and P. B. Baltes (eds.): *International Encyclopedia of the Social and Behavioral Sciences*. Oxford: Pergamon, 8126–32.

De Angelis, G. 2007. *Third or Additional Language Acquisition*. Clevedon: Multilingual Matters.

de Bot, K. 2008*a*. 'The imaging of what in the multilingual mind?' *Second Language Research* 24/1: 111–33.

—— 2008*b*. 'Second language development as a dynamic process'. *Modern Language Journal* 92: 166–78.

—— W. Lowie, and M. Verspoor 2005. *Second Language Acquisition: An Advanced Resource Book*. London: Routledge.

—— —— —— 2007*a*. 'A Dynamic Systems Theory approach to second language acquisition'. *Bilingualism: Language and Cognition* 10/1: 7–21.

—— —— —— 2007*b*. 'A dynamic view as a complementary perspective'. *Bilingualism: Language and Cognition* 10/1: 51–5.

De Raad, B. 2000. 'Differential psychology' in A. E. Kazdin (ed.): *Encyclopedia of Psychology*. Oxford: American Psychological Association and Oxford University Press, iii. 41–4.

De Wolf, T., and T. Holvoet 2005. 'Emergence versus self-organization: Different concepts but promising when combined' in S. A. Brueckner, G. Di Marzo Serugendo, A. Karageorgos, and R. Nagpal (eds.): *Engineering Self-Organising Systems: Methodologies and Applications* Berlin: Springer, 1–15.

DeKeyser, R. M. 1997. 'Beyond explicit rule learning: Automatizing second language morphosyntax'. *Studies in Second Language Acquisition* 19: 195–221.

—— 2000. 'The robustness of critical period effects in second language acquisition'. *Studies in Second Language Acquisition* 22/4: 493–533.

—— 2001. 'Automaticity and automatization' in P. Robinson (ed.): *Cognition and Second Language Acquisition*. New York: Cambridge University Press, 125–51.

—— 2005. 'What makes second-language grammar difficult? A review of issues'. *Language Learning* 55 (Suppl. 1): 1–25.

—— 2007*a*. 'Introduction: Situating the concept of practice' in R. M. DeKeyser (ed.): *Practice in Second Language: Perspectives from Applied Linguistics and Cognitive Psychology*. New York: Cambridge University Press, 1–18.

—— (ed.) 2007*b*. *Practice in Second Language: Perspectives from Applied Linguistics and Cognitive Psychology*. New York: Cambridge University Press.

—— 2007*c*. 'Skill acquisition theory' in B. VanPatten and J. Williams (eds.): *Theories in Second Language Acquisition: An Introduction*. Mahwah, NJ: Lawrence Erlbaum, 97–113.

—— and A. Juffs 2005. 'Cognitive considerations in L2 learning' in E. Hinkel (ed.): *Handbook of Research in Second Language Teaching and Learning*. Mahwah, NJ: Lawrence Erlbaum, 437–54.

—— and J. Larson-Hall 2005. 'What does the critical period really mean?' in J. F. Kroll and A. M. B. De Groot (eds.): *Handbook of Bilingualism: Psycholinguistic Approaches*. Oxford: Oxford University Press, 88–108.

Dewaele, J.-M. 2002. 'Individual differences in L2 fluency: The effect of neurobiological correlates' in V. Cook (ed.): *Portraits of the L2 User*. Clevedon: Multilingual Matters, 221–49.

—— 2005. 'Investigating the psychological and emotional dimensions in instructed language learning: Obstacles and possibilities'. *Modern Language Journal* 89/3: 367–80.

Dewaele, J.-M., K. V. Petrides, and A. Furnham Forthcoming. 'The effects of trait emotional intelligence and sociobiographical variables on communicative anxiety and foreign language anxiety among adult multilinguals: A review and empirical investigation'. *Language Learning* 58/4.

Dienes, Z., and R. Fahey 1995. 'Role of specific instances in controlling a dynamic system'. *Journal of Experimental Psychology: Learning, Memory, and Cognition* 21/4: 848–62.

Dijkstra, T., and W. J. B. van Heuven 2002. 'The architecture of the bilingual word recognition system: From identification to decision'. *Bilingualism: Language and Cognition* 5/3: 175–97.

Dobbs, D. 2005. 'Fact of phrenology'. *Scientific American Mind* (April): 24–31.

Dörnyei, Z. 1994. 'Motivation and motivating in the foreign language classroom'. *Modern Language Journal* 78: 273–84.

—— 2000. 'Motivation in action: Towards a process-oriented conceptualisation of student motivation'. *British Journal of Educational Psychology* 70: 519–38.

—— 2001*a*. *Motivational Strategies in the Language Classroom*. Cambridge: Cambridge University Press.

—— 2001*b*. *Teaching and Researching Motivation*. Harlow: Longman.

—— 2002. 'The motivational basis of language learning tasks' in P. Robinson (ed.): *Individual Differences in Second Language Acquisition*. Amsterdam: John Benjamins, 137–58.

—— 2005. *The Psychology of the Language Learner: Individual Differences in Second Language Acquisition*. Mahwah, NJ: Lawrence Erlbaum.

—— 2006*a*. 'Individual differences in second language acquisition'. *AILA Review* 19: 42–68.

—— 2006*b*. 'Non-native speakers exist!' *TESL-EJ* 10/1.

—— 2007*a*. 'Creating a motivating classroom environment' in J. Cummins and C. Davison (eds.): *International Handbook of English Language Teaching*. New York: Springer, ii. 719–31.

—— 2007*b*. *Research Methods in Applied Linguistics: Quantitative, Qualitative and Mixed Methodologies*. Oxford: Oxford University Press.

—— 2009. 'The L2 Motivational Self System' in Dörnyei and Ushioda (2009: 9–42).

—— and J. Kormos 1998. 'Problem-solving mechanisms in L2 communication: A psycholinguistic perspective'. *Studies in Second Language Acquisition* 20: 349–85.

—— and T. Murphey 2003. *Group Dynamics in the Language Classroom*. Cambridge: Cambridge University Press.

—— and I. Ottó 1998. 'Motivation in action: A process model of L2 motivation'. *Working Papers in Applied Linguistics* (Thames Valley University, London) 4: 43–69.

—— and P. Skehan 2003. 'Individual differences in second language learning' in C. J. Doughty and M. H. Long (eds.): *The Handbook of Second Language Acquisition*. Oxford: Blackwell, 589–630.

—— and S. Thurrell 1990. *Expressions on Your Own*. Budapest: Belvedere Ötlet.

—— and W.-T. Tseng Forthcoming. 'Motivational processing in interactional tasks' in A. Mackey and C. Polio (eds.): *Multiple Perspectives on Interaction: Second Language Research in Honor of Susan M. Gass*. Mahwah, NJ: Lawrence Erlbaum.

—— and E. Ushioda (eds.) 2009. *Motivation, Language Identity and the L2 Self*. Bristol: Multilingual Matters.

Doughty, C. J. 2003. 'Instructed SLA: Constraints, compensation, and enhancement' in C. J. Doughty and M. H. Long (eds.): *The Handbook of Second Language Acquisition*. Oxford: Blackwell, 256–310.

—— and J. Williams 1998. 'Issues and terminology' in C. Doughty and J. Williams (eds.): *Focus on Form in Classroom Second Language Acquisition*. New York: Cambridge University Press, 1–11.

Dufva, M., and M. J. M. Voeten 1999. 'Native language literacy and phonological memory as prerequisites for learning English as a foreign language'. *Applied Psycholinguistics* 20: 329–48.

Dweck, C. S., J. A. Mangels, and C. Good 2004. 'Motivational effects on attention, cognition, and performance' in D. Y. Dai and R. J. Sternberg (eds.): *Motivation, Emotion, and*

Cognition: Integrative Perspectives on Intellectual Functioning and Development. Mahwah, NJ: Lawrence Erlbaum, 41–55.

Egbert, J. 2003. 'A study of flow theory in the foreign language classroom'. *Modern Language Journal* 87/4: 499–518.

Ehrman, M. E., and Z. Dörnyei 1998. *Interpersonal Dynamics in Second Language Education: The Visible and in-Visible Classroom*. Thousand Oaks, Calif.: Sage.

Ellis, N. C. (ed.) 1994a. *Implicit and Explicit Learning of Languages*. New York: Academic Press.

—— 1994b. 'Vocabulary acquisition: The implicit ins and outs of explicit cognitive mediation' in Ellis (1994a: 211–82).

—— 2001. 'Memory for language' in P. Robinson (ed.): *Cognition and Second Language Acquisition*. New York: Cambridge University Press, 33–68.

—— 2002a. 'Frequency effects in language processing: A review with implications for theories of implicit and explicit language acquisition'. *Studies in Second Language Acquisition* 24: 143–88.

—— 2002b. 'Reflections on frequency effects in language processing'. *Studies in Second Language Acquisition* 24: 297–339.

—— 2003. 'Constructions, chunking, and connectionism: The emergence of second language structure' in C. J. Doughty and M. H. Long (eds.): *The Handbook of Second Language Acquisition*. Oxford: Blackwell, 63–103.

—— 2005a. 'At the interface: Dynamic interactions of explicit and implicit language knowledge'. *Studies in Second Language Acquisition* 27: 305–52.

—— 2005b. 'Introduction to Part I: Acquisition' in J. F. Kroll and A. M. B. De Groot (eds.): *Handbook of Bilingualism: Psycholinguistic Approaches*. Oxford: Oxford University Press, 3–8.

—— 2006a. 'Cognitive perspectives on SLA: The associative-cognitive CREED'. *AILA Review* 19: 100–21.

—— 2006b. 'Language acquisition and rational contingency learning'. *Applied Linguistics* 27/1: 1–24.

—— 2007a. 'The associative-cognitive CREED' in B. VanPatten and J. Williams (eds.): *Theories in Second Language Acquisition: An Introduction*. Mahwah, NJ: Lawrence Erlbaum, 77–95.

—— 2007b. 'Dynamic systems and SLA: The wood and the trees'. *Bilingualism: Language and Cognition* 10/1: 23–5.

—— 2007c. 'The weak interface, consciousness, and form-focused instruction: Mind the doors' in S. S. Fotos and H. Nassaji (eds.): *Form-Focused Instruction and Teacher Education*. Oxford: Oxford University Press, 17–34.

—— 2008. 'Usage-based and form-focused language acquisition: The associative learning of constructions, learnt-attention, and the limited L2 endstate' in Robinson and Ellis (2008b: 372–405).

—— and D. Larsen-Freeman 2006. 'Language emergence: Implications for applied linguistics—Introduction to the Special Issue'. *Applied Linguistics* 27/4: 558–89.

—— 2008. 'An introduction to cognitive linguistics, second language acquisition, and language instruction' in Robinson and Ellis (2008b: 3–24).

Ellis, R. 2003. *Task-Based Language Learning and Teaching*. Oxford: Oxford University Press.

—— 'Measuring implicit and explicit knowledge of a second language'. *Studies in Second Language Acquisition*. 27: 141–72.

—— 2008. *The Study of Second Language Acquisition*, 2nd edn. Oxford: Oxford University Press.

Elman, J. L. 2001. 'Connectionism and language acquisition' in M. Tomasello and E. Bates (eds.): *Language Development: The Essential Readings*. Oxford: Blackwell, 295–306.

Eubank, L., and K. R. Gregg 2002. 'News flash—Hume still dead'. *Studies in Second Language Acquisition* 24: 237–47.

Evans, J. L. 2007. 'The emergence of language: A dynamical systems account' in E. Hoff and M. Shatz (eds.): *Blackwell Handbook of Language Development*. Oxford: Blackwell, 128–47.

Fabbro, F., M. Skrap, and S. Aglioti 2000. 'Pathological switching between languages after frontal lesions in a bilingual patient'. *Journal of Neurology, Neurosurgery and Psychiatry* 68: 650–2.

Fauconnier, G. 2003. 'Cognitive linguistics' in L. Nadel (ed.): *Encyclopedia of Cognitive Science*. London: Nature Publishing, i. 539–43.

Fenstermacher, S. K., and K. J. Saudino 2006. 'Understanding individual differences in young children's imitative behavior'. *Developmental Review* 26: 346–64.

Ferguson, C. A. 1994. 'Dialect, register, and genre: Working assumptions about conventionalization' in D. Biber and E. Finegan (eds.): *Sociolinguistic Perspectives on Register*. New York: Oxford University Press, 15–30.

Fernald, A., and V. A. Marchman 2006. 'Language learning in infancy' in M. J. Traxler and M. A. Gernsbacher (eds.): *Handbook of Psycholinguistics*, 2nd edn. London: Academic Press, 1027–71.

Fillmore, C. J. 1979. 'On fluency' in C. J. Fillmore, D. Kempler, and W.-S. Y. Wang (eds.): *Individual Differences in Language Ability and Language Behavior*. New York: Academic Press, 85–101.

Fitts, P. M. 1964. 'Perceptual-motor skill learning' in A. W. Melton (ed.): *Categories of Human Learning*. New York: Academic Press, 243–85.

—— and M. I. Posner 1967. *Human Performance*. Belmont, Calif.: Brooks/Cole.

Flege, J. E., G. H. Yeni-Komshian, and S. Liu 1999. 'Age constraints on second-language acquisition'. *Journal of Memory and Language* 41: 78–104.

—— D. Birdsong, E. Bialystok, M. Mack, H. Sung, and K. Tsukada 2006. 'Degree of foreign accent in English sentences produced by Korean children and adults'. *Journal of Phonetics* 34: 153–75.

Fotos, S. S., and H. Nassaji (eds.) 2007. *Form-focused Instruction and Teacher Education*. Oxford: Oxford University Press.

Frenck-Mestre, C. 2005. 'Eye-movement recording as a tool for studying syntactic processing in a second language: a review of methodologies and experimental findings'. *Second Language Research* 21/2: 175–98.

Frensch, P. A. 1998. 'One concept, multiple meanings: On how to define the concept of implicit learning' in M. A. Stadler and P. A. Frensch (eds.): *Handbook of Implicit Learning*. Thousand Oaks, Calif.: Sage, 47–104.

Frisch, S., A. Hahne, and A. D. Friederici 2004. 'Word category and verb–argument structure information in the dynamics of parsing'. *Cognition* 91: 191–219.

Funder, D. C. 2006. 'Towards a resolution of the personality triad: Persons, situations, and behaviors'. *Journal of Research in Personality* 40: 21–34.

Gahl, S., and A. C. L. Yu (eds.) 2006. 'Exemplar-based models in linguistics', Special Issue. *Linguistic Review*.

Ganis, G., W. L. Thompson, and S. M. Kosslyn 2005. 'Understanding the effects of task-specific practice in the brain: Insights from individual-differences analyses'. *Cognitive, Affective, & Behavioral Neuroscience* 5/2: 235–45.

Garcia, T. 1999. 'Maintaining the motivation to learn: An introduction to the Special Issue'. *Learning and Individual Differences* 11/3: 231–2.

García Mayo, M. P., and M. L. García Lecumberri 2003. 'Introduction' in eid. (eds.): *Age and the Acquisition of English as a Foreign Language*. Clevedon: Multilingual Matters, pp. vii–xii.

Gardner, R. C. 1985. *Social Psychology and Second Language Learning: The Role of Attitudes and Motivation*. London: Edward Arnold.

—— 2001. 'Integrative motivation and second language acquisition' in Z. Dörnyei and R. Schmidt (eds.): *Motivation and Second Language Acquisition*. Honolulu: University of Hawai'i Press, 1–20.

—— and W. E. Lambert 1959. 'Motivational variables in second language acquisition'. *Canadian Journal of Psychology* 13: 266–72.

—— —— 1972. *Attitudes and Motivation in Second Language Learning*. Rowley, Mass.: Newbury House.

Garlick, D. 2002. 'Understanding the nature of the general factor of intelligence: The role of individual differences in neural plasticity as an explanatory mechanism'. *Psychological Review* 109/1: 116–36.

Gass, S. M. 2003. 'Input and interaction' in C. J. Doughty and M. H. Long (eds.): *The Handbook of Second Language Acquisition*. Oxford: Blackwell, 224–55.

—— and A. Mackey 2006. 'Input, interaction, and output'. *AILA Review* 19: 3–17.

—— —— 2007. 'Input, interaction, and output in second language acquisition' in B. VanPatten and J. Williams (eds.): *Theories in Second Language Acquisition: An Introduction*. Mahwah, NJ: Lawrence Erlbaum, 175–99.

Gatbonton, E., and N. Segalowitz 1988. 'Creative automatization: Principles for promoting fluency within a communicative framework'. *TESOL Quarterly* 22/3: 473–92.

—— —— 2005. 'Rethinking communicative language teaching: A focus on access to fluency'. *Canadian Modern Language Review* 61/3: 325–53.

Gazzaniga, M. S., R. B. Ivry, and G. R. Mangun 2002. *Cognitive Neuroscience: The Biology of the Mind*. New York: W. W. Norton.

Genesee, F., and E. Nicoladis 2007. 'Bilingual first language acquisition' in E. Hoff and M. Shatz (eds.): *Blackwell Handbook of Language Development*. Oxford: Blackwell, 324–42.

Gernsbacher, M. A., and M. P. Kaschak 2003. 'Psycholinguistics' in L. Nadel (ed.): *Encyclopedia of Cognitive Science*. London: Nature Publishing, iii. 783–6.

Gibson, E. 1992. 'On the adequacy of the Competition Model'. *Language* 68/4: 812–30.

Giles, H., and J. L. Byrne 1982. 'The intergroup model of second language acquisition'. *Journal of Multilingual and Multicultural Development* 3: 17–40.

Gobet, F. 2005. 'Chunking models of expertise: Implications for education'. *Applied Cognitive Psychology* 19: 183–204.

—— P. R. C. Lane, S. Croker, P. C.-H. Cheng, G. Jones, I. Oliver, and J. M. Pine 2001. 'Chunking mechanisms in human learning'. *Trends in Cognitive Sciences* 5/6: 236–43.

Goldstein, J. 1999. 'Emergence as a construct: History and issues'. *Emergence* 1/1: 49–72.

Graham, C. 1978. *Jazz Chants*. Oxford: Oxford University Press.

Green, D. W. 2001. 'Introduction'. *Bilingualism: Language and Cognition* 4/2: 101–3.

—— 2005. 'The neurocognition of recovery patterns in bilingual aphasics' in J. F. Kroll and A. M. B. De Groot (eds.): *Handbook of Bilingualism: Psycholinguistic Approaches*. Oxford: Oxford University Press, 516–30.

Gregg, M., and C. Hall 2006. 'Measurement of motivational imagery abilities in sport'. *Journal of Sports Sciences* 24/9: 961–71.

Grigorenko, E. L. 2007. 'How can genomics inform education?' *Mind, Brain, and Education* 1/1: 20–7.

Grosjean, F., P. Li, T. F. Münte, and A. Rodriguez-Fornells 2003. 'Imaging bilinguals: When the neurosciences meet the language sciences'. *Bilingualism: Language and Cognition* 6/2: 159–65.

Guastello, S. J., E. A. Johnson, and M. L. Rieke 1999. 'Nonlinear dynamics of motivational flow'. *Nonlinear Dynamics, Psychology, and Life Sciences* 3/3: 259–73.

Gullberg, M., and P. Indefrey (eds.) 2006. *The Cognitive Neuroscience of Second Language Acquisition*. Malden, Mass.: Blackwell.

Halliday, M. A. K. 1985. *An Introduction to Functional Grammar*. London: Edward Arnold.

Hamers, J. F., and M. H. A. Blanc 2000. *Bilinguality and Bilingualism*, 2nd edn. Cambridge: Cambridge University Press.

Han, Z. 2008a. 'On the role of meaning in focus on form' in Z. Han (ed.): *Understanding Second Language Process*. Clevedon: Multilingual Matters, 45–79.

—— 2008b. 'Preface' in Z. Han (ed.): *Understanding Second Language Process*. Clevedon: Multilingual Matters, pp. xi–xiii.

Harklau, L. 2005. 'Ethnography and ethnographic research on second language teaching
and learning' in E. Hinkel (ed.): *Handbook of Research in Second Language Teaching and
Learning*. Mahwah, NJ: Lawrence Erlbaum, 179–94.

Harley, B., and W. Wang 1997. 'The critical period hypothesis: Where are we now?' in
A. de Groot, M. B. Kroll, and J. F. Kroll (eds.): *Tutorials in Bilingualism: Psycholinguistic
Perspectives*. Mahwah, NJ: Lawrence Erlbaum, 19–51.

Harrington, A., and G. Oepen 1989. ' "Whole brain" politics and brain laterality research'.
European Archives of Psychiatry and Clinical Neuroscience 239/3: 141–3.

Harrington, M., and S. Dennis 2002. 'Input-driven language learning'. *Studies in Second
Language Acquisition* 24: 261–8.

Hawkins, R. 2008a. 'Can innate linguistic knowledge be eliminated from theories of SLA?'
Lingua 118/4: 613–19.

—— (ed.) 2008b. 'Current emergentist and nativist perspectives on second language
acquisition', Special Issue. *Lingua* 118/4.

Heeger, D. J., and D. Ress 2002. 'What does fMRI tell us about neuronal activity?' *Nature
Reviews Neuroscience* 3: 142–51.

Henson, R. N. 2005. 'What can functional neuroimaging tell the experimental psychologist?'
Quarterly Journal of Experimental Psychology 58a/2: 193–233.

—— 2007. 'Efficient experimental design for fMRI' in K. Friston, J. Ashburner, S. Kiebel,
T. Nichols, and W. Penny (eds.): *Statistical Parametric Mapping: The Analysis of Functional
Brain Images*. London: Elsevier, 193–210.

Herdina, P., and U. Jessner 2002. *A Dynamic Model of Multilingualism: Perspectives of
Change in Psycholinguistics*. Clevedon: Multilingual Matters.

Hernandez, L. M., and D. G. Blazer 2006. *Genes, Behavior, and the Social Environment:
Moving Beyond the Nature/Nurture Debate*. Washington, DC: National Academies Press.

Herschensohn, J. 2007. *Language Development and Age*. Cambridge: Cambridge University
Press.

Higgins, E. T. 1987. 'Self-discrepancy: A theory relating self and affect'. *Psychological Review*
94: 319–40.

—— 1996. 'The "self-digest": Self-knowledge serving self-regulatory functions'. *Journal of
Personality and Social Psychology* 71/6: 1062–83.

—— 1998. 'Promotion and prevention: Regulatory focus as a motivational principle'.
Advances in Experimental Social Psychology 30: 1–46.

—— R. Klein, and T. Strauman 1985. 'Self-concept discrepancy theory: A psychological model
for distinguishing among different aspects of depression and anxiety'. *Social Cognition*
3/1: 51–76.

—— C. J. R. Roney, E. Crowe, and C. Hymes 1994. 'Ideal versus ought predilections for
approach and avoidance: Distinct self-regulatory systems'. *Journal of Personality and Social
Psychology* 66/2: 276–86.

Higham, P. A. 1997. 'Chunks are not enough: The insufficiency of feature frequency-based
explanations of artificial grammar learning'. *Canadian Journal of Experimental Psychology*
51/2: 126–37.

Hirschman, M. 2000. 'Language repair via metalinguistic means'. *International Journal of
Language and Communication Disorders* 35/2: 251–68.

Howatt, A. P. R. 2004. *A History of English Language Teaching*, 2nd edn. Oxford: Oxford
University Press.

Howe, M. L., and M. D. Lewis 2005. 'The importance of dynamic systems approaches for
understanding development'. *Developmental Review* 25: 247–51.

Hoyle, R. H., and M. R. Sherrill 2006. 'Future orientation in the self-system: Possible selves,
self-regulation, and behavior'. *Journal of Personality* 74/6: 1673–96.

Hull, R., and J. Vaid 2005. 'Clearing the cobwebs from the study of the bilingual brain:
Converging evidence from laterality and electrophysiological research' in J. F. Kroll and
A. M. B. De Groot (eds.): *Handbook of Bilingualism: Psycholinguistic Approaches*. Oxford:
Oxford University Press, 480–96.

Hulstijn, J. H. 2002a. 'Towards a unified account of the representation, processing and acquisition of second language knowledge'. *Second Language Research* 18/3: 193–223.

—— 2002b. 'What does the impact of frequency tell us about the language acquisition device?' *Studies in Second Language Acquisition* 24: 269–73.

—— 2003. 'Incidental and intentional learning' in C. J. Doughty and M. H. Long (eds.): *The Handbook of Second Language Acquisition*. Oxford: Blackwell, 349–81.

—— 2005. 'Theoretical and empirical issues in the study of implicit and explicit second-language learning'. *Studies in Second Language Acquisition* 27: 129–40.

—— 2007a. 'Fundamental issues in the study of second language acquisition' in L. Roberts, A. Gürel, S. Tatar, and L. Marti (eds.): *EUROSLA Yearbook 7*. Amsterdam: John Benjamins, 191–203.

—— 2007b. 'Psycholinguistic perspectives on language and its acquisition' in J. Cummins and C. Davison (eds.): *International Handbook of English Language Teaching*. New York: Springer, ii. 783–95.

Hunt, E. 2005. 'Information processing and intelligence: Where we are and where we are going' in R. J. Sternberg and J. E. Pretz (eds.): *Cognition and Intelligence: Identifying the Mechanisms of the Mind*. Cambridge: Cambridge University Press, 1–25.

Hyltenstam, K., and N. Abrahamsson 2001. 'Age and L2 learning: The hazards of matching practical "implications" with theoretical "facts"'. *TESOL Quarterly* 35/1: 151–70.

—— —— 2003. 'Maturational constraints in SLA' in C. J. Doughty and M. H. Long (eds.): *The Handbook of Second Language Acquisition*. Oxford: Blackwell, 539–88.

Hymes, D. H. 1972. 'On communicative competence' in J. B. Pride and J. Holmes (eds.): *Sociolinguistics*. Harmondsworth: Penguin, 269–93.

Ionin, T. 2007. 'DST vs. UG: Can DST account for purely linguistic phenomena?' *Bilingualism: Language and Cognition* 10/1: 27–9.

Ioup, G. 2005. 'Age in second language development' in E. Hinkel (ed.): *Handbook of Research in Second Language Teaching and Learning*. Mahwah, NJ: Lawrence Erlbaum, 419–35.

Jacobs, B. 2004. 'Foreword' in J. H. Schumann, S. E. Crowell, N. E. Jones, N. Lee, S. A. Schuchert, and L. A. Wood (eds.): *The Neurobiology of Learning: Perspectives from Second Language Acquisition*. Mahwah, NJ: Lawrence Erlbaum, pp. ix–x.

Jay, T. B. 2003. *The Psychology of Language*. Upper Saddle River, NJ: Prentice Hall.

Jessner, U. 2008. 'A DST model of multilingualism and the role of metalinguistic awareness'. *Modern Language Journal* 92: 270–83.

—— and J. Cenoz 2007. 'Teaching English as a third language' in J. Cummins and C. Davison (eds.): *International Handbook of English Language Teaching*. New York: Springer, 155–67.

Jia, G., and D. Aaronson 2003. 'A longitudinal study of Chinese children and adolescents learning English in the United States'. *Applied Psycholinguistics* 24: 131–61.

—— and A. Fuse 2007. 'Acquisition of English grammatical morphology by native mandarin-speaking children and adolescents: Age-related differences'. *Journal of Speech, Language, and Hearing Research* 50/5: 1280–99.

—— D. Aaronson, and Y. Wu 2002. 'Long-term language attainment of bilingual immigrants: Predictive variables and language group differences'. *Applied Psycholinguistics* 23: 599–621.

Johnson, T. R., H. Wang, and J. Zhang 2003. 'Skill acquisition: Models' in L. Nadel (ed.): *Encyclopedia of Cognitive Science*. London: Nature Publishing, iii. 30–6.

Jones, P. E. 1995. 'Contradictions and unanswered questions in the Genie case: A fresh look at the linguistic evidence'. *Language & Communication* 15/3: 261–80.

Juffs, A. 2001. 'Psycholinguistically oriented second language research'. *Annual Review of Applied Linguistics* 21: 207–20.

—— and R. M. DeKeyser 2003. 'Psycholinguistics' in L. Nadel (ed.): *Encyclopedia of Cognitive Science*. London: Nature Publishing, iii. 1022–8.

Kane, M. J., D. Z. Hambrick, and A. R. A. Conway 2005. 'Working memory capacity and fluid intelligence are strongly related constructs: Comment on Ackerman, Beier, and Boyle (2005)'. *Psychological Bulletin* 131/1: 66–71.

Kelso, J. A. S. 1995. *Dynamic Patterns: The Self-Organization of Brain and Behavior*. Cambridge, Mass.: MIT.

Keltner, D., and P. Ekman 2000. 'Emotion: An overview' in A. E. Kazdin (ed.): *Encyclopedia of Psychology*. Oxford: American Psychological Association and Oxford University Press, iii. 162–7.

Kirsner, K. 1994. 'Second language vocabulary learning: The role of implicit processes' in N. C. Ellis (ed.): *Implicit and Explicit Learning of Languages*. London: Academic Press, 283–311.

Klein, W. 2001. 'Second language acquisition' in N. J. Smelser and P. B. Baltes (eds.): *International Encyclopedia of the Social and Behavioral Sciences*. Oxford: Pergamon, 13768–71.

Knudsen, E. I. 2004. 'Sensitive periods in the development of the brain and behavior'. *Journal of Cognitive Neuroscience* 16/8: 1412–25.

—— 2007. 'Fundamental components of attention'. *Annual Review of Neuroscience* 30: 57–78.

Koch, C. 2004. *The Quest for Consciousness*. Englewood, Colo.: Roberts & Co..

—— and F. Crick 2001. 'Neural basis of consciousness' in N. J. Smelser and P. B. Baltes (eds.): *International Encyclopedia of the Social and Behavioral Sciences*. Oxford: Pergamon, 2600–4.

—— and N. Tsuchiya 2007. 'Attention and consciousness: Two distinct brain processes'. *Trends in Cognitive Sciences* 11/1: 16–22.

Koch, I., and J. Hoffmann 2000. 'Patterns, chunks, and hierarchies in serial reaction-time tasks'. *Psychological Research* 63: 22–35.

Kohonen, T. 2001. *Self-Organizing Maps*, 3rd edn. Berlin: Springer.

Kormos, J. 2006. *Speech Production and Second Language Acquisition*. Mahwah, NJ: Lawrence Erlbaum.

Kosslyn, S. M. 1999. 'If neuroimaging is the answer, what is the question?' *Philosophical Transactions of the Royal Society of London: Biological Sciences* 354: 1283–94.

—— and E. E. Smith 2000. 'Introduction to Part VIII: Higher cognitive functions' in M. S. Gazzaniga (ed.): *The New Cognitive Neurosciences*, 2nd edn. Cambridge, Mass.: MIT, 961–63.

—— W. L. Thompson, and G. Ganis 2006. *The Case for Mental Imagery*. New York: Oxford University Press.

—— J. T. Cacioppo, R. J. Davidson, K. Hugdahl, W. R. Lovallo, D. Spiegel, and R. Rose 2002. 'Bridging psychology and biology: The analysis of individuals in groups'. *American Psychologist* 57/5: 341–51.

Kövecses, Z. 2005. *Metaphor in Culture: Universality and Variation*. Cambridge: Cambridge University Press.

Krashen, S. D. 1981. 'Aptitude and attitude in relation to second language acquisition and learning' in K. C. Diller (ed.): *Individual Differences and Universals in Language Learning Aptitude*. Rowley, Mass.: Newbury House, 155–75.

—— 1982. *Principles and Practice in Second Language Acquisition*. Oxford: Pergamon.

—— 1985. *The Input Hypothesis: Issues and Implications*. London: Longman.

—— 2003. *Explorations in Language Acquisition and Use*. Portsmouth, NH: Heinemann.

Kuhl, P. K. 2000. 'A new view of language acquisition'. *Proceedings of the National Academy of Sciences of the United States of America (PNAS)* 97/22: 11850–7.

—— 2004. 'Early language acquisition: Cracking the speech code'. *Nature Reviews Neuroscience* 5: 831–43.

—— B. T. Conboy, D. Padden, T. Nelson, and J. Pruitt 2005. 'Early speech perception and later language development: Implications for the "Critical Period"'. *Language Learning & Development* 1(3/4): 237–64.

Kumaravadivelu, B. 1994. 'The postmethod condition: (E)merging strategies for second/ foreign language teaching'. *TESOL Quarterly* 28: 27–48.

—— 2006. *Understanding Language Teaching: From Method to Postmethod*. Mahwah, NJ: Lawrence Erlbaum.

Kutas, M., C. K. VanPatten, and R. Kluender 2006. 'Psycholinguistics electrified II (1994–2005)' in M. J. Traxler and M. A. Gernsbacher (eds.): *Handbook of Psycholinguistics*, 2nd edn. London: Academic Press, 659–724.

Lado, R. 1957. *Linguistics across Cultures: Applied Linguistics for Language Teachers*. Ann Arbor, Mich.: University of Michigan Press.

—— 1964. *Language Teaching: A Scientific Approach*. New York: McGraw Hill.

Lafford, B. A. (ed.) 2007. 'Second language acquisition reconceptualized? The impact of Firth and Wagner (1997)', Focus Issue. *Modern Language Journal* 91.

Lamb, S. M. 1999. *Pathways of the Brain: The Neurocognitive Basis of Language*. Amsterdam: John Benjamins.

Lantolf, J. P., and S. L. Thorne 2006. *Sociocultural Theory and the Genesis of Second Language Development*. Oxford: Oxford University Press.

Larsen-Freeman, D. 1997. 'Chaos/complexity science and second language acquisition'. *Applied Linguistics* 18: 141–65.

—— 2000. *Techniques and Principles in Language Teaching*, 2nd edn. Oxford: Oxford University Press.

—— 2002. 'Making sense of frequency'. *Studies in Second Language Acquisition* 24: 275–85.

—— 2003. *Teaching Language: From Grammar to Grammaring*. Boston: Thomson/Heinle.

—— 2006. 'The emergence of complexity, fluency, and accuracy in the oral and written production of five Chinese learners of English'. *Applied Linguistics* 27/4: 590–619.

—— 2007a. 'On the complementarity of Chaos/Complexity Theory and Dynamic Systems Theory in understanding the second language acquisition process'. *Bilingualism: Language and Cognition* 10/1: 35–7.

—— 2007b. 'Reflecting on the cognitive-social debate in second language acquisition'. *Modern Language Journal* 91: 773–87.

—— and L. Cameron 2008. *Complex Systems and Applied Linguistics*. Oxford: Oxford University Press.

Laufer, B., and J. H. Hulstijn 2001. 'Incidental vocabulary acquisition in a second language: The construct of task-induced involvement'. *Applied Linguistics* 22/1: 1–26.

Lee, N. 2004. 'The neurobiology of procedural memory' in J. H. Schumann, S. E. Crowell, N. E. Jones, N. Lee, S. A. Schuchert, and L. A. Wood (eds.): *The Neurobiology of Learning: Perspectives from Second Language Acquisition*. Mahwah, NJ: Lawrence Erlbaum, 43–73.

Lenneberg, E. H. 1967. *The Biological Foundations of Language*. New York: Wiley.

Lennon, P. 2000. 'The lexical element in spoken second language fluency' in H. Riggenbach (ed.): *Perspectives on Fluency*. Ann Arbor, Mich.: University of Michigan Press, 25–42.

Leow, R. P. 2007. 'Input in the l2 classroom: An attentional perspective on receptive practice' in R. M. DeKeyser (ed.): *Practice in Second Language: Perspectives from Applied Linguistics and Cognitive Psychology*. New York: Cambridge University Press, 21–50.

Leung, Y.-K. I. 2007. 'Third language acquisition: Why it is interesting to generative linguists'. *Second Language Research* 23/1: 95–114.

Lewin, K. 1943. 'Defining the field at a given time'. *Psychological Review* 50: 292–310.

—— 1951. *Field Theory in Social Science*. New York: Harper & Row.

—— 1952. 'Field theory and learning' in D. Cartwright (ed.): *Field Theory in Social Science: Selected Theoretical Papers by Kurt Lewin*. London: Tavistock, 60–86.

Lewis, M. 1993. *The Lexical Approach: The State of ELT and a Way Forward*. Hove: Language Teaching Publications.

—— 1997. *Implementing the Lexical Approach: Putting Theory into Practice*. Hove: Language Teaching Publications.

—— 2005. 'Bridging emotion theory and neurobiology through dynamic systems modeling'. *Behavioral and Brain Science* 28/2: 169–245.

—— and R. M. Todd 2005. 'Getting emotional: A neural perspective on emotion, intention, and consciousness'. *Journal of Consciousness Studies* 12/8–10: 210–35.

Lewontin, R. 2000. *The Triple Helix: Gene, Organism, and Environment*. Cambridge, Mass.: Harvard University Press.

Lightbown, P. M. 2000. 'Classroom SLA research and second language teaching'. *Applied Linguistics* 21/4: 431–62.

—— 2008. 'Transfer appropriate processing as a model for classroom second language acquisition' in Z. Han (ed.): *Understanding Second Language Process*. Clevedon: Multilingual Matters, 27–44.

—— and N. Spada 2006. *How Languages Are Learnt*, 3rd edn. Oxford: Oxford University Press.

Linnenbrink, E. A., and P. R. Pintrich 2004. 'Role of affect in cognitive processing in academic contexts' in D. Y. Dai and R. J. Sternberg (eds.): *Motivation, Emotion, and Cognition: Integrative Perspectives on Intellectual Functioning and Development*. Mahwah, NJ: Lawrence Erlbaum, 57–87.

Litman, L., and A. S. Reber 2005. 'Implicit cognition and thought' in K. J. Holyoak and R. G. Morrison (eds.): *The Cambridge Handbook of Thinking and Reasoning*. Cambridge: Cambridge University Press, 431–53.

Littlewood, W. 1981. *Communicative Language Teaching: An Introduction*. Cambridge: Cambridge University Press.

Logan, G. D. 1988. 'Toward an instance theory of automatization'. *Psychological Review* 95/4: 492–527.

—— 2005. 'Attention, automaticity, and executive control' in A. F. Healy (ed.): *Experimental Cognitive Psychology and Its Applications*. Washington, DC: American Psychological Association, 129–39.

—— S. E. Taylor, and J. L. Etherton 1999. 'Attention and automaticity: Toward a theoretical integration'. *Psychological Research* 62: 165–81.

Long, M. H. 1991. 'Focus on form: A design feature in language teaching methodology' in K. de Bot, R. B. Ginsberg, and C. Kramsch (eds.): *Foreign Language Research in Cross-Cultural Perspective*. Amsterdam: John Benjamins, 39–52.

—— 2007. *Problems in SLA*. Mahwah, NJ: Lawrence Erlbaum.

—— and C. J. Doughty 2003. 'SLA and cognitive science' in C. J. Doughty and M. H. Long (eds.): *The Handbook of Second Language Acquisition*. Oxford: Blackwell, 866–70.

Lozanov, G. 1979. *Suggestology and Outlines of Suggestopedy*. New York: Gordon & Breach.

—— 2005. *Suggestopaedia—Desuggestive Teaching: Communicative Method on the Level of the Hidden Reserves of the Human Mind*. Vienna: International Centre for Desuggestology.

Lubinski, D. 2004. 'Introduction to the special section on cognitive abilities: 100 years after Spearman's (1904) *General Intelligence, Objectively Determined and Measured*'. *Journal of Personality and Social Psychology* 86/1: 96–111.

—— and R. M. Webb 2003. 'Individual differences' in L. Nadel (ed.): *Encyclopedia of Cognitive Science*. London: Nature Publishing, ii. 503–10.

McCrone, J. 1999, 3 July. 'Left brain right brain'. *New Scientist* 2193.

McGuffin, P., B. Riley, and R. Plomin 2001. 'Genomics and behavior: Toward behavioral genomics'. *Science* 291/5507: 1232–49.

MacIntyre, P. D. 2002. 'Motivation, anxiety and emotion in second language acquisition' in P. Robinson (ed.): *Individual Differences in Second Language Acquisition*. Amsterdam: John Benjamins, 45–68.

—— S. P. Mackinnon, and R. Clément 2009. 'The baby, the bathwater, and the future of language learning motivation research' in Z. Dörnyei and E. Ushioda (eds.): *Motivation, Language Identity and the L2 Self*. Bristol: Multilingual Matters, 43–65.

Mackey, A. 2007. 'Interaction as practice' in R. M. DeKeyser (ed.): *Practice in Second Language: Perspectives from Applied Linguistics and Cognitive Psychology*. New York: Cambridge University Press, 85–110.

—— and C. Polio (eds.) Forthcoming. *Multiple Perspectives on Interaction: Second Language Research in Honor of Susan M. Gass*. Mahwah, NJ: Lawrence Erlbaum.

McMahon, C. E. 1973. 'Images as motives and motivators: A historical perspective'. *American Journal of Psychology* 86/3: 465–90.

MacWhinney, B. 2001a. 'The competition model: The input, the context, and the brain' in P. Robinson (ed.): *Cognition and Second Language Acquisition*. New York: Cambridge University Press, 69–90.

—— 2001*b*. 'Emergentist approaches to language' in J. Bybee and P. Hopper (eds.): *Frequency and the Emergence of Linguistic Structure*. Amsterdam: John Benjamins, 449–70.

—— 2001*c*. 'Psycholinguistics: Overview' in N. J. Smelser and P. B. Baltes (eds.): *International Encyclopedia of the Social and Behavioral Sciences*. Oxford: Pergamon, 12343–9.

—— 2004. 'New directions in the competition model' in M. Tomasello and D. I. Slobin (eds.): *Beyond Nature-Nurture: Essays in Honor of Elizabeth Bates*. Mahwah, NJ: Lawrence Erlbaum, 81–110.

—— 2005. 'A unified model of language acquisition' in J. F. Kroll and A. M. B. De Groot (eds.): *Handbook of Bilingualism: Psycholinguistic Approaches*. Oxford: Oxford University Press, 49–67.

—— 2006. 'Emergentism: Use often with care'. *Applied Linguistics* 27/4: 729–40.

—— 2008. 'A unified model' in N. C. Ellis and P. Robinson (eds.): *Handbook of Cognitive Linguistics and Second Language Acquisition*. New York: Routledge, 341–71.

—— and E. Bates 1994. 'The Competition Model and UG' (unpublished manuscript). Pittsburgh: Carnegie Mellon University.

—— and C. Pléh 1988. 'The processing of restrictive relative clauses in Hungarian'. *Cognition* 29: 95–141.

—— —— and E. Bates 1985. 'The development of sentence interpretation in Hungarian'. *Cognitive Psychology* 17: 178–209.

Manning, C. D. 2003. 'Probabilistic syntax' in R. Bod, J. Hay, and S. Jannedy (eds.): *Probabilistic Linguistic*. Cambridge, Mass.: MIT, 289–341.

Mäntylä, T. 2001. 'Incidental versus intentional memory' in N. J. Smelser and P. B. Baltes (eds.): *International Encyclopedia of the Social and Behavioral Sciences*. Oxford: Pergamon, 7262–5.

Marinis, T. 2003. 'Psycholinguistic techniques in second language acquisition research'. *Second Language Research* 19/2: 144–61.

Marinova-Todd, S. H., D. B. Marshall, and C. E. Snow 2000. 'Three misconceptions about age and second language acquisition'. *TESOL Quarterly* 34: 9–34.

—— —— —— 'Missing the point: A response to Hyltenstam and Abrahamsson'. *TESOL Quarterly* 35: 171–6.

Markus, H. 2006. 'Foreword' in C. Dunkel and J. Kerpelman (eds.): *Possible Selves: Theory, Research and Applications*. New York: Nova Science, pp. xi–xiv.

—— and P. Nurius 1986. 'Possible selves'. *American Psychologist* 41: 954–69.

—— and A. Ruvolo 1989. 'Possible selves: Personalized representations of goals' in L. A. Pervin (ed.): *Goal Concepts in Personality and Social Psychology*. Hillsdale, NJ: Lawrence Erlbaum, 211–41.

Matthews, G., and M. Zeidner 2004. 'Traits, states, and the trilogy of the mind: An adaptive perspective on intellectual functioning' in D. Y. Dai and R. J. Sternberg (eds.): *Motivation, Emotion, and Cognition: Integrative Perspectives on Intellectual Functioning and Development*. Mahwah, NJ: Lawrence Erlbaum, 143–74.

—— D. R. Davies, S. J. Westerman, and R. B. Stammers 2000. *Human Performance: Cognition, Stress and Individual Differences*. Hove: Psychology Press.

Mayberry, R. I. 1998. 'The critical period for language acquisition and the deaf child's language comprehension: A psycholinguistic approach'. *Bulletin d'Audiophonologie: Annales Scientifiques de L'Université de Franche-Comté* 15: 349–58.

—— 2006. 'Second language acquisition of sign' in B. Woll and K. Brown (eds.): *Encyclopedia of Language and Linguistics*, 2nd edn. Oxford: Elsevier, vi. 739–43.

—— 2007. 'When timing is everything: Age of first-language acquisition effects on second-language learning'. *Applied Psycholinguistics* 28: 537–49.

—— and E. Lock 2003. 'Age constraints on first versus second language acquisition: Evidence for linguistic plasticity and epigenesis'. *Brain and Language* 87: 369–84.

Mayberry, R. I. and H. Kazmi 2002. 'Linguistic ability and early language exposure'. *Nature* 417/38.

Mayer, J. D., H. F. Chabot, and K. M. Carlsmith 1997. 'Conation, affect, and cognition in personality' in G. Matthews (ed.): *Cognitive Science Perspectives on Personality and Emotion*. Amsterdam: Elsevier, 31–63.

Menard, S. 2002. *Longitudinal Research*, 2nd edn. Thousand Oaks, Calif.: Sage.

Miller, G. A. 1956. 'The magical number seven, plus or minus two: Some limits on our capacity for processing information'. *Psychological Review* 63/2: 81–97.

Miller, R. B.,and S. J. Brickman 2004. 'A model of future-oriented motivation and self-regulation'. *Educational Psychology Review* 16/1: 9–33.

Mitchell, R., and F. Myles 2004. *Second Language Learning Theories*, 2nd edn. London: Hodder Arnold.

Miyake, A., and D. Friedman 1998. 'Individual differences in second language proficiency: Working memory as language aptitude' in A. F. Healy and L. E. Bourne (eds.): *Foreign Language Learning: Psycholinguistic Studies on Training and Retention*. Mahwah, NJ: Lawrence Erlbaum, 339–64.

Modell, A. H. 2003. *Imagination and the Meaningful Brain*. Cambridge, Mass.: MIT.

Morrow, K. 1981. 'Principles of communicative methodology' in K. Johnson and K. Morrow (eds.): *Communication in the Classroom*. Harlow: Longman, 59–69.

Moyer, A. 2004. *Age, Accent, and Experience in Second Language Acquisition: An Integrated Approach to Critical Period Inquiry*. Clevedon: Multilingual Matters.

Mueller, J. L. 2005. 'Electrophysiological correlates of second language processing'. *Second Language Research* 21/2: 152–74.

Muñoz, C. 2006. 'The effects of age on foreign language learning: The BAF project' in C. Muñoz (ed.): *Age and the Rate of Foreign Language Learning*. Clevedon: Multilingual Matters, 1–40.

Murre, J. M. J. 2005. 'Models of monolingual and bilingual language acquisition' in J. F. Kroll and A. M. B. De Groot (eds.): *Handbook of Bilingualism: Psycholinguistic Approaches*. Oxford: Oxford University Press, 154–69.

Naccache, L., and S. Dehaene 2001. 'The priming method: Imaging unconscious repetition priming reveals an abstract representation of number in the parietal lobes.' *Cerebral Cortex* 11: 966–74.

Nadel, L., and M. Piattelli-Palmarini 2003. 'What is cognitive science?' in L. Nadel (ed.): *Encyclopedia of Cognitive Science*. London: Nature Publishing, i. pp. xiii–xli.

Nattinger, J. R., and J. S. DeCarrico 1992. *Lexical Phrases and Language Teaching*. Oxford: Oxford University Press.

Newell, A., and P. S. Rosenbloom 1981. 'Mechanisms of skill acquisition and the law of practice' in J. R. Anderson (ed.): *Cognitive Skills and Their Acquisition*. Hillsdale, NJ: Lawrence Erlbaum, 1–55.

Nikolov, M. and M. J. Djigunović 2006. 'Recent research on age, second language acquisition, and early foreign language learning'. *Annual Review of Applied Linguistics* 26: 234–60.

Noels, K. A. 2003. 'Learning Spanish as a second language: Learners' orientations and perceptions of their teachers' communication style' in Z. Dörnyei (ed.): *Attitudes, Orientations, and Motivations in Language Learning*. Oxford: Blackwell, 97–136.

Norman, S. 2006, July. 'Desuggestopedia: Interview with Dr Georgi Lozanov'. *English Teaching Professional*: 4–7.

Norris, J. M., and L. Ortega 2000. 'Effectiveness of L2 instruction: A research synthesis and quantitative meta-analysis'. *Language Learning* 50/3: 417–528.

Nowak, A., R. R. Vallacher, and M. Zochowski 2005. 'The emergence of personality: Dynamic foundations of individual variation'. *Developmental Review* 25: 351–85.

Oatley, K. 2000. 'Emotion: Theories' in A. E. Kazdin (ed.): *Encyclopedia of Psychology*. Oxford: American Psychological Association and Oxford University Press, iii. 167–71.

Oberauer, K., R. Schulze, O. Wilhelm, and H. M. Süss 2005. 'Working memory and intelligence—their correlation and their relation: Comment on Ackerman, Beier, and Boyle (2005)'. *Psychological Bulletin* 131/1: 61–5.

Obler, L. K., and K. Gjerlow 1999. *Language and the Brain*. Cambridge: Cambridge University Press.

O'Connor, T., and H. Y. Wong 2006. 'Emergent properties' in E. N. Zalta (ed.): *The Stanford Encyclopedia of Philosophy (Online)*: <http://plato.stanford.edu/archives/win2006/entries/properties-emergent/>, accessed 20 August 2008.

O'Grady, W. 2008. 'The emergentist program'. *Lingua* 118/4: 447–64.

Ortega, L. 2007a. 'Meaningful L2 practice in foreign language classrooms: A cognitive-interactionist SLA perspective' in R. M. DeKeyser (ed.): *Practice in Second Language: Perspectives from Applied Linguistics and Cognitive Psychology.* New York: Cambridge University Press, 180–207.

—— 2007b. 'Second language learning explained? SLA across nine contemporary theories' in B. VanPatten and J. Williams (eds.): *Theories in Second Language Acquisition: An Introduction.* Mahwah, NJ: Lawrence Erlbaum, 225–50.

Oyserman, D., and H. R. Markus 1990. 'Possible selves and delinquency'. *Journal of Personality and Social Psychology* 59: 112–25.

—— D. Bybee, and K. Terry 2006. 'Possible selves and academic outcomes: How and when possible selves impel action'. *Journal of Personality and Social Psychology* 91/1: 188–204.

Page, M. P. A. 2006. 'What can't functional neuroimaging tell the cognitive psychologist?' *Cortex* 42: 428–43.

Paivio, A. 1985. 'Cognitive and motivational functions of imagery in human performance'. *Canadian Journal of Applied Sport Sciences* 10: 228–88.

Papadopoulou, D. 2005. 'Reading-time studies of second language ambiguity resolution'. *Second Language Research* 21/2: 98–120.

Paradis, M. 2004. *A Neurolinguistic Theory of Bilingualism.* Amsterdam: John Benjamins.

—— 2005. 'Introduction to Part IV: Aspects and implications of bilingualism' in J. F. Kroll and A. M. B. De Groot (eds.): *Handbook of Bilingualism: Psycholinguistic Approaches.* Oxford: Oxford University Press, 411–15.

Parasuraman, R., and P. Greenwood 2006. 'Individual differences in attention and working memory: A molecular genetic approach' in A. F. Kramer (ed.): *Attention: From Theory to Practice.* Oxford: Oxford University Press, 59–72.

Parrott, W. G. 2004. 'The nature of emotion' in M. B. Brewer and M. Hewstone (eds.): *Emotion and Motivation.* Oxford: Blackwell, 5–20.

Pawley, A., and F. H. Syder 1983. 'Two puzzles for linguistic theory: Nativelike selection and nativelike fluency' in J. C. Richards and R. W. Schmidt (eds.): *Language and Communication.* London: Longman, 317–31.

Penfield, W., and L. Roberts 1959. *Speech and Brain-Mechanisms.* Princeton, NJ: Princeton University Press.

Peper, E. 1979. 'The possible uses of biofeedback in Education' in E. Peper, S. Ancoli, and M. Quinn (eds.): *Mind/Body Integration: Essential Readings in Biofeedback.* New York: Plenum, 111–17.

Perani, D., J. Abutalebi, E. Paulesu, S. Brambati, P. Scifo, S. F. Cappa, and F. Fazio 2003. 'The role of age of acquisition and language usage in early, high-proficient bilinguals: An fMRI study during verbal fluency'. *Human Brain Mapping* 19: 170–82.

Perrig, W. J. 2001. 'Cognitive psychology of implicit memory' in N. J. Smelser and P. B. Baltes (eds.): *International Encyclopedia of the Social and Behavioral Sciences.* Oxford: Pergamon, 7241–5.

Phelps, E. A. 2005. 'The interaction of emotion and cognition: Insights from studies of the human amygdala' in L. F. Barrett, P. M. Niedenthal, and P. Winkielman (eds.): *Emotion and Consciousness.* New York: Guilford, 51–66.

Pintrich, P. R., and D. H. Schunk 1996. *Motivation in Education: Theory, Research, and Applications.* Englewood Cliffs, NJ: Merrill.

Plaza-Pust, C. 2008. 'Dynamic Systems Theory and Universal Grammar: Holding up a turbulent mirror to development in grammars'. *Modern Language Journal* 92: 250–69.

Plomin, R., Y. Kovas, and M. A. Haworth 2007. 'Generalist genes: Genetic links between brain, mind, and education'. *Mind, Brain, and Education* 1/1: 11–19.

Poeppel, D., and G. Hickok 2004. 'Introduction: Towards a new functional anatomy of language'. *Cognition* 92: 1–12.

Poldrack, R. A., and M. G. Packard 2003. 'Competition among multiple memory systems: Converging evidence from animal and human brain studies'. *Neuropsychologia* 41: 245–51.

322 *References*

Prinz, J. 2005. 'Are emotions feelings?' *Journal of Consciousness Studies* 12/8–10: 9–25.

Pulvemüller, F. 2002. *The Neuroscience of Language: On Brain Circuits of Words and Serial Order*. Cambridge: Cambridge University Press.

Raichle, M. E., J. A. Fiez, T. O. Videen, A.-M. K. MacLeod, J. V. Pardo, P. T. Fox, and S. E. Petersen 1994. 'Practice-related changes in human brain functional anatomy during nonmotor learning'. *Cerebral Cortex* 4: 8–26.

Ramat, P. 2001. 'Grammaticalization' in N. J. Smelser and P. B. Baltes (eds.): *International Encyclopedia of the Social and Behavioral Sciences*. Oxford: Pergamon, 6353–7.

Ramsøy, T., D. Balslev, and O. Paulson 2007. 'Methods for observing the living brain' in B. J. Baars and N. M. Gage (eds.): *Cognition, Brain, and Consciousness: Introduction to Cognitive Neuroscience*. London: Academic Press, 477–511.

Ranta, L., and R. Lyster 2007. 'A cognitive approach to improving immersion students' oral language abilities: The Awareness–Practice–Feedback sequence' in R. M. DeKeyser (ed.): *Practice in Second Language: Perspectives from Applied Linguistics and Cognitive Psychology*. New York: Cambridge University Press, 141–60.

Reber, A. S. 1967. 'Implicit learning of artificial grammars'. *Journal of Verbal Learning and Verbal Behavior* 5: 855–63.

—— 1993. *Implicit Learning and Tacit Knowledge: An Essay on the Cognitive Unconscious*. New York: Oxford University Press.

—— 2003. 'Implicit learning' in L. Nadel (ed.): *Encyclopedia of Cognitive Science*. London: Nature Publishing, ii. 486–91.

Reber, P. J., and L. R. Squire 1998. 'Encapsulation of implicit and explicit memory in sequence learning'. *Journal of Cognitive Neuroscience* 10/2: 248–63.

Richards, J. C., and T. S. Rodgers 2001. *Approaches and Methods in Language Teaching*, 2nd edn. Cambridge: Cambridge University Press.

Richardson, A. 1994. *Individual Differences in Imaging: Their Measurement, Origins, and Consequences*. Amityville, NY: Baywood.

Rieder, A. 2003. 'Implicit and explicit learning in incidental vocabulary acquisition'. *Vienna English Working Papers* 12/2: 24–39.

Riggenbach, H. (ed.) 2000. *Perspectives on Fluency*. Ann Arbor, Mich.: University of Michigan Press.

Ritter, F. E., and L. J. Schooler 2001. 'The learning curve' in N. J. Smelser and P. B. Baltes (eds.): *International Encyclopedia of the Social and Behavioral Sciences*. Oxford: Pergamon, 8602–5.

Robinson, P. 2001. 'Individual differences, cognitive abilities, aptitude complexes and learning conditions in second language acquisition'. *Second Language Research* 17/4: 368–92.

—— 2002a. 'Effects of individual differences in intelligence, aptitude and working memory on adult incidental SLA: A replication and extension of Reber, Walkenfield and Hernstadt (1991)' in P. Robinson (ed.): *Individual Differences and Instructed Language Learning*. Amsterdam: John Benjamins, 211–66.

—— 2002b. 'Learning conditions, aptitude complexes and SLA: A framework for research and pedagogy' in P. Robinson (ed.): *Individual Differences and Instructed Language Learning*. Amsterdam: John Benjamins, 113–33.

—— 2003. 'Attention and memory during SLA' in C. J. Doughty and M. H. Long (eds.): *The Handbook of Second Language Acquisition*. Oxford: Blackwell, 631–78.

—— 2007. 'Aptitudes, abilities, contexts, and practice' in R. M. DeKeyser (ed.): *Practice in Second Language Learning: Perspectives from Linguistics and Cognitive Psychology*. Cambridge: Cambridge University Press, 256–86.

—— Forthcoming. *Aptitude in Second Language Learning*. Oxford: Oxford University Press.

—— and N. C. Ellis 2008a. 'Conclusion: Cognitive linguistics, second language acquisition, and L2 instruction—Issues for Research' in Robinson and Ellis (2008b: 489–545).

—— —— (eds.) 2008b. *Handbook of Cognitive Linguistics and Second Language Acquisition*. New York: Routledge.

Rodriguez-Fornells, A., M. Rotte, H.-J. Heinze, T. Nösselt, and T. F. Münte 2002. 'Brain potential and functional MRI evidence for how to handle two languages with one brain'. *Nature* 415: 1026–9.

Rose, C., and M. J. Nicholl 1998. *Accelerated Learning for the 21st Century.* New York: Dell.

Rosenbaum, L. 1989. *Biofeedback Frontiers: Self-Regulation of Stress Reactivity.* New York: AMS.

Rosenberg, E. L. 1998. 'Levels of analysis and the organization of affect'. *Review of General Psychology* 2/3: 247–70.

—— and B. L. Fredrickson 1998. 'Overview to Special Issue: Understanding emotions means crossing boundaries within psychology'. *Review of General Psychology* 2/3: 243–6.

Rumelhart, D. E., and J. L. McClelland 1986. *Parallel Distributed Processing: Explorations in the Microstructure of Cognition.* Cambridge, Mass.: MIT.

Russell, J. A. 2005. 'Emotion in human consciousness is built on core affect'. *Journal of Consciousness Studies* 12/8–10: 26–42.

Ruvolo, A. P., and H. Markus 1992. 'Possible selves and performance: The power of self-relevant imagery'. *Social Cognition* 10/1: 95–124.

Saffran, J. R., and E. D. Thiessen 2007. 'Domain-general learning capacities' in E. Hoff and M. Shatz (eds.): *Blackwell Handbook of Language Development.* Oxford: Blackwell, 68–86.

—— R. N. Aslin, and E. L. Newport 1996. 'Statistical learning by 8-month-old infants'. *Science* 274: 1926–8.

—— S. D. Pollak, R. L. Seibel, and A. Shkolnik 2007. 'Dog is a dog is a dog: Infant rule learning is not specific to language'. *Cognition* 105: 669–80.

Sakai, K., K. Kitaguchi, and O. Hikosaka 2003. 'Chunking during human visuomotor sequence learning'. *Experimental Brain Research* 152: 229–42.

Samuda, V., and M. Bygate 2008. *Tasks in Second Language Learning.* Basingstoke: Palgrave Macmillan.

Savignon, S. J. 1990. 'Communicative language teaching: Definitions and directions' in A. J. E. (ed.): *Georgetown University Round Table on Language and Linguistics.* Washington, DC: Georgetown University Press, 207–17.

—— 2005. 'Communicative language teaching: Strategies and goals' in E. Hinkel (ed.): *Handbook of Research in Second Language Teaching and Learning.* Mahwah, NJ: Lawrence Erlbaum, 635–51.

Saville-Troike, M. 2006. *Introducing Second Language Acquisition.* New York: Cambridge University Press.

Schacter, D. L. 1987. 'Implicit memory: History and current status'. *Journal of Experimental Psychology: Learning, Memory, and Cognition* 13/3: 501–18.

Scherer, K. R. 1995. 'Plato's legacy: Relationships between cognition, emotion, and motivation'. *Geneva Studies in Emotion and Communication* 9/1: 1–7, <http://www.unige. ch/fapse/emotion/publications/pdf/plato.pdf>, accessed 22 August 2008.

—— 2000. 'Emotions as episodes of subsystem synchronization driven by nonlinear appraisal processes' in M. D. Lewis and I. Granic (eds.): *Emotion, Development. and Self-Organization: Dynamic Systems Approaches to Emotional Development.* Cambridge: Cambridge University Press, 70–99.

—— 2001. 'Psychological structure of emotions' in N. J. Smelser and P. B. Baltes (eds.): *International Encyclopedia of the Social and Behavioral Sciences.* Oxford: Pergamon, 4472–7.

Schieffelin, B., and E. Ochs (eds.) 1986. *Language Socialization across Cultures.* New York: Cambridge University Press.

Schmidt, R. 1992. 'Psychological mechanisms underlying second language fluency'. *Studies in Second Language Acquisition* 14: 357–85.

—— 1995. 'Consciousness and foreign language learning: A tutorial on the role of attention and awareness in learning' in R. Schmidt (ed.): *Attention and Awareness in Foreign Language Learning.* Honolulu: University of Hawai'i Press, 1–63.

Schmidt, R. 2001. 'Attention' in P. Robinson (ed.): *Cognition and Second Language Acquisition.* New York: Cambridge University Press, 3–32.

Schmitt, N. (ed.) 2004. *Formulaic Sequences.* Amsterdam: John Benjamins.

Schmitt, N. 2008. 'Instructed second language vocabulary learning'. *Language Teaching Research* 12/3: 329–63.

Schumann, J. H. 1978. 'The acculturation model for second language acquisition' in R. Gingras (ed.): *Second Language Acquisition and Foreign Language Teaching*. Arlington, Va.: Center for Applied Linguistics, 27–107.

—— 1986. 'Research on the acculturation model for second language acquisition'. *Journal of Multilingual and Multicultural Development* 7: 379–92.

—— 1990. 'The role of the amygdala in mediating affect and cognition in second language acquisition' in J. E. Alatis (ed.): *Georgetown University Round Table on Language and Linguistics*, 169–76.

—— 1994. 'Where is cognition? Emotion and cognition in second language acquisition'. *Studies in Second Language Acquisition* 16: 231–42.

—— 1997. *The Neurobiology of Affect in Language*. Oxford: Blackwell.

—— 1999. 'A neurobiological perspective on affect and methodology in second language learning' in J. Arnold (ed.): *Affect in Language Learning*. Cambridge: Cambridge University Press, 28–42.

—— 2001. 'Appraisal psychology, neurobiology, and language'. *Annual Review of Applied Linguistics* 21: 23–42.

—— 2004a. 'Conclusion' in Schumann *et al.* (2004a: 175–80).

—— 2004b. 'Introduction' in Schumann et al. (2004a: 1–6).

—— 2006. 'Summing Up: Some Themes in the cognitive neuroscience of second language acquisition' in M. Gullberg and P. Indefrey (eds.): *The Cognitive Neuroscience of Second Language Acquisition*. Malden, Mass.: Blackwell, 313–19.

—— and L. A. Wood 2004. 'The neurobiology of motivation' in Schumann *et al.* (2004a: 23–42).

—— S. E. Crowell, N. E. Jones, N. Lee, S. A. Schuchert, and L. A. Wood 2004a. *The Neurobiology of Learning: Perspectives from Second Language Acquisition*. Mahwah, NJ: Lawrence Erlbaum.

—— —— —— —— —— —— (2004b). 'Preface' in Schumann *et al.* (2004a: pp. xi–xii).

Schutz, P. A., and R. Pekrun 2007. 'Introduction to emotion in education' in P. A. Schutz and R. Pekrun (eds.): *Emotion in Education*. Burlington, Mass.: Elsevier, 3–10.

Scovel, T. 2006. 'Age in L2 acquisition and teaching' in C. Abello-Contesse, R. Chacón-Beltrán, L.-J. M. D. and M. M. Torreblanca-López (eds.): *Age in L2 Acquisition and Teaching*. Bern: Peter Lang, 31–48.

Searle, J. R. 1969. *Speech Acts*. Cambridge: Cambridge University Press.

Segalowitz, N. 2001. 'On the evolving connections between psychology and linguistics'. *Annual Review of Applied Linguistics* 21: 3–22.

—— 2003. 'Automaticity and second languages' in C. J. Doughty and M. H. Long (eds.): *The Handbook of Second Language Acquisition*. Oxford: Blackwell, 382–408.

—— 2007. 'Access fluidity, attention control, and the acquisition of fluency in a second language'. *TESOL Quarterly* 41/1: 181–6.

—— and J. H. Hulstijn 2005. 'Automaticity in bilingualism and second language learning' in J. F. Kroll and A. M. B. De Groot (eds.): *Handbook of Bilingualism: Psycholinguistic Approaches*. Oxford: Oxford University Press, 371–88.

Seliger, H. W. 1978. 'The implications of a multiple critical period hypothesis for second language learning' in W. C. Ritchie (ed.): *Second Language Acquisition Research. Issues and Implications*. New York: Academic Press, 11–19.

Selinker, L. 1972. 'Interlanguage'. *International Review of Applied Linguistics* 10: 209–31.

Servan-Schreiber, E., and J. R. Anderson 1990. 'Learning artificial grammars with competitive chunking'. *Journal of Experimental Psychology: Learning, Memory, and Cognition* 16/4: 592–608.

Shatz, M. 2007. 'On the development of the field of language development' in E. Hoff and M. Shatz (eds.): *Blackwell Handbook of Language Development*. Oxford: Blackwell, 1–15.

Shore, C. M. 1995. *Individual Differences in Language Development*. Thousand Oaks, Calif.: Sage.

Sinclair, J. 1991. *Corpus, Concordance, Collocation.* Oxford: Oxford University Press.

Singleton, D. 2005. 'The Critical Period Hypothesis: A coat of many colours'. *IRAL* 43: 269–85.

—— and L. Ryan 2004. *Language Acquisition: The Age Factor*, 2nd edn. Clevedon: Multilingual Matters.

Skehan, P. 1998. *A Cognitive Approach to Language Learning.* Oxford: Oxford University Press.

—— 2002. 'Theorising and updating aptitude' in P. Robinson (ed.): *Individual Differences and Instructed Language Learning.* Amsterdam: John Benjamins, 69–93.

—— 2007. 'Language instruction through tasks' in J. Cummins and C. Davison (eds.): *International Handbook of English Language Teaching.* New York: Springer, i. 289–301.

—— and P. Foster 2001. 'Cognition and tasks' in P. Robinson (ed.): *Cognition and Second Language Acquisition.* New York: Cambridge University Press, 183–205.

Skinner, B. F. 1957. *Verbal Behavior.* New York: Appleton-Century-Crofts.

Smith, L. B., and L. K. Samuelson 2003. 'Different is good: Connectionism and dynamic systems theory are complementary emergentist approaches to development'. *Developmental Science* 6/4: 434–9.

Snow, R. E., L. Corno, and D. N. Jackson 1996. 'Individual differences in affective and conative functions' in D. C. Berliner and R. C. Calfee (eds.): *Handbook of Educational Psychology.* New York: Macmillan, 243–310.

Spada, N. 2007. 'Communicative language teaching: Current status and future prospects' in J. Cummins and C. Davison (eds.): *International Handbook of English Language Teaching.* New York: Springer, i. 271–88.

—— and P. M. Lightbown 2008. 'Form-focused instruction: Integrated or isolated?' *TESOL Quarterly* 42/2 181–207.

Squire, L. R. 2004. 'Memory systems of the brain: A brief history and current perspective'. *Neurobiology of Learning and Memory* 82: 171–7.

—— 2007. 'Memory systems: A biological concept' in H. L. Roediger, Y. Dudai, and S. M. Fitzpatrick (eds.): *Science of Memory: Concepts.* Oxford: Oxford University Press, 339–43.

Standing, L. 1973. 'Learning 10,000 pictures'. *Quarterly Journal of Experimental Psychology* 25: 207–22.

Stephan, A. 1999. 'Varieties of emergentism'. *Evolution and Cognition* 5/1: 49–59.

Sternberg, R. J. 2002. 'The theory of successful intelligence and its implications for language-aptitude testing' in P. Robinson (ed.): *Individual Differences and Instructed Language Learning.* Amsterdam: John Benjamins, 13–43.

Stevens, G. 1999. 'Age at immigration and second language proficiency among foreign-born adults'. *Language in Society* 28: 555–78.

Taguchi, N. 2007. 'Chunk learning and the development of spoken discourse in a Japanese as a foreign language classroom'. *Language Teaching Research* 11/4: 433–57.

Talmy, L. 2007. 'Foreword' in M. Gonzalez-Marquez, I. Mittelberg, S. Coulson, and M. J. Spivey (eds.): *Methods in Cognitive Linguistics.* Amsterdam: John Benjamins, pp. xi–xxi.

Thelen, E., and E. Bates 2003. 'Connectionism and dynamic systems: Are they really different?' *Developmental Science* 6/4: 378–91.

—— and L. B. Smith 1994. *A Dynamic Systems Approach to the Development of Cognition and Action.* Cambridge, Mass.: MIT.

Thompson, E., and F. J. Varela 2001. 'Radical embodiment: Neural dynamics and consciousness'. *Trends in Cognitive Sciences* 5/10: 418–25.

Thompson-Schill, S. L., T. S. Braver, and J. Jonides 2005. 'Individual differences: Editorial'. *Cognitive, Affective & Behavioral Neuroscience* 5/2: 115–16.

Tomasello, M. 2000. 'The item-based nature of children's early syntactic development'. *Trends in Cognitive Sciences* 4/4: 156–63.

—— 2003. *Constructing a Language: A Usage-Based Theory of Language Acquisition.* Cambridge, Mass.: Harvard University Press.

Tomlinson, B. 2007. 'Introduction: Some similarities and differences between L1 and L2 acquisition and development' in B. Tomlinson (ed.): *Language Acquisition and Development: Studies of Learners of First and Other Languages* London: Continuum, 1–12.

Toohey, K. 2008. 'Ethnography and language education' in K. King and N. Hornberger (eds.): *Encyclopedia of Language and Education*, x. *Research Methods*. New York: Springer, 177–88.

Turner, J. E., and R. M. Waugh 2007. 'A dynamical systems perspective regarding students' learning processes: Shame reactions and emergent self-organizations' in P. A. Schutz and R. Pekrun (eds.): *Emotion in Education*. Burlington, Mass.: Elsevier, 125–45.

Ullman, M. T. 2001. 'A neurocognitive perspective on language: The declarative/procedural model'. *Nature Reviews Neuroscience* 2: 717–26.

—— 2004. 'Contributions of memory circuits to language: The declarative/procedural model'. *Cognition* 92: 231–70.

—— 2005. 'A cognitive neuroscience perspective on second language acquisition: The declarative/procedural model' in C. Sanz (ed.): *Mind and Context in Adult Second Language Acquisition: Methods, Theory, and Practice* Washington, DC: Georgetown University Press, 141–78.

—— 2006. 'Language and the brain' in R. Fasold and J. Linton-Connor (eds.): *An Introduction to Language and Linguistics*. Cambridge: Cambridge University Press, 235–74.

Ushioda, E. 1996. 'Developing a dynamic concept of motivation' in T. J. Hickey and J. Williams (ed.): *Language, Education and Society in a Changing World*. Clevedon: Multilingual Matters, 239–45.

—— 2001. 'Language learning at university: Exploring the role of motivational thinking' in Z. Dörnyei and R. Schmidt (eds.): *Motivation and Second Language Acquisition*. Honolulu: University of Hawaii Press, 91–124.

—— 2003. 'Motivation as a socially mediated process' in D. Little, J. Ridley, and E. Ushioda (eds.): *Learner Autonomy in the Foreign Language Classroom: Teacher, Learner, Curriculum, Assessment*. Dublin: Authentik, 90–102.

—— 2007. 'Motivation, autonomy and sociocultural theory' in P. Benson (ed.): *Learner Autonomy 8: Teacher and Learner Perspectives*. Dublin: Authentik, 5–24.

—— 2009. 'A person-in-context relational view of emergent motivation and identity' in Dörnyei and Ushioda (2009: 215–28).

Uttal, W. R. 2001. *The New Phrenology: The Limits of Localizing Cognitive Processes in the Brain*. Cambridge, Mass.: MIT.

Vallacher, R. R., and A. Nowak 1999. 'The dynamics of self-regulation' in R. S. J. Wyer (ed.): *Perspectives on Behavioral Self-Regulation*. Mahwah, NJ: Lawrence Erlbaum, 241–59.

van Geert, P. 2007. 'Dynamic systems in second language learning: Some general methodological reflections'. *Bilingualism: Language and Cognition* 10/1: 47–9.

—— 2008. 'The Dynamic Systems approach in the study of L1 and L2 acquisition: An introduction'. *Modern Language Journal* 92: 179–99.

—— and H. Steenbeek 2005a. 'The dynamics of scaffolding'. *New Ideas in Psychology* 23: 115–28.

—— —— 2005b. 'Explaining after by before: Basic aspects of a dynamic systems approach to the study of development'. *Developmental Review* 25: 408–42.

van Gelder, T., and R. F. Port 1995. 'It's about time: An overview of the dynamical approach to cognition' in R. F. Port and T. van Gelder (eds.): *Mind as Motion: Explorations in the Dynamics of Cognition*. Cambridge, Mass.: MIT, 1–43.

van Lier, L. 1988. *The Classroom and the Language Learner: Ethnography and Second Language Research*. London: Longman.

VanPatten, B., and J. Williams (eds.) 2007. *Theories in Second Language Acquisition: An Introduction*. Mahwah, NJ: Lawrence Erlbaum.

Vigneau, M., V. Beaucousin, P. Y. Hervé, H. Duffau, F. Crivello, O. Houdé, B. Mazoyer, and N. Tzourio-Mazoyer 2006. 'Meta-analysing left hemisphere language areas: Phonology, semantics, and sentence processing'. *NeuroImage* 30: 1414–32.

Wallach, D., and C. Lebiere 2003. 'Implicit and explicit learning in a unified architecture of cognition' in L. Jiménez (ed.): *Attention and Implicit Learning*. Amsterdam: John Benjamins, 215–50.

Walters, J. 2005. *Bilingualism: The Sociopragmatic-Psycholinguistic Interface*. Mahwah, NJ: Lawrence Erlbaum.

Watson-Gegeo, K. A. 1997. 'Classroom ethnography' in N. Hornberger and D. Corson (eds.): *Encyclopedia of Language and Education*, viii. *Research Methods in Language and Education*. Dordrecht: Kluwer, 135–44.

—— 2004. 'Mind, language, and epistemology: Toward a language socialization paradigm for SLA'. *Modern Language Journal* 88/3: 331–50.

Weiner, B. 2007. 'Examining emotional diversity in the classroom: An attribution theorist considers the moral emotions' in P. A. Schutz and R. Pekrun (eds.): *Emotion in Education*. Burlington, Mass.: Elsevier, 75–88.

Wenger, E. 1998. *Communities of Practice: Learning, Meaning, and Identity*. Cambridge: Cambridge University Press.

White, L. 2003. *Second Language Acquisition and Universal Grammar*. Cambridge: Cambridge University Press.

—— 2007. 'Linguistic theory, Universal Grammar, and second language acquisition' in B. VanPatten and J. Williams (eds.): *Theories in Second Language Acquisition: An Introduction*. Mahwah, NJ: Lawrence Erlbaum, 37–55.

Widdowson, H. G. 1972. 'The teaching of language as communication'. *ELT Journal* 27/1: 15–19.

—— 1978. *Teaching Language as Communication*. Oxford: Oxford University Press.

—— 1989. 'Knowledge of language and ability for use'. *Applied Linguistics* 10: 128–37.

—— 2003. *Defining Issues in English Language Teaching*. Oxford: Oxford University Press.

Williams, J. 2005. 'Form-focused instruction' in E. Hinkel (ed.): *Handbook of Research in Second Language Teaching and Learning*. Mahwah, NJ: Lawrence Erlbaum, 671–91.

Williams, M., and R. Burden 1997. *Psychology for Language Teachers*. Cambridge: Cambridge University Press.

Willingham, D. T. 2006, Fall. ' "Brain-based" learning: More fiction than fact'. *American Educator*: (Available online: <http://www.aft.org/pubs-reports/american_educator/issues/fall2006/cogsci.htm>, accessed 20 August 2008.)

Wong-Fillmore, L. 1979. 'Individual differences in second language acquisition' in C. J. Fillmore, W.-S. Y. Wang, and D. Kempler (eds.): *Individual Differences in Language Ability and Language Behavior*. New York: Academic Press, 203–28.

Wray, A. 2002. *Formulaic Language and the Lexicon*. Cambridge: Cambridge University Press.

—— 2008. *Formulaic Language: Pushing the Boundaries*. Oxford: Oxford University Press.

Yowell, C. M. 2002. 'Dreams of the future: The pursuit of education and career possible selves among ninth grade Latino youth'. *Applied Developmental Science* 6/2: 62–72.

Zeidner, M. 2007. 'Test anxiety in educational contexts: Concepts, findings, and future directions' in P. A. Schutz and R. Pekrun (eds.): *Emotion in Education*. Burlington, Mass.: Elsevier, 165–84.

Zuengler, J., and K. Cole 2005. 'Language socialization and second language learning' in E. Hinkel (ed.): *Handbook of Research in Second Language Teaching and Learning*. Mahwah, NJ: Lawrence Erlbaum, 301–16.

—— and E. R. Miller 2006. 'Cognitive and sociocultural perspectives: Two parallel SLA worlds?' *TESOL Quarterly* 40/1: 35–58.

—— and J. Mori 2002. 'Microanalyses of classroom discourse: A critical consideration of method—Introduction to the Special Issue'. *Applied Linguistics* 22/3: 283–8.

Subject Index

(Rather than identifying every single occurrence of a term in the text, the following page numbers refer only to those places where there is a substantial discussion or a significant mention of the concept in question.)

Author Index